Feminist Theological Ethics

A Reader

Lois K. Daly, editor

Westminster John Knox Press
Louisville, Kentucky

Book design by Drew Stevens

First edition

Published by Westminster John Knox Press
Louisville, Kentucky

This book is printed on acid-free paper that meets the American National Standards Institute Z39.48 standard. ♾

PRINTED IN THE UNITED STATES OF AMERICA

94 95 96 97 98 99 00 01 02 03—10 9 8 7 6 5 4 3 2 1

Library of Congress Cataloging-in-Publication Data

Feminist theological ethics : a reader / Lois K. Daly, editor.—1st ed.
    p. cm.
  Includes bibliographical references.
  ISBN 0-664-25327-X (alk. paper)
    1. Feminist ethics.   2. Feminist theology.   I. Daly, Lois K.
BJ1395.F45   1994
241'.082—dc20   94-15935

For the women in my family:

Nellie Stipp Daly (1899–1988)
Charlotte Stevens Holtman (1906–1993)
Joan Brown Daly
Diane Brown Comegys
Alice Daly Garrett
Susan Yaden Morgan
Catherine Elisabeth Zimmerman
Bryn Catherine Daly
Maren Elisabeth Daly

CONTENTS

PART 2. TAKING ON THE TRADITIONS

PART 3. EXPLORING OUR LIVES TOGETHER

LIBRARY OF THEOLOGICAL ETHICS

GENERAL EDITORS' INTRODUCTION

The field of theological ethics possesses in its literature an abundant inheritance conerning religious convictions and the moral life, critical issues, methods, and moral problems. The Library of Christian Ethics is designed to present a selection of important texts that would otherwise be unavailable for scholarly purposes and classroom use. The series will engage the question of what it means to think theologically and ethically. It is offered in the conviction that sustained dialogue with our predecessors serves the interest of responsible contemporary reflection. Our more immediate aim in offering it, however, is to enable scholars and teachers to make more extensive use of classic texts as they train new generations of theologians, ethicists, and ministers.

The volumes included in the Library will comprise a variety of types. Some will make available English-language texts and translations that have fallen out of print; others will present new translations of texts previously unavailable in English. Still others will offer anthologies or collections of significant statements about problems and themes of special importance. We hope that each volume will encourage contemporary theological ethicists to remain in conversation with the rich and diverse heritage of their discipline.

ROBIN W. LOVIN
DOUGLAS F. OTTATI
WILLIAM SCHWEIKER

ACKNOWLEDGMENTS

Grateful acknowledgment is made for permission to reprint the following material:

Eleanor Humes Haney, "What Is Feminist Ethics: A Proposal for Continuing Discussion," reprinted by permission of Religious Ethics, Inc., from the *Journal of Religious Ethics* 8, no. 1 (spring 1980): 115–24.

Carol S. Robb, "A Framework for Feminist Ethics," reprinted by permission of Religious Ethics, Inc., from the *Journal of Religious Ethics* 9, no. 1 (spring 1981): 48–68.

Katie G. Cannon, "Hitting a Straight Lick with a Crooked Stick: The Womanist Dilemma in the Development of a Black Liberation Ethic," *Annual of the Society of Christian Ethics* (1987).

Delores S. Williams, "The Color of Feminism: Or Speaking the Black Woman's Tongue," *The Journal of Religious Thought* 43 (1986): 42–58.

Katie G. Cannon and Carter Heyward, "Can We Be Different But Not Alienated? An Exchange of Letters," 35–59, as published in *God's Fierce Whimsy: Christian Feminism and Theological Education,* The Mud Flower Collective, copyright 1985, The Pilgrim Press.

Ada María Isasi-Díaz, "Solidarity: Love of Neighbor in the 1980's," in *Lift Every Voice* (31–40), edited by Susan Brooks Thistlethwaite and Mary Potter Engel. Copyright © 1990 by Susan Brooks Thistlethwaite and Mary Potter Engel. Reprinted by permission of HarperCollins Publishers Inc.

Toinette M. Eugene et al., "Appropriation and Reciprocity in Womanist/Mujerista/Feminist Work," *Journal of Feminist Studies in Religion* 8 (fall 1992): 91–122.

Mary Daly, "The Spiritual Revolution: Women's Liberation as Theological Re-education," *Andover Newton Quarterly* 12 (1972): 163–72.

Anne McGrew Bennett, "Overcoming the Biblical and Traditional Subordination of Women," *Radical Religion* 1 (1974): 26–31. Used by permission of John C. Bennett.

Barbara Hilkert Andolsen, "Agape in Feminist Ethics," reprinted by permission of Religious Ethics, Inc., from the *Journal of Religious Ethics* 9, no. 1 (spring 1981): 69–83.

Toinette M. Eugene, "Moral Values and Black Womanists," *The Journal of Religious Thought* 41 (1984–85): 23–34.

Carter Heyward, "Heterosexist Theology: Being Above It All," *Journal of Feminist Studies in Religion* 3 (1987): 29–38.

Clare Benedicks Fischer, "Let Her Works Praise Her," reprinted from *Women in a Strange Land* by Clare Benedicks Fischer, copyright © 1975 Fortress Press. Used by permission of Augsburg Fortress.

Margaret A. Farley, "Feminist Theology and Bioethics," in *Theology and Bioethics: Exploring the Foundations and Frontiers,* ed. by E. E. Shelp, © 1985 by D. Reidel Publishing Company, Dordrecht, Holland, 163–85. Reprinted by permission of Kluwer Academic Publishers.

"Theology and Morality of Procreative Choice" from *Making the Connections,* by Beverly Wildung Harrison. Copyright © 1985 by Beverly Wildung Harrison and Carol Robb. Reprinted by permission of Beacon Press.

Janice G. Raymond, "Reproductive Gifts and Gift Giving: The Altruistic Woman," *Hastings Center Report* (Nov/Dec 1990): 7–11, copyright © The Hastings Center.

Karen Lebacqz, "Love Your Enemy: Sex, Power, and Christian Ethics," *Annual of the Society of Christian Ethics* (1990).

Elizabeth Bettenhausen, "The Moral Landscapes of Embodiment," *Annual of the Society of Christian Ethics* (1991).

Joan L. Griscom, "On Healing the Nature/History Split in Feminist Thought," is reprinted by permission of the author. First published in *Heresies: A Feminist Journal of Art and Politics* 4, no. 1 (1981): 4–9.

Catherine Keller, "Women Against Wasting the World: Notes on Eschatology and Ecology," in *Reweaving the World: The Emergence of Ecofeminism* edited by I. Diamond and G. Orenstein, Sierra Club Books, is reprinted with permission of Sierra Club Books, copyright © 1990 by Irene Diamond and Gloria Feman Orenstein.

Lois K. Daly, "Ecofeminism, Reverence for Life, and Feminist Theological Ethics," in *Liberating Life: Contemporary Approaches to Ecological Theology* edited by Charles Birch et al., 1990, is reprinted with permission of Orbis Books.

Mary E. Hunt, "Medals on Our Blouses? A Feminist Theological Look at Women in Combat," is reprinted by permission of the author.

My thanks also go to the editors of this series, William Schweiker, Douglas Ottati, and Robin Lovin. This volume would not have been completed without their vision and support. Thanks go also to Davis Perkins of Westminster John Knox Press, thanks especially for his patience. Although I have dedicated this book to all the women in my family, I also want to acknowledge the men. All these individuals, as well as my circle of friends, have played important roles in shaping the woman who could edit such an anthology as this. In particular I want to thank Kate and my two daughters, Bryn and Maren, for their playfulness, nurture, and good humor.

PREFACE

Explicitly feminist theological ethics has developed in the last twenty-plus years. It emerged as a reaction against the traditional, male-dominated modes of doing ethics as it became clear to more and more women, and to some men, that those modes refused to acknowledge the reality and the value of people whose experience differs from the typical white, middle- to upper-strata man; namely, most women, all people of color, and the poor. At the same time, feminist writings are not simply reactive or negative; they are also constructive. They are attempts to envision a different world, one in which patterns of domination and subordination, of hierarchy, of injustice are replaced by reciprocity, coalition, and justice.

Yet "feminist" is a contested word. Even a cursory reading of the twenty-two articles in this volume reveals this. In part, this is because there is no single "universal" feminism. Rather, there are feminisms. In some of the articles, for example, the word "feminist" is carefully defined and located; in others it is not. In some, "feminist" is not intended by the author to refer to *all* women; in others it is clear that "feminist" has in fact referred only to some—especially to white, heterosexual middle- to upper-strata women—while assuming it applied to all. In several there are clearly laid out positions that name the particularity of some women's experience with a word other than "feminist." What womanists, mujeristas, and others are doing is unmasking the universalizing assumptions of white women and, more important, self-consciously asserting the value of their own particularity.

This anthology is a collection of "snapshots" or "moments" in theological ethics written by women over the last twenty years. It is intended to bring together in one volume key articles or articles about key issues in women's theological and moral reflections. Its focus is on the writings of women who speak out of the Christian tradition, but perhaps no longer to it. Briefly stated, the aim of this anthology is to capture some of the important episodes: those that later generations might call formative, influential, or historic.

The anthology is divided into three sections, "Changing and Challenging Assumptions," "Taking on the Traditions," and "Exploring Our Lives Together." These roughly correspond to three separable but interconnected kinds of writings: methodological, critical, and "practical." In each section the articles are organized by their prior publishing dates, and in the third section, by topic as well.

The first section is the most explicitly methodological. It is placed at the beginning *not* because method precedes content but because it explains why the rest of the articles look the way they do. These articles lay out the assumptions that make these writings different from the theological ethics of earlier generations, and/or they propose different frameworks for doing ethics. They argue that the author's social location matters not only for how the tasks of theology and ethics are construed but also for which authorities are honored, which resources are chosen, and how they are used.

Articles in the second section continue to explore some of these methodological issues, but they do so primarily in the context of critiquing a received tradition. "Tradition" or "traditional" are terms used loosely here to indicate dominant patterns or issues. For the most part these articles are critical of some aspect of the male-dominated tradition, including liberal theology's neutrality, the way biblical texts have been used, the meaning of *agape,* the meaning of church. One of the articles critiques not only a received male tradition but also the emerging feminist "tradition," which fails to acknowledge the values black women have been living out.

The third section includes articles that examine issues traditionally called practical—issues such as work, bioethics, sexual ethics, and war. Three things need to be said about this section. First, it does make clear what happens when attention is paid to women's perspectives on these issues. It also includes two issues that have often been associated more with women writers, namely, nature and embodiment. However, and this is the second point, that women have reflected so much on so-called traditional practical issues illustrates how closely tied feminist theological ethics is to the tradition it criticizes. Clearly, this has both a positive and a negative side to it. On the positive side, sexual ethics, work, bioethics, and war are important, real, lived issues for women. But they are not the only issues women, or men, need to address. Hence, on the negative side, when so much attention is paid to the issues identified by the "tradition," in other words, by a male-dominated tradition, then less time and effort goes toward identifying other issues that may be equally or more important for those attempting to envision a different world.

Finally, the third point: that most feminist (read "white feminist") theological ethical reflection has remained so closely tied to traditional issues, or to issues that the tradition identifies with women (e.g., nature), is a clear illustration of the arguments of womanists, mujeristas, and others that white women have also been blinded by universalistic assumptions. The fact that little womanist or mujerista work has been published on bioethics, war, and the like is an indication that these "traditional" issues are not issues these communities feel compelled to address. In fact, for the most part, these women have had to expend so much time and effort justifying their very existence that only now is a body of literature appearing that not only identifies but addresses the issues these communities face. Volumes that collect this work will be valuable additions.

In short, this anthology has limitations, not least of which are the idiosyncrasies of its editor. In a sense, this volume contains a kind of public syllabus. It includes the articles and the issues that I, a white, academically trained, middle- to upper-strata woman, would begin with in a course on Christian feminist theological ethics. Just as a syllabus is never totally exhaustive or comprehensive, neither is this collection. Nor is this a systematic attempt to trace some "development" in thought or style in one woman's thought or in women's thought. At the same time, perhaps there is some evidence of an evolution of sorts as the years pass. That is for the reader to decide. What this collection of articles attempts to illustrate are the ongoing tensions, strains, struggles *and* joys that take place as voices emerge and women name themselves: feminist, womanist, mujerista.

CONTRIBUTORS

Barbara Hilkert Andolsen is the Helen Bennett McMurray Professor of Social Ethics at Monmouth College in New Jersey.

Anne McGrew Bennett was a pioneer feminist theologian who coedited *Women in a Strange Land* (Fortress Press, 1975). She died in 1986.

Elizabeth Bettenhausen coordinates the Study-Action Program at the Women's Theological Center in Boston.

Katie G. Cannon is associate professor of religion at Temple University.

Lois K. Daly is professor of religious studies at Siena College in Loudonville, New York.

Mary Daly is a radical feminist philosopher who teaches feminist ethics at Boston College.

Toinette M. Eugene is associate professor of social ethics at Garrett-Evangelical Seminary in Evanston, Illinois.

Margaret A. Farley holds the Gilbert L. Stark Chair in Christian Ethics at Yale University Divinity School.

Clare Benedicks Fischer is the Aurelia Henry Reinhardt Professor of Religion and Culture at the Starr King School for the Ministry.

Joan L. Griscom teaches courses in race, gender, and sexuality at William Paterson College in New Jersey.

Eleanor Humes Haney works with The Center for Vision and Policy and teaches courses in ethics and issues of race, gender, class, and ecology at the Maine College of Arts.

Beverly Wildung Harrison is the Caroline Williams Beard Professor of Christian Ethics at Union Theological Seminary in New York City.

Carter Heyward is the Howard Chandler Robbins Professor of Theology at the Episcopal Divinity School in Cambridge, Massachusetts.

Mary E. Hunt is the co-director of the Women's Alliance for Theology, Ethics and Ritual (WATER) in Silver Spring, Maryland.

Ada María Isasi-Díaz is assistant professor of ethics and theology at Drew University.

Catherine Keller is associate professor of constructive theology at Drew University.

Kwok Pui-lan is associate professor of theology at Episcopal Divinity School in Cambridge, Massachusetts.

Karen Lebacqz is professor of Christian ethics at Pacific School of Religion in Berkeley, California.

Judith Plaskow is professor of religious studies at Manhattan College.

Janice G. Raymond is professor of women's studies and medical ethics at the University of Massachusetts at Amherst.

Carol S. Robb is associate professor of Christian social ethics at San Francisco Theological Seminary.

Emilie M. Townes is assistant professor of Christian social ethics at St. Paul School of Theology in Kansas City, Missouri.

Ellen M. Umansky teaches at Hebrew Union College–Jewish Institute of Religion in New York City.

Delores S. Williams is associate professor of theology and culture at Union Theological Seminary in New York City.

PART 1

Changing and Challenging Assumptions

1

WHAT IS FEMINIST ETHICS?

A Proposal for Continuing Discussion

Eleanor Humes Haney

INTRODUCTION

For nearly two thousand years what has been called the Judeo-Christian ethic has been developing. What is becoming increasingly clear to feminists is that much of that ethic represents only a part of Christian and human reality—that of men, called to an ideal of celibacy, men largely in positions of status and dominance within the church and who, however critical they may have been within the church and who, however critical they may have been of their society, nevertheless were an intrinsic part of it. Little of the ethics held significant by the church and by divinity schools has been written by women, by non-whites, by the poor, and by those whose expressed sexual orientations deviated from a heterosexual and marital one.

Those of us aware of the parochialism of the past and its arrogance in claiming universality can neither continue to "do" ethics as it has been done nor take seriously the questions it deals with. It does not matter, because the debate is not informed by the insights and experience of the majority of people in and often now outside that tradition. Neither what is "natural" nor what is "revealed" is necessarily the same for those in a subordinate position in a society as it is for those in a position of dominance. Until, therefore, we have redefined what is indeed natural and what is revealed, until we have drawn on the insights and experience of all of us for articulating our theological and ethical bases, many of the traditional questions are irrelevant.

It does not matter, also—and even more importantly—because of immoralities that are a part of that tradition.[1] Claiming to speak about human nature and revelation and God, when that speech is not informed by the realities of life for all, is immoral. Accepting the oppressive consequences of so much of that speech is also immoral. Women, gay people, minorities, and the earth itself have suffered in part because of the theology and ethics the church has articulated and lived. And as some of us have been denied our humanity and the earth its integrity, so others—those who have been the articulators—also bear scars. There has been so much wounding and scarring in the name of a gospel of alleged liberation that the gospel itself is scarred.

The more aware many of us become of the injustices, oppression and dehumanization that have attended traditional "ethics," therefore, the more that past must be called into question. Women's experiences are not mere addenda to theological and ethical reflection, but critiques of all other reflection. We cannot simply "do" ostensible liberation theology, for instance, and extend it to women. It simply is not liberating if it is done by men only and if it is not profoundly informed by feminist perception and values. Nor can we simply return to biblical or Lutheran or Thomistic sources and seek to "make them come out right" with respect to women. For women to go back to some starting point in the past or to some already defined authority is to do little more than think men's thoughts after them. In this respect, Mary Daly was right when she was reported to have exclaimed, "Who the hell cares what Paul thought!"

Such an awareness is exciting, sometimes frightening, but more and more compelling. It is difficult still for many of us to take seriously our own experiences and insights, difficult not to believe deep down that we are wrong or that we are not qualified to challenge two thousand years of apparent wisdom, indeed "inspiration." But then we recall that that "inspired wisdom" is of far less than half of the people in the church, we recall the less than inspired consequences of it for those who are "other," and we know that we must speak, that we must be faithful to the vision that is emerging and developing in our lives; we can, indeed do no other.

A FEMINIST CONTEXT FOR
ETHICAL ACTION AND REFLECTION

To be faithful to the vision emerging and developing in lives of many women and men is a key, perhaps *the* key, to understanding feminist ethics. Feminist ethics is not only a matter of supporting economic justice by and for women, for instance, or for eliminating sex-role stereotyping. These are essential, and a feminist ethic includes them; but they are included in a larger context—that of fidelity to a vision emerging and developing in our lives.

The vision is one of a new community, indeed of a new heaven and earth. It is a vision of women in all areas of life, in the legislatures and parliaments of the world as well as in the homes, villages, and cities of the earth, sharing with men and perhaps children all the opportunities, responsibilities and privileges of citizenship. It is, at the same time, a vision of a transformation of the way women and men relate to each other and to the earth. It is a vision of a transformation of leadership, of power, and of the criteria by which decisions are made. Feminist vision, and thus feminism, is a values—a moral—revolution.

A feminist ethics seeks to articulate and make real that vision; it is thus rooted in specific communities of women and men faithful to one another, to a new and powerful awareness of what it means to be human, and to the struggle to realize that awareness. In kitchens and women centers, in all the institutions of the country, women and some men are "putting off" more traditional ways of being women and men and exploring alternatives, seeking more humane ways.

This twofold context of feminist ethics—vision and present community— means that "doing" ethics involves being a part of the envisioning and struggling. The ethic very much emerges out of the concrete, sometimes painful, often joyous activity on the part of individuals and groups both to embody that vision and to create it in and through concrete decision and action. The material for feminist ethics at this point in its history is not primarily a body of concepts or a philosophy, but the experiences and stories about and by women. Biography, autobiography—including the ethicist's—fiction, poetry and oral history are the data of feminist ethics. If vision is the warp of feminist ethics, the lives of women are its woof.[2]

REDEFINING THE GOOD

Something new is breaking into our lives, and we call that newness good. Although we can be grateful for intimations of the good in other communities, religious and secular, and for consistencies between the good as discerned elsewhere and as discussed in feminist community, our discernment of the good is intrinsic to this community. By attending to patterns emerging in our lives and to a creative exploration of alternatives, we discover what is good:

> We removed fifty brass screws
> stripped canvas to skeleton canoe
> and laid the gunnels down
> like long thin modern s's.
> We scraped away the painted years
> green, white, and battle grey
> until we got down eventually
> to brass tacks and two women
> rebuilding from raw wood
> a slim-skinned, silent boat
> that puts upon the waters
> nothing but its weight.
>   (Hazlewood-Brady, 1972)

The good, then, in some sense is there, even if we have to remove screws, strip canvas, and scrape paint. And as we perceive it, it compels our allegiance. It fits, and on its basis a new, "slim-skinned, silent boat" can be built.

The good we discern is a common good, not simply the private good of an individual or a group, not even of women. It is not the whole good; that requires the contributions and insights of children and men, of the poor and the aged, of dolphins and cats, perhaps of plants and rocks, and beneath and beyond all of these the matrix of being—physical and spiritual—out of which we come. Nevertheless, the good that we discover is central to an articulation of what is good for all, and how we should live together.

The good that emerges can be described with the paradigms of nurture and friendship. That is good which nurtures us, all of us. More specifically, that is good which makes us, human beings, more humane towards ourselves and one another; at the same time, although humaneness is a central norm it is not the only overarching one because it would then perpetuate a hierarchical perception of humanity in relation to the rest of being. The rest of the world need not and ought not to exist *for us;* their value ought not to be primarily utilitarian. We are to nurture one another. The second paradigm, friendship, points us in that direction. We are able to be friends with one another, and the earth, and all that is and can be. Friendship, in other words, helps us to remember that our good must fit in significant ways with the good of the rest of being.

To make nurture central to a feminist ethic is to make central those values and tasks that have traditionally been relegated to women (and indeed to the church) and have correspondingly in fact been devalued in the public realm as inappropriate, unrealistic, and unmasculine.[3] To make nurture central, then, is to restore those values and tasks to their rightful place and to offer them as valid human activities and attitudes toward others, particularly men. We are saying, among other things, "Damn it, you can stop worrying about proving your manhood, defending your honor, consolidating your power, demonstrating your scholarship by dispassionate—and cold—rational analysis! You can nurture yourself and others—feed your own spirit and body and offer yourself for the nurture of others."

To make friendship central is both to transform the power relations that most often hold between individuals, groups, and people and the earth, and to be a participant in that transformation. Friendship is a relation of mutuality, respect, fidelity, confidence, and affection. It is impossible in, and therefore a rejection of, most competitive patterns, adversarial patterns, exploitive patterns, authoritarian patterns, and paternalistic patterns of relating. To begin to make friendship a reality is to begin acting as a friend. That is, to demonstrate in one's speech and behavior that one is not superior or inferior and that one will no longer countenance being related to in those ways.

IMPERATIVE TO SOCIAL ACTION

The paradigms of friendship and nurture, therefore, enable and require serious and sustained collective social action. Far from being privatistic concepts, paradigms of interpersonal life withdrawn from the ambiguities and complexities of public existence, they plunge us into the midst of ongoing corporate existence, challenging at every point what is happening and offering, at every point, alternatives.

The paradigms enable and require concrete action for the liberation of all oppressed people and of the earth. They require action by the oppressed themselves and by those in positions of advocacy for the oppressed. At their heart, they require concrete action by and for women. Women's oppression historically has preceded the oppression of others and has been used as a way of conceptualizing and justifying the oppression of others. Without attending to that oppression and making the connections between the oppression of women and others and between sexism and violence, poverty and imperialism, we will not respond adequately to the oppression of any.

At the same time, the paradigms of friendship and nurture enable and require that we be fully aware of and attentive to the indivisibility of all oppression and of all human and natural rights. We do not have to waste energy or time in trying to claim that one form is worse or more important to overcome than another, and we can be appreciative of all who are committed to the liberation of any oppressed group.

Nevertheless, as feminists, our primary responsibility is the liberation of and by women, liberation from an ethos that corrupts our hearts and minds, from the religious and philosophical constructs that support and reflect that ethos, and from the concrete institutional and physical expressions of that ethos. The specific agendas of liberation will appropriately vary around the world, and we can support as well as critique one another's agendas. Loyalty to one another and to all that is, demands no less.

As we work on our agendas, it is important to remind ourselves that commitment to friendship and nurture commits us to address both concrete human imperatives of food, clothing, and shelter and also intrinsically takes us beyond survival to willing actively the well-being of all. Such an ethic commits us, for instance, not only to a goal of adequate income for women as well as others, but also to one of work or another source of income that is not "too petty for the human spirit," to use Studs Terkel's phrase.

In the process of liberation, we are constantly seeking and experimenting with personal and institutional changes and exploring alternative goals and plans that might be more consistent with these paradigms than the status quo is. We do not necessarily agree on which alternatives are more consistent, and there are no doubt others that we have yet to think of. We do insist, however, that how we go about change is as important as seeking the changes we want. The means not only shape the ends—they may be more important than the ends, and whatever the specific action we may take, there are two fundamental criteria that guide our decisions about what action is appropriate. They are (*a*) that they must be consistent with our integrity and (*b*) that they open up alternatives. What we do should demonstrate what we value and who we are. In order to do that, we may—and probably often do—have to bring conflicting values out into the open. Perhaps only then can alternatives be genuinely explored and new possibilities emerge. As the exasperated minister said to one of his "uppity" parishioners, "Elaine, why can't you be more ladylike?" She replied, "Well, I try. I've borne nine children, and I'm a good cook." She is right. The world needs people who are willing to act on a different set of values. The world needs friends more than it needs ladies.

To act, to take the initiative, however much the knees may be trembling and the heart pounding, to act courageously and confidently has been considered a masculine characteristic, and not a feminine one—certainly not one appropriate for ladies. To nurture has been considered one—to mother, to serve, to care for. Feminism brings those together. The good that feminists seek is one which acknowledges the potential goodness in many of those characteristics considered feminine and masculine, but is a good which transcends their goodness either individually or in combination, and it is a good for all, not only for women and children. Feminist ethics brings other characteristics together also and transcends them. For instance, there are features of autonomy that are necessary if people are to be friends and nourish our lives, but there is much about that concept that isolates us and commends an illusory sense of self-sufficiency. Dependency and relatedness also have qualities that are valuable and qualities that are destructive. In the effort to name that way of being that is both independent and responsible and yet related and interdependent, I and some other feminists use the term *centering*. That seems to come closest to describing a way of being that is neither autonomous nor dependent nor, somehow, both, but a finding and living out of the still point, the axis the center of one's own life. The centering self lives on her own terms, out of her own roots, in tune with the reasons of her heart and head, competent and capable of shaping, in concert with others, our individual and corporate lives with all the resources we have gathered through the centuries. A centering woman can and does take the hand of other women, not along the edges of one's life but as a stance toward the world. In doing so, in an androcentric world, she becomes a revolutionary.

There are others, of course, some of which we hardly have words for. My use of *centering* is illustrative, not inclusive; and my point is that feminist community is and must be a norm-creating community. The virtues and principles do not come to us often as legacies of the past. We must both create them and discover them.

Even those principles from the past—principles of love, justice and mercy, for instance—to some extent must be redefined or held as suspect about how they are valid or ethical. When people who have had generations of privileged treatment can cry "reverse discrimination" when asked simply to share some of that privilege, one does become suspicious about the use of the principle of justice and, whether we like it or not, use—to a very large extent—shapes, if not determines, meaning.

The paradigms of friendship and nurture, then, help us to hold together what too often have been split asunder—being and doing, the personal and the political, means and ends. Only in holding them tightly together does the moral life have significance and power. When they become separated, the moral life short-circuits: action becomes ineffective or a denial of fundamental human values, actors become discouraged or cynical, and (to change the metaphor) the moral life skids between privatization and prudential pragmatism.

PRINCIPLES AND RULES IN FEMINIST ETHICS

As we learn to hold together the various components of moral life and action, we are able to see the significance of imperatives and rules to inform action and our own becoming. The iconoclasm in feminist action is directed at actions and rules that are destructive of human and natural well-being; this does not mean either that feminist ethics is a do-your-own-thing ethic or that, somehow, in each situation that calls for decisions we can intuit the good or the right thing to do. Rules and relatively concrete principles are necessary both for guiding decisions and calling us to action, to our doing what we have to do whether we feel like it or not.

Honesty, for instance, is central to a feminist ethic. And by honesty, I mean both telling the truth (reporting accurately) and integrity (living in such a way that there is consistency between what one says one values and believes, and what one does). Perhaps only by being honest can we begin to cut through the habits of generations of equivocations, "dealing," hypocrisy, and the hiatus between being "moral" and being "realistic."

A second principle in feminist ethics is respect for nurturing life in whatever form it appears. Whether fetal life, the life of a friend, one's own life, the life of one whose intentions and desires contradict one's own, or the life of a cow, it is worthy of respect and nurture. This does not mean that there are no occasions when life can and perhaps should be terminated, but it does mean that our present policy of allegedly striving for peace while preparing for war, no matter how discriminate the weapons may be, reflects the profound lack of real commitment to respect for and nurture of life. When we as a country have made a commitment to respect for life that is reflected in the way we deal with conflict and in our economic and social policies, when we have taken significant steps to transform the power realities that presently exist among the peoples and nations of the world, and indeed in the very definition and service of power, then we can begin to explore under what circumstances, if any, life can and should be terminated and indeed what kind of legislation might be appropriate for that.

Such rules and principles, however, do not exist in a vacuum. They exist as part of the fabric of an ethos which can either be destructive or nurturing of human and non-human well-being. The feminist task is to wrench these rules and principles from their destructive context. This means, for instance, that respect for life becomes first of all an "unmasking" of the profound lack of respect for life in this country. Since much of the approach to conflict resolution to women, to the poor, to children, to minorities, does not reflect a commitment to life, much less the quality of life, we will not allow that it be then used to reinforce the powerlessness of women. We will not allow its continuing to play a part in forcing women to pay the price of the way in which this ethos institutionalizes sexual violence and treating one another as objects to be used, and then denies us healthy and positive support for rearing the children that, still, inevitably do come.

Such rules and principles, therefore, when put in a different context, may well lead to a new set of commandments or a new list of imperatives that we must act upon. For the sake of human beings and the welfare of all, we can do no less.

RELATIONSHIPS WITH OTHER ETHICS

Feminist ethics is not an extension of Christian ethics or Marxist ethics or some other shape of ethical reflection. The kinds of connections that can occur between feminist ethics and one or more of these others need much more analysis than I can engage in here. It seems clear that connections can and ought to be made; feminists can find some resources and do find problems in other traditions.

Briefly, however, I wish to conclude this essay by suggesting that a feminist ethic is first of all appropriately related to traditional Christian ethics, as a critique and an alternative. The concept of centering, for instance, is on the one hand a critique of, and indeed a contradiction to, the emphasis on self-sacrifice and centering in God characteristic of Christian ethics because it places the self in a position of importance and authority. From that perspective, centering in one's self smacks of egotism, greed, and all the ills the flesh is heir to. Yet, on the other hand, self-centering is precisely that movement of one's personal existence that brings women into an at-homeness with the universe. It is one pole of a graceful relationship with all that is, it is one extremely important step in a process of coming into congruence with others, of becoming whole. As such, then, it illuminates alternative ways for conceptualizing our relation with what we have traditionally called *God,* in a non-hierarchical and interdependent fashion.

But just as it offers alternatives, a feminist perspective on Christian ethics can, secondly, help us uncover and indeed enrich themes in the latter tradition. Although the model for human excellence is not given once and for all in the past, dimensions of Jesus Christ's teaching and life are consistent with and enrich a feminist ethic. I think it is overstating the case to call Christ a feminist, as Leonard Swidler does, since sexism was hardly an issue then, so far as we know. What Christ did was to redefine God for his time, and his relationships with women seem consistent with that redefinition of God. He sought to eliminate a separatist and adversarial view of God and to replace that with a gracious and graceful view that freed people to become friends with Romans and Samaritans and even to begin to interact with one another as women and men. In Christ's redefinition, God was not the Holy One who demanded exclusion and purity, so much as the Gracious One, the One with Whom the self could be on intimate terms.

The moral significance of Christ for us, then, lies in his re-interpretation of God, a redefinition that I think Paul was largely faithful to as he sought to make connections between that view of God and the social, religious, and political fabric of Hellenistic life. Nevertheless, that redefinition remains limited, and necessarily so, until it is informed by and then transformed by the experiences and vision of women.

In an ironic way the moral significance of Christ also lies in his Crucifixion. Loyalty to God brought him death—in part, perhaps in large part, because the values that loyalty reflected were feminine (*i.e.,* nurturing and serving the needs and well-being of the neighbor), values associated with responsibilities of subordinates. In the patriarchy of first-century Judaism, that had to be terribly threatening. The Crucifixion, in other words, helps to reinforce what we already know—that the feminine is both devalued and that it is necessary to human well-being. The continuing resistance to feminist presence in the church remains, then, a cruel and ironic paradox.

A concept in the tradition that I find particularly rich for feminist thought is that of grace, even as it, too, needs a combination of redefinition and recovering of lost dimension. Grace is not so much forgiveness, although it can include that; nor is it a rescue operation by God for us helpless victims. Rather, it is the twofold reality of being at-home-in-the-universe and of living freely—graciously, gracefully. It is the reality of being a host as well as a guest, a resident as well as a stranger and pilgrim. It is the experience of moving through one's life and the world with ease and authority, rather than with timidity or aggression.

As feminists, therefore, we are open to and responsive to that which nurtures and enriches our lives and that which is consistent with our experiences in the past as well as in the present and future. Further, openness to the past reminds us that as its perspective was relative, so ours is also. In religious language, we may indeed reflect a Second Coming, but we do not yet reflect the Final Coming.

There are further strands and themes in the past, including very much the sectarian past and also the heretical past, consistent with feminist insights and concerns; and we can be open to any or all of those. There are indeed strands, stories, and themes in the other religious traditions of the world, particularly in those Israel sought to subdue. Whatever continuing or enduring truth that any of this—our story—has, rests finally on the extent to which it can and does facilitate justice and the well-being of women, men, and the rest of being. And to facilitate justice and well-being, it must help us to integrate means and ends, person and society, character and deed as they have seldom been in the past. We simply can no longer afford to compartmentalize our lives with different criteria, policies, and virtues for each area.

In conclusion, feminism offers us hope (perhaps historically, our last hope) that we can move away from fundamentally life-denying values, principles, and policies to life-giving ones. Indeed, humanity literally yearns for what feminism intends. It offers us individually and collectively the possibility of making connections with ourselves, one another, the earth, and all that is and can be. It offers us the possibility, thus, of making connections with the rhythms and powers of life. Feminist ethics, finally, is fidelity to being.

At the same time, fidelity to being does not mean acceptance of the status quo, much less compliance with it. Such fidelity may well make of us a troublemaker, an outcast, a martyr, by the definitions of others. It does make us angry, but our anger is generative, not destructive anger. At the same time, in making connections, we are empowered to transform the status quo as we move across the land with authority and ease, with integrity and guilelessness. And no force on the face of the earth can stop us.

NOTES

1. Whether these immoralities are an inherent part of Christian ethics remains to be seen. Certainly there is and has been a continuing source of power and life that can serve to correct injustices as they are recognized. Hope for the ongoing vitality of the tradition lies in part, at least, in this source.

2. In this effort to describe feminist ethics, I am drawing on my own experiences and struggles, those shared by many others through reading and discussions and in particular what Wilma Scott Heide, for many years an activist in human rights and responsibilities from a feminist perspective, has done and has discussed with other women and men.

3. To find an ethical resource in women's experiences, perceptions, and responsibilities is not to assume that the values in that resource are an intrinsic part of women's nature as distinct from men's. I am not operating with a theory of two natures but with the reality of a pluralistic ethos.

REFERENCE

Hazelwood-Brady, Anne
    1972 "Bonded," *Unwritten Testament.* Camden: Camden Herald Publishing Company.

2

A FRAMEWORK
FOR FEMINIST ETHICS

Carol S. Robb

INTRODUCTION

The diversity among feminist perspectives is reflected in the diversity of feminist ethical theories. A major indicator of this diversity is the way feminists answer the question, who is accountable to feminist ethics? The seat of accountability rests in some of the following areas: to women solely, according to radical feminists; to families and schools, for sex-role theorists; to the working class, according to Marxist-Leninist feminists; to all women and the working class, for socialist-feminists. Considering these responses, this paper takes the position that feminists are making claims on social structures and aggregates of people—government, child care systems, families, schools, churches, and the corporate sphere. In this light, feminist ethics are social ethics, and can guide our reflection with the tools and questions which pertain to the discipline of social ethics.

On the other side, social ethics is a discipline still in the forge, in process, with some of its outlines yet to be shaped. Developments in feminist ethical theory provide the basis for a contribution to the formation of social ethics: a vision of the breadth of scope that the discipline must encompass. Without a scope broad enough to include, among other things, the task of analyzing the roots of women's oppression, our ethical reflection is subject to a major difficulty, to fail to account for the systemic quality of the grounds for women's complaints and claims. Secondarily, without recognizing the importance of that analysis to feminist ethics, we will miss understanding a major reason why feminists take such diverse and even conflicting normative stances, ranging from separatism to institutional reformism to commitment to socialist revolution.

Yet the analysis of women's oppression is only one aspect of feminist ethics, as the analysis of the root of any situation is only one aspect of social ethics in general. Several factors constitute ethical theories, and ethicists, including feminist ethicists, may differ along any or all of these factors, thus expressing different normative stances. In this paper I propose a schema which can make explicit how ethical theories differ from each other and share points of commonality. This schema can be shared by feminist ethics and social ethics.

This schema contains many factors which appear in contemporary and traditional ethical theory, though this particular configuration is one which I propose to encourage viewing the ethical enterprise in a broad way. Ethicists in general, including feminist ethicists, tend to focus their attention on one or a few of these factors, as the notes will indicate, making contributions to the total enterprise in the context of others' contributions in different ways.

ELEMENTS OF ETHICAL THEORIES

Proposing this schema necessitates attentiveness to a dialogue between the traditions of the discipline of ethics and new voices which are both appropriating and challenging the traditions. One of the outcomes of this dialogue is an awareness of the impact on ethical reflection of the analysis of the roots of oppression. We have seen attention to analysis before in the ethics of Latin American liberation theology. My concern is to make this aspect of ethical reflection explicit, since to do so confronts us with the importance of making explicit the social theories at the base of our various social ethics.

Specifically in relation to feminist ethics, analyses among feminists differ, as I shall take some care to show. Thus, while all feminist ethics begins with or assumes a criticism of the historical, including contemporary, roles of women in society, or a complaint about those roles, the attempt to understand the grounds for the criticism and the requirements for liberation requires analysis. Because the analyses of the roots of women's oppression yield such divergent normative stances, I will make the case that this particular factor is heavily weighted in relation to all the other factors.

Starting Point for Ethical Reflection

The starting point is the first of nine analytically distinct aspects of ethical reflection. In the tradition of ethics we have learned the significance of how people define problems appropriate for ethical reflection, or pose issues, and in this sense *start* the ethical enterprise.

On the one hand, one can proceed by reflecting on very concrete historical experiences, and attempt to arrive at more general understandings of the ethical situation by that "reflection on praxis," to borrow liberation theology terminology. On the other hand, one can begin with a definition of the good life, the virtuous person, the "nature" of anything in an idealist sense, and deduce the definition of an ethical situation from that basis.[1]

To date there has been a nearly consistent tendency for feminist ethicists to take as their starting points reflection upon very concrete situations. This procedure is one way, and a main way, in which dominant ideology is unmasked. In this procedure, there is commonality or at least a basis for commonality with those who articulate ethical reflections from other oppressed groups. For until the dominant ideology of a social structure can be exposed as manufactured instead of natural, the terms of an ethical problem will tend to reflect assumptions which support a dominant ideology. For this reason, the act of defining a problem is a political act; it is an exercise of power to have accepted one's terms of a "problem."[2]

Data about the Historical Situation

Ethical decisions must take into account all of the relevant data. Social ethicists are accountable for basing their definition of the ethical situation on inclusive data. Those formulating feminist ethical theory are inclined to challenge social ethicists in two ways, as to the *sufficiency* of the data to be considered, whether it adequately reflects what is happening to women and what it is that women are doing, and as to the *weight given* to the data which reflects or impacts women's lives.[3]

Analysis of the Roots of Oppression

Dependent upon but not collapsible to the data about the historical situation, the location of the roots of oppression informs all aspects of ethical reflection. The purpose of this factor is to locate causal dynamics.[4]

Feminist ethical theory reflects at least four different analyses of the roots of oppression which I will examine later. They share one perspective, however: that the causative factors in women's situation, whether prehistorical, historical, or currently operative, are not collapsible to, even if they are related to, causes of other social inequalities. Women's oppression cannot be "liquidated" by abolishing the class structure alone, racism alone, or the need for democratic reforms alone.

Loyalties

On whose behalf ought we to make ethical judgments? Some ethicists have treated this factor as a pre-ethical factor, one about which persons have made some judgment when they enter into ethical reflection. However, the approach I suggest is that one may intentionally and after reflection take a position of partiality, or loyalty to a particular group, and consequently it is appropriate to treat "loyalties" as an ethical factor.

Feminist ethical theory confronts all proponents of justice in the social-ethical tradition as to whether loyalty to women *as women* is operative. It is not sufficient to espouse justice for women solely or even primarily as a means to achieve justice for the underdeveloped, a racial or ethnic group, or a nationality. On the other hand, there is among feminist ethicists a continuing search for the relationship between loyalty to women and loyalty to other oppressed groups. With some exceptions, feminist ethicists are loyal to women in a way which is consistent to a loyalty to all of humanity.

Theory of Value

Value theories contain rank orders of values according to priority. Rank orderings are based on an assumption that many if not all ethical decisions are made in situations in which some values must be chosen at the expense of some others. Thus theories of value may posit how to choose between life and freedom, unity and justice, affiliation and autonomy, to name some examples of choices often posed. Theories of value are often implied in anthropologies, theologies, and visions of future social orders as they are expressed in utopic science fiction, for example.

An ongoing discussion among those developing theories of feminist values concerns whether feminists have claim to any values independent of either a theory that biology is determinative, or a commitment to social justice shared with others with commitments to racial or economic justice. The substance of feminist value theory remains an open discussion.[5]

Mode of Making Ethical Decisions

The discipline of social ethics generally recognizes three primary models for decision-making, and there is some discussion about whether there are in fact only two. That is, in reflecting upon the teleological, deontological, and situation-response modes, one can detect within the third mode aspects which are essentially teleological or deontological, depending on the ethicist in question.

Feminist ethics is in large part done in the teleological mode when the understanding of teleology allows for inclusion of the relational mode. Feminist ethics is oriented toward the liberation of women and weighs the value of acts or policy in those terms, but it is important to distinguish teleology from utilitarianism.[6] For while utilitarian theories are teleological, not all teleological theories are subject to the difficulties of utilitarianism. That is, when utilitarianism calculates the greater good, it can be done in such a way as to make minority groups, including women, pay the cost for social policy. There are trends of feminist ethics which view the liberation of women as inclusive of or consistent with the liberation of other oppressed groups, and also of white men.[7]

Source or Justification of Ethical Claims

Some typical sources of ethical claims have traditionally included reference to the revelation of God, tradition, rational reflection, history, or lived experience.

When lived experience is the source of ethical claims, further questions must be asked to clarify *whose* experience and under what interpretation. A further issue involves how persons are able to claim objectivity for their ethical sources when cultural, personal, and political perspectives on those claims are significant.

In relation to the various modes of making ethical decisions, it appears unlikely that those using a teleological mode would claim revelation as the source or justification of ethical claims, whereas those using a deontological or relational mode might do so. There is no rigid relation between the various sources and modes. For instance, one might claim natural law as the source for ethical claims and use either a teleological or a deontological mode of making ethical decisions, or justifying them.

Those developing feminist ethical theory are overwhelmingly inclined to refer to lived experience as the source for ethical claims, granting the complexities of this method.[8]

Presupposition of Ethical Action, Autonomy

The theory with regard to autonomy must necessarily be complex if it is to take seriously both the meaning of ethical propositions as well as behavioral research uncovering the very powerful forces which limit autonomy. While a measure of autonomy is necessary before moral choice can be exercised—and in this sense is an important goal—the notion of the moral agent as dispassionate and disengaged is distinct from the former notion of autonomy, and has come under criticism for its failure to recognize the social foundation of self.

Feminist ethical theory, in general terms, presupposes a criticism of the forces which limit women's autonomy in the ethical realm. In this sense, the economic dependency of women in the family, the inequality of pay and promotion in the labor force tied to women's role as child-bearer and child-rearer, the possibility of sexual harassment or physical abuse from a stranger or an intimate, and further, in psychological terms, the tendency toward lack of ego differentiation in women's personality formation, are all factors impinging upon women's sense of self which can be autonomous confronting or defining ethical situations.[9]

Motivation

How do we view the way ethical action begins and what keeps it going, recognizing that knowledge of what is the right thing to do does not necessarily result in the will to do the right? This is a classical question in the ethical tradition. Developing feminist perspectives bring to light the energy unleashed when women become engaged in collective efforts of self-definition, an energy which overcomes or at least mitigates against the alienation between the will and the right.[10]

To include all these factors in the ethical reasoning process is significant in itself, as there is not general agreement that the scope of social ethics should be so broadly conceived. While ethicists have proposed schemas including some of these factors, or more factors than these, it has been only recently, in relation to Latin American theologians of liberation, that the analysis of the roots of oppression has been suggested as necessary (Robb, 1979). In the field of social ethics we have had no trouble viewing "data" as a significant factor in ethical theory. However, *analysis* is the process of organizing data according to a theory which attempts to locate the historical causes of the situation. Some of the most important work impacting ethical reflection on women's experience is explicitly in this area, as I will presently outline.

In addition, there is another reason to broaden the scope of ethics to include this factor alongside the others. It provides a framework in which we can see the way the divergent agendas relate to each other. For instance, the work of Daly, Haney, and Pellauer, emphasizing heretofore ignored data and reversing value systems in which women have no honor, can be seen *in relation to* work which emphasizes sources and justification in ethics, as in Lebacqz and Harrison, or the analysis of the roots of oppression, as in Lenin (1978), Gordon (1978), Ehrenreich (1978), or Vogel (1979), or the method of deciding what is to be done, as in Gilligan.

In sum, to do feminist ethics we need a view of ethics in this broad scope. And in particular, we need to recognize analysis of the roots of oppression as an ethical factor.

DIVERGENT FEMINIST SOCIAL-POLITICAL THEORIES

This discussion should illustrate the value of this scope of the discipline of social ethics. One basis from which all feminists begin doing social-political theory is by reflecting upon what is happening to women and what it is that women are doing. Our starting point is in our own experience, as that is revealed in women of different races, classes, religions, and nationalities. Socialist feminists in particular have contributed a wonderful way of talking about this in terms of reuniting the personal and the political. To reunite the personal and the political means two things. First, it means that the areas of women's lives heretofore thought to be "private" and "personal"—for instance; her relations to individual men or women—were part of a systematic division of labor between men and women (male supremacy). This division of labor is reinforced by a set of attitudes and ideas (male chauvinism), that serve to justify and maintain this division. The home, for instance, is considered the personal and private domain of a family, and women often exercise what control they have only in the context of the home. Men, on the other hand, have had more control in the public sphere or the marketplace. "Women's work" is then systematically undervalued. To recognize that the personal is political is a challenge to that equation of women and personal, men and public or political.

Second, if the personal is political, the attempt by women to understand our personal lives within small groups is political. It is a political action for a woman to say what she believes or is coming to believe about her life instead of what she has always been told to say (Judis, 1971).

In a fundamental way, feminist ethical theory criticizes the alienation of the personal from the political, and seeks both to integrate these aspects of personality and to institutionalize this integration. In order to institutionalize the integration of the personal and the political, however, we need more than the integration of women into the paid labor force, or the proliferation of women's support groups. While these measures heighten women's awareness of the weaknesses in the ideology of male chauvinism, they do not constitute a far-reaching strategy to liberate or emancipate women in the broadest sense. Arriving at such a strategy requires careful attention to the history of women in different societies, an assessment of the current situation, an analysis of the causal or key factors in the oppression of women, and a program to guide our action together.

What follows are four contemporary social-political analyses of the oppression of women, chosen to illustrate the importance of such analysis for ethics. The major limitation to the following outline of these analyses is that they appear to be mutually exclusive. In fact, women often identify with parts of several of these four descriptions. Nevertheless, they are representative of major feminist political formations which are significant within the women's movement in the U.S. and internationally.

Radical Feminism

One very important perspective is radical feminism.[11] According to the analysis of radical feminism, the roots of women's oppression are very simply *men*. Men have in their make-up some tendencies, say brutishness or weak egos, for instance, which result in goals for social organization which are different from women's. At some historical moments, perhaps different moments in different parts of the populated globe, men overthrew egalitarian social orders and through physical strength consolidated political and economic control. They continue to use that strength to maintain their control.

According to radical feminists, women have their own culture which has not been recognized by the dominant culture since the patriarchal revolt. Women have different aesthetics, priorities, and perceptions. Men have feared, and in their fear reviled, women's culture and therefore have kept women isolated and ignorant of their sisterhood. Daly (1978:39) writes concerning this fear:

All of the so-called religions legitimating patriarchy are mere sects subsumed under its vast umbrella/canopy. They are essentially similar, despite variations. All—from buddhism and hinduism to islam, judaism, christianity, to secular derivatives such as freudianism, jungianism, marxism, and maoism—are infrastructures of the edifice of patriarchy. All are erected as parts of the male's shelter against anomie.

Eventually, according to radical feminist arguments, women will have to take power away from men in order to establish a truly egalitarian society, because egalitarianism is only possible under matriarchy. But for now, women must create our own enclaves to nurture and support each other. By living out in the present the freedom of the future, the revolution will grow *by example* to other women. And if we decide that it will never be worthwhile to reestablish the egalitarian society, at least we have a parallel nation, regardless of the patriarchal order.

According to this analysis, racism, capitalism and imperialism are results of male supremacy and can only be eliminated by eliminating male supremacy:

> We identify the agents of our oppression as men. Male supremacy is the oldest, most basic form of domination. All other forms of exploitation and oppression (racism, capitalism, imperialism, etc.) are extensions of male supremacy: men dominate women, a few men dominate the rest. . . . Attempts have been made to shift the burden of responsibility from men to institutions or to women themselves. We condemn these arguments as evasions. Institutions alone do not oppress; they are merely tools of the oppressor. (Redstocking, 1970)

The weakness in this argument is that it does not in itself offer the prospect of dismantling the society that is being criticized. Political program in this view is masculist. Therefore, the only real option for women who adopt this line is to withdraw from the struggle for liberation for themselves and for other women who can't take the option of withdrawal.

On the other hand, a major insight of this analysis must be taken seriously: the institution and ideology of heterosexuality in its historical development is a cornerstone of male supremacy. As long as the majority of adult women allow themselves to be linked in intimate and emotionally sustaining relationships primarily with men, it will be difficult for us to engage in a long-term struggle to destroy male supremacy.

Though the notion that heterosexuality is a cornerstone of male supremacy is an important notion to be considered and tested, another approach may offer the basis for broader political unity; it is not heterosexuality *per se* that must be conquered. Rather, we must target the ideology which limits appropriate sexual expression and relationships to heterosexual ones. In addition, we must dismantle the various material support systems of male supremacy, which tie women's economic support to husbands and make child rearing women's work.

Sex-rolism

A second perspective on women's oppression focuses on the importance of sex roles. A broad base of the population first engages feminist thought through the investigation of the notions of "masculine" and "feminine" as socially-defined role expectations, discovering the extent to which such notions are social constructions, and then identifying feminism with a critical perspective on sex roles.

In its simplest version, this line absolves men from any but psychological responsibility for the oppression of women, and blames it all on "sex roles" or society. According to this version, the program for change is primarily education, with complementary incremental reforms in schooling practices and workplace/home relationships. Women should learn how to fix automobiles and other machines, and men should learn how to maintain the home. Women should take courses in college that are oriented toward specific careers, and men should take equal responsibility for parenting. Women should practice acting assertively and self-consciously check behaviors reflecting internalized oppression, and men should try to exercise some restraint over their typically domineering and hierarchical interaction patterns.

Clearly, education and incremental reforms do fit into a strategy of changing society and behavior, including sexist behavior. And the attempts at destroying stereotypical sex roles are important for obvious reasons. But this analysis has several weaknesses if it stands by itself. The qualities that sex-rolists say are ascribed to all women are really only ascribed to middle and upper class women. Sarah Small, a campus minister at the University of Massachusetts–Boston, has often said that America creates two kinds of women: those who can't take care of themselves and those who have to. The existence of the second group indicates that sex roles are not the basis of women's oppression, but rather the result of other factors. Sex roles are symptoms of male supremacy, not the cause or the cure (Williams, 1978).

A second and closely related weakness is that adherents to this perspective never articulate a political program to ensure that all races and classes will benefit from the educational and incremental reforms. They fail to do so because they *assume* that their goals can be achieved by working within constitutional means, given the current political process and the current general view of the rights and responsibilities of individuals. Those who work within these assumptions do not feel the necessity of articulating a political program, because they accept the existing one. While, on the other hand, those who work within the other perspectives have the double burden of articulating their analyses of the roots of oppression and the vision of the new society, sex-role feminists do not perceive the need to envision radically new social-political arrangements.[12]

There is a second and deeper version of this analysis of the roots of the new gender system which, while calling for similar programmatic commitments, describes the psychological dynamics of sex-role divisions of labor in the home and public spheres. For example, in attempting to account for demonstrated tendencies for boys to be oriented toward achievement and self-reliance and girls toward nurturance and responsibility, Chodorow (1974), and Dinnerstein (1977) cite in a somewhat different way the identification process between mother and daughter and the lack of such identification between mother and son as the factor which results in daughters differentiating less, while sons are encouraged to separate and individuate. Therefore, cultural definitions of personality and behavior are not simply taught. The structural situation of child rearing, wherein women are universally the primary child rearers, produces these differences. Women lactate, and for convenience, not biological necessity, mothers, and females in general, have tended to take care of all babies. Social and self-help reforms will not succeed, ultimately, unless there is a shift in the quality of the very early social environment of child rearing. It is Chodorow's (1974:66) perspective that

> Daughters and sons must be able to develop a personal identification with more than one adult, and preferably one embedded in a role relationship that gives it a social context of expression and provides some limitation upon it. Most important, boys need to grow up around men who take a major role in child care, and girls around women who, in addition to their child-care responsibilities, have a valued role and recognized spheres of legitimate control. These arrangements could help to ensure that children of both sexes develop a sufficiently individuated and strong sense of self, as well as a positively valued and secure gender identity, that does not bog down either in ego-boundary confusion, low self-esteem, and overwhelming relatedness to others, or in compulsive denial of any connection to others or dependence upon them.

This second version of sex-rolism is explicit in the work of Gilligan (1977; 1979), who draws on Chodorow's contributions and concludes that women not only define themselves in a context of human relationship but also judge themselves in their ability to care, while men devalue that care and define moral excellence in terms of male development up to the period of adolescence.[13]

To recapitulate an earlier point, the weakness of both versions of this analysis is that they never ask about the broad social-political conditions, costs, and consequences of restructuring child-rearing practices to allow for the recommended role redefinitions. The contribution of this analysis, however, is to hold up as essentially irrational the basis for the sexual division of labor and for gender-defined behavioral expectations in the current day.

Marxist-Leninist Feminism

The social-political theory of Marxist-Leninist feminism stands within the tradition of Marx, Engels, Lenin, Luxembourg, Zetkin, and Kollontai, all of whom were committed to leading the working class and its allies to overthrow the dictatorship of the bourgeoisie, to establish socialism under the dictatorship of the proletariat, and eventually to achieve communism. This tradition sees private property as the basis of all alienation in the social sphere and thus holds that the struggle for women's rights must be linked with the *principal aim:* the conquest of power and the establishment of the dictatorship of the proletariat. "At present, this is, and will continue to be, our alpha and omega" (Lenin, 1978:113).

Engels' and Marx's writings acknowledge that sexual domination preceded capitalist economic formation. Their documents have historically served as part of the basis for commitment to the liberation of women within the socialist agenda. But it is to Lenin that we look for the manner in which such a commitment took shape in the midst of political struggles for socialism. In his speeches, articles, and conversations, aspects of the woman question, as it is put in this tradition, include the struggle for equal rights under the law, both in bourgeois and socialist countries; freeing women from slavery to the home and small farm (in Russia) because housework is drudgery and degrading, and because when she is isolated under the rule of the father or husband she cannot broaden herself or her view of the world; the politicization of women whose lives have been so dominated, so that,

> We say that the emancipation of the workers must be effected by the workers themselves, and in exactly the same way the emancipation of working women is a matter for the working women themselves. (Lenin, 1978:70)

Other aspects involve drawing women into various social spheres, such as social production, the administration of socialized enterprises, and of the state, as well as the reconstruction of the economy and of sexist ideology (Lenin, 1978:112):

> We demonstrate thereby that we are aware of these needs and of the oppression of women, that we are conscious of the privileged position of the men, and that we hate—yes, hate—and want to remove whatever oppresses and harasses the working women, the wife of the worker, the peasant woman, the wife of the little man, and even in many respects the woman of the propertied classes. (Lenin, 1978:110)

The implementation of these measures requires a mass movement of women before, during, and after seizing state power, and Lenin encouraged systematic political work among women. He inveighed against separate organizations of communist women, but declared that within the Party there must be organs— working groups, commissions, and committees with the special purpose of rousing the broad masses of women and integrating them into political work under the influence of the Party.

But the relationship between revolutionary struggle and feminist organizing is not simple. An exchange between Lenin and Zetkin gives some indication of the historical importance of the woman question in revolutionary Europe. When Zetkin organized evening study groups for women in Germany, Lenin called her to account why she was focusing on sex and marriage problems as main objects of interest in her political and educational work. She defended her work, saying that knowledge of the historical modifications of the forms of marriage and family and their dependence on economics was important in politicizing women. Such knowledge served to rid women's minds of the notion that bourgeois society structured marriage and family along natural and eternal lines. Lenin's concern was that Zetkin was treating sex and marriage problems as the *main* social problem, rather than as *part* of the main social problem. One of the ongoing issues for Marxist-Leninist feminists is how to acknowledge that "sex and marriage problems" are part of the main social problem—the dominance of industrial monopoly capital—without implying that they are *secondary* issues.

Lenin perceived the broad-ranging character of the woman question, though the politics of sexuality was not developed either in his own thinking or in western thought in general in the early part of the twentieth century (Row-botham, 1974:107). Lenin was aware of sexuality as a political issue. He characterized bourgeois marriage and legislation on the family as perverse, because they treated women as property and thus gave license to forms of violence against women. Communism would not, should not breed asceticism, but rather "joy and strength, stemming among other things from a consummate love life" (Lenin, 1978:107). He was distressed that some of the communist youth subscribed to the theory that satisfying sexual needs was as simple as taking a drink of water. But he recognized that new sexual values in keeping with the proletarian revolution were being formed, and that the process was a part of the liberation of women.

In summary, then, Lenin's program for the liberation of women referred to production, housework, legal rights, sexism as the ideology of male supremacy, sexuality, and governance. But all these aspects are related to one foundation, "wherever there is capitalism, wherever there is private property in land and factories, wherever the power of capital is preserved, the men retain their privileges" (Lenin, 1978:67).

The distinctiveness of feminism within the context of Leninism is that it poses the need for a Marxist-Leninist party organized according to the principles of democratic centralism, and engaged in building a mass political base to seize state power, as the prerequisite for the liberation of women. The major weakness of this analysis is that it has not sufficiently grasped and criticized the way that democratic centralism became *bureaucratic* centralism in the history of major Marxist-Leninist parties, the Communist Party of the U.S.A. and the Commu-nist Party of the Soviet Union. The past practices of the socialist movements with regard to women's leadership and commitment to women's issues do not warrant our trust in the context of bureaucratic leadership—a leadership that has historically been shown to be insensitive to the concerns and the wisdom of the base.

The strength of this analysis is that it is the most clear of all those presented herein about the implications of the demands of feminism for social reorganization.

Socialist Feminism

Socialist feminism stands in the tradition of socialist struggles, but criticizes this tradition for not being able to account for the reality of patriarchy, the near universal domination of men over women, existing in all societies regardless of economic organization. The criticism is aimed at two aspects of socialism: the practice of socialists which often reflects the sexism of the surrounding society; and the theory of Marxism, which is unable to account for relations within the mode of reproduction (sexuality, home, family) or the deep significance of sexuality in the formation of human social relations (Graff, 1978:32).

Socialist feminists build on the radical feminist empirical data regarding male supremacy. But they criticize radical feminists for having a nonhistorical understanding of what patriarchy is, equating the effects of male supremacy across cultures and across historical eras, and not making qualitative distinctions between female infanticide and under-representation on the central committee (Ehrenreich, 1978:5).

In general terms, socialist feminism is not a uniform theory with consistency in its formulations. Theorists ally themselves with that trend within Marxist theory which emphasizes the connections between culture, politics, and the economic base, with attendant organizing implications, and oppose that trend which emphasizes the primacy of workplace organizing on economic issues. This is a strength in their perspective. A weakness, however, is that when socialist feminists criticize leftist theory and practice, mechanical Marxism, or econ-omism, their criticisms are rarely linked closely to texts or events. Thus, it is difficult to assess their criticisms.

The distinction between socialist feminism and mechanical Marxism is de-scribed by advocates of the former in terms of their intent to transform the sphere of reproduction as well as the sphere of production. Rather than collapse the issues involved in reproduction—family, child rearing, socialization, cooking, house-work—into a category of relations which will *automatically* change after the control of the productive forces has passed to the proletariat, socialist feminists contend that they should be bases for organizing in the working class now. Since the rise of monopoly industrial capitalism, these issues together with sexuality have become the last domain of control of workers, who have lost control over the productive or public sphere. Zaretsky (1978:17), who has developed this aspect of the "personal is political" slogan, theoretically dates this split as a process that took most of the nineteenth century and culminated around 1900.

With the rise of corporate capitalism the family became the major institution in society given over to the personal needs of its members. Within it new needs began to take shape: for intimacy, self-understanding and emotional connection. . . . A special concern for personal life has been called a "petit bourgeois" or "middle-class" preoccupation, but in fact it is only with the full scale development of a proletariat that we can truly speak of personal life in the modern sense.

The implication of Zaretsky's analysis is that "the personal is political" should not be seen as an addition to a Marxism manqué. Rather it should be seen as a reflection of historical developments within industrial capitalism, which we are compelled to understand and compute into our political theory and organizing, *using* the theory and method of historical materialism.

What this means for organizational structure, however, is unclear; for socialist feminists, while claiming that a socialist revolution is a necessary though not sufficient condition for the liberation of women (with which Marxist-Leninist feminists would agree), do not advocate party-building in Leninist perspective. Political formations tend to be described as autonomous groups, characterized by democracy, consensus decision-making, but not democratic centralism. Just how autonomous groups of women, blacks, gays, lesbians, poor people, and the elders will relate to each other in mass-based political struggle to make a revolution is not made explicit in socialist feminist documents, and this unclarity is another weakness.

Mitchell (1971) and Rowbotham (1974) are theorists of some import for the development of early socialist feminist theory. Mitchell put forward the view that women are oppressed in terms of their roles in production, reproduction, socialization, and sexuality, and that any program which does not address all these aspects will not fully liberate women. Because such views do not clearly identify the primary contradiction with women's liberation, their adherents lend only qualified support to socialist programs and organizations.

Rowbotham is credited with having reviewed much of the history of women's struggles within socialist struggles in Britain and Europe. Her work underlines the necessity of maintaining a strong women's movement within socialist organizing efforts as well as in socialist countries after revolutions. She is critical of feminist movements which do not have a social commitment.

CONCLUSION

In the preceding discussion, my purpose was to indicate why the term "feminist ethics" does not by itself indicate the content of feminist ethical theory. Indeed, there are at least four different social-political theories and programs which could provide a foundation for feminist ethics. However, the analysis of the roots of oppression is a key factor in feminist ethics. It has a direct bearing on the way we pose problems, gather data, commit our loyalties, rank values, engage in moral reasoning, justify claims, structure autonomy, and heighten motivation. Some examples might point to the validity of the exercise.

I made the point earlier that feminist ethicists generally agree that the appropriate starting point for ethical reflection is to attend to the very concrete situations, the fabric of women's lives. But just as few ethicists use the inductive mode at the expense of the deductive mode, feminists take into their reflection some assumptions which affect how they define the problem. Consequently, one can compare a radical feminist way of posing the problem, "In what ways are problematic situations the results of patriarchal control?" to a sex-rolist approach, "Is this a problem for both women and men, or do the conditions which resolve it apply equally for women and men?" A socialist feminist approach might look for concrete ways in which race and sexual dynamics benefit the owners of capital in the situation, and Marxist-Leninist feminists would probably share this starting point. Thus, at a fundamental level, the analysis of women's oppression affects the way the problem is posed.

Again, earlier I made the point that feminist ethicists have a loyalty to women *as women*, but that there is not across-the-board agreement as to how this loyalty relates to loyalties to other oppressed groups. Hence, the loyalties of radical feminists are to women, and perhaps even to radical feminist women, whereas the loyalties of sex-rolists are to all people, in the vision of situation-specific behaviors rather than sex-defined behaviors. Marxist-Leninist feminists have loyalties to women and men in the working class, and to all groups exploited by capital, as well as to those women and men who swing in their class allegiance toward the working class, thereby committing class suicide. Socialist feminists, because of a class analysis which views many professionals and white collar workers as working class, would view their loyalties in similar but broader terms than Marxist-Leninist feminists.

Values take on new meaning when they are defined in terms of the different political theories. "Control over our own bodies" can evoke images of the petit bourgeoisie, a class of individualists, in light of a Marxist-Leninist feminist position on reproductive rights. On the other hand, reproductive rights as democratic rights needed by working class women to participate in the revolutionary struggle can sound like a mask of male hegemony in the context of a socialist feminist or a radical feminist perspective.

Yet there is no necessary disagreement among feminists about a value theory. Self-determination for women, autonomy, and an inviolable sense of embodiedness figure prominently in all feminists' visions of a new social order. There might be disagreement, however, on the understanding about why to articulate a feminist value theory, which would determine the weight it is given. Ethicists who have integrated an historical materialist world view are likely to articulate a value theory as one task to be accomplished in addition to other, more social-structural tasks. It could be that ethicists who do not operate with an historical materialist world view project the reordering of values as primary among the tasks involved in creating new structures for social relations. This thesis explains in some measure the emphasis given to value theory among radical feminists and sex-role theorists. However, some sex-role theorists actually place more emphasis on restructuring the institutions of family and school than socialist or Marxist-Leninist feminists. Since the sex-role theorists do not face the task of restructuring the economy and political relations, they can attend to and focus on a limited range of institutions.

In the radical feminist perspective, motivation to ethical activity is a function of coming to awareness of being female in a woman-hating culture. In sex-rolism, motivation is the result of having insight as to all the levels of experience which have been defined as socially inappropriate by virtue of an irrational factor, gender. Socialist feminism and Marxist-Leninist feminism acknowledge a motivation of commitment to justice for all victims of private property, even if one has race, class, or sex privilege.

And so on. These paragraphs should be suggestive of further possibilities in connecting the analysis of the roots of oppression to other factors in ethical theory. The emphasis on the role of this factor in feminist ethics reflects two things: first, that social-political theory contains a broad range of ethical factors, and, second, that ethicists, in the narrow sense of this term, do have social-political analyses, often unacknowledged.

By implication, ethicists are accountable to make clear their analyses of the roots of oppression, so that they can be held accountable for adequacy to the full range of data. In so doing we are broadening the range of accountability for attending to such analyses in two directions: to all ethicists, insofar as their work is in any way related to the social sphere; and to claims for adequacy to women regardless of race and class. In the context of such claims we can sense that the discipline of social ethics is full of possibilities for people seeking to take control of their lives in the midst of community formation.

NOTES

1. For an illustration of this particular distinction in terms of the abortion question, see English (1977) and Cohen (1977).

2. Gilligan (1977) claims that the proclivity of women to reconstruct hypothetical dilemmas in terms of the real, to request or supply the information missing about the nature of people and the places where they live, shifts their judgment away from the hierarchical ordering of principles and the formal procedures of decision-making that are critical for scoring at Kohlberg's highest level.

3. Card (1978) claims we cannot presuppose a requisite publicity of the data for our inquiries, thus the need for autobiographies. Lebacqz (1979) says that if only logical analysis of "facts" is considered appropriate data, one takes the decision away from those most intimately involved, and obfuscates the value-laden nature of data. Mary Pellauer

teaches a course, "Violence and Violation," at Union Theological Seminary which organizes often-ignored data about various forms of violence against women.

4. For an illustration of the significance of analysis of a common data fund, compare Ehrenreich and Ehrenreich (1977) with Daly (1978) on the treatment of the development of gynecology in the medical profession. The Ehrenreichs argue that that development was part of the de-skilling of the working class. Midwifery, which played an important role in the culture of European immigrant groups and rural black and white Americans, was outlawed or discredited in the early 1900s and replaced by professionally-dominated care. De-skilling the working class was involved in the rise of the professional managerial class, whose function is to reproduce capitalist class relations. Daly views the rise of the professional field of gynecology as a reactionary response of men to the first wave of feminism. "For of course the purpose and intent of gynecology was/is not healing in a deep sense but violent enforcement of the sexual caste system." (See p. 227.)

5. Haney (1980) has articulated a notion of feminist ethics as a vision for a values revolution, and proposes the paradigm nourishment-friendship as the central values. It is the task of feminists, she claims, to redefine moral excellence, virtue, and the good person, and to hold suspect definitions from the past of justice, love, and mercy.

6. Just as H. Richard Niebuhr is credited by Gustafson (1978:13) as having claimed that ethics is reflection upon ethos, when that means that his task is to analyze "ethos," to lay bare the roots and fundamental character of a community's moral life, so too might the metaethics of Daly (1978:12) be understood: "I would say that radical feminist metaethics is of a *deeper intuitive* type than 'ethics.' The latter, generally written from one of several (but basically the same) patriarchal perspectives, works out of hidden agendas concealed in the texture of language, buried in mythic reversals which control 'logic' most powerfully because unacknowledged. Thus for theologians and philosophers, Eastern and Western, and particularly for ethicists, woman-identified women do not exist. The metaethics of radical feminism seeks to uncover the background. . . . It is able to do this because our primary concern is *not* male ethics and/or ethicists, but our own Journeying." Further considering the mode of decision-making, Gilligan (1979) characterizes women's patterns of moral reasoning in terms of an ethic of responsibility: "Sensitivity to the needs of others and the assumption of responsibility for taking care lead women to attend to voices other than their own and to include in their judgment other points of view. Women's moral weakness, manifest in an apparent diffusion and confusion of judgment, is thus inseparable from women's moral strength, an overriding concern with relationships and responsibilities. The reluctance to judge itself can be indicative of the same care and concern for others that infuses the psychology of women's development. . . ."

7. I am indebted to a March 1980 discussion within the Consultation on Social Ethics in Feminist Perspective, at Andover Newton Theological School, Newton Centre, Massachusetts, in which Lisa Cahill made the point that the inclusiveness of ends may distinguish teleological ethics from utilitarian ethics.

8. Lived-world experience, feminist consciousness, "our bodies ourselves," women's efforts to achieve full recognition as persons—all serve as sources for norms in the work of Beverly Harrison (1975; 1978).

9. In response to this and related issues, Ruth Smith, doctoral candidate at Boston University, is developing a notion of the social self as moral agent, and Kate Cannon, doctoral student at Union Theological Seminary, is judging the applicability of the autonomous self to survival ethics of black women.

10. Ehrenreich (1978:3) says that Marxism and feminism are both outlooks which

"lead to conclusions which are jarring and disturbing at the same time that they are liberating. There is no way to have a Marxist or feminist outlook and remain a spectator. To understand the reality laid bare by these analyses is to move into action to change it."

11. The term "radical feminism" is used here because it is a nomenclature of persons with this perspective. Where there is disagreement with radical feminists about the roots of women's oppression, and hence strategy, there will be reluctance to grant such usage of this term.

12. Barbara Hilkert Andolsen, doctoral candidate at Vanderbilt University, contributed this perspective on the political program of sex-rolism at the above-mentioned consultation.

13. To summarize and paraphrase her description of moral patterns in men and women, Gilligan (1979) claims that the morality of rights, characteristic of men's moral reasoning, differs from the morality of responsibility, characteristic of women's, in its emphasis on separation rather than attachment, in its consideration of the individual rather than the relationship as primary. When the categories of women's thinking are examined, the moral problem is seen to arise from conflicting responsibilities rather than competing rights and to require for its resolution a mode of thinking which is contextural and inductive rather than formal and abstract. This reconstruction of moral understanding is based not on the primacy of and universality of individual rights, but rather on a very strong sense of being responsible to the world. This orientation focuses on the limitations of any particular resolution and describes the conflicts that remain, whereas the rights conception of morality that informs Kohlberg's principled stages is geared toward arriving at an objectively fair or just resolution to the moral dilemma to which all rational men could agree.

REFERENCES

Card, Claudia
    1978 "Feminist ethical theory: a lesbian perspective." Unpublished manuscript.
Chodorow, Nancy
    1974 "Family structure and feminine personality." Pp. 43–66 in Michelle Zimbalist
        Rosaldo and Louise Lamphere, eds., Woman, Culture, and Society. Stanford:
        Stanford University Press.
Cohen, Howard
    1977 "Abortion and the quality of life." Pp. 429–440 in Mary Vetterling-Bragin,
        Frederick A. Elliston, and Jane English, eds., Feminism and Philosophy. Totowa,
        New Jersey: Littlefield, Adams, and Company.
Daly, Mary
    1978 Gyn/Ecology: The Metaethic of Radical Feminism. Boston: Beacon Press.
Dinnerstein, Dorothy
    1977 The Mermaid and the Minotaur. New York: Harper and Row.
Ehrenreich, Barabara
    1978 "What is socialist feminism?" New American Movement Working Papers on
        Socialism and Feminism. Chicago: National office.
Ehrenreich, Barabara, and Ehrenreich, John
    1977 "The professional-managerial class." Radical America 11:7–31.
English, Jane
    1977 "Abortion and the concept of a person." Pp. 417–428 in Mary Vetterling-

Bragin, Frederick A. Elliston, and Jane English, eds., *Feminism and Philosophy*. Totowa, New Jersey: Littlefield, Adams, and Company.

Gilligan, Carol
1977 "In a different voice: women's conceptions of self and of morality." *Harvard Educational Review* 47 (November): 481–517.
1979 "Woman's place in man's life cycle." *Harvard Educational Review* 49 (November):431–446.

Gordon, Linda, and Hunter, Allen
1978 "Sex, family and the new right: anti-feminism as a political force." *Radical America* 11, 12 (November–February):9–25.

Graff, Holly
1978 "The oppression of women." *New American Movement Working Papers on Socialism and Feminism*. Chicago: National office.

Gustafson, James
1978 "Introduction" to H. Richard Niebuhr, *The Responsible Self*. San Francisco: Harper and Row.

Haney, Eleanor
1980 "What is feminist ethics? a proposal for continuing discussion." *Journal of Religious Ethics* 8/1 (Spring): 115–124.

Harrison, Beverly
1975 "The new consciousness of women: a socio-political resource." *Cross Currents* (Winter):445–461.
1978 "Toward a just social order." *Journal of Current Social Issues* 15 (Spring): 63–70.

Judis, John
1971 "The personal and political." *Socialist Revolution* 2 (January–February): 9–29.

Lebacqz, Karen
1979 "Bioethics: some challenges from a liberation perspective." World Council of Churches, Conference on Faith, Science, and the Future, July 12–24, 1979, Cambridge, Massachusetts.

Lenin, Vladimir
1978 *The Emancipation of Women*. New York: International Publishers.

Mitchell, Juliet
1971 *Woman's Estate*. New York: Vintage Books.

Muelder, Walter
1966 *Moral Law in Christian Social Ethics*. Richmond, Virginia: John Knox Press.

Potter, Ralph
1972 "The logic of moral discourse." Pp. 93–114 in Paul K. Deats, Jr., ed., *Towards a Discipline of Social Ethics: Essays in Honor of Walter George Muelder*. Boston: Boston University Press.

Redstocking
1970 "The redstocking manifesto." Pp. 109–110 in Leslie B. Tanner, ed., *Voices From Women's Liberation*. New York: Signet.

Robb, Carol S.
1979 "Ethical procedures of Gutierrez and Alves." The American Society of Christian Ethics, *Selected Papers*.

Rowbotham, Sheila
1974 *Women, Resistance, and Revolution*. New York: Vintage Books.

Vogel, Lise
    1979 "Questions on the woman question." *Monthly Review* 31 (June):39–59.
Williams, Brooke L.
    1978 "What's wrong with sex-rolism." *Feminist Revolution.* Redstocking, P. O. Box
        413, New Paltz, New York, 12561.
Zaretsky, Eli
    1978 "Socialist politics and the family." *New American Movement Working Papers on
        Socialism and Feminism.* Chicago: National office.

3

HITTING A STRAIGHT LICK
WITH A CROOKED STICK

The Womanist Dilemma in the
Development of a Black Liberation Ethic

Katie G. Cannon

As a Black womanist ethicist I have been invited to be the first speaker in a three-part concurrent session entitled "Towards a Black Liberation Ethic." This invitation places me in a most precarious predicament. On the one hand, my task as a *Christian social ethicist* is to transcend my blackness and femaleness, and draft a blueprint of liberation ethics that somehow speaks to, or responds to, the universality of the human condition. On the other hand, my assignment as a *womanist liberation ethicist* is to debunk, unmask, and disentangle the historically conditioned value judgments and power relations that undergird the particularities of race, sex, and class oppression. Zora Neale Hurston described this dilemma as trying to hit a straight lick with a crooked stick. In essence, I have been invited to speak as "one of the canonical boys" and as "the noncanonical other" at one and the same time. These two tasks stand in opposition to each other.[1] Thus, the question which has evolved from wrestling with this dilemma is the following: what importance do race and gender have as meaningful categories in the development of a Black liberation ethic?

BLACK WOMAN ETHICIST AS
ONE OF THE CANONICAL BOYS

Even though there is no clearly written statement among Christian social ethicists regarding the nature of scholarship, enough areas of agreement do exist within the guild to make reasonable generalizations regarding the ethicist as scholar. Most of these have nothing to do with the realities of Black women. For instance, membership in this highly complex fraternity means investigation of abstract metatheory, traditional philosophical thought, and the established canon of ethical inquiry with supposedly calm and detached objectivity.[2]

To prove that she is sufficiently intelligent, the Black woman as Christian ethicist must discount the particularities of her lived experiences and instead focus on the validity of generalizable external analytical data. The dilemma she faces in joining the canonical boys is that of succumbing to the temptation of only mastering the historically specified perspective of the Euro-American masculine preserve.[3] In order to be a respected scholar in the discipline, the Black woman is placed under a double injunction. She has to face a critical jury, primarily white and male, that makes claims for gender-neutral and value-free inquiry as a model for knowledge.[4] The Black female scholar will have little opportunity to expand her creative energy in the direction of liberation ethics if she concentrates on searching for universal truths unhampered by so-called incidental matters such as race, sex, and class differences. In other words, there is an unspoken informal code within the guild that the Black woman academician must engage in this type of abstract moral discourse or else she runs the risk of being misunderstood, misinterpreted, and frequently devalued as a second-class scholar specializing in Jim Crow subject matter.[5]

What is important to grasp here is that both the inclusion of Black women and the inclusion of Black women's moral reasoning within the structure of traditional ethics are pioneering endeavors.[6] Black women's experience has been overlooked, neglected, or distorted in most of the existing ethical scholarship. For instance, Black women as subjects for scholarly research have been given little attention. Little writing in ethics focuses on the moral agency of Black females. Unfortunately, this situation is not peculiar to ethics; Black women as worthy subjects of study are ignored in most areas of scholarship.

From behind the veil of race and sex neutrality, the Black female scholar understands that the metaphysical and ethical issues are mutually connected. The accepted canonical methods of moral reasoning contain deeply hidden biases that make it exceedingly difficult to turn them to the service of the best interest of Black women.[7] Universality does not include the Black female experience.

Why does the discipline of ethics have so little to say about Black women's role in church and society? What value does the academy place on the history, culture, and traditions that Black women have created? Do we see Black women's moral wisdom as making a poor virtue of survival?

In scanning the canon in ethical studies, one finds that this omission of Black women provides continuing ideological support for conditions and public policies oppressive to Black women. The white masculine orientation that characterizes the field of study leaves Black women out. This type of academic invisibility reinforces racist/sexist stereotypes and justifies misapprehensions that lock Black women into marginal status. In other words, the concepts used by the majority of white male ethicists to discuss moral agency implicitly devalue Black women's contribution. Chanzo Tallamu in her review of *Slipping Through the Cracks: The Status of Black Women* argues that as long as current research methods do not reflect or pay enough attention to the needs of Black women, the policies and programs that result may benefit white women or Black men but not Black women.[8]

When ethical discourse provides truncated and distorted pictures of Black women, the society at large uses these oppressive stereotypes to define what it is to be Black and female in America. An even more basic manifestation of this trivialization of Black women has been the traditional practice of generalizing about Black women on the information gathered from white women or Black men.[9] The emphasis has to be placed on information derived from Black women talking about their own lives and religious experiences.

Until the advent of the civil rights movement in the 1960s and the women's movement in the 1970s, Black women were virtually ignored and their questions reduced to marginal absurdity as a result of sexist/racist assumptions. Black women's contributions to the academy have been considered incidental to the substance of theology and ethics—mere asides, insignificant to the conceptual framework that defines the body of thought as a whole.[10] Black women's moral agency must be understood on their own terms rather than being judged by essentially abstract external ideological norms and squeezed into categories and systems which consider white men the measure of significance. Lives of Black women cannot be fully comprehended using analytical categories derived from white/male experience. Oftentimes such concepts covertly sustain a hierarchy of white supremacy, patriarchy, and exploitative power.[11]

BLACK WOMAN ETHICIST AS NONCANONICAL OTHER

The dilemma of the Black woman ethicist as the noncanonical other is defined as working in opposition to the academic establishment, yet building upon it. The liberation ethicist works both within and outside the guild. The Black womanist scholar receives the preestablished disciplinary structures of intellectual inquiry in the field of ethics and tries to balance the paradigms and assumptions of this intellectual tradition with a new set of questions arising from the context of Black women's lives.[12] The tension is found in the balancing act of simultaneously trying to raise the questions appropriate to the discipline while also trying to understand what emphasis ought properly to be placed on the various determinants influencing the situation of Black women. In order to work towards an inclusive ethic, the womanist struggles to restructure the categories so that the presuppositions more readily include the ethical realities of Black women.

The womanist scholar identifies the pervasive white and male biases deeply embedded in the field of study. As a liberationist, she challenges and reshapes the traditional inquiry and raises candid questions between the two locales of whiteness and maleness. She insists that new questions guide the research so that

Black women's moral wisdom can provide the answers. In essence, she seeks to determine why and how Black women actively negotiate their lives in a web of oppression.[13]

The Black woman's ethical analysis distinguishes between "possibilities in principle" and "possibilities in fact." She extends Black women's existential reality above the threshold of that frustrating and illusory social mobility which forms the core of the American dream. That is, she strips away false, objectified conceptualities and images that undergird the apparatuses of systemic oppression.

The intersection of race, sex, and class give womanist scholars a different ethical orientation with a different ideological perspective. The experience of being both the participant from within and the interpreter from without results in an inescapable duality to the character of womanist ethics. Beginning with her own historical, socio-ethical situation, the Black woman scholar cuts off what is untrue and adds what is most urgent. In other words, she refutes what is inimical and co-opts the positive. This task is difficult since Black women in general are dealing with vague, amorphous social ideals, on the one hand, and with the long-standing effects of American racism, sexism, and class elitism on the other.[14]

For example, Black female ethicists endure with a certain grace the social restrictions that limit their own mobility, and at the same time they demand that the relationships between their own condition and the condition of those who have a wide range of freedom be recognized. They bring into clear focus the direct correlation of economic, political, and racial alienation. As participant-interpreters, their direct contact with the high and the lowly, the known and the unrecognized, the comic and the tragic, makes them conscious of the myriad value systems which are antithetical to Black survival. To demystify large and obscure ideological relations, social theories, and, indeed, the heinous socio-political reality of tri-dimensional oppression is a moral act. To do ethics inside out and back again is the womanist norm.

In other words, as the noncanonical other, these women rightly recognize how family life, cultural expression, political organization, social and economic roles shape the Black community. Furthermore, they identify the way Black women as moral agents persistently attempt to strip away the shrouding of massive dislocation and violence exacerbated in recent years by the nation's fiscal crisis.[15] Under extremely harsh conditions, Black women buttress themselves against the dominant coercive apparatuses of society. Using a series of resistance modes, they weave together many disparate strands of survival skills, styles, and traditions in order to create a new synthesis which, in turn, serves as a catalyst for deepening the wisdom-source which is genuinely their own.[16]

Black women ethicists use this framework of wisdom to compare and contrast Black female moral agency with the agency of those in society who have the freedom to maximize choice and personal autonomy. The womanist scholar focuses on describing, documenting, and analyzing the ideologies, theologies, and systems of values that perpetuate the subjugation of Black women. At the same time, she emphasizes how Black women are shaping their own destinies within restricted possibilities, resisting and overthrowing those restrictions, and sometimes, in the interest of survival, acting in complicity with the forces that keep them oppressed.[17]

To make this point clearer: Black women ethicists constantly question why Black women are considered merely ancillary, no more than throwaway superfluous appendages in a society that claims "life, liberty, and the pursuit of happiness" as "inalienable rights." What theological systems relegate Black women to the margins of the decision-making mainstream of American religious, political, and economic life? And, what qualitative judgments and social properties establish a chasm between the proposition that Black women, first and foremost, are human beings and the machinations that allow glaring inequities and unfulfilled promises to proceed morally unchecked?

The womanist scholar stresses the role of emotional, intuitive knowledge in the collective life of the people. Such intuition enables moral agents in situations of oppression to follow the rule within, and not be dictated to from without. Untrammeled by external authority, Black female moral agents' intuitive faculties lead them toward a dynamic sense of moral reasoning. They designate the processes, the manners, and subtleties of their own experiences with the least amount of distortion from the outside. They go below the level of racial, sexual structuring and into those areas where Black people are simply human beings struggling to reduce to consciousness all of their complex experiences. Communion with one's own truths makes one better able to seize and delineate with unerring discrimination the subtle connections among people, institutions, and systems that serve as silent accessories to the perpetuation of flagrant forms of injustice.[18]

Intrigued by the largely unexamined questions that have fallen through the cracks between feminist ethics and Black male theology, the womanist scholar insists on studying the distinctive consciousness of Black women within Black women's institutions, clubs, organizations, magazines, and literature.[19] Appropriating the human condition in their own contexts, Black women collectively engage in revealing the hidden power relations inherent in the present social structures. A central conviction is that theo-ethical structures are not universal, color-blind, apolitical, or otherwise neutral. Thus, the womanist ethicist tries to comprehend how Black women create their own lives, influence others, and understand themselves as a force in their own right. The womanist voice is one of deliverance from the deafening discursive silence which the society at large has used to deny the basis of shared humanity.

CONCLUSION

In order to move towards a Black liberation ethic, attention must be paid to an ethical vision that includes Black women. The substantial omission of Black women from theological discourse flows quite naturally from male theologians using analytical concepts and frameworks that take the male experience as the norm.[20] An inclusive liberation ethic must focus on the particular questions of women in order to reveal the subtle and deep effects of male bias on recording religious history.[21] As scholars, we must demonstrate the hidden assumptions and premises that lie behind our ethical speculations and inferences. Our task is to change the imbalance caused by an androcentric view, wherein it is presumed that only men's activities have theological value. If we are willing to unmask the male assumptions that dominate religious thought, we will discover whole new areas of ethical inquiry.

Secondly, in moving towards a Black liberation ethic we must examine Black women's contributions in all the major fields of theological studies—Bible, history, ethics, mission, worship, theology, preaching, and pastoral care. The Black male biases operate not so much to omit Black women totally as to relegate Black church women to the position of direct object instead of active subject.[22] Too often Black women are presented in a curiously impersonal dehumanizing way as the fused backbone in the body of the church.

A womanist liberation ethic requires us to gather information and to assess accurately the factual evidence regarding Black women's contribution to the Black church community.[23] Black women organized voluntary missionary societies, superintended church schools, led prayer meetings, took an active part in visiting and ministering to the sick and needy, and raised large amounts of money to defray the expenses of the Black church. Black women are conscious actors who have altered the theological picture in significant ways. Furthermore, this second area of research does more than increase our understanding of Black women in the church community; it also elicits reinterpretation of old conclusions about the church universal.

Finally, the development of an inclusive ethic requires us to recognize and condemn the extent to which sex differences prevail in the institutional church, in our theological writings, and in the Black church's practices.[24] A womanist liberation ethic directs critical attention not only to scholarship in the fields of study but also to its concrete effects on women in the pews. The work has to be done both from the basis of church practices and from the basis of continuing academic investigation. For instance, we need to do an analysis of sexist content of sermons in terms of reference to patriarchal values and practices. Particular attention needs to be given to the objectification, degradation, and subjection of the female in Black preaching.[25] At the same time, we need to analyze the social organization of the Black Church[26]—curricula, music, leadership expectation, pastor-member interactions—as well as outright sex discrimination. Far too often, the organization of the church mirrors male dominance in the society and normalizes it in the eyes of both female and male parishioners.

Whether the discipline of ethics has almost completely neglected Black women (as in white male scholarship) or treated them as incidental to central issues (as in Black male scholarship) or considered gender as the important factor for research (as in white feminist scholarship), the cumulative effect of womanist scholarship is that it moves us towards a fundamental reconceptualization of all ethics with the experience of Black women at center stage.

NOTES

1. For a provocative critique of this dilemma, see Vincent Harding, "Responsibilities of the Black Scholar to the Community," in *The State of Afro-American History: Past, Present, and Future,* ed. Darlene Clark Hine (Baton Rouge: Louisiana State University Press, 1986), 277–84; Oliver C. Cox, "The New Crisis in Leadership Among Negroes," *Journal of Negro Education,* 19/4 (Fall 1950), 459–65; also Cox "Leadership Among Negroes in the United States," in Alvin W. Gouldner, ed., *Studies in Leadership* (New York: Russell & Russell, 1950), 228–71.

2. Robert K. Merton, "Insiders and Outsiders: A Chapter in the Sociology of Knowledge," *American Journal of Sociology* 78 (July 1972).

3. For example, read the essays in *Norm and Context in Christian Ethics,* edited by Gene H. Outka and Paul Ramsey (New York: Charles Scribner's Sons, 1968), and critique them in relation to this concern. Use the same process with Paul Ramsey, *Basic Christian Ethics* (New York: Charles Scribner's Sons, 1950); and Alasdair MacIntyre, *After Virtue* (Notre Dame: University of Notre Dame Press, 1981).

4. For a selection of early works on this topic from the perspective of the Black male scholar, see John Hope Franklin, "The Dilemma of the American Negro Scholar," in Herbert Hill, ed., *Soon, One Morning: New Writing by American Negroes, 1940–1962* (1963), 64–69 passim and 73–74; Carter G. Woodson, *The Mis-Education of the Negro* (Washington, D.C.: The Associated Publishers, Inc., 1933); W.E.B. Du Bois, *The Education of Black People: Ten Critiques, 1906–1960,* ed. Herbert Aptheker (Amherst: University of Massachusetts Press, 1973); and Harry Washington Greene, *Holders of Doctorates Among American Negroes* (1946).

5. For recent and comprehensive critique, see Mary Francis Berry, "Blacks in Predominantly White Institutions of Higher Learning," in National Urban League, *The State of Black America 1983* (New York: 1983); Robert Staples, "Racial Ideology and Intellectual Racism: Blacks in Academia," *The Black Scholar* 15/2 (March–April 1984): 2–17; and John Wideman, "Publish and Still Perish: The Dilemma of Black Educators on White Campuses," *Black Enterprise* 10 (September 1978): 44–49.

6. This sort of observation has been made in numerous contexts. See for example, Harold Cruse, *The Crisis of the Negro Intellectual* (New York: William Morrow and Co., 1967); Betty D. Maxwell, *Employment of Minority Ph.D.'s: Changes Over Time* (Washington, D.C.: Commission on Human Resources of the National Research Council, 1981); Jeanne Noble, *The Negro College Woman Graduate* (New York: Columbia University Press, 1954); and Oliver C. Cox, "Provisions for Graduate Education Among Negroes," *Journal of Negro Education,* 11/1 (January, 1940): 222–27.

7. Sheila Ruth, "Methodocracy, Misogyny, and Bad Faith: Sexism in the Philosophical Establishment," *Metaphilosophy* 10 (1979): 48–61; Delores Williams, "Women's Oppression and Life-Line Politics in Black Women's Religious Narratives," *Journal of Feminist Studies in Religion* 1/2 (Fall 1985):59–71.

8. Chanzo Tallamu, Review of *Slipping Through the Cracks: The Status of Black Women, Black Scholar* (July/August 1986): 59.

9. Chandra Talpade Mohantz, "On Difference: The Politics of Black Women's Studies," *Women's Studies International Forum* 6 (1983): 243–47; Margaret A. Simons, "Racism and Feminism: A Schism in the Sisterhood," *Feminist Studies* 5 (1979): 384–401; and The Mud Flower Collective, *God's Fierce Whimsy: Christian Feminism and Theological Education* (New York: Pilgrim Press, 1985).

10. See John E. Fleming, *The Lengthening Shadow of Slavery: A Historical Justification for Affirmative Action for Blacks in Higher Education* (Washington, D.C.: Howard University Press, 1976).

11. Theodore Caplow and R. McGee, *The Academic Marketplace* (New York: Basic Books, 1958); Pierre Van den Berghe, *Academic Gamesmanship: How to Make a Ph.D. Pay* (New York: Abelard-Schuman, 1970); and Alvin W. Gouldner, *The Future of Intellectuals and the Rise of the New Class* (New York: Seabury Press, 1979).

12. Without doubt the most influential womanists who take this approach are: Angela Davis, *Women, Race and Class* (New York: Random House, 1981); June Jordan, *On Call: Political Essays* (Boston: South End Press, 1985); Alice Walker, *In Search of Our Mothers' Gardens: Womanist Prose* (New York: Harcourt Brace Jovanovich, 1983); Audre Lorde, *Sister Outsider: Essays and Speeches* (Trumansburg, N.Y.: Crossing Press, 1984).

13. For examples, see Bernice Johnson Reagon, "The Borning Struggle: The Civil Rights Movement," in Dick Cluster, ed., *They Should Have Served That Cup of Coffee* (Boston: South End Press, 1979); Barbara Smith, ed., *Home Girls: A Black Feminist Anthology* (Watertown, Mass.: Persephone Press, 1983); Bell Hooks, *Ain't I a Woman? Black Women and Feminism* (Boston: South End Press, 1981).

14. This kind of moral reasoning is delineated in Filomina C. Steady, ed., *The Black Woman Cross-Culturally* (Cambridge, Mass.: Schenkman Pub. Co., 1981); Toni Cade, ed., *The Black Woman: An Anthology* (New York: The New American Library, 1970); and Gloria T. Hull, Patricia Bell Scott, and Barbara Smith, eds., *All the Women Are White, All the Blacks Are Men, But Some of Us Are Brave* (Old Westbury, N.Y.: Feminist Press, 1982).

15. Coalition on Women and the Budget, *Inequality of Sacrifice: The Impact of the Reagan's Budget on Women* (Washington, D.C., 1983).

16. All these works are either implicit or explicit analyses of this position: Dorothy Sterling, *We Are Your Sisters: Black Women in the Nineteenth Century* (New York: Norton Books, 1984); Jacqueline Jones, *Labor of Love, Labor of Sorrow: Black Women, Work and the Family from Slavery to the Present* (New York: Basic Books, 1985); Bert Loewenberg and Ruth Bogin, eds., *Black Women in Nineteenth Century American Life: Their Words, Their Thoughts, Their Feelings* (University Park, Penn.: Pennsylvania State University, 1976); and Rosalyn Terborg-Penn and Sharon Harley, eds., *The Afro-American Woman: Struggles and Images* (New York: Kennikat, 1978).

17. See, in particular, Ellen N. Lawson, "Sarah Woodson Early: Nineteenth-Century Black Nationalist 'Sister,' " *Umoja: A Scholarly Journal of Black Studies* 5 (Summer 1981); Gerda Lerner, ed., *Black Women in White America: A Documentary History* (New York: Random House, 1972); and Dorothy Sterling, *Black Foremothers: Three Lives* (Old Westbury, N.Y.: Feminist Press, 1979).

18. Rennie Simson, "The Afro-American Female: The Historical Context of the Construction of Sexual Identity," in Ann Snitow, Sharon Thompson, and Christine Stausa II, eds., *The Powers of Desire: The Politics of Sexuality* (New York: Monthly Review Press, 1983), 229–35.

19. Darlene Clark Hine, "Lifting the Veil, Shattering the Silence: Black Women's History in Slavery and Freedom," in Darlene Clark Hine, ed., *The State of Afro-American*

History: Past, Present, and Future (Baton Rouge: Louisiana State University Press, 1986), 223–49.

20. For examples, see Gayraud S. Wilmore and James H. Cone, eds., *Black Theology: A Documentary History, 1966–1979* (Maryknoll, New York: Orbis Books, 1979); and Preston N. Williams, "Impartiality, Racism, and Sexism," *The Annual of the Society of Christian Ethics,* 1983: 147–59.

21. Ellen Carol DuBois et al., *Feminist Scholarship: Kindling in the Groves of Academe* (Urbana: University of Illinois Press, 1985); Beverly W. Harrison, *Making the Connections,* edited by Carol Robb (Boston: Beacon Press, 1985); Barbara H. Andolsen, Christine E. Gudorf, and Mary D. Pellauer, eds., *Women's Consciousness, Women's Conscience* (New York: Seabury Press, 1985).

22. For historical works, see W.E.B. Du Bois, *The Negro Church* (Atlanta: Atlanta University Press, 1903); Benjamin E. Mays, *The Negro's God as Reflected in His Literature* (Boston: Chapman and Grimes, Inc., 1958); Benjamin E. Mays and Joseph W. Nicholson, *The Negro's Church* (New York: Institute of Social and Religious Research, 1933); and Carter G. Woodson, *The History of the Negro Church* (Washington, D.C.: The Associated Pub., 1921).

23. Katie G. Cannon, "The Sign of Hope in Three Centuries of Despair: Women in the Black Church Community," in *Human Rights and the Global Mission of the Church,* Boston Theological Institute Annual Series, vol. 1 (Cambridge, Mass., 1985), 44–50.

24. For examples, see Edward M. Brawley, ed., *The Negro Baptist Pulpit* (Philadelphia: American Baptist Publication Society, 1890); Charles V. Hamilton, *The Black Preacher in America* (New York: Morrow, 1972); Henry Beecher Hicks, *Images of the Black Preacher* (Valley Forge: Judson Press, 1977).

25. Henry H. Mitchell, *Black Preaching* (Philadelphia: Lippincott, 1970); William M. Philpot, ed., *Best Black Sermons* (Valley Forge: Judson Press, 1972); Henry J. Young, ed., *Preaching the Gospel* (Philadelphia: Fortress Press, 1976); and Samuel Proctor and William D. Watley, *Sermons from the Black Pulpit* (Valley Forge: Judson Press, 1984).

26. Harry V. Richardson, *Dark Glory: A Picture of the Church Among Negroes in the Rural South* (New York: Friendship Press, 1947); William L. Banks, *The Black Church in The United States: Its Origin, Growth, Contribution and Outlook* (Chicago: Moody Press, 1972); C. Eric Lincoln, *The Black Experience in Religion* (Garden City: Doubleday, Anchor, 1974); Albert J. Raboteau, *Slave Religion: The "Invisible Institution" in Antebellum South* (New York: Oxford University Press, 1978).

4

THE COLOR OF FEMINISM

Or Speaking the Black Woman's Tongue

Delores S. Williams

The title of my address issues from two sources. The first part of the topic—"The Color of Feminism"—came from the editors of *Christianity and Crisis* who used these words to title my response to an article written by feminist theologian, Rosemary Ruether.[1] The second part of the title—"Speaking the Black Woman's Tongue"—came from my experience with two groups of black Christian women who asked me to speak to them about feminism and feminist theology. When I finished discussing feminism (its source and contemporary character) and describing the positions of representative feminist theologians, one woman in each group gave a response that has plagued me from that day until this. For the purposes of this address, I will refer to these women as group "A" and group "B." The black woman in group "A" said:

> "Honey [addressing me], I want to say something about this feminism if you can bear with me. [I nodded my head indicating I could.] This all reminds me of the day I went into a fancy dress shop downtown and saw a real pretty dress. The colors in the dress blended right. The design was modern and fashionable. The buttons in front looked real pretty with the material. Everything about that dress looked just right. There was only one problem when it came right down to me. The dress was size five, and I wear size twenty. The saleslady told me that shop didn't carry no dresses over size thirteen. I can sew real good, but I knew there was no way for me to alter that dress and still have the same thing. There just wasn't enough material in that dress to make it fit me. Now that's my point, honey. This feminism looks real pretty, but there just ain't enough in it to fit me. And what I'm wondering is: if you black feminists try to make feminism fit me, will you have the same thing?"

The woman in group "B" asked questions that were even more probing. In this group, I had used the work of Bell Hooks (*Ain't I a Woman?*) and Angela Davis (*Women, Race and Class*) to present some black female scholars' views of the politics of some of the leading nineteenth and twentieth century feminists. Instantly, the women in the group became interested in Davis' and Hooks' descriptions of the racist ideas and actions of some of the white feminists. Then a small black woman in the group walked up to the front. She faced me and asked the following questions:

> "If the work of women's liberation in this country has always accomplished white supremacy and the work of the Ku Klux Klan is for white supremacy, is the label 'feminist' comparable to the label 'klansman'? Do the words 'black feminist' equal the same kind of terrible contradiction as the words 'black klansman'? Since you are a feminist, ma'am, are you advancing the cause of white supremacy? Are you extending white woman's privilege rather than fighting for the liberation of black women and all other black people? What are your feminist politics about?"

I could discern that my responses to these women left them uneasy, unsatisfied. While I could make some correlations between white and black women's oppression and could point to the work of individual white feminists who also struggled for all women's liberation, I could not deliver on the "biggies" that Bell Hooks pointed out in *Ain't I a Woman?* For instance, I could not convince them that the contemporary feminist movement was any more *seriously concerned* about black women's liberation than the early white suffragettes were *seriously concerned* about black women getting the vote. Like many poor, oppressed people who cannot afford to live above the level of practical reality, these Afro-American Christian women apparently believed the truth of feminism lay in the incongruity between feminist rhetoric and feminist action.

These experiences (i.e., having *Christianity and Crisis* editors title my article "The Color of Feminism," and hearing the response of black Christian women to feminism) have caused me to shape some questions which are now at the center of my work. As I teach religious studies; as I participate in the life of the church; as I struggle with groups of women caught up in the problems generated by racist social structures, low self-esteem, and abusive men, I ask myself: "Is it only the racism of a few white feminists that causes most black women not to become involved in the feminist movement in church and society? How (or can) feminism be 'colorized' so that it also speaks the black woman's tongue, so that it tells the very truth of the black woman's historical existence in North America? What are the materials that have to be put into feminism to make it fit black women? If feminism is 'colorized' so that it also speaks the black woman's tongue, so that it (feminism) does not reinforce white supremacy, will feminism still be feminism?"

Tonight, I will share with you my reflections upon these questions. Though my observations and analysis are far from conclusive, they do represent my first public attempt to respond to the call for accountability that undergirded the questions of the black Christian women in groups "A" and "B."

IS IT ONLY RACISM?

Within the last five years, black female scholars have documented the biases toward black women that have existed in the women's liberation movements in America since their beginning in the nineteenth century. Angela Davis describes the first women's rights convention held in America at Seneca Falls in 1848. She comments on the white women's lack of concern for the slave women:

> While at least one Black man was present among the Seneca Falls conferees, there was not a single Black woman in attendance. Nor did the convention's documents make even a passing reference to Black women. In light of the organizers' abolitionist involvement it would seem puzzling that slave women were entirely disregarded.[2]

At the 1851 Women's Convention held in Akron, Ohio (when Sojourner Truth delivered her famous "Ain't I a Woman?" speech), some of the white women ". . . had been initially opposed to a Black Woman having a voice in their convention." Davis claims, however, that by 1869 when the Equal Rights Association was ending its life, Sojourner Truth had begun to recognize:

> . . . the dangerous racism underlying the feminists' opposition to Black male suffrage. . . . When Sojourner Truth insisted that "if you bait the suffrage-hook with a woman, you will certainly catch a black man," she issued yet another profound warning about the menacing influence of racist ideology.[3]

Another black female scholar, Bell Hooks, declares that "every women's movement in America from its earliest origin to the present day has been built on a racist foundation. . . ."[4] Hooks claims "the first white women's rights advocates were never seeking social equality for all women; they were seeking social equality for white women."[5] Refuting the contemporary white poet, Adrienne Rich, who said that white women's activity in the Abolitionist movement provides a ". . . strong anti-racist female tradition" for the contemporary feminist movement, Hooks says:

> They [the nineteenth century white women's rights' advocates] attacked slavery, not racism. The basis of their attack was moral reform. . . . While they strongly advocated an end to slavery, they never advocated a change in the racial hierarchy that allowed their caste status to be higher than that of black women or men. In fact, they wanted that hierarchy to be maintained. Consequently, the white women's rights movements, which had a lukewarm beginning in earlier reform activities, emerged in full force in the wake of efforts to gain rights for black people precisely because white women wanted to see no change in the social status of blacks until they [white women] were assured that their demands for more rights were met.[6]

Even more devastating for black women and black men in the nineteenth century were the racist strategies individual white feminists employed to gain white women's rights. Paula Giddings describes some of the debased activities of women's suffrage leaders Susan Anthony and Elizabeth Cady Stanton. Giddings says:

> More revealing—and disturbing—was the vicious campaign launched by Anthony and Stanton. Black women like [Francis] Harper may have had their complaints against Black men, but they must have looked down on White women using them as fodder to further their own selfish ends. That this was Anthony and Stanton's strategy became clear when they allied with a millionaire Democrat, George Train, who financed their feminist newspaper, *The Revolution*. Within its pages was venom of the worst kind.[7]

The Revolution carried Susan Anthony's observation that the Republican Party had elevated two million black men and given them the dignity of citizenship by giving them the vote. "With the other hand," Anthony claimed, "they [the Republicans] dethroned FIFTEEN MILLION WHITE WOMEN—their own mothers and sisters, their own wives and daughters—and cast them under the heel of the lowest orders of manhood."[8] Elizabeth Cady Stanton was more vicious. She wrote about a black man lynched in Tennessee. "The point of the story," says Giddings, "wasn't the awful injustice of lynching, but that giving black men the vote was virtually a license to rape."[9] Stanton also attempted to use class as a weapon in her battle to secure voting rights for white, upper-class women. When she announced she would run for the New York Legislature in 1866, Stanton had this to say:

> In view of the fact that the freed men of the South and the millions of foreigners now crowding our shores, most of whom represent neither property, education nor civilization, are all in the progress of events to be enfranchised, the best interests of the nation demand that we outweigh this incoming pauperism, ignorance and degradation, with the wealth, education, and refinement of the women of the republic.[10]

When Stanton was pressured to clarify this position, she condescendingly responded: "We prefer Bridget and Dinah at the ballot box to Patrick and Sambo."[11]

It is no wonder that subsequent feminists made racist statements equal to those of Anthony and Stanton. In 1903, a leading southern feminist, Belle Kearney, proclaimed:

> Just as surely as the North will be forced to turn to the South for the nation's salvation, just so surely will the South be compelled to look to its Anglo-Saxon women as the medium through which to retain the supremacy of the white race over the Africans.[12]

Apparently the contemporary feminist movement—in both its secular and religious manifestations—is no less infested with racism than its predecessor, the women's suffrage movement. Feminists of color are protesting. In the book *This*

Bridge Called My Back, a Chicana woman declares that ". . . women of color are veterans of a class and color war that is still escalating in the feminist movement." Black feminist poet Audre Lorde chides Mary Daly, a white feminist scholar in religious studies, about using her words (Lorde's) to corroborate her (Daly's) analysis of what she sees as sexist practices in black cultures. In "An Open Letter to Mary Daly" about Daly's book *Gyn/Ecology,* Lorde says, "For my part, I felt . . . you . . . misused my words, utilized them only to testify against myself as a woman of color. . . . For my words you used were no more, or less, illustrative of this chapter than . . . any number of my other poems might have been." Lorde asks Daly, "So the question arises in my mind, Mary, do you ever really read work of black women?"[13] In a recent issue of *Christianity and Crisis,* a black female minister, the Reverend Angelique Walker-Smith, directed some questions to white feminist theologian Rosemary Ruether about an article she (Ruether) wrote. Walker-Smith expressed serious concern over what she saw as Ruether's use of the term "Christian feminism" to signify only white feminism. Walker-Smith says:

> I am very disturbed about Ruether's labeling of "Christian Feminism" in her article [Ruether's "Feminist Theology and the Academy" appearing in *Christianity and Crisis,* March 4, 1985]. Why does she use the term "Christian Feminism" to label what really is "Christian feminism for white women"? Is she trying to suggest that Asian Christian feminism and black Christian feminism or any other minority Christian feminism is somehow subject to "white woman Christian feminism"? The insinuation that "white woman feminism" is somehow the true Christian feminism is clearly made when it is made to look synonymous with "Christian feminism. . . ."[14]

On the basis of the preceding evidence, one can conclude that the racist activity of white feminists has been prevalent enough to discourage many Afro-American women from participating in the feminist movement. However, I want to suggest an additional problem that might account for black women's absence from the feminist movement. This problem centers upon an idea that is significant for feminist thought and action. My discussion here will also touch on the second and third questions I am considering tonight—i.e., "How (or can) feminism be 'colorized' so that it also speaks the tongue of black women . . . ?" and, "if feminism can so speak, what additional materials have to be added to make it fit black women's experience?"

SPEAKING BLACK WOMEN'S TONGUE?

For feminist thinking, an important idea is that patriarchy is the major source of all women's oppression. However, this idea becomes limited and problematic when one attempts to use it to understand the Afro-American woman's *total* experience of oppression in North America.

In feminist literature, patriarchy is the power relation between men and women and between women and society's institutions controlled by men. White-American feminist Adrienne Rich describes it as:

> . . . the power of the fathers: a familial-social, ideological, political system in which men—by force, direct pressure, or through ritual, tradition, law, and language, customs, etiquette, education, and division of labor, determine what part women shall or shall not play, and in which the female is everywhere subsumed under the male.[15]

While Mary Daly, in *Beyond God the Father,* reveals how the patriarchal religions (e.g., Judaism and Christianity) reinforce women's oppression and validate male supremacy, her understanding of patriarchy apparently concurs with Rich's definition. It is not reductionist, I think, to suggest that most feminist writing on the subject does support Rich's understanding of the meaning of patriarchy.[16]

However, a simple interpolation of Rich's definition reveals its limitation as far as black women are concerned. To be congruent with the Afro-American woman's experience of oppression in this country, patriarchy would have to be defined as:

> . . . the power of . . . [white men and white women]: a familial-social, ideological, political system in which [white men and white women]—by force, direct pressure, or through ritual, tradition, law and language, customs, etiquette, education, and division of labor, determine what part [black women] shall or shall not play, and in which the [black female] is everywhere subsumed under the [white female] and white male.[17]

Thus defined, patriarchy loses its identity. It is no longer just the power of fathers, or men, to oppress women. It is also the power of a certain group of females to oppress other groups of females. This inclusion of a group of women as oppressors—an assessment that speaks the truth of the Afro-American woman's history in North America—renders the feminist patriarchal critique of society less valid as a tool for assessing black women's oppression *resulting from their relation to white-controlled American institutions.* Therefore, one cannot claim that patriarchy, as it is understood by feminists, is the major source of all women's oppression.

Another limitation of the feminist understanding of patriarchy is that it fails to place emphasis upon what appears to be a positive side of patriarchy with regard to the development of white-American women. It is also the operation of this positive side that indicates a clear distinction between white women's and black women's oppression.

White American patriarchy, in its institutional manifestations, affords many white female children and white female adults (as groups) the care, protection, and resources necessary for intellectual development and physical well-being.[18] White American patriarchy has thus provided white women with the education, skills, and support (and often financial resources) they need to get first chance at the jobs and opportunities for women resulting from the pressures exerted by the civil rights movements in America. White American patriarchy, in its private and institutional manifestations, also intends to support the life, physical growth, intellectual development, and economic well-being of the female and male fruit of the white woman's womb—*When That Fruit Issues From Her Sexual Union With White Males.* From a black female perspective, then, it is possible to speak of *the productive patriarchal intent of white patriarchy* for the female and male fruit of the white woman's womb. And this productive patriarchal intent permeates the relation between white women (as a group) and the white-controlled institutions of American society.

However, the same institutions have no such productive intent for black women or for the fruit of black women's wombs (even if that fruit derived from sexual union between a black female and a white male).[19] Rather, these institutions intend the retardation of the intellectual, emotional, spiritual, economic, and physical growth of black women and the fruit of their wombs, male and female. This is partly demonstrated in the current operation of the white-controlled public school system in America. The black struggle for equality through integration into that system has exposed black children to a host of white male and white female teachers who daily undermine (often through ignorance of their own racism) the confidence, the intellectual stamina, the spirit, and the leadership development of black children. Convinced that black people are intellectually inferior to whites, many of these white teachers and school administrators "do not encourage black children to excel like they do white children," a black female student in my freshman English class once told me. "If you keep quiet, act nicely, and do a little work they will pass you," she said. "It doesn't matter that nobody taught you to read or write a theme."

In my own dealings with the white-controlled public school system, I have often come face-to-face with the "exclusion tactics" some white female and white male teachers use to retard black children's interest in the school's talent-shaping activities. I am reminded of the time my daughter wanted to try out for a role in a school play. The assistant drama coach, a white female, told her there was no need for her to try out because there were no black parts in the play. To this day, I have trouble understanding the term "black parts" in relation to Shakespeare's "A Midsummer Night's Dream." In my encounter with this school's drama department, I discovered any white child, male or female, could try out for roles in plays. Black children were discouraged from trying out for all plays except those designating that a black character was needed—usually a nurse for white children, or a maid, janitor, or jester.[20] The drama coach (white) tried to console the aspiring young black actresses and actors by telling them the drama department would put on a black play at the end of the year. Later, the same teacher told the black children that her department had decided not to put on a black play because nobody would come to see it; the school population was mostly white. In this school, white children interested in acting did not experience this kind of humiliation. The white drama coaches were not retarding the development of white female and male children. Some of the black children became discouraged and gave up their interest in acting.

With regard to black women's oppression and the feminist idea that patriarchy is the primary source of women's oppression, two points should be reiterated. The first is that the feminist understanding of the patriarchal relation between women and society's institutions does not include black women's oppression resulting from *their relation to the white-controlled American institutions governing their lives*. As far as black women's experience is concerned, it is a misnomer to name oppressive-rule with words that only identify men as oppressors of women. Since white women join white men in oppressing black women (and in maintaining white supremacy), black women need nomenclature and language which reflect this reality. One cannot accept the argument that white women, in their affiliation with American institutions, are forced by patriarchal structures (or by patriarchal conditioning) to oppress black women, and therefore, patriarchy—in male role—ally is responsible for the oppression of all women relating to society's institutions. Davis, Hooks, and Giddings have shown how independent white feminists (at odds with and supposedly rejecting patriarchal rule) did, of their own volition and for their own political benefit, oppress black women and other black people. White American women cannot be relieved of the responsibility for choices they made/make in their roles as oppressors.

The second point to be reiterated here is that while white patriarchy may ultimately cause the oppression of white women, it constantly provides resources for the development of white women. Many black women who work in white settings have seen white feminist groups use the positive side of white patriarchy to gain political, economic, and educational advantages that mostly benefit white women. The positive side of patriarchy provides the media and means for keeping white women's issues at the forefront of the liberation movement and at the forefront of American conscience.[21]

The failure of white feminists to emphasize the *substantial difference* between their patriarchally-derived-privileged-oppression and black women's demonically-derived-annihilistic-oppression renders black women invisible in feminist thought and action. It is no wonder that in most feminist literature written by white-American women, the words "woman" and "women" signify only the white woman's experience. By failing to insert the word "white" before "woman" and "women," some feminists imperialistically take over the identity of those rendered invisible. Therefore, one can encounter instances in white feminist literature when feminists make appropriations from Afro-American culture without identifying the source of the appropriation and without admitting that American feminism has roots deep in black culture. This is glaringly obvious in the following claim made by white feminist scholar Jo Freeman:

The most prevalent innovation developed by the younger branch [of feminism] has been the "rap group." Essentially an education technique, it has spread far beyond its origins and become a major organizational unit of the whole movement, most frequently used by suburban housewives. From a sociological perspective, the rap group is probably the most valuable contribution by the women's liberation movement to the tools for social change.[22]

Even the most casual student of black culture knows that the "rap" and the "rap group" have been alive in the oral tradition of the Afro-American Community (nation-wide) for more than fifty years. During the civil rights movements in the late 1950s and early 1960s, rap groups were held in black homes and in black churches. These groups had several purposes. One major purpose was to educate black people about the various strategies to be used in demonstrations. Another purpose was to allow black people to share their experiences so that the black community could see how racism had affected every area of black life. Before the 1950s and 1960s, individual blacks used the rap to expound on social and moral issues. Today, in Afro-American and some Hispanic communities, the "rap" provides the rhythmic accompaniment for the famous "break dancing" which originated among northern Hispanic and black youth forming the street cultures of both communities. The "rap" and the "rap group" certainly did not originate among white feminists. If anything, the rap was *borrowed* from black people by white women who touched black culture, perhaps through the civil rights movements or through one-on-one involvements with black men and women.

The implication of all the preceding discussion is that black women, *in their relation to white-controlled American institutions,* do not experience patriarchy.[23] It is necessary, then, for black women—when describing their own oppressed relation to white-controlled American institutions—to use new words, new language, and new ideas that fit their experience. These new words, language, and ideas will help black women develop an appropriate theoretical foundation for the ideology and political action needed to obtain the liberation of black women and the black family.[24]

Therefore, as a beginning, I suggest that there are at least two ways of institutional white-rule effecting the oppression of many American women. Certainly one of these is patriarchy as described by Adrienne Rich earlier in this paper. There is also the demonic way of institutional white-rule which controls black women's lives. This way can be named demonarchy.[25] Patriarchy, *in its white institutional form,* can also be understood as the systemic governance of white women's lives by white women's fathers, brothers, and sons using care, protection, and privilege as instruments of social control. Demonarchy can be understood as the demonic governance of black women's lives by white male and white female ruled systems using racism, violence, violation, retardation, and death as instruments of social control. Distinguished from individual violent acts stemming from psychological abnormalities on the part of the perpetrator, demonarchy is a traditional and collective expression of white government in relation to black women. It belongs to the realm of normalcy. It is informed by a state of consciousness that believes white women are superior to and more valuable than any woman of color and that white men are the most valuable and superior forms of life on earth. While sexism is a kind of women's oppression issuing from patriarchy, racist-gender oppression of black women issues from demonarchy. Black women cannot disjoin race and gender as they describe their oppression resulting from their relation to white-controlled American institutions.

Demonarchy has its roots in American slavery in the governance that allowed black women to be used as breeder women, that allowed black women to be indiscriminately raped by white men of every class, that allowed black women to be used as work-horses for white females controlling the domestic/private sphere of the slavocracy.[26] Note the following example of the demonic governance (demonarchy) of the Afro-American slave woman's life:

> Women [on the slave ships] were lashed severely for crying. They were stripped of their clothing and beaten on all parts of their body. Ruth and Jacob Weldon, an African couple who experienced the horrors of the slave passage, saw "mothers with babes at their breast basely branded and scarred, till it would seem as if the very heavens might smite the infernal tormentors with the doom they so richly merited." After the branding all slaves were stripped of any clothing. . . . Rape was a common method of torture slavers used to subdue recalcitrant black women. The threat of rape or other physical brutalization inspired terror in the psyches of displaced African females. Robert Shufeldt, an observer of the slave trade, documented the prevalence of rape on slave ships. He asserts, "In those days many a negress was landed upon our shores [sic] already impregnated by some one of the demonic crew that brought her over."[27]

Demonarchy prevailed beyond slavery as white men continued to rape black women and as both white males and white females put the blame for this rape on the alleged ". . . immorality of black women."[28] Demonarchy prevailed in World War II America as white women severely exploited the labor of black female domestic workers. In *Women, Race and Class,* Angela Davis reports that:

> . . . in the 1940's, there were street-corner markets in New York and other large cities—modern versions of slavery's auction block—inviting white women to take their pick from the crowds of Black women seeking work.

Quoting from Louise Mitchell's account, Davis describes the actual situation:

> Every morning, rain or shine, groups of [black] women with brown paper bags or cheap suitcases stand on street corners in the Bronx and Brooklyn waiting for a chance to get some work. . . . Once hired on the "slave market," the women often find after a day's backbreaking toil, that they worked longer than was arranged, got less than was promised, were forced to accept clothing

instead of cash, and were exploited beyond human endurance. Only the urgent need for money makes them [black women] submit to this routine daily.[29]

During the Second World War, northern white women were not alone in their desire to exploit black women's labor so that the domestic/private sphere of white American life could offer comfort and well-being for white families. Discussing black female employment in the defense industries in America during the 1940s Paula Giddings reports that:

> . . . a Black newspaper, "The Baltimore Afro-American," ran a story in 1945 about Black women struggling to be hired by the Naval Ordnance Plant in Macon, Georgia: "The chief opposition to employment of colored women did not come from management or the employees . . . but from white local housewives, who feared lowering the barriers would rob them of maids, cooks and nurses."[30]

As a way of controlling black women's lives, demonarchy thrives today in white-controlled American institutions where *racist-gender* oppression not only affects black women. It also affects the economic well-being of the black family. As Paula Giddings reminds us:

> Both the past and the present tell us it is not a question of race *versus* sex, but race *and* sex. In a time when so many Black women and children need sufficient income, the concerns about sex are necessary for the progress— indeed, the economic survival—of Afro-Americans as a group.[31]

As the source of the *racist-gender* oppression black women experience in their relation to white-controlled American institutions, demonarchy causes a qualitative difference between the oppression of black women and white women. Therefore, black women, understanding the demonic character of their oppression, are apt to emphasize issues different from those emphasized by white feminists informed by the patriarchal critique of women's oppression. White feminists struggle for women's liberation *from male domination* with regard for such *priority* issues as rape, domestic violence, women's work, female bonding, inclusive language, the gender of God, economic autonomy for women, and heterosexism. Black women liberators would perhaps consider *women's liberation and family liberation from white-male-white-female domination* with regard for such priority issues as physical survival and spiritual salvation of the family (with equality between males and females); the re-distribution of goods and services in the society (so that white families no longer get the lion's share of the economic, educational, political, and vocational resources available in every social class); encountering God as family (masculine and feminine, father, mother, and child); ending white supremacy, male supremacy (or any gender supremacy), and upper-class supremacy in all American institutions.

This does not mean that black women are not concerned about such issues as rape, domestic violence, and women's work. Neither does this mean that white feminists should refrain from indicating these issues as priorities for *white* women. Nor does this mean that black women liberators should refrain from supporting white feminist action to alleviate domestic violence, rape, and exclusion of women. All black women should support the abolition of these atrocities. However, these issues are not priorities for Afro-American liberators who understand the demonic nature of their oppression resulting from their relation to white-controlled American institutions.

Inasmuch as Afro-American women's history shows that black women have struggled *simultaneously* for their own liberation and that of other black people (males, females, and children), it is appropriate to suggest that a women's movement, informed by an understanding of demonarchy, would have at least three primary goals. These would be (1) liberation of women and the family simultaneously; (2) establishing a positive quality of life for women and the family simultaneously; (3) forming political alliances with other marginal groups struggling to be free of the oppression imposed by white-controlled American institutions. Hence, the black women's issues clud above emerge from these goals. Liberation of black women and black families involves survival, salvation of black people's spirits and equality between males and females. A positive quality of life is achieved through the redistribution of goods and services and new encounters with God. As they form the appropriate political alliances, black women liberators raise the issue of ending white supremacy, gender supremacy, and class bias. (It must be emphasized that a positive quality of life for black women and the family should be based upon *both* a reinforcement of Afro-American cultural and religious heritage *and* a realistic/scientific analysis of black people's relation to the means of production in the societies in which Afro-Americans live.)

Hence, if black women's tongue is to be spoken within feminism, i.e., if feminism is also to be "colorized," feminist consciousness must be raised to:

1) understand the limitation of the feminist patriarchal critique for assessing the nature of black women's oppression derived from black women's *relation to white-male-white-female dominated social systems;*

2) recognize the need to assess the ethical significance of white feminists using "white patriarchal power" to gain privileges that benefit mostly white women;

3) realize that black American women and white American women are apt to use different linguistic configurations to express the terms of their oppression. For instance, white women may claim that women's primary oppression issues from male subjugation of females; therefore, women must struggle for their liberation which, when achieved, also liberates oppressor-men. Afro-American females may say that white American families (fathers, mothers, children) in every social class have the power to oppress the black family (mothers, fathers, and children). Black women must struggle for the liberation of women within the context of the broader struggle for the liberation of the black family where equality must exist between females and males. Therefore, feminist consciousness must also be raised to:

4) consider women's liberation and family liberation as *inseparable* goals;

5) realize that the family (whether nuclear or extended) can be an effective unit for consciousness-raising with regard to gender, racial, and class oppression.

The multi-racial feminist collective called Mud Flower has already begun to suggest what it means to color feminism so that black women and other women of color are seriously included. They say, "An analysis of sexism that is not also an assessment of racism, ethnic prejudice, and economic injustice is not . . . a feminist analysis."[32] In accord with this Mud Flower statement, black female liberators might want to make an additional affirmation—i.e., that an analysis of racial oppression which is not also an assessment of women's oppression, of the black family's oppression, and of the economic injustices in society is not a valid assessment of black oppression in North America. Mud Flower reminds us that "We do not have to be economists, anthropologists, or sociologists to know that race, class and gender are critical, even determinative, forces in the ordering of human life and religion."[33] We merely have to be determined to confront the forces in our society that create and perpetuate oppression based on race, gender, and class.

MATERIALS TO BE ADDED?

While the preceding discussion suggests that additional "materials" must be added to feminism to make it also fit black women's experience, there are parts of feminism that "sound pretty," as the black Christian woman observed in group "A" above. Hence, some aspects of feminism are already attractive to some Afro-American women. Certainly, the feminist emphasis upon equal pay for equal work done by men and women in the work place is appealing—as is also the feminist claim that women should have control of their own bodies and that nurturing responsibilities within the family should be shared equally by males and females.

Even though there is a split between rhetoric and action in some feminist approaches to the Afro-American woman's rights and liberation, the feminist movement in America has provided some useful tools for black women to begin to evaluate their relationship to black men, to the black family, and to the institutions in the Afro-American community where black males have the authority (e.g., the black church). Some Afro-American female thinkers have shown that the feminist understanding of sexism—oppression of a person because of gender—aptly describes the oppression black women receive in their relationships with some black men and with black male dominated Afro-American institutions, e.g., the black church. This means, then, that even though the feminist understanding of patriarchy (from which sexism derives) is limited when one attempts to use it to describe black women's oppression *resulting from their relation to white-male-white-female dominated social systems*, it is useful for assessing black women's relation to black males and to those institutions where black males have the authority. This state of affairs exists because black males, since slavery, have tended to re-create their manhood to conform to the model of manhood sanctioned in American society. Of course, this sanctioned manhood was white and was understood by white people to be patriarchal. So, while we add the demonarchal critique to feminism, we must maintain relevant aspects of the patriarchal critique feminists have provided. But some caution must be exercised. We must insist that our feminist definitions of patriarchy be adjusted so that they show clearly (and not by inference) that white people have the power and authority to oppress black men, and they exercise this authority in every area of American life.

The question of whether these new additions will distort feminism is an open one. Feminists, themselves, will have to deal with the questions. But we can say that feminism as a language of women's experience will become stagnant unless new concepts are added to its linguistic store of word and wisdom.

ECCLESIOLOGICAL IMPORT

In conclusion, some brief consideration must be given to the significance of the demonarchal critique for the life and mission of the black church. The naming of demonic rule (i.e., demonarchy) suggests new ways to talk about black worship and new biblical foundations for the mission of the church. Informed by the demonarchal critique of black women's relation to white-controlled American institutions, one can now understand the black church's shouts, rhythms, and music not as uncontrolled frenzy, but as its way of casting out the intolerable pain demonic rule *instills* in its victims. This process of casting out pain in the worship space of the black church happens in a transactional relation between the rhythm of song, the rhythm of words, the black preacher's charisma, and the black woman. Time, in its ordinary sense, is suspended as black women give up their pain in the rhythm of the flow of music, of word, and of charisma. The joyful noise that results—e.g., shouts, moans, claps, etc.—represents the black woman's thanks to God for the re-vitalization of her spirit which demonarchy has tried to destroy. The deep spirituality that often characterizes the black church results from this process of casting out pain and women giving thanks to God for the spirit.

In terms of its mission to the black community and to the world, the black church (informed by the demonarchal critique) will be about the business of casting out the demonic—the socially, politically, economically, and spiritually demonic rule that threatens the life of black people and the life of the human spirit. This casting out of demonic rule can be named "the church's liberation activity" which finds its biblical validation in such texts as: Mark 3:14–15 (Jesus ". . . appointed twelve—designating them apostles—that they might be with him and that he might send them out to preach and to have authority to drive out demons. . . ."); Matthew 10:1 ("He called his twelve apostles to him and gave them authority to drive out evil spirits. . . ."); Matthew 10:7–8 ("As you [the disciples] go preach this message: 'The kingdom of heaven is near.' Heal the sick, raise the dead, cleanse those who have leprosy, drive out demons. . . ."); Luke 9:1 ("When Jesus had called the twelve together, he gave them power and authority to drive out all demons. . . .").[34] The importance of this emphasis upon casting out the work of the demonic is that it allows the black church to understand its liberation action in terms of the connection between the spiritual and political dimensions of its life and history.

Apart from modern psychological theory which understands the demonic as a constitutive element of human personality, the black church (if informed by the demonarchal critique) will see the demonic in socio-political-spiritual terms. The church will understand that social organization based upon racist-gender oppression, economic oppression, and oppression of the human spirit does not intend merely to maim. It intends to destroy the very lives of black women and black peoplehood. For this reason, the church cannot be naive, nor can it underestimate the *power* of the demonic governance it challenges. The black church's mission of casting out the demonic in the social world can only be successful if the church realizes that its liberation encounter is with *nothing less* than radical evil.

Finally, if the black church is to understand its mission to itself, it must see that part of its mission is to enlighten its congregations so that the oppression of women in the church is alleviated—so that black male imitations of white manhood and white male patriarchy are discarded. Due to the split in the black church between power and authority, this oppression is reinforced. Black women are the economic, spiritual, numerical powers in the churches while black males have the authority. When black women *take* the lead and heal the split by giving authority to black women (especially black women ministers), the black church will indeed become a more representative model of the kingdom in our midst. But in order to do this, the black church—like feminism—must add materials to its life and thought which speak the black woman's tongue— materials that show women and men to be equal in both power and authority— materials that speak in new, meaningful, and inclusive theological categories.

NOTES

1. Delores S. Williams, "The Color of Feminism," *Christianity and Crisis,* vol. 45, no. 7 (April 29, 1985), pp. 164–165.

2. Angela Davis, *Women, Race and Class* (New York: Vintage Books, 1983), p. 57.

3. Ibid., p. 83.

4. Bell Hooks, *Ain't I a Woman?: Black Women and Feminism* (Boston: South End Press, 1981), p. 124.

5. Ibid.

6. Ibid., pp. 125–126.

7. Paula Giddings, *Where and When I Enter: The Impact of Black Women on Race and Sex in America* (New York: William Morrow & Company, 1984) p. 66.

8. Ibid.

9. Ibid.

10. Ibid., p. 67.

11. Ibid.

12. Quoted by Elizabeth Hood, "Black Woman, White Woman: Separate Paths to Liberation," *The Black Scholar,* vol. 4, no. 7 (April 1978), p. 49.

13. Audre Lorde, "Open Letter to Mary Daly," in *This Bridge Called My Back,* Cherrie Moraga and Gloria Anzaldúa, eds. (Watertown, Massachusetts: Persephone Press, 1981).

14. Angelique Walker-Smith, "Exclusive Language Reflects Inner Beliefs," *Christianity and Crisis,* vol. 45, no. 7 (29 April, 1985), p. 146.

15. Adrienne Rich, *Of Woman Born: Motherhood as Experience and Institution* (New York: W. W. Norton & Company, 1976), p. 40.

16. For a discussion of patriarchy in several contexts see Kate Millett, *Sexual Politics* (Garden City, N.Y.: Doubleday, 1970); see also Bell Hooks' discussion in *Ain't I a Woman?;* Elizabeth Dodson Gray, *Patriarchy as a Conceptual Trap* (Wellesley, Massachusetts: Roundtable Press, 1982).

17. Rich, *Of Woman Born,* author's interpolations.

18. While many feminists are to be admired for refusing to take the white woman's traditional place upon the pedestal, few have turned down the privileges bestowed upon them by fathers, brothers, and sons.

19. Afro-American slave narratives contain many accounts about slave owners who fathered children by slave women and then sold these children as slaves.

20. In the October 27, 1985 issue of *The New York Times Magazine* a black middle-class mother expressed her anger about a play performed by students at a predominantly white school her child attended. In the play, all the black children were cast as monkeys and wore no masks. A little white boy was cast as a gorilla and he wore a mask.

21. For some time now, black women have been complaining about the nature of the women's studies programs planned by feminists but financed by white male money. Black women say these programs are primarily about white women. See *Some of Us Are Brave,* edited by Gloria T. Hull, Barbara Smith, and Patricia Bell Scott. Pay special attention to the article written by Barbara Smith.

22. Jo Freeman, "The Women's Liberation Movement: Its Origins, Structures, Import and Ideas," in *Women: A Feminist Perspective,* Jo Freeman, ed. (New York: Mayfield Publishing Company, 1975), p. 451.

23. Black women should, as they name their experience, consider the following: "White males experience the world from the top side of history. White females experience the world from the underside of history. Black men experience the world from the underside of the underside of history. Black women experience the world from rock-bottom." Such a position for black women logically suggests a different naming of reality and certainly a different view of history.

24. For some years now, I have heard many black women say that they could not conceive of their own liberation apart from the liberation of the black family because black children, female and male, are as oppressed by white-controlled American institutions as they (black women) are.

25. Democracy has no relation to demonarchy which posits beings intermediate between humans and the divine.

26. Much literature about black women describes the inhumane treatment that black women received as they worked for white women as domestics and as housekeepers.

27. Hooks, *Ain't I a Woman?*, p. 18.

28. See Bell Hooks' discussion of this in *Ain't I a Woman?*, pp. 36–37.

29. Angela Davis, *Women, Race and Class*, p. 95.

30. Giddings, *Where and When I Enter*, p. 237.

31. Ibid.

32. Katie G. Cannon, Beverly W. Harrison, Carter Heyward et al., *God's Fierce Whimsy* (New York: The Pilgrim Press, 1985), p. 34.

33. Ibid.

34. From *The New International Version* of the Bible.

5

CAN WE BE DIFFERENT BUT NOT ALIENATED?

An Exchange of Letters

Katie G. Cannon
Carter Heyward

> I will flow, not censor or edit, but let the innermost part of me speak.
> —Katie Cannon

> I'm pulled between excitement and anxiety over what you say.
> —Carter Heyward

Often candor is born between friends who already share a bond of assurance that speaking the truth of one's life will not be futile. In this spirit, Katie, a black woman, and Carter, a white woman, corresponded after our first meeting in the fall of 1982. On the basis of the original outline we had drawn up for our work, Carter had asked each of us to do some thinking about particular issues that had been of special interest to us. The correspondence between Katie and Carter grew out of this request. The rest of us did not know about the letters until after they had been written. During our second weekend meeting, in the winter of 1983, we shared what Katie and Carter had written. We offer it here with few alterations, because it reflects teaching/learning in the praxis of particularities.

A little background: Katie refers to *The Color Purple* by Alice Walker.[1] At Kate's suggestion, Carter had read this novel, and the two of them had discussed its theological value as a narrative of a rural black woman who is cut off from all love, relationality, and God until she has a friend who takes her seriously.

October 31, 1982

Dear Carter,

I will respond to the parts of the outline you've asked me to think about by writing a letter much like Celie in *The Color Purple* wrote letters to God and Nettie. By this I mean that I will flow, not censor or edit, but let the innermost part of me speak.

Can we be different but not alienated? Only if there is mutuality in our relating. The analogy for me is the difference between the miracle of dialogue and bilateral conversations. When two parties, people, races, nations, etc., are dialoguing, they respect whatever their intellect, spirit, culture, and traditions tell them is sound in each other, with an attitude of openness for growth and change that comes with the moving of God's spirit. The open-flowing energy between the two removes alienation. But when one of the parties tries to listen only long enough to tell the others what to do, to control, to obtain power or superiority, the result has to be alienation. It is like what Alice Walker says about Church. We come to Church to share with others the God we have found in ourselves, not to find God.

When we, as various people, can claim the beauty of our innerselves, then we do not have to exploit, oppress, disenfranchise other people in some kind of hierarchical, vertical, sadomasochistic pecking order.

Racism, sexism, class elitism are all false, institutionalized systems of the abortive search for somebodiness (meaning). Therefore, in such systems there cannot be acceptance of difference. Difference is interpreted by those in power as *less than*. Conformity is the norm, and anyone who cannot be bleached out and neutered has to be isolated, alienated, and eventually exterminated. It is no mere coincidence that hard and destructive drugs flow freely in our black communities. The self-defense that comes from the side of the oppressed is to maintain the alienation that is already in place, because history bears out that whenever any of us try to heal the breach, they either get co-opted and become a token pet in the system or they get assassinated as a threat to the status quo: academic excellence, national security, etc.

As Zora Neale Hurston says, our survival in the black community is to let those researchers probe—but *not* to give them the information, because the very data shared will be used as the boomerang to destroy us.[2] The beauty of living is appreciating the various differences in God's creation, but, for those in power and control, that very difference is the seed of negation that demands a spontaneity in relating which they refuse to give. Race/class and gender oppressions are based on removing the intelligence, the source of feelings, aspirations, and achievements of those who are different by closeting, categorizing, burying, and cremating them, so that those who reap the privileges of superiority and supremacy do not have to confront their futile and anachronistic gestures of success, progress, or their inability to live any other way.

The particular relation between white and black women. My mama always says that black people must remember that all white people have white mamas. She makes several points with this proverb.

First, the hand that rocks the cradle is the hand that rules the world. We may question the validity and truth of such assumptions, but we cannot deny the impact that racist child-rearing practices have had on sustaining and perpetuating white supremacy.

Second, the volatile relationship between the majority of white women and the majority of women of color has to do with the pedestaled position that white women allow themselves to be placed upon, always at the expense of other women. When white women buy into the privileges of white supremacy and the illusive protectiveness of their superiority, women of color are forced to pick up their slack.

Third, white women are the only ones to guarantee the purity of the white race. They are the white man's most important treasure. George Frederickson makes a strong historical case for white supremacy in South Africa and in the United States, with the bottom-line motivation for the oppression of people of color: white men protecting the virtue and virginity of white women, resulting in the objectification of white women and all others.[3]

Fourth, white women in particular are always seeking blessings of assurance from women of color. By this I mean that, even as a teenager when I worked as a domestic, I was asked by the white kids that I tended to, who were sometimes my age and sometimes older, for advice. (My confusion was always about the injustice of why, if we were the same age, I was their caretaker.) They would sometimes ask me what I thought about washing their hair with beer and other white folk phenomena. Learning, knowing, and remembering my place was critical to my job security. If I responded "What in the hell do I care?" or any milder version of that feeling, I would have been written off as uppity and therefore disrespectful—and fired. If I dumbed-up and numbed-out, ignoring them completely, just continuing my menial, low-paying work, such silence would have been read either the same way or as reinforcing my so-called inferiority and ignorance. It really was that precarious situation my mama describes: when you have your head in the lion's mouth, you have to treat the lion very gently.

Economic/work relationships cannot be minimized in discussing and under-standing the relationship between white women and women of color. Also this same kind of blessing of assurance has been manifested in my experience with white women when they don't want to participate in an equal, reciprocal process of give and take.

I remember once at a party lots of folks relaxing and having a good time. Black and white together. My conversation with a white woman appeared to be fairly open and honest. She said that she had always been taught that black people had a foul odor and asked for permission to smell me. (I didn't even flinch. I just registered the request in my category of weird-things-white-people-do.) After she sniffed and smelled and got her nose full of me, she concluded that all that time she had been living with a racist myth, which, as far as she could tell from her experiment with me, was not true.

I then reciprocated the experiment by saying that I, too, had heard some smell-myths about white people. I had been taught that when white people wash their hair or get wet, they smell like dogs. I then proceeded to smell her. She jumped back, appalled, infuriated. How dare I have the audacity to smell her. This is when I was shocked. It was good enough for me to be the object of her examination, but it was not OK when the tables were turned.

And that white woman, huffing and puffing, got up and stormed out of the party. This is often what white women do when they're not in front of the line, calling the shots, or in charge of the dynamics between themselves and women of color. They take their toys, their funds, their programs, their printing press, and go home, where they can perch on a ledge and not have their boat rocked. This in itself is privilege.

My relationship with white feminists and women of color, who may or may not be feminists, is radically different. White feminists are aware of racism. White feminists are aware of their own subjugation and oppression as females. White feminists are beginning to claim their biases, their elitist values, and their assumptions about life. And not only are they aware; they are engaged, actively, in justice-making. This, to me, is the hope. White feminists and women of color are changing the directions and the quality of their relations to each other.

White women who are not about the above, even if they call themselves feminists, are not feminists to me, but only white women with white mamas perpetuating systems of oppression by continuing to participate in them.

I believe that, as women, we need each other. We need to cross race lines and class lines, join forces to stop this messing up of lives by the racist, patriarchal systems and structures steeped in a greed for power and domination, all toward the maximizing of profits.

White feminists are standing over against their privileges inherent in an oppressive system to be in mutual relation with others. Women of color often need to test and retest the authenticity of white women's willingness to relate. The question before us is whether our timing and tolerance will sustain the processes of change.

I wholeheartedly believe that "godding is relating."[4] I only know the essential nature of God when I as an individual, and my people as a race, are not permitted—but command by the respect of our very being—space to engage in the most rigorously honest confrontation. When we confront and are confronted so that all might have life and have life more abundantly—this is what it's all about. And this is why, when I hear of "postfeminist" movements, I quake and shake.[5] The hands that rocked the cradle now cradle the rock, so that, together, we can change the powers and principalities of this world.

Studying our lives in relation to the lives of other women. I respond to this by adapting a metaphor of Amari Baraka:[6]

A black woman is locked up in one room of a large house by an oppressor (white male/female and/or racial/ethnic male) who never enters that room. When the isolated woman finally comes out, she is able to talk about the whole house, whereas her oppressor who imprisoned her is not.

Women who are in touch with their oppression may be more fit to handle the totality of the ethical ambiguities in their lives than their oppressors. Since the oppression of women is the oldest oppression, and since no anthropologist, feminist or otherwise, has ever come up with convincing evidence of a culture in which some form of male dominance does not exist, we, as women, have a wealth of wisdom in our stories, many which have never been told.

The metaphor about the woman in the locked room depicts the "epistemological privilege" of *women of color.* Langston Hughes sums it up in his book *The*

Ways of White Folks.[7] The class and economic location of women of color affords them the inside scoop on the nemeses, the jugular veins, and the Achilles' heels of those in power. But the catch-22 is that by the time they get through slaving, with no reflective time for analysis, they don't know how to fight, only how to stay alive. The privilege to reflect in order to prevail beyond survival is not granted to them, so their epistemological privilege either lies dormant, in some kind of state of denial or self-delusion, or it is acted out in ways that get black women beaten up, incarcerated, mutilated. How to channel this wisdom is the essential concern of the ongoing survival of women of color.

Do black women and white women experience a common dilemma? A common possibility? I wholeheartedly respond, Yes. The difference is that white women tend to have more layers of veneer with which they deny our common bond. Racism as idolatry teaches them that they are somebody in spite of the violence in the home, the beatings, rapes, incest, conspiracies of silence, because their white skin makes them better than any black person. The "culture of inequality" teaches them that if they obtain certain material objects, they are far superior to those who have not obtained them. Not until white women and women of color are aware and willing to accept our common dilemma can there be any possible common action for liberative change.

A demon that divides us. You asked about these demons. I've mentioned some, but one that we have to name is the hidden injuries of class.[8] The more economic security one has, the more one can buy illusive myths and distance herself from reality. In other words, money can give those who have it the false security and illusory worth that their personhood is more valuable because of their finances. They then set up and manipulate systems to undergird their uniqueness so that those at the bottom of the pyramid also get on the treadmill of wanting that same shallowness always available in the shadows of the golden ghettoes. A case in point is professionalism. The more one goes to school, the more elite one is supposed to be. The farce of so many of our systems cannot be exposed because those of us struggling for upward mobility, once we see the light, cannot speak; or else we have nothing to sustain our energy and effort after the sacrifices that have put us where we are. So many of our class locations are based on the story line of the emperor who has no clothes. But who will dare name this?—because the namer will be discredited either as a liar and a fool, or as a failure who has a bone to pick, or as a traitor to the guild. A few of us marginated people are tolerated to show the equality of the system, but only a limited quota can survive.

I'll stop here because my brain needs to rest.

Kate

November 2, 1982

Dear Carter,

I haven't heard from you, so I will continue this dialogue in my head, assuming you have asked me to elaborate a little more about my mother's statement that all white people have white mamas. Whether this is your question or not, I think it is where a little more clarification is needed. My line of reasoning is not to establish white women or women of color either as the evil ones or as the victims of patriarchal oppression and exploitation but to lift up the rape of the psyche that causes all of us to internalize our own destruction so that "if there is not a backdoor our very nature will demand one."[9]

Rosa D. Bowser, an outstanding black woman of the late nineteenth and early twentieth century, coined the words my mother used to accept her accountability: "Men are what the women make them."[10] One of Bowser's contemporaries, Sarah Dudley Pettey, said; "Men go from home into the world to execute what women have decreed."[11] George Jackson in *Soledad Brother* drove this point home for me.[12] Reading his life story about how his mother made him a black man/child, I was struck with my own reality, which is—if I were to choose to bring forth a child from my womb or raise a child as an adoptive parent, I would have the responsibility to teach that child the rudiments of surviving a racist world. The only way that can be done is to set up a schizoid, push-pull, give-take child-rearing pattern, wherein I rape the psyche of my own offspring or immerse the child in the bleaching-vat process myself. Parenting is difficult in a racist patriarchal capitalist society.

Maybe I am totally off target in holding white women accountable for their role in white families in the same way; if so, I think there needs to be some honest communication with me and other women of color about the paralyzing nature of oppression of white females. I do know that black women have a sayso in child-rearing and the goings-on in the black family, and I believe white women have some sayso too, for perpetuating white privilege. Black women are not solely responsible for pathology in the black community. Poverty, drug abuse, low educational achievement, prostitution, and unemployment are real. But we are, like Bernice Johnson Reagan said, holding up the wall of society so that it doesn't crush the next generation—and simultaneously taking from that wall the essentials of survival. Black women, therefore, have neither the privilege nor the leisure to analyze the changing reality and the changing needs of the very people they claim that they are accountable to. If I don't accept some of the responsibility for the perpetuation of my own oppression, I can never be free. Whether I use the analogy of holding up the wall with my back, or the rape of my psyche, once the violence has happened, and even when it becomes routinized in well-documented, insidious institutional systems, the people in my community and I have a responsibility to the God who has created us in God's image to face and explore the terror, so as to militate the radicality of our own rebirth.

My commitment to finishing my Ph.D. degree comes from owing the black female community all that I had obtained and been exposed to in this privileged process. Since the masses cannot have reflecting and reading time to analyze, those of us who do are indebted to the very ones who called us forth "to discover

books, desks, a place for [those] who know nothing of these things themselves."[13]

Now to pick up again on the demons that divide us.

Co-opting and rendering invisible our contributions and histories. The most
devastating reality of writing my dissertation is having to face the fact that black
women have been omitted from the writing of black history. As I try to
reconstruct the "Black Woman's Moral Situation," the glaring vacancies make
my endeavor extremely difficult. The oral tradition and its validity sustain me,
however. My grandmother, who lived from Reconstruction until 1975, told me
many of the tales that I have pieced together like quilted patchwork. The
literature on black women in American history is so sparse (Noble, Lerner, and
maybe two others) that one can establish only a skeletal framework of the past.
Gloria Hull, Patricia Scott, and Barbara Smith hit the nail squarely on the head
when they titled their book *All the Women Are White, All the Blacks Are Men, But
Some of Us Are Brave.*[14]

Now to respond to the white privilege of co-opting and rendering invisible
black experience: There is one scene in the Broadway musical *Dreamgirls* that
dramatically depicts this kind of co-optation, when whites rip off the black
musical tradition. This also relates to what I shared in the first letter about so
little tolerance and appreciation for differences. Those in power tend to render
things "universal" in a cloning fashion or else to define their worth, value, and
quality out of existence by assessing them as liabilities and inferior. It has to do
with superiority and arrogance again, wherein dominant oppressors structure life
so that they are always taking control, never appreciating the color purple.
Sometimes I hear people in the black community talking about not trusting
white folks because they (whites) just want to study us enough to write about us,
continuing the exploitation of our very lives by monopolizing the publishing of
our history and experiences.

In essence what I am asking, given these systems of inequality, is how do we
maximize them for a more equitable distribution of wealth in society? Well, we
can begin as feminists by understanding our interconnectedness, our interdependency, and therefore lifting each other as we climb.

Another demon: marginalization of women's studies and interests. To marginal-
ize is to disempower, to push to the outer edge of the hub of the life-decision-
making-center. When one—as an individual, a group, a race—has to hang on to
the edge, white-knuckling all the way, there is little time to confront authorities
and demand change in the system. It is to the advantage of those who maintain
the power in society to keep those who think differently about themselves and
their rights engaged in all kinds of cliff-hanging activities. It is very much like a
crushing wall that's caving in on the sustaining forces of life. Marginality also
means that one is removed from the nurturing and sustaining sources of life's
energy. It can render one docile, ignorant of self and therefore willingly
susceptible to whatever comes down the pike. Marginality places women's

communities and racial/ethnic interests in throwaway, expendable positions, diluting our potency.

Another demon: exceptional women as tokens. Depending on which side of tokenism one is on, one can either lose by losing or lose by winning, but all the time losing just the same. When strong, positive, God-centered women confront their male counterparts, they are usually afforded a subtle, institutionalized option to conform to whatever those in power have defined as normative or to become a slightly "deformed" one of the boys. I was quite successful in seminary because I knew how to behave in men's space so as to not threaten them. My stance was primarily that of the fly on the wall—a fly with many privileges granted to me as long as I remembered my place/space. Sometimes I was permitted to soar like a mighty eagle and at other times I sat quietly like a bump on a log. Knowing the difference made me constantly feel as if I was driving with one foot on the accelerator and the other one simultaneously on the brakes. This meant that even though I was producing at top quality on one side of my brain, my soul sagged and ached with the heavy load of precariousness of my tokenism.

Another one of my mother's proverbs is that if you let people make you at will, they can break you at whim. Martin Luther King, Jr. said that all a token is good for is a one-way ride on a subway. I have tried to keep myself sensitized to this so that, when in token positions, I understand that it is a place to bring about change for a few until the revolution comes. The privileged inside circle can serve as a vantage point for some change only if those who are allowed into such holy-of-holies stay mindful of our call, our commitment, and our community. What happens so often is that tokens behave like doorkeepers. The system uses the token, like the main character in Sam Greenlee's novel *The Spook Who Sat by the Door,* to screen out whoever is unacceptable to the functioning of the status quo and, thereby, to nullify the legitimacy of calls for justice.

Well, Carter, I think these responses take care of my thoughts for now. If I have anything to share on the other theme you asked about—embodied learning—I will drop it in the mail. Take care.

                                                                                      Kate

                                                                      November 18, 1982

Dear Kate,

I've reread your letters many times, and only now, having had them with me for several weeks, can I begin to try to articulate a response, and not only a response to you but to myself. Responding to my own feelings, questions, confusions, and delights. Even now I'm pulled between excitement and anxiety over what you say, what I read, what we're doing, especially as women of different colors. You see, I find that I want to be a color! I'd always, even as a little girl, thought there was something weird about the implication that white people have no color—unlike "colored" people. White seemed to me to be a color, but then someone told me that whiteness is the absence of color—sort of like evil is the absence of good? I have serious reservations about whether this is true ethically and politically. Isn't it crucial for white people to own up to our whiteness (read: privilege in a racist society) and to acknowledge the difference our color makes?

I don't think this is nitpicking but rather that it's one more example of racial privilege looked at through the lens of liberalism—color doesn't make any difference and shouldn't matter; we shouldn't even notice it—because, in the world of God, color (like sex, etc.) is transcended, a nonissue, a nonreality. That sounds to me like the sort of logic that could only bounce out of the brain of a race/a people that thinks of itself as "colorless," folks like my people who distance ourselves from the difference color makes.

I'm excited to be writing this to you, Kate, because I like you and I know you like me, which makes it a little easier to speak my mind. But I would be lying if I said that I'm comfortable discussing race—even with you, or maybe especially with you. My fear is that you'll leave; that you'll notice my racism—which I certainly notice—and that you'll leave, close the door.

Surely I've told you about Bessie. Bessie was our maid. I was about four years old, living with Mamma and Daddy; at the time still the only child. Bessie came every several days, maybe once a week, to clean the house and cook fried chicken, my favorite food, and look after me. And I adored her. Sometimes she'd take me to the movie theater in Hendersonville, North Carolina, where "colored" people had to sit in the balcony and white people downstairs. I can remember begging her to let me go with her to the balcony! And I remember asking Mamma and Daddy why we never went to Bessie's house, except to drop her off at the end of the driveway; and why Bessie's house looked so poor, like a shack, and ours didn't. My memory is fuzzy, but I think I recall both my parents' very pained and strained expressions as they tried to explain racism to a four-year-old white child. I will go to my grave grateful that they told me racism was wrong and that it was not God's will and that we, all of us, were living in a sinful society. Those were the lessons my parents tried to teach, and they were, even then, considered by most folks who knew them to be moderate to liberal white southerners.

But they didn't try to teach me, explicitly, that we should do something about ending racism. I suppose, like most, they didn't know what to do. They felt powerless. They did tell me that I must always be kind to colored people and respect them as God's children. And they also told me that I should never ever call a colored person a nigger—that this was a bad word that only ignorant and racist white people used (notice the class bias of dominant white culture here—white folks' sense of "poor white trash").

But one day my friend Elliott (a white girl) and I were playing jump rope in the front yard and Bessie was watching over us. And I began that infamous little jingle: "Eenie, meenie, miny mo, catch a nigger by its toe." I still to this day have no sense of whether I knew what I was saying, whether I was making the connection between "nigger" and "colored person" or between "nigger" and

Bessie; but Bessie walked into the house, got her coat and walked out again, slowly down the driveway. I never saw her again.

That was 1950. Mamma and Daddy explained to me that I had hurt Bessie's feelings and that it was wrong for me to have done it, but that Bessie shouldn't have taken such offense at a five-year-old girl. Recollecting this story is still painful for me, and I haven't fully unloaded it. I do know that it represents my fear—but of what? Of someone leaving? But who? Necessarily a black person? Or might it be anyone? And as I've gotten older, the story has begun to make me angry—to put me in touch with my feelings of having been betrayed—by Bessie. My fantasy now is not to watch silently as she walks down the driveway, but to run after her and ask her to stop, turn around, come back—even demand—that she tell me why she's going, what she feels like, and that, even at age five, if I could do something about it, I would. I also want her to know that I'm sorry, that I am ashamed, that I didn't know what I was doing—at least not consciously or willfully.

It is almost more than I can bear to imagine that Bessie didn't give a damn about me, and yet now, over thirty years later, I can say, for certain, that if I were black, a black woman, I would be burning with an unquenchable fire of rage against white people—including the five-year-old girls and boys I had been expected to nurture at the expense of my own.

As I've told you before, sexism makes racism all the more complicated for me to try to sort out—especially my own attitudes and actions. Sometimes I think that if there were only black women and white women in the world (and of course women of other colors too), racism wouldn't be a problem—for *me*, that is. I don't mean to be idealizing womanhood, because I don't believe women are morally superior to men. What I do mean is that, for me, it's in relation to black men that I get confused about the ways in which I am or am not racist. I do not like for any man of any color or ethnic group to harass me sexually. My experience has been that in relation to most (not all) white men who've come on to me sexually, when I brush them off or say no, they back off and rather quietly get out of my way. In relation to black men (again, not all of them) who've come on to me, when I say no or brush them off, there's usually a big scene about my being racist or about chocolate being better than vanilla—"if only you weren't too hung up to taste it"—and on it goes.

Furthermore, since I came out as a lesbian, I've felt (paranoid or not) that a good many black men have wanted to do to me what the guys in Brewster Place did to one of "The Two."[15] I'll never forget the contemptuous look in the eyes of Mr. —— when a gay man and I gave a five-minute speech on behalf of lesbians and gays at the Theology in the Americas Conference in 1980. He and a dozen or so other black men, together with the men in the Native American group, were the only people, out of some six hundred, who chose to sit there with stone faces after the gay/lesbian presentation rather than to rise and applaud. I understand this from a sociological, historical perspective, of course.

But even to write about it makes me angry. And I find that at times—much to my chagrin, actually—my image of black men is of people I cannot trust, people who scare me, people who'll use me—whether physically, professionally, whatever—to bolster themselves. It's really clear to me that these feelings of mine combine simple truth-telling (black men and white women have at best a strained relationship historically that none of us individually can transcend absolutely) and flashy remnants of my own racism (really believing that black men are more violent than white men; being afraid, for example, that a black male mugger would kill me whereas a white male mugger would simply take my money . . .).

I didn't mean to go on about my relations with black men—that's not exactly the point of this correspondence. And yet, it does relate to us, you and me, does it not?

Can we be different but not alienated? I agree totally, Kate, that the answer lies in the quality of our relation; whether real dialogue, the "miracle of dialogue" as you say, is possible and desired between us and around us, among our sisters, black and white. The problem with white liberalism (I don't know about black liberalism) is that liberal white men and women do not advocate real relation, not mutual relation, but rather a patronizing sort of relation based on hand-me-down affections. White liberals "love" black people; white liberal men "love" all women (white women and women of color)—as long as we're not threatening to change the name of the power game. There's really not much difference between white liberals and white conservatives when it comes to race relations or any relations. There may be a different attitude or worldview—but the actions seem to me, when all is said and done, pretty much the same.

I would distinguish between conservatives and reactionaries. Conservatives are very much like liberals—it's just that their patronizing is attached more explicitly to the value of the past. But both liberal and conservative white people (and I suppose their black clones) really don't want to see things shaken up. Change? Maybe, very gradually, very cautiously, and very amicably. No disruptions, no riots, no violence. Whereas reactionaries in white communities are today in this country very much an incarnation of fascism. They do want to see things change and they do want to see things shaken up—and all in the service of what they believe either once was (the American Dream) or what ought to be—because it's God's will (Moral Majority, for example).

The point of this little digression is that, in my opinion, among us white people, we have very few models of mutual relation—people helping show the way. Most of the white people I know (myself included) grew up as more or less liberal—and, as such, really not very relational in any authentic sense. Even our primary, most intimate relations—parent-child, spouse-spouse, lover-lover, friend-friend—have been characterized more by a "let me give you what's good for you" attitude and less by a "let's try to see what's good for ourselves and then work together for what we see" way of being together. As far as I am concerned, the former is destructive of human well-being, whether between two lovers or two races of people. The latter may be redemptive, or so it seems to me. And it seems to me that that's exactly what we need to be about, we white women and women of color.

Women of color and white women need to own up to our own respective situations, getting ourselves together *as white* women or *as black* women or *as Hispanic* women—so our racial/ethnic womanness and particularity is clear. We need to be clear about who we are *as a people*—which is why white people like me have to own up to our whiteness and not be always bouncing ourselves off people who are black or brown or yellow, as if somehow we are looking to you for our definition—which could only be a sham.

We have to work together—as we are doing right now on this project. I don't believe these two steps of being separate, and also working together, follow in any neat sequence. Rather they can go on simultaneously under the right conditions, sometimes in crisis situations in which solidarity becomes mandatory; or through friendship when solidarity has become thinkable or at least a common dream.

It seems to me that we can work together only if we are willing to risk being candid with each other—about what we need, how we affect each other, how we experience the difference our race makes even in the instant we are acting together for what we believe is our common good.

As you know—I've heard you discuss this—being candid is more difficult for white liberal women than for just about anyone else, because (1) liberals don't like conflict; (2) whites don't like to get in touch with the difference our race makes; and (3) women, white women at least, have been cultivated to be reconcilers—although I should add that such attitudes are also class related. The sort of candor that involves conflict is especially hard for white, upper-middle-strata, liberal women like me raised to think that we must be "ladies." I thought a lot about this when Grace Kelly died. When I was a child, she was my role model of what a "lady" should be; in recent years, I had grown to find Grace Kelly a rather dreary archetype of passivity, a woman who did not interest me in any way, except that once upon a time I had wanted to be like her.

And so what is it I'm afraid of? What do I fear my candor may unleash or cause? Several things: I've already mentioned my fear that you, rather than struggling through issues with me, will simply walk away—not because you won't want to have anything to do with me but rather because I will have become a source of great pain for you, a pain you won't feel that you should have to bear. I'm also afraid that you'd be right to leave, to say "To hell with you," because I'm afraid that my own racism is deeper and more pervasive than I realize, and such that no black person would really want to be with me if ever she were to see this nasty wad of remnant racism, from generations past and present, which I have swallowed, and which, like a giant furball, has infected my gut.

And why am I afraid that I'm the most racist person in the Northeast? Because it's clear to me that racism is far more pervasive, far more odious, far more sinful and outrageous than any of us white children were ever taught to believe or imagine, even those of us who had white "ladies and gentlemen" for parents. Racism is so obnoxious, so unspeakably devastating to each white personality and psyche, that I, no less than any white sister or brother, must surely have been infected by this gross malaise in ways that I still cannot comprehend.

Yes, indeed, every white person has a white mama—and a white papa too. And while I do hear the particular poignancy and responsibility in the black mama-child relation you articulate, Kate, it's the white daddy/white papa/white father image, symbol, and reality that cuts to the core of what I see the problem to be in the white world I know. It's interesting, isn't it, that the white woman would say, "But let's talk about the white father instead"? Interesting to me—in that it may have something to do with some of the tensions between black and white women. Something we need to sort out?

You see, for me, in my white culture it's the *father* who's been responsible for a kind of headship of family, which the mother simply passes on, passively. She is to nurture and coddle the father's values—including racism. This sounds simplistic, if what I am saying is interpreted on the basis of individual personalities, because, within lots of families—including my own—individual white mothers are as assertive and strong as white fathers. But among white folks in my world, the prevailing, *public* assumption is that father does indeed know best—and even in families where there is no father at home, or in which the mother personally rules the roost, there looms large this image of "the man"/"the father"/"God," in whose service this life is being lived. Which makes for a complex and often intense relation between the white mother and the white child.

Often this means that the white mama must be manipulative if she's ever to have her own way, because wives and mothers do not live for themselves. To be manipulative is to be indirect, circuitous. It means that the mama must never let the daddy think that the children love her more, even if they do. Because, in fact, she is simply the channel through which the children's feelings get passed to daddy. Which means, again, that the mother must be coy, mysterious, enigmatic when it comes to appropriating the child's feelings for her; moreover, it means that she seldom ever really feels loved by the children—even though they may adore her. What this means is that many white mamas live frantic emotional lives in relation to their children—trying always not to love them too much, but at the same time desperate to feel loved by them. And so it is that white mothers "hang on" or "won't let go"—or so the stories suggest, and I think, to be honest, it is often true.

And while black mamas have to teach their kids how to survive in a racist world, white mamas—if they are women of goodwill—have to teach their kids something similar: on one hand, how to reject patriarchal values of racism, sexism, and economic greed; and, on the other hand, how to pretend to accept these values in order not to be destroyed. So white mothers, if they believe in justice, and white fathers too, if they advocate justice, find themselves in the roles of teaching schizophrenia to the kids in order to help them learn to cope humanely and responsibly in—and still survive—a racist, sexist, classist, war-mongering situation.

I'll probably write to you more later. Right now I'm spent. Your words bear witness to some deep and abiding truths—and I don't often speak of "eternals." Thank you for the gift of you.

Carter

November 20, 1982

Dear Carter,

I feel so grateful for the honesty of sharing that is occurring in these letters. It reminds me of my childhood, when I habitually watched Red Buttons on TV. I gathered a host of imaginary friends around me for comfort, all named HiHi, HoHo, HeHe, based on the characters I remembered that Red Buttons talked about a great deal. My sister, Sara, who is twenty-three months older than I, refused to play with me because I insisted that my imaginary friends be allowed to play too. At that point she announced to the world (which consisted of my younger sister, Doris, and the neighborhood children, all blood relatives) that I was crazy. But I didn't really care, because my imaginary friends were with me through thick and thin, they never left; and when I raised questions about the fundamental order of life, especially as to what the curse of blackness was all about, they (the imaginary friends) raised the same question. I knew in my heart of hearts that they knew I wasn't crazy, just extremely delicate and sensitive.

I feel that you are one of those imaginary friends who is now present in the flesh. The bond between us has been there before we were born. I just remembered I wrote a poem about such a bond on the day that the Feminist Theological Institute came into existence—November 22, 1980.

> Strolling down the sidewalk
>   a woman-pair
> Holding quadraphonic conversations
>   in our heads
> Sure of words
>   not sure of the genus of our souls
> Agonizing the same truths
> Embedded in the common womb
>   of wrestling supplications
> Posing difficult questions
>   with piercing X-ray vision
>   inherent in the friendship
>
>   before the beginning.

The poem goes on, but the point I am making is that the covenant of relating is mutual. I know that if I tried to lift or erase the fear you have about your racism hanging out that I would be trespassing on God's territory. However, I do believe that only in experiencing the new heaven and the new earth do we develop convictions about what is really possible as well as renewed commitment to keep the covenant alive and ever-expanding.

I don't know whether you are familiar with Lillian Smith's book, *Killers of the Dream,* written in the 1940s and revised and reissued in 1961.[16] I urge you to read it and add it to our book discussion for the collective, along with *The Color Purple.* We discussed Smith's book in the RSAC (Race, Sex, and Class) meeting yesterday.[17] I only wish that more women in my age group had been present. There was such a need for reality checking with counterparts of my generation, and maybe that day will come soon. What you talked about in your last letter resonated exactly with Lillian Smith's discussion of her childhood. For instance, she says:

> The mother who taught me what I know of tenderness and love and compassion taught me also the bleak rituals of keeping Negroes in their "place." The father who rebuked me for an air of superiority toward schoolmates from the mill and rounded out his rebuke by gravely reminding me that "all men are brothers," trained me in the steel-rigid decorum I must demand of every colored male. They who so gravely taught me to split my body from my mind and both from my "soul," taught me also to split my conscience from my acts and Christianity from southern tradition.[18]

I need to respond to another issue you raised. Carter, I ask that you separate your experience of black men from everything else right now because as long as those two (men, plus all else) stay tangled inside you, we cannot get on with the conversation that will take both of our lifetimes, and then some, to complete anyway. You and I have shared with each other the experience of being molested as children.[19] It just dawned on me that when you shared your experience with me, I identified so readily with what happened to you that it may be that only in my imagination did I share my experience with you! Do you recall my telling you about being repeatedly molested by an older boy when I was about five years of age? If you don't recall it, then it is probably because I told it to you when you still existed only in your "imaginary" state!

Your fear, feelings, and response to black men are not abstract racist ideology and doctrine but come from that place inside of you that has not healed from violation. I say that from my own space/place. The teenage boy who molested me several times died soon afterwards and I believed, until my early adulthood, that God did that especially for me, that I was special and that if someone hurts Kate, I could ask "Friend-God" to zap that person—and in seconds my will would be done. That theological narrowness of imagining a controlled/controlling God has changed for me, but it sustained me through some of the abuse I endured from men, including that childhood violation.

Think about the incident with your heart, not your mind. Here's a little white girl who shared what she thought was harmless. Then when she spoke of it, she had to endure the response of angry, frightened parents and the retaliation by the white community to the black man. And, all along, Carter gets lost in the shuffle, denying the good feeling, feeling unclean, having confused-as-hell feelings, assuring everybody that she is okay, and remembering we must love "those" people. No wonder your fear of black males is deep and still confusing to you: but it is like I said in our discussion of *The Color Purple: rebirth is only possible when we face terror face to face.* That experience was terror in your life, just as my experience of being molested was. It wreaked havoc in our psyches. What I have learned in facing terror, sometimes day by day, is that I don't go to certain people for affirmation, especially to those who remind me of the boy who molested me.

I hope that the challenge I am presenting to you is not too threatening. I hope that it is simple and clear to you. I think of the pain of violation like the woman in the scriptures who had the issue of blood for seven long years. (Remember all that the number seven symbolizes in the Bible, especially that seven means "complete.") Think of the woman as bleeding away her life energy and life substance, that they flowed from her in wasteful ways. The story affirms that the woman was healed by her awareness of her situation, an acceptance of the help that was available, and the courage to take the action to touch God in the person of Jesus. And even though Jesus was being pressed by the crowd, he knew that he had been touched by this woman in a significant way.

It is like all the healing-touching between Celie and Shug in *The Color Purple.* The people who hurt you in all kinds of ways cannot do the healing. Nor can those who act like our violators act today. For you still to worry so much about black men or the Native American men who did not stand in support of the lesbian/gay presentation at TIA meeting is to long for and look for healing from the source from whence it will not and cannot come. To focus on the walking dead means that you may miss out on the powerful healing touch and touching healing of the six hundred people who stood with you in love and commitment and cheered.

I want to say more about this healing at some later date. For now I will close with a story that I heard recently. Before doing that I affirm that I enter this covenant of friendship with you because I am thoroughly convinced that I cannot be all that I can be as a black woman if I dismiss you from the community of humanity just because you are a white woman. I cannot be in an I-It relationship with anyone and call myself Christian. And the more I-Thous in my life, the more I feel, experience, and know the Eternal Thou who lives and breathes in each one of us in beautiful and unique ways. (I never thought I would reach the day when I'd say that I need white people in my life, just like I need black people and the other people in the world because we are all part of the whole!) On with the story.

As a child, I was a lover of baby dolls. I yearned to the point of experiencing physical pain in my body for a black doll. I always got white dolls because they were more plentiful and cheaper. But my sister, Doris, who is thirteen months younger than I, got a beautiful black doll one Christmas, and the next year we used it for Jesus in the Christmas play at the church. Back in 1956–57 that was a revolutionary, radical thing to do, but we did it, and it felt so good to me, to know that this little black female doll symbolized the boy Jesus. After that point I didn't care whether I got a black doll, because if the baby Jesus was black, then the boy Jesus and the grownup Jesus could also be black, and it all started to make sense in my little ever-churched Sunday school mind. Of course I only acknowledged this radical truth to HiHi, HoHo, and HeHe, and they, of course, agreed with me. (Believe it or not, this is not the story I started out to tell. The above story is the one that flowed from the miracle of dialogue. Now, for the story I heard recently . . .)

A woman was asked by her therapist to imagine that she was a child in a crib who had pushed her favorite toy onto the floor so that it rolled out of sight. When no one came to return this beloved object of pleasure to her, what, she was asked, would she do? The young woman started crying, saying no one had ever been there for her. She insisted that people, places, and things had rolled out of her sight and life repeatedly, and, as a result, she was now terrified to trust anyone to be there with and for her. When we have been intentionally or unintentionally hurt by others, it is not enough to have had someone there to return our lost toy on several occasions, randomly, at their convenience. It would not be enough to assure the wounded child that there is somebody who cares. The sexual abuse against you and me, Carter, caused a part of us to roll out of sight. Even though we have done a lot to put ourselves together again, the healing only happens for each of us, I believe, when we embrace God in ourselves and each other. When I touch other individuals, they feel touched by me, and in a miraculous way the healing happens, slowly but surely. The issue of blood stops flowing out of me. Instead it flows through me, in new and invigorating ways, so that I can be present when the next touch connects with me. When my blood stays inside me, flowing in me, I am more sensitive to the press from the crowd, and I am also in tune with myself to know when "somebody has touched me. And, oh, what joy floods my soul, something happened, and now I know, somebody touched me and made me whole." (This is a paraphrase of a popular gospel song in the black church tradition.)

Have a great Thanksgiving.

Kate

NOTES

1. Alice Walker, *The Color Purple* (New York: Harcourt Brace Jovanovich, 1982).

2. Zora Neale Hurston, *Mules and Men* (Philadelphia: Lippincott, 1935; reprint ed., New York: Collier Books, 1970), pp. 18–19.

3. George Frederickson, *White Supremacy: A Comparative Study in American and South African History* (New York: Oxford University Press, 1981).

4. See Carter Heyward, *The Redemption of God,* especially pages 25–59 and 149–72, for the source of my use of the term "godding."—KGC

5. Cherrie Moraga, and Gloria Anzaldúa, eds., *This Bridge Called My Back: Writings by Radical Women of Color* (Watertown, Mass.: Persephone Press, 1981), pp. 27–37, 71–75, 94, 101.

6. See Amari Baraka, "Philistinism and the Negro Writer," in *Anger and Beyond: The Negro Writer in the United States,* ed. by Herbert Hill (New York: Harper & Row, 1966).

7. Langston Hughes, *The Ways of White Folks* (New York: Knopf, 1934).

8. See Richard Sennett and Jonathan Cobb, *The Hidden Injuries of Class* (New York: Vintage Books, 1972).

9. Carter Godwin Woodson, *The Mis-Education of the Negro* (New York: The Associated Publishers, 1933).

10. Cynthia Neverdon-Morton, "The Black Woman's Struggle for Equality in the South, 1895–1925," in *The Afro-American Woman: Struggles and Images,* ed. by Sharon Harley and Rosalyn Terborg-Penn (Port Washington, N.Y.: Kennikat Press, 1978), p. 43.

11. Ibid., p. 44.

12. George Jackson, *Soledad Brother: The Prison Letters of George Jackson* (New York: Bantam Books, 1970).

13. Alice Walker, *Revolutionary Petunias and Other Poems* (New York: Harcourt Brace Jovanovich, 1973), p. 5.

14. Gloria Hull, Patricia Scott, and Barbara Smith, *All the Women Are White, All the Blacks Are Men, But Some of Us Are Brave* (Old Westbury, N.Y.: Feminist Press, 1982).

15. Gloria Naylor, *The Women of Brewster Place* (New York: Viking Press, 1982), pp. 129–73.

16. Lillian Eugenia Smith, *Killers of the Dream,* rev. ed. (New York: W.W. Norton & Co., 1961).

17. RSAC is a network of professional women in New York City, mostly denominational executives, who have been meeting for the past ten years to discuss, analyze, and strategize around issues related to the intersection of race, sex, and class.

18. Smith, *Killers of the Dream,* p. 27.

19. This reference is to an incident in Carter's childhood when she was molested by the black yardman who was employed by her family. As Carter recalls, "I was five or six and I liked Jeff. I knew he wouldn't hurt me and his fondling of me in the garage never bothered me. What did bother me was the reaction of the police captain, and all the other white men when my parents called them. I couldn't understand why all the fuss. What had Jeff done that was so wrong? And I felt guilty because I had told on him."

6

SOLIDARITY

Love of Neighbor in the 1980s

Ada María Isasi-Díaz

CONTEXT AND COMMITMENT

I am a Cuban activist theologian struggling to develop a *Mujerista* theology that is rooted in and has as its source the experience of Hispanic women. I have lived away from my country most of my adult life because of circumstances beyond my control and I think of myself as living in exile. This is the context within which I have struggled to find my voice and my mission. I now know that finding my voice has been part of my mission, a mission which now calls me to struggle to create a platform in the theological world for my voice and the voices of my Hispanic sisters.

As a *Mujerista* I do not see myself as part of a minority group, a marginalized group. It is a fact that at present *Mujeristas,* as well as all Hispanics, have no way of influencing the society in which we live; our values and ideals are not part of the norm of society. As a *Mujerista* I believe that we need to change radically the society in which we live. Simply influencing society will not result in the changes that are needed to bring about peace with justice in our world. That is why we *Mujeristas* understand ourselves along the lines of the biblical concept of the "remnant." Like the biblical remnant we are not an integral part of society. Our mission is to challenge oppressive structures which refuse to allow us to be full members of society while preserving our distinctiveness as Hispanic women.

We also apply this understanding of ourselves as a remnant to our theological task and to our role as theologians. We see *Mujerista* theology as a distinctive contribution to the theological enterprise at large which challenges particularly nonliberative theological understandings. For us theology is a praxis—a liberative praxis having as its goal the liberation of Hispanic women which cannot take place at the expense of any other oppressed group. As *Mujerista* theologians we straddle the academic theological world and the Hispanic women's community. Hispanic women are indeed my community of accountability. But I am an academically trained theologian and wish to maintain a dialogue with all liberation theologies. Therefore, *Mujerista* theology must be understandable both to Hispanic women and to liberation theologians. Our theological method must be a liberative praxis; at the same time we must be able to explain our methodology in such a way that it impacts in no matter how limited a degree the whole theological world.

For me the struggle is life, *la vida es la lucha.* To do *Mujerista* theology is an intrinsic part of my struggle for liberation. To do *Mujerista* theology is to attempt to live life to the fullest, to be about justice and the self-determination of all peoples. To do *Mujerista* theology is to believe that God stands in solidarity with us, Hispanic women.

CONSTRUCTION

Solidarity must replace charity as the appropriate Christian behavior—ethical behavior—in our world today. This constitutes a significant methodological shift, for there is an essential difference between solidarity and charity. Charity, the word we have used most often when talking about love of neighbor, has been implemented mainly by giving of what we have in abundance, a one-sided affair. Obviously that is not all that charity means, but I think that, in general, this is how it is understood and used. I am not saying that giving is never an appropriate and even necessary way of loving. I do believe, however, that giving is an ethical behavior today only if it is understood and carried out within the context of solidarity.

Solidarity is the appropriate present-day expression of the gospel demand that we love our neighbor. This demand, I contend, is what salvation is all about— the goal of Christianity.[1] Therefore, if salvation depends on love of neighbor, and if love of neighbor today is expressed through solidarity, then solidarity is a *sine qua non* of salvation. And who is our neighbor? Our neighbor, according to Matthew 25, is the least of our sisters and brothers. Our neighbor is the poor, the oppressed, with whom we must stand in solidarity.[2]

The Meaning of Solidarity

The true meaning of solidarity is under serious attack and runs the risk of being drastically changed. The proof of this is how fashionable its usage has become, how easily it rolls off the tongues of all sorts of speakers, how unthreatening it is. If the true meaning of solidarity were understood and intended, visible radical change would be happening in the lives of those who endorse it with their applause. Solidarity is *not* a matter of agreeing with, of being supportive of, of liking, or of being inspired by, the cause of a group of people. Though all these might be part of solidarity, solidarity goes beyond all of them. Solidarity has to do with understanding the interconnections among issues and the cohesiveness that needs to exist among the communities of struggle.

Solidarity is "the union of fellowship [sic] arising from the common responsibilities and interests, as between classes, peoples, or groups; community of interests, feelings, purposes, or action; social cohesion."[3] Solidarity moves away from the false notion of disinterest, of doing for others in an altruistic fashion. Instead it is grounded in "common responsibilities and interests," which necessarily arouse shared feelings and lead to joint action.

The true meaning of solidarity can best be understood if it is broken down into its two main interdependent elements: mutuality and praxis. Both of these elements will be examined at length later in the chapter, but from the very beginning it must be clear that neither of them is to be considered more important, central, or necessary than the other. Mutuality and praxis are inexorably bound; they have a dialogic, circular relation in which one is always understood in view of the other. There is no dichotomy between them, nor are they to be understood in a dualistic fashion. Furthermore, mutuality and praxis as intrinsic elements of solidarity cannot be conceived or understood as abstractions. They are grounded in the historical situation; their specificity is defined by the socio-economic-political circumstances of the persons involved.

The goal of mutuality and praxis, of solidarity, is to create participation in the ongoing process of liberation through which Christians become a significantly positive force in the unfolding of the "kin-dom"[4] of God. At the center of the unfolding of the kin-dom is the salvific act of God. Salvation and liberation are interconnected. Salvation is gratuitously given by God: it flows from the very essence of God—love. Salvation is the love between God and individual human beings and among human beings. This love relationship is the goal of all life—it constitutes the fullness of humanity. Therefore, love sets in motion and sustains the ongoing act of creation in which the person necessarily participates, since love requires, per se, active involvement of those who are in relationship.

Our ongoing act of creation, our work to transform the world, is both cause and effect of the struggle to have a love relationship with others, including God. This work of transformation—to become a full person and to build the human community—is the work of salvation.[5] There can be no salvation without liberation, though no single act of liberation can be totally identified with salvation in its fullness. As Gustavo Gutiérrez has said, "Without liberating historical events, there would be no growth of the Kingdom [sic] . . . we can say that the historical, political, liberating event is the growth of the Kingdom [sic] and *is* a salvific event; but it is not *the* coming of the Kingdom [sic], not *all* of salvation."[6]

The main obstacle to the unfolding of the kin-dom is the alienation from God and from each other experienced by all persons and understood only through social categories.[7] This alienation is what in theology has been traditionally called sin. Sin always affects the totality of the person and the relationship with God and with others for which the person was created and, therefore, sin always affects society and is a concrete historical reality. "Sin appears, therefore, as the fundamental alienation, the root of a situation of injustice and exploitation."[8]

In order for the person to become fully human—to be in a love relationship with God and with others—justice has to prevail. "As virtue, justice is a trait of character empowering and disposing an agent to act in ways constitutive of human flourishing."[9] This is why the unfolding of the kin-dom of God is made possible when just structures and situations exist. "This is the reason why effort to build a just society is liberating."[10] This is why "action on behalf of justice and transformation of the world fully appear . . . as a constitutive element of the preaching of the Gospel."[11] And, finally, this is why Christianity can be reaffirmed as containing some truth, "not because of its origins, but because it liberates people now from specific forms of oppression."[12]

Solidarity with the oppressed and among the oppressed has to be at the heart of Christian behavior, because the oppression suffered by the majority affects everyone. This solidarity demands a preferential option for the poor. This preferential option is not based on the moral superiority of the poor; it does not mean that personally those who are oppressed are better, or more innocent, or purer in their motivations. The preferential option is based on the fact that the point of view of the oppressed, "pierced by suffering and attracted by hope, allows them, in their struggles, to conceive another reality. Because the poor suffer the weight of alienation, they can conceive a different project of hope and provide dynamism to a new way of organizing human life *for all.*"[13]

The epistemological privilege of the poor makes it possible for them to conceive of a new nonalienating reality for all. Oppression and poverty limit love since love cannot exist in the midst of alienation. Oppression and poverty are "a slap in the face of God's sovereignty."[14] The alienation brought about and maintained by oppressive structures is a denial of God. Gutiérrez recalls, "as a Bolivian campesino, Paz Jimenez, put it . . . with an insight that is profoundly biblical: 'an atheist is someone who fails to practice justice toward the poor.' "[15]

Who are the poor and oppressed? First of all, the poor and the oppressed in this context "always implies collective and social conflict."[16] The poor and the oppressed are those who are marginalized, whose participation in the sociopolitical life is severely restricted or totally negated. The poor are living persons whose struggle for survival constitutes their way of life. "Concretely, to be poor means to die of hunger, to be illiterate, to be exploited by others, not to know that you are being exploited, not to know you are a person."[17] The poor and the oppressed suffer from very specific forms of oppression—sexism, racism, classism. These specific oppressions, however, are not self-contained realities in the world today, but are interconnected parts of a worldwide system of domination in which the few oppress the many.[18] This system of domination permeates every aspect of society: ideology, religion, social mores, government, businesses, families, relationships.

In order to effectively change such a worldwide reality, solidarity is a must both as a theory and as a strategy.[19] As a theory solidarity stands against the theory of oppression[20] and reconceptualizes every aspect of society in every part of the world. As a strategy solidarity indicates the path to follow in order to change society radically. The magnitude of this task is such that only worldwide action can effectively undo and replace oppression.

The starting place of solidarity as a theory is the particularity of the oppressions suffered by those who are exploited and marginalized. As a theory solidarity insists on the interconnections of the oppression. This creates a commonality of interests among the oppressed and between the oppressed and those who stand in solidarity with them. Solidarity as a theory insists on the centrality of mutuality, on the importance of a new order of relationships opposed to any and all forms of domination. This constructive task has to go hand in hand with the deconstructive task of denouncing the understandings and theories which support the present structures of domination. Therefore, solidarity must continuously denounce hierarchy as a structure which sets a few, eventually only one, over the many.

As a strategy solidarity has to be politically effective. Though there is no place for purist understandings in strategical considerations, solidarity as a strategy must not sacrifice any one group of oppressed people for the sake of another group. As a strategy solidarity must be about radical structural change. The goal is not the participation of the oppressed in present societal structures but rather the replacement of those structures by ones in which full participation of the oppressed is possible. No strategy can wait for a perfect time to be carried out, or until all the internal problems and inconsistencies are solved. As with all strategies, there is risk involved; as with all human realities, the understanding and implementation of solidarity is and will always be imperfect. But this should never delay creating a community of solidarity committed to change oppressive structures.

The theoretical aspect of solidarity is intrinsically linked to its strategic component.[21] The theoretical and strategic considerations of solidarity correspond to its two main elements: mutuality and praxis. The strategy of solidarity carries out the theoretical understandings at the same time that it provides the ground for the reflection needed to elaborate the theory. The theory of solidarity provides the goal for the strategy of solidarity at the same time that it gives the strategy an inherent way of evaluating its progress and critiquing itself. It is solidarity as a strategy which demands of the theory an ever greater clarity and demands that it be historically rooted. The internal relation of theory to strategy within solidarity demands a dialogic, circular understanding of the elements of solidarity—mutuality and praxis.

The Praxis of Mutuality: Friendship

Common interests—the heart of solidarity—are what move Christian behavior from the one-sidedness of charity to mutuality. These common interests are a reality in our world today. Two world wars, multinational corporations, the threat of global annihilation, the global spread of AIDS, the worldwide political influence and control of the superpowers, acid rain, the deterioration of the ozone layer—all of these are examples of the bases for common interests today.

What about mutuality among the oppressed? Mutuality among the oppressed is set in motion by becoming aware, by a moment of insight which creates a suspicion about oppression. Almost anything can create the spark which moves people "from a 'naive awareness,' which does not deal with problems, gives too much value to the past, tends to accept mythical explanations, and tends toward debate, to a 'critical awareness,' which delves into problems, is open to new ideas, replaces magical explanations with real causes, and tends to dialogue."[22]

Paulo Freire calls this process "conscientization" and insists that it involves praxis and is not just an intellectual understanding apart from action.[23] Critical awareness makes the oppressed understand the real causes of oppression and the need to engage with others in changing the situation which marginalizes them. This process of conscientization is not something that happens once and for all. Conscientization is a "permanent effort of man [sic] who seeks to situate himself [sic] in time and space, to exercise his [sic] creative potential, and to assume his [sic] responsibilities."[24]

Mutuality among the oppressed is not a given. Though it is true that many of the oppressed do depend on other oppressed people to survive, frequently the oppressed do not see their common interests because they have to fight each other for the few crumbs that fall from the table of the oppressors. In many ways the oppressed depend for their survival on those who control the society in which they live—their oppressors. To even begin to envision the possibilities that they can create when they stand in solidarity with each other, the oppressed have to be willing to stop looking for and accepting the "charity" of their oppressors. To turn from the "charity" of the oppressors to solidarity among themselves requires great willingness to take risks. This going beyond the isolated self is followed by creating strategies, solidarity among them, in order to carry out their struggle for liberation. The implementation of these strategies will keep their hopes alive and, together with the vision of their own liberation, it will give them the courage to risk and sustain the struggle.

Mutuality between the oppressed and the oppressor also starts with a process of becoming aware. To become aware does not stop with individual illumination but necessarily moves to establish dialogue and mutuality with the oppressed.[25] The first word in this dialogue is uttered by the oppressed. The oppressors who are willing to listen and to be questioned by the oppressed begin to cease being oppressors—they become "friends" of the oppressed.[26] This word spoken by the oppressed is "at times silent, at times muzzled; it is the face of the poor . . . of oppressed people who suffer violence."[27] This word is often spoken through demonstrations, boycotts, and even revolution. This word imposes itself "ethically, by a kind of categorical imperative, which is well determined and concrete, which the 'friend' as 'friend' listens to freely. This word . . . appeals to the 'friend's' domination and possession of the world and even of the other, and questions the desire for wealth and power."[28]

This word uttered by the oppressed divests those who allow themselves to be questioned by it of whatever they have totally appropriated. This word carries in its very weakness the power to judge the desire for wealth and power. It also is able to signify effectively the real possibility of liberation for those oppressors who allow themselves to be questioned. The leap the oppressors must take in order to be questioned is also made possible by the efficacious word uttered by the oppressed. The word uttered by the oppressed carries the real possibility of this qualitative jump and can be the liberating force which pushes the "friends" to take the leap that will put them in touch with the oppressed. This word also makes it possible for the "friends" to question and judge the oppressive structures which they support and from which they benefit, and to become cocreators with the oppressed of new liberating structures.

The "friends" answer the initial word uttered by the oppressed not only by questioning their own lives but also by responding to the oppressed. This response is born of the critical consciousness of those who allowed themselves to be critiqued and who take responsibility for their own consciousness. This response therefore becomes a word and an action which helps the oppressed in their process of conscientization. The response of the "friends" is one of the enabling forces which help the oppressed to become agents of their own history. This response of the "friends" enables the oppressed to rid themselves of the oppressor they carry within themselves. This moves the oppressed away from seeking vengeance, from wanting to exchange places with the oppressors. This response of the "friends" enables the oppressed to understand that they must not seek to participate in oppressive structures but rather to change radically those structures.

In many ways the "friends" are often harshly victimized by society at large because they have been part of the oppressors and know how to thwart the control and domination which keeps the oppressors in power. Furthermore, "friends" can prick the conscience of the oppressors in ways the oppressed cannot, because the "friends" know the manipulations and the betrayals that the oppressors must make to stay in power. The "friends" are able to demystify the world of the oppressors from within, to expose its weakness and incoherence, to point out its lies. One must not lose sight, however, that it is not the word uttered by the "friends" which initiates the process of conscientization for the oppressor. It is the word uttered by the oppressed, the one which starts the dialogic process which results in mutuality based on common interests— especially liberation. The oppressors who have become "friends" and the oppressed derive their courage to persist in the long struggle which begins with conscientization from their vision of liberation.

Mutuality among the oppressed and between the oppressed and their "friends" is not simply a matter of mutual understanding and support, though that is or could be a very positive side effect. Mutuality as an element of solidarity must push the oppressed and their "friends" to revolutionary politics.[29] Mutuality must urge them to envision and work toward alternative systems, or they will not be able to sustain the revolutionary momentum that makes liberation possible.[30] Mutuality must enable the oppressed and their "friends" to stay away from easy, partial solutions which might alleviate the situation of oppression but do not lead to liberation.

In order to maintain the revolutionary momentum the oppressed and their "friends" must work constantly to maintain the commitment to mutuality alive and strong. Commitment to mutuality means "*willingness to do something* for or about whatever it is we are committed to (at least to protect it or affirm it when it is threatened),"[31] and this follows upon a "sense of *being bound* to whomever or whatever is the object of [this] commitment."[32] Commitment gives other persons or a cause claim over oneself, thus establishing or strengthening mutuality between the self and the other. It is, as Margaret Farley argues, "a relation of binding and being-bound, giving and being-claimed."[33]

Commitment to the mutuality established among the oppressed and between the oppressed and the "friends" is essential because it provides assurance to others and strength to the person who is committed. Commitment is required if mutuality as an element of solidarity is to be the basis for praxis, because "it undergirds the very possibility of human communication."[34] Mutuality as an element of solidarity based in commonality of interests demands commitment to action. Without action mutuality becomes a "soft word," a passing whimsical reaction which is often privatized and removed from the public sphere, from the political reality of the struggle for liberation.[35] The actions resulting from true commitment become the framework of mutuality; they are the signs and deeds of mutuality and the efforts that ensure the future of mutuality.[36] It is precisely these actions which express and constitute mutuality that in a limited but real way begin to make liberation present. Actions born out of commitment to mutuality are eschatological glimpses which clarify the vision of liberation and make faithfulness to the vision possible. Liberation is not a condition that already exists and is simply waiting for the oppressed to grasp it. Rather, liberation is a historical possibility that takes form and shape according to the actions of the oppressed and their "friends." Liberative actions born out of commitment to mutuality, therefore, are not only glimpses of the future but eschatological actions making parts of the future present.

Commitment to mutuality among the oppressed and between the oppressed and their "friends" cannot be taken lightly because of the eschatological actions which are part of its framework. This commitment involves all aspects of one's life and has a lifelong permanency. The way in which the commitment is lived out might change. At times the person might be much more intentional about carrying out the implications of the commitment than at others. How the commitment is carried out might also vary according to circumstances. But to betray the mutuality established by placing oneself in a position of control and domination over others is to betray the commitment made. This is a betrayal of the other and a betrayal of oneself, because of the commonality of interests that exists whether one recognizes it or not. The betrayal, which most of the time occurs by failing to engage in liberative praxis rather than by a formal denunciation of the commitment, results in the "friends" becoming oppressors once again and in the oppressed losing their vision of liberation. Such betrayal, then, effectively delays liberation and, therefore, at least makes more difficult the unfolding of the kin-dom of God.[37]

CONCLUSION

Solidarity as a praxis of mutuality is indeed an intrinsic element of the process of liberation and salvation. It is through solidarity with the "least" of our sisters and brothers (Matt. 25) that the gospel command to love our neighbor as ourselves finds expression in our world today. By examining the process through which solidarity is established and the politically effective praxis through which it is expressed, we come to understand what our ethical behavior is to be today, if we are to call ourselves Christian.

NOTES

Author's note:

I dedicate this chapter to Blanche Marie Moore, a sister in the Order of St. Ursula who died in the Bronx, New York, on December 10, 1987, as I was typing it. Blanche Marie was my high school teacher in Cuba. A person of great strength of character, her dedication and strong will caught my imagination and strongly influenced me. I will always be most grateful to her for imbuing in me a love of reading and studying. *In paradisum perducant te angeli,* Blanche.

1. See Isabel Carter Heyward, *The Redemption of God* (Washington, DC, 1982), 1–18.

2. In this chapter the terms *the poor* and *the oppressed* are at times used interchangeably and at times together. I would have preferred to use the term *nonperson*—those human beings who are considered less than human by society, because that society is based on privileges arrogated by a minority (Gustavo Gutiérrez, *The Power of the Poor in History* [Maryknoll, NY: Orbis, 1984], 92). But I am concerned that the ontological meaning of the word, "nonentity," would be read into my use of *nonperson,* regardless of the explanation provided. I thought of using only *the oppressed* but felt that some specificity needed to be added to that term for fear of creating the illusion that the oppressed are a classification, an abstraction, instead of concrete persons.

I then needed to decide what term to add to *the oppressed.* I thought of the term I use to identify my own oppression, *Hispanic women,* but felt that it was too specific and that what I say here could be understood to apply only to us. I decided to use *the poor* because, though the restricted meaning of the term relates to those who are economically oppressed, it often goes beyond that meaning and closely parallels the meaning of *the oppressed* even in everyday language. In the Bible, at least in the Book of Zephaniah 2:3, 3:12–13, "the poor" are identified with the *anawim*. The *anawim,* the poor, are "the portion of the community . . . upon which the possible future existence of the community depends" (E. Jenni, "Remnant," *The Interpreter's Dictionary of the Bible,* ed. George Arthur Buttrick [Nashville, TN: Abingdon, 1965], 32–33). My usage of *the poor* in this chapter definitely includes this meaning.

3. *The Random House Dictionary of the English Language,* 2d unabridged ed. (New York: Random, 1987).

4. There are two reasons for not using the regular word employed by English Bibles, *kingdom.* First, it is obviously a sexist word that presumes that God is male. Second, the concept of kingdom in our world today is both hierarchical and elitist—which is why I do not use the word *reign.* The word *kin-dom* makes it clear that when the fullness of God becomes a day-to-day reality in the world at large, we will all be sisters and brothers—kin to each other.

5. Gustavo Gutiérrez, *A Theology of Liberation* (Maryknoll, NY: Orbis, 1973), 159.

6. *Ibid.,* 177.

7. Rebecca S. Chopp, *Praxis of Suffering* (Maryknoll, NY: Orbis, 1986), 25.

8. Gutiérrez, *Theology of Liberation,* 175.

9. William Werpehowski, "Justice," *The Westminster Dictionary of Christian Ethics,* ed. James F. Childress and John Macquarrie (Philadelphia: Westminster, 1986), 338.

10. Gutiérrez, *Theology of Liberation,* 177.

11. Synod of Bishops Second General Assembly, November 30, 1971, "Justice in the World," *The Gospel of Peace and Justice,* ed. Joseph Gremillion (Maryknoll, NY: Orbis, 1976), 514.

12. Sharon D. Welch, *Communities of Resistance and Solidarity* (Maryknoll, NY: Orbis, 1985), 53.

13. José Míguez Bonino, "Nueves Tendencias en Teología," in *Pasos* (1985), 22.

14. Gustavo Gutiérrez, *The Power of the Poor in History* (Maryknoll, NY: Orbis, 1984), 140.

15. *Ibid.*

16. *Ibid.,* 96.

17. Gutiérrez, *Theology of Liberation,* 289.

18. I use these three "isms" as inclusive categories and paradigms of oppression. Under sexism, for example, I include exclusive heterosexism. Under racism I include ethnic prejudice. Under classism I include militarism, etc.

19. I use strategy instead of practice here because of my insistence on the intrinsic unity between reflection and practice in praxis—which is what I claim solidarity is. I also use strategy because it carries with it the implication of political effectiveness which is intrinsic to solidarity as a praxis of liberation.

20. Janice Raymond, *A Passion for Friends* (Boston: Beacon, 1986), 22.

21. *Ibid.,* 214–5.

22. Gutiérrez, *Theology of Liberation,* 92.

23. Paulo Freire, *Pedagogy of the Oppressed* (New York: Seabury, 1973), 3.

24. Gutiérrez, *Theology of Liberation,* 92.

25. I have based this section about the relationship between the oppressor and the

"friend" on Juan Carlos Scannone, *Teología de la Liberación y Praxis Popular* (Salamanca: Ediciones Sigueme, 1976), 133–86.

26. Scannone uses the word *brother*. I have used *friend* in translating into English in order to avoid a sexist term.

27. *Ibid.*

28. Scannone, 164. In translating I have used inclusive language even though the original uses sexist language.

29. Bell Hooks, *Feminist Theory: From Margin to Center* (Boston: South End, 1984), 159.

30. *Ibid.*

31. Margaret Farley, *Personal Commitments* (San Francisco: Harper & Row, 1986), 14.

32. *Ibid.*, 15.

33. *Ibid.*, 18–19.

34. *Ibid.*, 19.

35. This is what I understood Joan Martin to say recently about why the Black community does not use the word *mutuality* in their struggles.

36. See Farley, 36

37. I find Gutiérrez wavering when he comes to this issue. In *Theology of Liberation*, 167, he says, "it is only in the temporal, earthly, historical event that we can open up to the future complete fulfillment." It is in this sense that I originally had written here that such betrayals *impede* the unfolding of the kin-dom of God. But Gutiérrez later insists on the contrary: "nor does it mean that this just society constitutes a 'necessary condition' for the arrival of the Kingdom, nor that they are closely linked, nor that they converge" (231). This is why I soften the claim I make here.

7

APPROPRIATION AND RECIPROCITY IN WOMANIST/MUJERISTA/FEMINIST WORK

Toinette M. Eugene,
Ada María Isasi-Díaz, Kwok Pui-lan,
Judith Plaskow, Mary E. Hunt,
Emilie M. Townes, and Ellen M. Umansky

On "Difference" and the Dream of Pluralist Feminism

Toinette M. Eugene

In discussing appropriation and reciprocity in womanist/mujerista/feminist work I intend to explore aspects of our differences as the key to what remains as yet for many of us a "dream" of pluralist feminism.[1] After rereading Lorraine Bethel's "What Chou Mean We, White Girl?" and June Jordan's "Where Is the Love?"[2] on the prompting of Maria Lugones, the witness of women of color is rekindled in my mind, reminding me that, although there are few women of color at the AAR, I am not alone in this gathering. The witnesses remind me: One does not make or remake anything alone; one cannot ignore the relations one has. To know one's self and one's situation is to know one's company (or lack of it), is to know oneself with or against others. With this chorus of voices surrounding me, this choir of witnesses, I feel empowered to comment on difference and the dream of pluralist feminism from my perspective as an African American liberation theologian.

I want to share with you some of the voices that commit me to this knowledge and ask you to keep them with you as I explain the difference that lack of this knowledge makes in theologizing and theorizing on women and religion. Audre Lorde offers us her visionary turn on this knowledge when she tells us that "interdependency between women is the only way to the freedom which allows the 'I' to 'be,' not in order to be used, but in order to be creative."[3]

Interdependency between women is necessary if we are to make ourselves into active, creative selves. Lorde knows the company she wants to keep and why.

These papers were originally presented at a session of the Women and Religion Section at the 1991 Annual Meeting of the American Academy of Religion.

Lorraine Bethel also knows the company she wants to keep, what comes from keeping this or that company, who she wants to be, and how that is related to the company she keeps.

> I am so tired of talking to others, translating my life for the deaf, the blind, . . . while we wonder where the next meal, job, payment on our . . . bills . . . are going to come from. They will come from us loving/speaking to our Black/Third World sisters, not at white women.[4]

June Jordan's understanding of anyone's "life supportive possibilities" is highly interactive.

> It is against such sorrow, . . . such deliberate strangulation of the lives of women, my sisters, and of powerless peoples—men and women—everywhere, that I work and live, now, as a feminist, trusting that I will learn to love myself well enough to love you (whoever you are), well enough so that you will love me well enough so that we will know, exactly, where is the love: that it is here, between us, and growing stronger and growing stronger.[5]

What women of color know is what I want to articulate and to encourage in feminist theorizing. To make it clearer what it is that we know and what difference it makes in theorizing and theologizing. I will take us back to Lugones's proposal for pluralist feminism and to Bethel's question, "What chou mean we, white girl?" In thinking about appropriation and reciprocity, I want to respond briefly to three questions: (1) What is the "problem of difference"? (2) What are some options for dealing with the "problem"? (3) How do we theologize once we recognize "the problem of difference"?

WHAT IS "THE PROBLEM OF DIFFERENCE"?

A number of feminists, womanists, and mujeristas are already asking the questions I am posing, and some theoretical shifts have already occurred. For example, *God's Fierce Whimsy,* the work of seven feminists who make up the Mud Flower Collective, contains an exchange of letters between Katie Cannon and Carter Heyward on the question, Can we be different but not alienated?[6] The focus of their conversation is on the difference color makes, on how assuming common bonds among all women amounts to a false liberalism, and on the problem this liberalism poses for feminist theory and theology.

Susan Thistlethwaite's *Sex, Race, and God: Christian Feminism in Black and White* argues that exploring difference is the only way white feminists and feminists of color will be able to develop a means of appropriation and reciprocity that has any integrity. She further argues that this exploration has to go beyond the easy appropriation of the fine lines of beauty available in richly nuanced fiction by women of color. Fiction can evoke truths that are obscured by social analysis, but sociology, anthropology, and economics—real social analysis must become key resources in a feminist theory that grapples with class and race privilege.[7]

Elizabeth Spelman, author of the provocative *Inessential Woman: Problems of Exclusion in Feminist Thought,* raises the same troubling question about the significance of difference in trying to offer reciprocity and to exercise integrity in appropriating one another's work.

> It certainly seems that if feminist inquiry and feminist political action are to have any coherent base at all, we have to have a solid answer to the following questions: What do I and can I know about women from whom I differ in terms of race, culture, class, ethnicity? (This question leaves out other closely related and also necessary questions such as what I in fact know about myself or about other women from whom I do not differ in terms of race, culture, etc.) We know that racism and other forms of oppression result in (as well as require) lack of knowledge, especially a lack in the oppressors of real knowledge of the oppressed.[8]

OPTIONS FOR DEALING WITH "THE PROBLEM OF DIFFERENCE"

Barbara Smith believes that, for those involved in studies focused on women, a major obstacle to changing individual racism and challenging racism institutionally is the pernicious ideology of professionalism.[9] The word *professionalism* covers a multitude of sins, because it is usually followed by an excuse for inaction or ethical irresponsibility. It is a word and concept I am trying to eschew because it is ultimately a way of dividing us from others and escaping reality.

In commenting on the kind of professionalism which fosters the "dream" of pluralist feminism, Barbara Smith says, "I think the way to be 'successful' is to do work with integrity and work that is good. Not to play cutthroat tricks and insist on being called 'Doctor.' "[10] When Smith got involved in women's studies she began to recognize what she calls "academic feminists": women who teach, research, and publish about women but who are not involved in any way in making radical social and political change; women who are not involved in making the lives of living, breathing women better. Smith raises powerful questions.

> The grassroots/community women's movement has given women's studies its life. How do we relate to it? How do we bring our gifts and our educational privilege back to it? Do we realize how very much there is to learn in doing this essential work? Ask yourself what the women's movement is working on in your . . . city. Are you a part of it? Ask yourself which women are living in the worst conditions in your town and how your work positively affects and directly touches their lives. If it doesn't, why not?[11]

There is a question regularly if quietly raised among the AAR constituency: should this guild be an activist association or an academic one? In many ways this is an immoral question, an immoral and false dichotomy. The answer to my question about the options for dealing with the problem of difference lies in the emphasis and the kinds of work that will lift oppression not only from women, but from all oppressed people: poor and working class people, people of color in this country and in the colonized Third World. If lifting this oppression is not a priority, then it is problematic whether we are really and authentically able to discuss appropriation and reciprocity in our work.

There are at least two other major obstacles to our making appropriation and reciprocity real. First, there is the antifeminism of many women of color, which I sense sometimes gets mixed up with opposition to white women's racism, and which is fueled by a history of justified distrust. As women of color, we must define a responsible and radical feminism for ourselves. We need not assume that white bourgeois female self-aggrandizement is all that feminism is and that therefore we are compelled to confront and challenge this feminism wholesale and without distinction.

The second major obstacle to reciprocity is homophobia, that is, antilesbianism, an issue that both white women and women of color have yet to address extensively in public dialogue with one another. In these times it does not seem necessary to argue that enforced heterosexuality is the extreme manifestation of male domination and patriarchal rule, or that women must not collude in the oppression of women who have chosen each other. For the same reasons, it is not a mystery to me why Alice Walker, in her landmark definition of what it means to be a womanist includes as a vital aspect for consideration:

> . . . A woman who loves other women, sexually and/or nonsexually. Appreciates and prefers women's culture, women's emotional flexibility . . . and women's strength. Sometimes loves individual men, sexually and/or nonsexually. Committed to survival and wholeness of entire people, male *and* female. Not a separatist, except periodically, for health.[12]

To move past the roadblocks to dealing with difference, I suggest we culti- vate those qualities and skills that can assist in bringing about change: integrity, awareness, courage, and redefining one's own "success." However, I know that the preference for a "professional/academic" as opposed to a "professional/ praxis" approach will, of necessity, determine how much appropriation or reci- procity will go on among us as we try to resolve the problem of difference.

HOW DO WE THEOLOGIZE
ONCE WE RECOGNIZE DIFFERENCE?

Many white feminists used to simply ignore differences among women. In their theorizing and theologizing, they used to speak as if all women *as women* were the same. Now some white feminists recognize the *problem* of difference.[13] Whether they recognize *difference* is another matter, as Maria Lugones points out in her reflections on the logic of pluralist feminism.[14] As white feminist theology increasingly acknowledges the problem, it is interesting to see that the acknowledgment is at present largely a noninteractive one.

"Noninteractive acknowledgment" can be summarized succinctly: "There are many ways of being, but we can still theorize about women if we acknowledge in some way or other that not everything we say is true of all women." This kind of disclaimer has become standard; it permits white feminists to disengage, to avoid interacting with the other. When I read theories about mothering, constructions of the moral domain, construction of the self, and so on, that are prefaced by disclaimers about the universality of the theoretical construct, I am left to conclude that difference is to be ignored.[15] After the disclaimer, nothing again indicates that difference is recognized. The logic of the discourse emphasizes ignoring difference and establishing a primacy for the singularity of the practice, discipline, or construction which is being offered from the dominant culture.

The disclaimer leaves the reader or audience either within or outside the limits of the discourse. From within these limits everything seems complete and rounded, the discourse gentle and comfortably safe. From outside the limits, the theoretical construction appears dangerous. The responsibility for corrections, the author tells us, is left to the reader or interlocutor who is outside, as if the logic of correcting views from outside were clear. So the disclaimer, in effect, serves as an announcement that the author will not accept responsibility for the effects on others of her own particular "social and sexual history."[16]

Most of the time what the theory proposes is not just a description of a particular practice or construction but also some prescription. But a prescription for whom? How is one who stands outside the limits of the discourse to correct the prescription? How is one to tell if the discourse that has produced this prescription is friendly to oneself? Lugones rightly and forthrightly challenges the omission of the interactive step:

> Why does the author just leave us to write another paper on the subject, but one that is dependent on hers even though she does not really acknowledge us? Why does she think she is justified in doing that? Why doesn't she realize that what she is doing is exercising authority, and that the authority she would exercise, if we are not careful, is authority over us?[17]

Resisting this omission and attacking the matrix of domination requires us to identify and engage in some revolutionary shifts on behalf of appropriation and reciprocity in feminist/womanist/mujerista theology. I would identify these paradigmatic shifts as radical alterations in the present format of our dialogues, and empathy, and truth telling[18] to one another from the perspectives of our particular social locations.

In order to know and then to change our heterosexist, racist, and classist ways of being and doing, what is always needed as Alice Walker maintains, "is the larger perspective." I would argue from the womanist perspective that what is critical is that "connections [must] be made, or at least attempted, where none existed before, the straining to encompass in one's glance at the varied world the common thread, the unifying theme through immense diversity."[19] Particularity and not universality is the condition of being heard and of expressing reciprocity and mutuality in womanist/mujerista/feminist work.

Investigating African American women's particular experiences thus promises to reveal much about the more universal process of domination, and about its antithesis in the reconstructive work of feminist/womanist/mujerista reciprocity and faithful appropriation which can be achieved *only* through honest recognition, acceptance, and hard dialogue about difference.

Eventually such dialogues may get us to a point where, as Elsa Barkley Brown claims, "all people can learn to center in another experience, validate it, and judge it by its own standards without need of comparison or need to adopt that framework as their own." In such dialogues, "one has no need to 'decenter' someone else; one has only to constantly, appropriately, 'pivot the center.' "[20]

Sharing a common cause fosters dialogue and encourages groups to transcend their differences. However, existing power inequities among groups must be addressed before an alternative epistemology or theology such as that described by Elsa Barkley Brown or Alice Walker is possible. The presence of subjugated knowledges[21] means that groups are not yet equal in making their standpoints known, either to themselves or to others.

"Decentering" the dominant group is essential. While it is unlikely the oppressor will relinquish privilege without a struggle, still the vision of appropriation and reciprocity in our common work remains. In particular, I subscribe to the verse in Genesis that invites us all to mirror the prophetic lifestyle and serve as change agents in religion and society. I am ultimately one who is willing to walk and to work with a dream announced of old in the words of Genesis, and brought to bear in the poetry and prose of people of color the world over: "Behold, the Dreamer cometh" (Gn. 37:19). I have a dream that womanists, mujeristas, and feminists can appropriate one another's work with integrity, and with true reciprocity. I do not believe that the dream needs to be deferred or that it need explode or dry up in the days to come.

I cherish the dream work that allows shamans and heroes and sisters of every race and class and culture to sit down with one another around the table of professionalism in the world of academe and around the table of solidarity with all the oppressed. I have a dream that the tables can overlap, that they must overlap—that the table of professionalism and the nourishment of academe must serve and become a table of solidarity and community for all those who are oppressed through lack of knowledge, or lack of empowerment in mind and in body.

In dealing honestly with the problem of difference and the dream of pluralist feminism, I trust that we can be together where the Holy Spirit, our Divine Wisdom, our Sancta Sophia is both Hostess and Guest. With this hope I advocate the vision and the perspective which encompasses our "coming to believe in the possibility of a variety of experiences, a variety of ways of understanding the world, a variety of frameworks of operation, without imposing consciously or unconsciously a notion of the norm."[22]

Viva la Diferencia!
Ada María Isasi-Díaz

I was born a feminist on Thanksgiving weekend 1975 at the first Women's Ordination Conference—the public launching in the United States of Catholic women's struggle for justice in our church. It was there that I realized for the first time how sexism had been a negative force in my life. During that conference María Iglesias, at that time coordinator of Las Hermanas,[23] and Shawn Copeland, then director of the Black Sisters Conference, took the stage for a few minutes to ask, plead, remind the participants that no justice would come to women if racial/ethnic women were not an intrinsic part of the movement. Using the story of Joshua at Jericho as a point of reference, Copeland asked the women assembled to remember that if they were able to break through the walls that keep us out of the church and take the city, they were not to rebuild the city.[24] It took me years to understand what they were talking about and even longer to grasp the importance and significance of "difference" in my work of articulating a *mujerista* theology, a Hispanic women's liberation theology.

The *mestizaje* that is an intrinsic element of Hispanic culture has been a strong influence in my life, teaching me not only to respect differences but to value them and embrace them. It is this positive sense of *mestizaje* that has made it difficult for me to understand the negative way in which being different is viewed in U.S. society, the way in which difference is understood as a problem. It is my contention that we will not be able to deal with each other's work as theologians in an appropriate way unless we recognize and embrace difference as a gift, not a problem.

EMBRACING DIFFERENCE, WELCOMING ENGAGEMENT

The way people react to me as a Hispanic woman has given me an insight into the significance, or lack of it, that difference has for the dominant culture. The way those in control—those from the dominant culture—react to a *mujerista* theologian (one who insists on articulating a theology using as its source the lived experience of Hispanic women) has taught me much about the understanding of difference operative in this society.

I noticed years ago that often the first reaction to my being a Hispanic woman is to totally ignore that fact. There is a difference between "ignoring" and "totally ignoring," and our lot as Hispanic women has been up to now the latter one. Elsewhere I have referred to this phenomenon as "invisible invisibility."[25] Those who totally ignore us do not even know they are doing so; they are incapable of acknowledging our presence. "Invisible invisibility" questions the very existence of Hispanic women; it makes us question not only the value of our specificity but the very reality of it.[26]

A second reaction I have encountered is that of "respect." This "respect" is not the profound awe that makes one value and grant importance to someone else. No, the "respect" I often experience is the quick-nod-of-the-head acknowledgment, the politically correct response one gets from those in control when they do not want to take one seriously. This is the reaction I get increasingly these days as Anglo feminists recognize and accept "the problem of difference." Anglo feminists do not want to be called racist, and so most of them have begun at least to mention difference. But, as María Lugones points out, Anglo feminists, who in general are willing to acknowledge that what they say does not necessarily apply to all women, are not willing to take differences into consideration. They fail to recognize that differences have to be embraced because they affect the very identity of white feminists as well as their theories and practices.[27]

What is missing in the respect I receive is engagement. That respect does not seem to include taking me seriously, allowing what I say to affect the other, recognizing that what the other says cannot ignore me and my praxis. The reaction I hunger for is one that takes difference seriously, recognizing plurality as something positive. Without that recognition no real respect is possible.

But to recognize difference not as a problem but as something good we have to be very intentional about how we relate to others. For difference to be positive we must allow the person who is different to be herself, and not require or demand that she be or act or present herself in a way that is intelligible to us. We need to enter into each other's world view as much as we can and help others open up to new perspectives. Unless we are willing to do this, the self we present to people who are different from us is a "pretend self." We will hide our real selves in order to protect ourselves from others' projections of us.

Respectful engagement and interaction require honesty, a willingness to see ourselves for who we are instead of who we would like to be and try to project. It also requires that we recognize and embrace difference but not because we want to avoid guilt or accusations of being noninclusive or of being falsely inclusive. In other words, true engagement and interaction are not matters of being politically correct but of accepting that "self requires self-conscious interaction."[28]

Engagement is a matter of realizing that those who are different

are mirrors in which you can see yourselves as no other mirror shows you. . . . It is not that we are the only faithful mirrors, but I think we *are* faithful mirrors. Not that we show you as you *really* are; we just show you as one of the people who you are. What we reveal to you is that you are many—something that may in itself be frightening to you. But the self we reveal to you is also one that you are not eager to know for reasons that one may conjecture.[29]

THE IMPACT OF DIFFERENCE ON OUR WORK

I believe that the way we deal with each other's work parallels the way we deal with difference. As women theologians from different racial/ethnic communities, with different sexual preferences, different faith traditions, and different economic strata, we have to embrace and value difference in order to be able to deal with each other's work seriously, respectfully. There are three very specific things that I think we will do with each other's work if we value and respect difference.

First, if we recognize difference, we will struggle to enter each other's work, to understand it from the inside. We will strive to find within it its own rules of validity, to appreciate the methods used and the assumptions operative within it. This is the way in which we allow others' work to engage us. We value difference if we allow each other's work to challenge us, to stretch us, instead of reducing it to our view of it.

Second, if we recognize and value difference and interaction we need to allow each other's work to be important in itself and not evaluate it according to how much we can use it. This requires a commitment to know each other's work, to know each other's struggles, to recognize that the oppressions our individual communities suffer are related while at the same time each has its own specificity. This demands we dialogue with each other, that we ask questions when we do not understand instead of dismissing the work of other people who struggle for liberation.

Third, if we recognize difference we will allow each other's work to be a mirror for our own work, reflecting in a way no other mirror can. This means that we let each other's work impact ours, question it, challenge it. We use each other's work to dialogue—knowing that any worthwhile dialogue is dialectic and creative, that it thrives on tension, on difference; that dialogue is not circular and that, therefore, the dialogue will lead us to a new place where we will not be afraid, for we will not be alone.

Embracing difference results in the kind of respect and appreciation for each other's work that we need to have if we are to appropriate it in a way that does not diminish it. To be willing to engage each other's work will keep us from co-opting it, it will keep us from making it say what we want it to say instead of what the author intends it to say. It will keep us from conquering each other's work, from ignoring its origin. To be willing to engage each other's work will keep us from assimilating it, from ignoring the specificities it describes that need to be always present.[30] Interacting with each other's work, which is only really possible if we stand in solidarity with each other, will lead us, I believe, to understand that, in itself, our struggle to develop theological discourses reflective of us and our communities can be, should be, indeed, will be a liberative praxis.

Speaking from the Margins
Kwok Pui-lan

The year I began my doctoral studies at Harvard, I went to a synagogue to listen to a lecture by a feminist theologian. The topic of the lecture was "Toward a Jewish Feminist Theology," and the speaker was Judith Plaskow. Plaskow's lecture, meant primarily for a Jewish audience, had a great impact on me, the only Asian in the audience.

As a Chinese Christian woman, I related to Plaskow's lecture on many levels. As a Chinese, I felt the anguish as she claimed her Jewish identity in spite of the patriarchal tradition. I, too, wished to claim my Chinese identity, in spite of the fact that we had a tradition of footbinding for over a thousand years. As a feminist, I shared her bitterness when I looked back to critical points and holy moments of my history and found that women were excluded. But as a Christian theologian, I asked myself what right I have to use Jewish myths, legends, and scriptures without sharing the pain Jewish women have experienced through the centuries. On what grounds can we Christians claim their stories as our own?

We must bear in mind these complexities and ambiguities as we listen to each other's stories and theologies. As women theologians trying to appropriate each other's work, we must come to terms with the differences shaped by our faith traditions, cultural presuppositions, and social locations. Our diversity must be seen as our strength and our particularity must be cherished as the unique gift each of us can bring to the dialogical table. We must cultivate our capacity for listening, so that we can have shared pain, shared anger, and shared strength.

We are all blessed by Jewish feminists' "Godwrestling,"[31] because they have clearly demonstrated that the patriarchal Torah is not the last word. Jewish women are writing women back into their history and are creating their own midrash and rituals. As Christians we can learn from them or appropriate their work only if we are prepared to be in solidarity with their pain and struggle. Otherwise we will again steal the sacred symbols from the Jews, appropriate them for our consumption, and use their symbols against them, as we have done in the past.

Religious symbols, sacred stories, great novels and literature emerge from peoples' yearnings, struggles, and visions. There is a holy dimension in them, because they illuminate the meaning of existence and the destiny of a people. If we take them out of context, we not only do injustice to the stories and symbols, but we also violate the integrity of the people. Both Mary Daly and Daphne

Hampson use Alice Walker's *The Color Purple* in their attempts to find another language to talk about God.[32] When I discussed their work in my class, one of my Afro-American students, Traci West, asked, "What right do they have to use Alice Walker's novel when their books do not even deal with the question of racism?"

I, too, have great difficulty when I hear white feminists use Asian resources in an uncritical way. The first time I attended an American Academy of Religion annual meeting, someone spoke about the wonderful nondual symbolism and philosophy in Tibetan Buddhism. I asked the speaker, "Where on earth can you find a truly egalitarian Buddhist community?" I wondered if she had heard the cry and anguish of Asian women living in a predominantly Buddhist society. The suffering and pain of Asian sisters become invisible if we romanticize Asian religious traditions.

I recognize the religious and spiritual need for people to appropriate myths and stories that are not their own. I have become a Christian, and some of my American friends are sincere followers of the Buddhist tradition. Wendy Doniger, a Jewish scholar who studies Hindu stories and myths, has pointed out that we sometimes recognize ourselves in other people's myths more vividly than we have ever recognized ourselves in the myths of our own culture. Adopting someone else's tradition as one's own must be done with extreme care and caution. Doniger challenges us to appropriate someone else's myths not just through the head, but through the heart and body too.[33] We, oriental people, agree with her because we understand it is the heart that matters, not the head.

As an Asian growing up in a non-Christian family, I live in the rich and diverse religious tradition of my people. Yet I have always felt that I am an *outsider-within,* to borrow a term from Afro-American feminist theorist Patricia Hill Collins.[34] As an Asian Christian, I do not feel I am readily accepted in the Christian tradition and I am an outsider-within there too. To articulate my theology and to nourish my faith in such a marginal position is not easy. Over the years my faith has been nourished by the work of other Christian feminists who also live on the margin.

From Katie Geneva Cannon I have learned the use of alternative resources for theology and ethics. Before meeting her I had never asked what ethics would look like if it were not articulated by free persons, but by persons who were not free. Cannon's work brought home to me that even though women were not free, they had struggled to be moral agents in their own right.[35]

As a Chinese feminist who experiences Marxism more as an oppressive tool of the Chinese Communist Party than a liberating ideology, I am not satisfied with the theological formulation of Latin American male theologians. Trying to articulate a new paradigm for Asian theology, I have benefitted from the insights of Delores S. Williams. In her study of black women's literature, she has found that black women do not use the language of liberation. Instead they speak of creating a context for survival and of the importance of quality of life.[36]

Williams's work challenges me to find the language used by Asian women and the ways through which they articulate their hope.

Inasmuch as I wish to identify with Afro-American sisters' work, I realize my experience of Christianity is radically different from theirs. While black religious communities historically provided black people with support for their struggle and served as a base for them to see an alternative reality, I cannot say this for many of our Asian churches. For many Asian folks, Christianity is the religion of the oppressors. My feminist critique, therefore, begins with the suspicion of such faith statements as "the Bible is the Word of God" or "Jesus is the savior of all people." Those who have read my article "Discovering the Bible in the Non-Biblical World" know how different my project is from that of womanist theologians.[37]

My friendship with Carter Heyward and other lesbians has helped me to see marginality in yet another way. Women as sensual, erotic, and passionate sexual beings are never accepted anywhere. Women loving women is taboo even to many women. To a certain extent, our lesbian colleagues and friends are outsiders-within their faith communities, the academy, and women's circles. As a heterosexual person from the Third World, I benefit from the privileges associated with heterosexism. As I learn to critique my own heterosexual privileges, I also challenge my lesbian friends to extend their passion and love for women to include all women living in inhuman and oppressive situations in the Third World. Our lesbian colleagues will help us immensely if they could show us the way to channel our erotic power in the struggle for justice for all.

Living on the margin is never lonely. Black folk wisdom says, "water finds its own way." People on the margin find each other and enjoy each other's company. We cannot do our feminist/womanist/mujerista work without simultaneously learning from and critiquing each other. We, women scholars in religion, must be present for each other and be accountable to each other. Sharon Welch was working on her book *A Feminist Ethic of Risk* while I was studying at Harvard. For years she has tried to learn from the moral insights of black women through their novels. I would like to conclude by quoting Welch: "We can see foundational flaws in systems of ethics from the outside, from the perspective of another system of defining and implementing that which is valued. In order to determine which interests or positions are more just, pluralism is required, not for its own sake, but for the sake of enlarging our moral vision."[38]

Appropriation, Reciprocity, and Issues of Power
Judith Plaskow

I assume that our discussion this afternoon is really a discussion about power: about how we read and make use of each other's work in a society based on relationships of domination and subordination—relationships that are reproduced within the community of womanists/feminists/mujeristas working in religion. I would like to talk about power from three perspectives: as a member of a dominated group borrowing from the dominant culture (that is, as a Jew learning from Christian theology), as a member of a dominated group whose tradition is appropriated by the dominant culture (that is, as a Jew whose tradition and work are used by Christians), and as a member of the dominant culture who uses the work of women from dominated cultures (that is, as a white middle-class woman who uses the work of women of color).

I

I first realized with a jolt that the issue of how we use each other's work is an issue of power when, several years ago, I participated in a heated debate about whether a white U.S. feminist Hindologist had the right to criticize a certain aspect of Hinduism's treatment of women. It struck me in the midst of the conversation that, like my colleague, I had begun my graduate career studying someone else's religious tradition. But no one had ever suggested to me that I was wrong to criticize Paul Tillich and Reinhold Niebuhr's doctrines of sin and grace. On the contrary, far from being attacked, I had on a number of occasions been incorporated into the dominant group—been placed on lists of Christian feminist theologians or ethicists. When I asked myself why I and my Hindologist friend found ourselves in such different situations, it became clear to me that we stood in different power relationships to the groups we were studying. As a white U.S. woman, she—and others—questioned her ability and right to stand in the place of Indian women. As a Jew in a Christian society, not only did I assume that I had the right to make use of the dominant discourse, but others accepted—perhaps expected—my use of this discourse, and indeed "rewarded" me for using it by making me an honorary Christian.

Ironically, my relationship to the dominant discourse became problematic when I stopped simply adopting its framework and tried to speak as a Jewish feminist. Then the fact that Christian feminists laid virtually all the important groundwork in feminist theology presented me with serious difficulties. On the one hand, it would be completely nonsensical, indeed impossible, to avoid using Christian feminist work. Christian feminists awakened me to the possibility of seeing my own tradition from a feminist perspective. Almost all that I know about feminist theology, I have learned from reading Christian feminists, womanists, and mujeristas. But on the other hand, if I attempt to translate Christian feminist/womanist/mujerista theory into Jewish terms, how do I avoid importing categories that are inappropriate to the Jewish experience, or even hostile to it? It is not easy to have come to feminist consciousness through the vocabulary and questions of Christian women and still do critical and constructive work that is addressed to and emerges out of the Jewish symbol system and world views.

II

As a Jew who uses the work of Christian women, whose tradition and work are in turn used by Christian women, I want to suggest a criterion for reciprocity in feminist/womanist/mujerista work that would allow Jewish feminists the distinctness of our perspective. When I use Christian material, I must continually be conscious of boundaries in order to preserve my identity—whether I find difference or similarity on the other side of the boundary. Sometimes I conclude that Jewish and Christian feminists have some important issue in common; other times, I feel our experiences diverge. But I am always aware of our commonalities and differences as commonalities and differences between different traditions. Because of the power differential between Jews and Christians, I want Christian women to draw boundaries from their side just as I need to draw them from my side. I want Christian women not to assume a commonality with my experience or my theory, but to acknowledge this commonality when it exists.

This criterion should apply when Christian women are using the work of Jewish feminists, and in the more difficult case when they are appropriating aspects of the Jewish tradition. For example, I recently read a paper by a Christian feminist who had obviously borrowed very directly and heavily from parts of my work without acknowledging the fact. I realized that much stronger for me than the general irritation at being appropriated without acknowledgment was my feeling that I wanted other Christian feminists to know that she got the concepts she was using from a Jew—that Jewish theology is alive and well and changing and developing, and that *as Jewish theology* it can be useful for Christian feminists. Not to acknowledge this indebtedness seemed to me not simply cheating but continuing a Christian pattern of swallowing Jewish tradition and experience without even noticing.

This issue arises for me on a more complex level when Christian feminists make use of the wider Jewish tradition. For example, every time I see the word *shalom* in Christian feminist work, or whenever a Christian feminist signs a letter to me with *shalom,* I feel a knot in my stomach. This knot has long puzzled me because I certainly believe that Hebrew Scripture is also the Old Testament and that Christians have the right to use and interpret it within their own framework. But as I analyze my reaction, I think there is something about the use of the Hebrew word that implies a kinship, familiarity, and sense of ease with Judaism, a feeling of "we're all in this together," that's false or premature. It's false in the general sense that one can use the term *shalom* as a biblical term and know nothing about Judaism as a postbiblical tradition. And it is also false in the more specific sense that Jews do not use the term *shalom* as a theological term evoking peace as wholeness.

In the past, I have seen my reaction to Christian use of *shalom* as irrational in that no Christian feminist I can think of claims to use the word *shalom* in a Jewish way. It's a biblical term being appropriated and elaborated in a Christian context. And yet it also seems to me that, without a specific *acknowledgment* of this context, the Christian feminist is ignoring the historical power differential between Jews and Christians. For two thousand years, Christian interpreters have read Hebrew Scripture in a way that renders invisible both Israelite religion and the subsequent history of rabbinic interpretation. Insofar as Christian feminists assume that scriptural terms like *shalom* form the basis of a common "Judeo-Christian tradition," they continue the process of effacing an independent Judaism. The need for boundaries I experience from the Jewish side is violated from the Christian side. In a feminist/womanist/mujerista context, however, I expect this boundary to be acknowledged. I need Christian feminists to say, "rightly or wrongly I am attempting to use this term in solidarity with Jewish feminists" or "Jewish feminists may not use the term in this way, but this is how I'm using it."

III

When I look at myself as a white middle-class woman using the work of women of color, I need to apply my concerns as a Jew with the shoe on the other foot. There are some places where I think I can translate my experience across the boundary of color and others where I have only questions. As a Jew, I have criticized certain modes of appropriation of Judaism by Christian women, and womanist, mujerista, and other minority feminists have made analogous criticisms from their perspectives. I am convinced that the point of these criticisms cannot be to rule out using each other's work. That would leave us speaking from the same narrow perspectives that feminist attention to difference was meant to undermine and overcome. I want Christian women to read my work and see where it intersects with and where it critiques their own, and I assume the same desire on the part of women of color.

Perhaps more problematically, I would also argue against reading each other's work simply in terms of difference. I want my difference acknowledged, and I believe we have a great deal to learn from differences, both critically and constructively. But I also believe that to see me simply in terms of difference—especially to see me primarily in terms of my oppression—continues to turn me into an Other. Just as Valerie Saiving argued (I think rightly) that women's experience can open up aspects of the human situation that have been neglected or ignored, so black or mujerista or other women's experiences can open to me as a white woman neglected dimensions of myself. I think knowledge of these commonalities is every bit as important as the knowledge of our differences and that these commonalities need to be named, not as universals pointing to some generic "women's experience," but as specific places of insight and connection. It is these connections, after all, that foster the personal friendships that feed our work and that enable us sometimes to be allies for each other as we confront an increasingly repressive political culture that aims to destroy all of us.

As we attend to these commonalities and differences, I assume that women of color feel the same need to have boundaries honored that I feel as a Jewish feminist. Yet as I look at my own use of the work of women of color, I see that I have often not acknowledged boundaries in the ways I would want them acknowledged in the work of Christian women. In *Standing Again at Sinai,* for example, I make heavy use of Audre Lorde's work on the power of the erotic, without following my own criterion of naming difference as a bottom line for feminist reciprocity. While Lorde's essay "Uses of the Erotic" provides the theoretical foundation for the constructive section of my chapter on sexuality, I do not name her blackness and lesbianism as essential sources out of which her work comes. This failure is significant on two counts: (1) because while I think I understand the lesbian roots of Lorde's essay, I do not explicitly name them in my work, and (2) because I do not know how Lorde's experience as a *black lesbian* shapes her perspective. While there is always the danger in using anyone's work that we misunderstand it or interpret it in ways the author never intended, in the case of a white woman using a black woman's work, there is the deeper danger of swallowing up and rendering invisible that I described in the context of Jewish-Christian relationships.

This is the point at which several questions arise for me. First, if I ask myself *why* I did not name the sources of Lorde's insight, I immediately become defensive. "It would interrupt the flow of thought." "It would shift the subject from sexuality to difference." "Everyone knows Lorde is a black lesbian." "Lorde is smarter than I am; that's why I'm using her work. So she is more powerful." How *do* I acknowledge that difference is *always* an issue without making it the central issue at a point I am exploring other issues? How do I keep structural power relationships always in view even while focusing on other questions? Second, is it *enough* to acknowledge the power differential between different groups of women and the ignorance that often accompanies it? When is this acknowledgment effective and substantial, and when is it part of a perfunctory litany of particularity that actually allows us to continue not knowing the other? Third, when we create an ethic for using the work of women in dominated groups, is there a quantitative element involved? I mentioned my use of Audre Lorde because she is the woman of color whose work I depend on most heavily. But if I quote three sentences from Audre Lorde or refer to her in a footnote, does that change my obligation to name our differences? Or, another aspect of the same question, if it is important that we read and learn from each other's work, is it a matter of the more we learn the better? Is there a quantitative point at which dependence becomes exploitation?

The issues that arise as we try to learn from each other's work emerge as mirror images of each other. As a Jewish woman, dependent on Christian feminist work, I need to find a way to create the boundaries that allow my own marginalized perspective to emerge. As a white woman using the work of marginalized women, how do I respect their boundaries and their voices at the same time allowing them to enter and affect my work?

RESPONDENTS

Mary E. Hunt

COMMENTARY

Appropriation and reciprocity is so important that I hope it will become in the academy like research and development in science and industry, an essential part of future strategizing. We continue the process in this exercise, indebted to the many women who, in earlier conversations of this sort, laid the foundation for the effort to mainline "A and R" in religion. My response consists of a respectful word to each of the presenters and a constructive footnote of my own.

I am in grateful agreement with Toinette Eugene when she insightfully names roadblocks to progress. The antifeminist/antiwomanist backlash is real and growing in a time I characterize as the "Skull and Bones Era." It is a time when the backlash against backlash is met by the secrecy and sense of entitlement that has made the Bush-Quayle administration so pernicious. The Anita Hill/ Clarence Thomas debacle showed the sinister nature of the complexities. The challenge is how to remain clear on the particularity of one's own struggles and, at the same time, build common strategies so that we are not divided and conquered.

I also agree with Dr. Eugene that one of the tried and untrue ways of dividing and conquering women has been the route of homophobia. I appreciate her lifting this up and pointing out the ways in which we need to work together to avoid it. I would even go the next step and argue that there are some important links between and among those of us who are lesbian which need to be explored for our mutual empowerment. Further, I believe that it is incumbent upon white, middle-class lesbian women who are "out" to exercise extreme caution in conversation and in expectations, respecting the real dangers that lurk for all lesbian women, especially lesbian women of color. Judith Plaskow's reflections on Audre Lorde are insightful here. I submit that there are conversations that some of us will, unfortunately, have to have in private for our collective survival.

I appreciate Ada María Isasi-Díaz's thoughtful epistemological work. My thanks are best expressed by naming what for me were the two central insights in her remarks. First, women do our best work when we are fully ourselves. This gives us a hermeneutical tool for saying when appropriation and reciprocity is honored: Do I need her to do the work or does she need to do the work in question in order to be fully herself? If the answer is the former, there is a good chance that the person and her work are being co-opted; if the latter, then there is a good chance that the woman and her work are being used positively.

Second, each woman's work needs to stand on its own terms. It is not to be wedged into fit with mine. But my work will change insofar as I take her work seriously. These insights shape the framework in which we ask questions about A + R, presenting some hope that communication and sharing with integrity are possible.

Kwok Pui-lan's helpful remarks lead me to name some of the pitfalls of this whole enterprise. "Adoption and romanticizing" are real dangers to be avoided. She reminds me of the uncritical use of Vatican Observatory materials by some liberal male theologians who are now interested in science. Collaborating uncritically with officials who use science to oppress women in the reproductive arena is precisely the dynamic we seek to avoid in our own work.

A second issue raised by Pui-lan is the global impact of the feminist/ womanist/mujerista work done in the United States. It is my experience that the particular roots of womanist/mujerista work in the survival needs of women and dependent children, as opposed to the roots of liberal feminism in seeking rights for women, make womanist/mujerista work more useful than feminism in many parts of the world for empowering women. It is important to give it widespread attention along with feminist work.

Judith Plaskow's cogent identification of power dynamics, the various permutations and layers of complexity, is a signal contribution. I agree that we need to draw boundaries and acknowledge commonality where and when it exists for strategic as well as ideological purposes. I especially appreciate Judith's concrete example of *shalom* which I suspect will cause many of us to change our linguistic habits.

Another important dimension of Judith's contribution is the insistence that we are defined by more than difference. We are also defined by those intersections of our various experiences as well as by some, albeit few, common threads. The challenge of this approach lies in ascertaining what difference difference makes and what and how commonalities can be acknowledged without forsaking their particularity. This is difficult terrain to traverse. But because I share Judith's questions I offer a constructive footnote.

CONSTRUCTIVE FOOTNOTE

Joan Martin and I worked together at a women-church conference some years ago, speaking from our varied experiences and ending up in quite different places theologically. I spoke as a white Catholic woman belonging to the women-church movement, and Joan spoke as an African American Presbyterian appreciating the movement but being absolutely clear that she did not wish to identify with it. Yet we were mutually fortified by each other's frankness. Joan summed up the dynamic by saying "You didn't steal my stuff. You did not make me be you." Hers was a pithy and understandable way of naming what happened and acknowledging that it was what should have happened given who we were.

The ethical problem at hand in the appropriation and reciprocity debate in my judgment is theft. Stealing ideas that are not our own, using materials, doing work, asking questions that do not belong to us is, in the vernacular, a rip off. Like white men doing womanist work, or even white women calling themselves womanist, the misuse of another's intellectual property is theft.

Of course there is in legal theory petty theft, in our circles the use of materials and sources without contextualizing or nuancing. There is also grand larceny, the wholesale taking over of people's ideas without any regard for the integrity of the work itself. The most blatant example of this is the endless repetitions of the name and work of Alice Walker, as if somehow just quoting Alice Walker will chase away the problem of racism. I use theft imagery advisedly to make an unmistakable point. I would not want extreme literalism to result in a debate over my metaphor instead of the problem to which it points, an obvious danger when one advances such bold words. The point is that such misuse must end if we are to work together with integrity.

These intellectual crimes are committed mostly by people who look like me, that is, white, middle-class, well-educated people, in order to appear politically correct, well informed and open. Such crimes are often done to give the appearance of diversity all the while maintaining the model, dynamic and framework that belong to the dominant culture into which have been shoved ideas and images that do not emerge from it. I respectfully urge that we name this dynamic honestly and stop it, period.

This theft, when viewed from the most practical level, results in the wearing out of sisters whose particularity we do not share, all in the name of inclusivity. On the theoretical level it means obliterating insights that we all need. It is time to say "basta" and get on with the hard work of social and intellectual change.

I suggest that the constructive ethical task among us is best conceptualized as how to borrow. The image that comes to my mind is the many women who have borrowed a cup of flour from their neighbors. The ground rules for borrowing give us some clues about how to appropriate and act with reciprocity with each other. I offer some common customs as a next step toward dealing with these matters.

First, we borrow only what we need. If I have what I need there is no need to borrow. But the question that shapes the exchange is do I need it or simply want it? A second dimension of borrowing is the need to ask permission, to explain why I need to borrow, why what I have won't do.

In most communities it is customary to repay the borrowed item with a little interest, giving back more than one took as a sign of goodwill and thanks. Further, borrowing is not the norm but the exception, what one does in a pinch, not something that is programmatic.

Borrowing can be part of children's education from early on. We teach them to be self-sufficient, but also how to live cooperatively, to share what we have because in fact it does finally belong to all of us or none of us. Survival is based on collective need fulfillment through lending and borrowing, while stealing will destroy us individually, thus doing patriarchy's work for it.

CONCLUSION

A good example of the integrity I hope to see proliferate was a recent ad in the *New York Times* entitled "African American Women in Defense of Ourselves," a creative and constructive response to the Anita Hill/Clarence Thomas set-up.[39] The ad was instructive because the signers made the direct claim that "No one will speak for us but ourselves." I can hear the impatient voices of some white women saying, "But when will we speak together for solidarity and creativity, for collective survival and individual expression?" It is an important question, but premature.

The issue at stake is timing, not simply when, but who decides when. It is not up to middle-class white women from the Christian tradition to set the grandmother clock of collaboration. Perhaps in a Jubilee Year white women can become equal partners in that decision making, but until then I submit that we simply have done it too long. The Jubilee Year, fifty years from now, will be 2041 when the youngest of the panelists will be nearly ninety years old. By then we may have gained, among us, the wisdom to know enough not to try. Meanwhile, efforts like this panel, without conclusions but with candor and rigor, are a good model for how to handle appropriation and reciprocity, so that we can try to make the dream to which Toinette Eugene referred come true.

Emilie M. Townes

for years, there was silence
    or more appropriately, few listened
whole worlds were left outside dominant discourse and analysis
    except as the occasional other
    who served the needs of oppression and dehumanization
cultures lapsed into deadly dualisms
    which carried with them
    difference and objectification
    and ultimately-domination
dubois and others named the experience

often felt by the other
doubleconsciousness
and as clarity about the nature of the blight:
that processes of objectification and subordination
defined whole peoples
categorized patterns of thought and behavior
and that ultimately, concrete history became the chimera
and counterfeit history became reality
african american women found that words
they had shouted to the winds
the lives they had lived *regardless*
found a place
albeit a small place
in normative discourse and inquiry
and around us all now rages the modernism/postmodernism debate
and within this debate
feminists, mujeristas, and womanists gather
to begin a much needed discussion
on appropriation and reciprocity
however, we stand within a context
which is volcanic
modernity radically alters the nature of everyday social lives
it seeks universal rationality
attempts to establish objective, value free established knowledge
ontologies
it speaks of the individual who then creates communities
rather than being birthed/formed by community
it seeks to institutionalize radical doubt
it insists that all knowledge is really hypothesis
postmodernism has a radical historicity
in which plurality
particularity
locality
context
the social location of thought
and a serious questioning of universal knowledge

are key features
it is in this molten, hot sand
    that i want to think out loud
    about the nature of the other
    and how each of us shifts in and out of this posture
    for at times, we are the subjects

I

the notion that we are aware of another person's feelings and experiences
    only on the basis of empathic inferences from our own
    veers into solipsism
self-consciousness and awareness of others
    are not natural dance partners
understanding the other
    is not predicated on how the individual (or the group) makes the
    shift from the certainty of her inner experiences
    to the unknowable person
when we make this kind of tenuous shift
    the outcome generally falls into two categories
        romanticization
        or trivialization
what we must be about as we approach one another's work
    is care-filled listening and observing and engagement
this takes time
        energy
        resources
        fortitude
        and a stout will-to-comprehend
the voice is salient
    yet this is not a disembodied voice
    but one in which rich traditions and histories
    have shaped it
    (and continue to be renewed and transformed)
it is a voice from a particular culture
    whose integrity and worth must be respected

if we rush in too quickly
   with our tools of correct analysis
   and sisterly solidarity
the voice we will hear is our own echo
   a distortion of the original
   but dolby in sound

II

naming is a powerful theo-ethical act
there is power in the naming
   black women are making a political choice when deciding between
         womanist and feminist
         colored and black
         black and african-american
   there is a history and culture of struggle
      dialogue
      arguments
      and peeling away imposed language
         to ponder and then utilize an articulate, indigenous witness
         to the absolute necessity
         that no one can speak for us but ourselves
there is power in the ability to take away a name
   being called girl when you are in your 60s, 70s, and, 80s by
      hegemonic culture
   being asked to speak, but not preach
and there is deadly power in taking away the ability to name
   in our conversation about appropriation and reciprocity
   take care when you name my reality
      for i am still discovering it myself
         african american women are yet in the process of naming our
         own reality
   discovering our own joys and pain
   re-membering the body of blackness and femaleness
      in a dominating culture
   and we are only just beginning to name
      the issues and points of tension that we must deal with internally

when considering our work from a position outside of our culture
   recognize that we speak in cultural codes and short hands
   many of us come from an oral tradition
   and not everything gets put into print
i *do* want you to hear my story
   take it in
   consider how you have been a part of it
   or not
but do this in contrast to your own traditions and cultures
   to understand and consider
   how your lives and history
   are a part of the fabric of creation
     with mine
guard against setting
   my story in your script
   having me illuminate points
     you must/should make on your own
     through the integrity of your witness
       your analysis
       your ability to critique and analyze
       from your perspective
each of us must begin with our own cognitive dissonance
   we cannot appropriate each other's
   and have a truly articulate and pithy analysis
we have much to learn from one another
   as we appropriate and reciprocate
   but we must not use each other up or down

III

this conversation does take place in the rise of postmodernism
i find it hard to believe that we are not
   in some way
responding to its themes of difference, disruption, marginality, otherness,
   transgression
   as we weigh each other's work
whatever we think about postmodernism itself

it can teach us an important lesson
    in our conversation today
it has been largely (and narrowly) focused on the west
    this is ironic
    given that it arises from
        the end of the age of europe
        the emergence of the u.s. as a world power
        and the decolonization of the third world[40]
there has been little mention of the black experience
    or particularly the writings of black women
    in postmodernist theory
yet the categories of otherness and difference stand
    central to its task
    of critical reflection
our conversation stands in a paradox
    which must be acknowledged
    and challenged
    as we appropriate and reciprocate
we must avoid collapsing "otherness" into a universal category
    much like we have done (and learned not to do) with "women"
    and "minorities"
or some of us will end up writing the second edition of "all the women
       were white, all the blacks are men, but some of us are brave"

IV

i do believe that the experience and critical analysis
    done by african american women
has much to offer feminist/mujerista/womanist reflections
    but i am also aware
that other voices have not yet joined
    (and there are those who are just pulling up to)
    our kitchen table
        the power to name and speak of native american women is a
           yawning silence
    and there are others . . .

the challenge for me
>   is as more women join what has largely
>   and ill-fittingly
>   been a black/white dialogue
> that i will take my words to heart
>   and not interrupt them
>   as they speak
> but listen
>   from a deep place
>   and challenge my scholarship
>   my emotions
>   my history
> to respond to them
>   with my voice
>   and not an imitation of theirs

Ellen M. Umansky

Like Judith Plaskow, I am a white, middle-class U.S. Jewish feminist who has learned a great deal about feminist theology from feminist theologians who are not Jewish, including Christian feminist and womanist theologians, Goddess thealogians, and feminist theologians who identify themselves as post-Christian or raised in the Christian tradition. I have also learned a great deal about theology from women and men, like Alice Walker and Elie Wiesel, who are not theologians at all. Like Judith, I, too, believe that there are important ways we can learn from one another and from one another's work and that when we do learn from one another, we must openly acknowledge what we have learned—in our classes, public lectures, and published works.

Yet unlike Judith, much of my own theological work has been historical rather than constructive, focusing on recovering the voices of Jewish women of the past as well as bringing to the attention of others the voices of contemporary Jewish women who have less access than I to publishers, less time to write, etc. Consequently, most of my work does not borrow either from the work of the dominant culture (i.e., white Christian feminists) or from the work of dominated cultures, insofar as that term applies to those women of color who are not Jewish.

Much of my own work, then, has been an attempt to recover and to reclaim the voices of Jewish women and to create a Jewish feminist theology that to a great extent reflects and builds upon women's experiences of Judaism over the last two thousand years. Yet this doesn't mean that our discussion of appropriation and reciprocity in womanist, mujerista, and feminist work has no bearing upon my work nor does it mean that my work has no bearing upon this discussion. For if one were to make the claim that *because* my work largely rests on and builds on the work of other Jewish women I do not appropriate the work of others, one would be ignoring the very real differences among Jewish women themselves. Indeed, if I were to use only the work of others who were "like me," I would probably quote no one but myself.

Those of us who question whether or when appropriation can be justified first need to ask ourselves: What factors constitute sufficient similarity or commonality in deciding whose work can be appropriated? To maintain, as some might, that the only works that I, as a Jewish feminist theologian, can justly appropriate are the works of other Jewish women fails to recognize the great differences— including differences of power—that exist among Jewish women. Let me elaborate further on my opening sentence. I am a white, middle-class, married with children, highly educated, third generation, twentieth-century Jewish woman born and raised in New York and religiously affiliated with Reform or Liberal Judaism. Yet I have learned a great deal from, and often quote, the works of Jewish women who are not from New York, who are not from the United States, who *are* from the United States but who are immigrants, second, or fourth generation; who are not middle class, are not well educated, do not have children, are lesbian, are not white, and/or are religiously traditional—women, in other words, whose experiences of being in the world and of being Jewish are very different from mine in many, significant ways.

Why, then, one might ask, if their experiences are so different from mine, do I cite their work at all? First, there is a real sense in which I have learned from all of these women. By citing their work, I openly acknowledge what they have taught me while at the same time acknowledging how our experiences and the contexts in which we write are different from one another. Second, since I am aware that I write from a position of relative power, it is important to me, indeed, I feel that it is my obligation, to bring to a new and/or wider audience the work of Jewish women who have less power and less privilege than I. Thus, much of my work attempts to make visible women who have been invisible, and make audible voices that have not yet been heard or that are heard but might conceivably gain a new audience by being cited or quoted in my work. I take it as a given that in doing so, I need to respect the integrity of the work that I am citing and to acknowledge both the differences and commonalities between the author in question and myself.

Finally, for me, at least, appropriating, while acknowledging, the work of others has enabled me to recognize and to openly acknowledge those aspects of my identity that are most central to me. If most of the women whose work I cite are religiously liberal Jews from the United States, it is because my being Jewish, religiously liberal, and an American are most central to my own sense of who I am. Given this sense of self, I have appropriated the writings of few womanist and mujerista theologians into my work (despite the fact that I have learned a great deal from them), not because these theologians are not white, but because those whose writings I am familiar with are not Jewish.

Despite all of the difficulties and inherent dangers of appropriation and reciprocity, I sincerely hope that we not feel ourselves so bound by our particularities and our multivocality that we feel hesitant to quote anyone else at all. Though differences among women need to be stated and respected, what has made feminism such an important part of my life and I suspect this is true for many others has been discovering those connections that *do* exist. Acknowledging both our differences and our connections is important, I believe, for doing so makes possible not only honest discussion, but also, in Mary Hunt's words, "justice-seeking" together.

NOTES

Toinette M. Eugene

1. Maria C. Lugones, an Argentinean philosopher, grassroots educator, and organizer who identifies herself as a U.S. Latina, has elaborated a theory that she calls *pluralist feminism* that honors many voices, many selves. I draw heavily upon her seminal essay on this topic and from her other works for my own commentary. Cf. "On the Logic of Pluralist Feminism," in *Feminist Ethics,* ed. Claudia Card (Lawrence: University of Kansas Press, 1991), 35–44; "Hablando Cara a Cara/Speaking Face to Face: An Exploration of Ethnocentric Racism," in *Making Face, Making Soul—Haciendo Caras: Creative and Critical Perspectives by Women of Color,* ed., Gloria Anzaldua (San Francisco: Aunt Lute, 1990), 46–54.

2. Lorraine Bethel, "What Chou Mean We, White Girl?" *Conditions: Five* (Autumn 1979): 86–92; June Jordan, "Where Is the Love?" in *Making Face, Making Soul,* 174–176.

3. Audre Lorde, "The Master's Tools Will Never Dismantle the Master's House," in *Sister Outsider: Essays and Speeches* (Trumansburg, N.Y.: Crossing Press, 1984), 111.

4. Bethel, 87.

5. Jordan, 176.

6. *God's Fierce Whimsy: Christian Feminism and Theological Education* (New York: Pilgrim Press, 1985), 36.

7. Susan Brooks Thistlethwaite, *Sex, Race, and God: Christian Feminism in Black and White* (New York: Crossroad, 1989), 7.

8. Elizabeth V. Spelman, *Inessential Woman: Problems of Exclusion in Feminist Thought* (Boston: Beacon Press, 1988), 178.

9. Barbara Smith, "Racism and Women's Studies," in *Making Face, Making Soul,* 25–28. I concur with this point, and reiterate the other two central tenets of her essay: the resistance of many women of color to what is perceived as a white feminist movement, and the problem of homophobia. The latter is often acknowledged limitation, concern, and a virulent prejudice which plagues nearly all communities of women engaged in the work of liberation.

10. Smith, 26.

11. Smith, 27.

12. Alice Walker, *In Search of Our Mothers' Gardens: Womanist Prose* (San Diego: Harcourt Brace Jovanovich, 1983), xi.

13. Notable examples of white feminist theologians and ethicists who directly acknowledge the problem of difference and attempt to deal with issues of reciprocity and mutuality which must be resolved between women of color and women of privilege are enumerated in Barbara Hilkert Andolsen, *Daughters of Jefferson, Daughters of Bootblacks: Racism and American Feminism* (Macon, Ga.: Mercer University Press, 1986).

14. Lugones, "On the Logic of Pluralist Feminism," 38.

15. Cf. Sara Ruddick, "Maternal Thinking," in Joyce Trebilcot, ed., *Mothering: Essays in Feminist Theory* (Totowa, N.J.: Rowman and Allanheld, 1983), 213–230.

16. Ruddick, 213.

17. Lugones, "On the Logic of Pluralist Feminism," 39.

18. Patricia Hill Collins, *Black Feminist Thought: Knowledge, Consciousness, and the Politics of Empowerment* (London: Harper Collins, 1990), discusses these shifts in detail and with great clarity from her perspective as a social scientist. Although she does not draw any theological or ethical conclusions, her work is foundational for those who would engage with critical interdisciplinary studies as an aspect of defining reciprocity and mutuality in a liberation form of womanist/mujerista/feminist work.

19. Collins, 5.

20. Elsa Barkley Brown, "African American Women's Quilting: A Framework for Conceptualizing and Teaching African American Women's History," *Signs* 14, 4 (1989): 922.

21. Michel Foucault, *Power/Knowledge: Selected Interviews and Other Writings 1972–1977,* ed. Colin Gordon (New York: Pantheon, 1980).

22. Brown, 921.

Ada María Isasi-Díaz

I dedicate this article to Rosalie Muschal-Reinhardt, who has always struggled to value difference and respects deeply my desire to be engaged. Thanks, Ro! I am grateful to Christine Walsh, my research assistant at Drew University, for her help with this article.

23. Las Hermanas is a national organization that advocates justice for Hispanic women in church, particularly in the Roman Catholic Church, and society and works to enable the development of leadership of Hispanic women. I have been involved with Las Hermanas since the late seventies and have been a member of its board for the last five years.

24. Anne Marie Gardiner, *Women and Catholic Priesthood: An Expanded Vision* (Paramus, N.J.: Paulist Press, 1976), 188–89.

25. Ada María Isasi-Díaz, "Toward an Understanding of *Feminismo Hispano,*" in *Women's Consciousness, Women's Conscience,* ed. Barbara Hilkert Andolsen, Christine Gudorf, and Mary D. Pellauer (Minneapolis: Winston-Seabury Press, 1985), 51–61.

26. I remember vividly the comment of an Anglo feminist with whom I have participated in the struggle for justice for women in the Roman Catholic Church for many years. As a great compliment she once said to me, "I never think of you as Hispanic."

27. María Lugones, "On the Logic of Pluralist Feminism," in *Feminist Ethics,* ed. Claudia Card (Lawrence: University of Kansas Press, 1991), 35–44.

28. Lugones, 43.

29. Lugones, 41–42.

30. We make a difference between assimilation and integration. Integration is what we aim for; assimilation, which we believe is behind the idea of the "melting pot," where one loses one's identity, is a concept we find oppressive.

Kwok Pui-lan

31. Judith Plaskow, *Standing Again at Sinai: Judaism from a Feminist Perspective* (San Francisco: Harper San Francisco 1990), 33.

32. Mary Daly, *Pure Lust: Elemental Feminist Philosophy* (Boston: Beacon Press, 1984), 399–400; Daphne Hampson, *Theology and Feminism* (London: Basil Blackwell Ltd., 1990), 163–67.

33. Wendy Doniger O'Flaherty, "The Uses and Misuses of Other People's Myths," *Journal of the American Academy of Religion* 54 (1986): 219–39.

34. Patricia Hill Collins, *Black Feminist Thought: Knowledge, Consciousness, and the Politics of Empowerment* (London: HarperCollins Academic, 1990), 11.

35. Katie G. Cannon, *Black Womanist Ethics* (Atlanta: Scholars Press, 1988).

36. Delores S. Williams, "Women's Oppression and Lifeline Politics in Black Women's Religious Narratives," *Journal of Feminist Studies in Religion* 1, no. 2 (1985). 59–71.

37. Kwok Pui-lan, "Discovering the Bible in the Non-Biblical World," in *Lift Every Voice: Constructing Christian Theology from the Underside*, ed., Susan Brooks Thistlethwaite and Mary Potter Engel (San Francisco: Harper & Row, 1990), 270–282.

38. Sharon D. Welch, *A Feminist Ethic of Risk* (Minneapolis: Fortress Press, 1990), 126.

Mary E. Hunt

39. *The New York Times* (November 17, 1991), 53.

Emilie M. Townes

40. For a piercing analysis, see Bell Hooks, *Yearning: Race, Gender, and Cultural Politics* (Boston: South End Press, 1990), and Cornel West, *The American Evasion of Philosophy: A Genealogy of Philosophy* (Madison, Wisconsin: University of Wisconsin Press, 1989), 237.

PART 2

Taking on the Traditions

8

THE SPIRITUAL REVOLUTION

Women's Liberation
as Theological Re-education

Mary Daly

Although there have been outstanding "exceptional women" in every period of Christian history, their existence has had almost no effect upon the official ideology and policies of the churches. This fact can be understood when it is realized that the Judaic-Christian tradition has functioned to legitimate male-dominated society.[1] The image of God as exclusively a father and not a mother, for example, was spawned by the human imagination under the conditions of patriarchal society and sustained as plausible by patriarchy. Then, in turn, the image has served to perpetuate this kind of society by making its mechanisms for the oppression of women appear right and fitting.[2] If God in "his" heaven is a father ruling "his" people, then it is in the "nature" of things and according to divine plan and the order of the universe that society be male-dominated. Within this context a mystification of roles takes place: the husband dominating his wife can feel that he represents God himself. A theologian such as Karl Barth could feel justified in writing that woman is "ontologically" subordinate to man. It might seem that intelligent people do not really think of God as an old man with a beard, but it is quite possible for the mind to function on two different and even contradictory levels at the same time. For example, many speak of God as spirit and at the same time, on the imaginative level, envisage "him" as male. The widespread concept of the Supreme Being has been a not very subtle mask of the divine father-figure, and it is not too surprising that it has been used to justify oppression, especially that of women, which is said to be "God's plan."[3] Doctrines about Jesus also have often reflected a kind of phallic obsession. Some theologians have argued that since Jesus was male, and called only males to become apostles, women should not be ordained. The doctrine of a unique "incarnation" in Jesus reinforced the fixed idea of patriarchal religion that God is male and that male is God. So also did the image of the Virgin kneeling in adoration before her own Son. The mechanism that can be seen in all of this is the familiar vicious circle in which the patterns of a particular kind of society are projected into the realm of religious beliefs and these in turn justify society as it is. The belief system becomes hardened and functions to resist social change which would rob it of its plausibility. (In a matriarchal or a diarchal society what credibility would the image of a divine patriarch have?)

Patriarchal religion tends to be authoritarian. Given the fact that the vicious circle is not foolproof, there is always the possibility that beliefs may lose their credibility. For this reason they are often buttressed by notions of "faith" that leave no room for dissent. For example, the believer is often commanded to assent blindly to doctrines handed down by authority (all male). The inculcation of anxieties and guilt feelings over "heresy" and "losing the faith" has been a powerful method used by institutional religion to immunize itself from criticism. Women especially have been victimized by this.

Traditional Christian ethics also has been to a great extent the product and support of sexist bias. Much of the theory of Christian virtue appears to be the product of reactions on the part of men—probably guilty reactions—to the behavioral excesses of the stereotypic male. There has been theoretical emphasis upon charity, meekness, obedience, humility, self-abnegation, sacrifice, service. Part of the problem with this moral ideology is that it became generally accepted not by men but by women, who have hardly been helped by an ethic which reinforced their abject situation. This emphasis upon the passive virtues, of course, has not challenged exploitativeness, but supported it. Part of the whole syndrome has been the reduction of hope to passive expectation of a reward from the divine Father for following the rules. Love or charity has been interpreted to mean that people should turn the other cheek to their oppressors. Within the perspective of such a privatized morality "sin" often becomes an offense against those in power, or against "God"—the two being more or less equated. The structures of oppression are not seen as sinful.

It is consistent with all of this that the traditional Christian moral consciousness has been fixated upon the problems of reproductive activity to a degree totally disproportionate to its feeble concern for existing human life. This deformity of perspective was summed up several years ago in Archbishop Roberts' remark that "if contraceptives had been dropped over Japan instead of bombs which merely killed, maimed and shriveled up thousands alive there would have been a squeal of outraged protest from the Vatican to the remotest Mass center in Asia." Pertinent also is Simone de Beauvoir's remark that the church has reserved its uncompromising humanitarianism for man in the fetal condition. Although both of these remarks are directed at the Catholic church, the same attitudes are widespread in Protestantism. Many theologians today do of course acknowledge that this passive and privatized morality has failed to cope with structures of oppression. However, few seriously face the possibility that the roots of this distortion are deeply buried in the fundamental and all-pervasive sexual alienation which the women's movement is seeking to overcome.

THE SPIRITUAL POTENTIAL OF THE MOVEMENT

As the women's revolution begins to have an effect upon the fabric of society, transforming it from patriarchy into something that never existed before—into a diarchal situation that is radically new—it will, I think, become the greatest single potential challenge to Christianity to rid itself of its oppressive tendencies or go out of business. Beliefs and values that have held sway for thousands of years will be questioned as never before. The movement, if it is true to its most authentic and prophetic dimensions, is possibly also the greatest single hope for the survival and development of authentic spiritual consciousness over against the manipulative and exploitative power of technocracy.

The caricature of a human being which is represented by the masculine stereotype depends for its existence upon the acceptance by women of the role assigned to them—the eternal feminine. By becoming whole persons women can generate a counterforce to polarization of human beings into these stereotypes, forcing men to re-examine their own self-definition. This movement toward the becoming of whole human beings, to the degree that it succeeds, will transform the values and symbols of our society, including religious symbols.

The women's liberation movement is a spiritual movement because it aims at humanization of women and therefore of the species. At its core it is spiritual in the deepest sense of the word, because it means the self-actualization of creative human potential in the struggle against oppression. Since the projections of patriarchal religion serve to block the dynamics of creativity, self-actualization, and authentic community by enforcing reduction of people to stereotyped roles, the challenge to patriarchy which is now in its initial stages is a sign of hope for the emergence of more genuine religious consciousness. The becoming of women may be not only the doorway to deliverance from the omnipotent Father in all of his disguises, but also a doorway to something, namely, the beginning for many of a more authentic search for transcendence, that is, for God.

Women's liberation is an event that can challenge authoritarian, exclusivist, and non-existential ideas of faith and revelation. Since women have been extra-environmentals, that is, since we have not been part of the authority structure which uses "faith" and "revelation" to reinforce the mechanisms of alienation, our emergence can unmask the idolatry often hidden behind these ideas. There could result from this becoming of women a remythologizing of Western religion. If the need for parental symbols for God persists, something like the Father-Mother God of Mary Baker Eddy will be more acceptable to the new woman and the new man than the Father God of the past. A symbolization for incarnation of the divine presence in human beings may continue to be needed in the future, but it is highly unlikely that women or men will find plausible that symbolism which is epitomized in the Christ-Mary image. Perhaps this will be replaced by a bisexual imagery which is non-hierarchical.[4]

The becoming of women can bring about a transvaluation of values. Faith can come to be understood in a non-authoritarian and universalist sense. Hope, rather than being restricted to expectation of rewards for conformity, can come to be experienced and understood as creative, political, and revolutionary. Love will mean uniting to overcome oppression. It will be understood that the most loving thing one can do for the oppressor is to fight the oppressive situation that destroys both the oppressor and the oppressed. Suffering, which has been so highly esteemed in Christianity, will be seen as acceptable, not when abjectly and submissively endured, but when experienced in the struggle for liberation.

The ethic emerging in the struggle has as its main theme not prudence but existential courage. This is the courage to risk economic and social security for the sake of liberation. It means not only risking the loss of jobs, friends, and social approval, but also facing the nameless anxieties encountered in new and uncharted territory. There is the anxiety of meaninglessness that can be overwhelming at times when the old simple meanings, role definitions, and life expectations have been rooted out and rejected openly and a woman emerges into a world without models.[5] There is also the anxiety of guilt over refusing to do what society demands, an anxiety which can still hold a woman in its grip long after the guilt has been recognized as false. To affirm oneself and one's sisters in the face of all this requires courage.

Such courage expresses itself in sisterhood, which is not at all merely the female counterpart of brotherhood. Sisterhood is a revolutionary fact. It is the bonding of those who have never bonded before, for the purpose of overcoming sexism and its effects, both internal and external. It is the coming together of those who are oppressed by sexual definition. The Christian churches have been fond of preaching the "brotherhood of man," which included women incidentally, as baggage. However, the concept has never been realized, because brotherhood in patriarchy, despite frequent attempts to universalize the term, is exclusive and divisive. "Brother" means us versus them. It begins by excluding women as "the other" and continues it divisiveness from there, cutting off "the other" by familial, tribal, racial, national, economic, and ideological categories. Women are learning to be aware that brotherhood, even when it attempts to be universal, means a male universalism. The Black Liberation Movement, the peace movement, the new left for the most part fail to notice the need for change in the situation of the more than 50% female membership of the groups to which they would extend their brotherhood.[6]

The "sisterhoods" of patriarchal society have really been mini-brotherhoods, following male models and serving male purposes. The religious sisterhoods within the Catholic Church, for example, have been male-dominated according to Canon Law. These communities, though they have offered an alternative to marriage and attracted many gifted women, have used the word "sister" in an elitist and divisive sense and have supported the ideology of sexism.

The sisterhood of women's liberation involves a strategic polarization which is different from all of this. It implies polarization for the sake of women's internal wholeness or oneness, because as in the case of all oppressed groups women suffer from a duality of consciousness. We have internalized the image that the oppressor has of us and are therefore divided against ourselves and against each other by self-hatred. We can only overcome this by bonding with each other. Sisterhood implies polarization also for the sake of political oneness, to achieve liberation. However, its essential dynamic is directed to overcoming the stereotypes that reduce people to the role of "the other." That is, it points toward a unity deeper than most theologians are capable of envisaging, despite the great amount of ink that has been spilled on the subject of "the bonds of charity."

Sisterhood is an event that is new under the sun. It is healing, revolutionary, and revelatory—which is what Christian brotherhood was claimed to be but failed to be. It is at war with the idols of patriarchal religion, but it is in harmony with what is authentic in the ideals of the religious traditions. In this sense, the movement in its deepest dimension is itself both antichurch and church. It has the potential to release the authentic values that have been distorted and suppressed by the sexism of synagogue and church.

SISTERHOOD AS ANTICHURCH

Women are a world-wide caste from whom the fact of low caste status has been hidden by several factors. It is masked, first of all, by role segregation, which is more subtle than spatial segregation, as in a ghetto. It makes possible the delusion that women should be "equal but different." It is masked also by the fact that women have various forms of derivative status as a consequence of their relationships with men. That is, women have duality of status, and the derivative aspect of this status, e.g., as daughters and wives, divides us from each other, and encourages identification with patriarchal institutions which do not serve the interests of women. Finally, it is hidden by ideologies that divide women. Patriarchal religion serves to support sexual caste and its masks; that is role segregation (for example, by insisting that "woman is the heart of the home"), the derivative status of women (for example, by symbolizing this status and glorifying it in the cult of Mary), and divisive ideologies (for example, its own doctrines by which women are called upon to submit their judgment to one male-dominated institution as opposed to another).

Despite the masks, women are experiencing a breakthrough to awareness of sexual caste as a universal phenomenon. As women revolt against this, a new sense of reality is emerging. That is, a counter-world to patriarchy is coming into being which is by the same token counter to religion as patriarchal. Sisterhood, then, by being the unique bonding of women against their reduction to low caste, is a radical form of antichurch. It is the evolution of a social reality that undercuts the credibility of sexist religion. Even without conscious attention to the church it is in conflict with it. There are, of course, other movements in contemporary society that threaten organized religion. In the case of other movements, however, it is not sexism that is directly under attack. The development of sisterhood is a unique threat, for it is directed against the basic social and psychic model of hierarchy and domination upon which authoritarian religion *as authoritarian* depends for survival. This conflict arises directly from the fact that women are beginning to overcome the divided self and divisions from each other.

Aside from the general way in which the movement simply by its own dynamic conflicts with sexist religion by setting up a counter-world to it, there is also a more specific and direct opposition developing to the sexism of the churches. This is related to the fact that some of the movement's leading figures as well as an increasing number of its adherents are women who know personally the experience of authoritarian religious conditioning and the experience of breaking through this. Many now recall in amazement their past acceptance of the exclusion of their sex from priesthood and ministry as if this were "natural." As long as the mask of role segregation was effective, it was possible to believe firmly that no inequality was involved: men and women were just "different." Women were able to accept the fact that a mentally retarded boy was allowed to serve Mass, whereas a woman with a Ph.D. was absolutely excluded from such a function. They could go through marriage ceremonies in which they promised to "obey" their husbands without reciprocal promises from men, and still think that no inequality was involved; they were "subordinate but not inferior." Now that the implications of role segregation in the wider society have received exposure in the media, however, inevitably more women, even the unradicalized, are seeing through the mystifications of religious sexism and their own resistances to consciousness. These women—whatever may be their relationship now to organized religion—are spiritual expatriates, and they bring to the movement intimate and precise knowledge of religion's role in reinforcing sexual caste, focusing criticism precisely upon this. In a particular way, they constitute sisterhood as antichurch.

There is yet another way in which sisterhood means thinking, feeling, and acting as antichurch. It is directly opposed to that contemporary ideology whose dogmas have partially replaced those of the church in the function of perpetuating sexual caste, that is, Freudian theory. Since psychoanalysis, with its creeds, priesthood, spiritual counseling, rules, and anathemas, functions as the mother church of contemporary secular patriarchal religions, it is a major target of the women's movement as antichurch.

The development of Freudian psychoanalysis began toward the end of the first wave of the women's revolution. It provided a powerful instrument for the male counter-revolution against feminism, supplying it with claims of "scientific" certitude (replacing the "God's plan" of theologians) and a vocabulary of

technical jargon which has cloaked prejudice. Its tremendous power of psychological intimidation not only has rivaled that of the churches but outstripped it
by far in this century.[7] Millions who would smile at being called "heretical"
could be cowed by the label "neurotic." This has rendered it nearly immune
from attack until recently. Its dogmas have been inserted as working principles
into the social sciences. Its missionaries have infiltrated the educational system
and used the mass media to spread the gospel of "mental health." Its priests have
converted their female penitents into acceptance of their male-imposed destiny.
As antichurch, the new sisterhood is exposing the bias of this "church" and the
fallibility of its "clergy."

BEYOND THE ANTICHURCH:
SISTERHOOD AS CHURCH

A purely negative evaluation of the impact of religion would be inaccurate.
With its help, many people have achieved a kind of autonomy, charity, and
peace, although these qualities—especially this peace—have generally been
achieved at the price of ignoring social problems, rather than working through
them. Women who have become alienated from institutional religion because of
its inadequacy have often retained from the tradition a sense of these values and
of transcendence. These are spiritual exiles with deeply radicalized consciousness. This quality of consciousness is not necessarily the unique property of
women who have been related to institutional religion, however. It is in many
women who are unable or unwilling to express it in religious terms. It is an
aspect of sisterhood that is consistent with the movement's functioning as
antichurch, but which points beyond this. It is the movement as church.

Contemporary theologians have claimed that the church should be a
community of freedom, assuming the role of inquiring about the assumptions
behind the ideologies and behavior patterns of the wider society, and constantly
criticizing these. It is possible for theologians to think of the church as learning
to function in this way when a distinction is made between the institutional
church as it is and the eschatological "kingdom of God" proclaimed by it. It is
claimed that when this split is courageously faced, that is, when the provisional
nature of the church as institution is acknowledged, then it will become possible
for it to assume the role of criticizing the prevailing culture, for its present
formulations and structures, which reflect the existing cultural situation and
legitimate it, will no longer be taken with ultimate seriousness.[8] The point which
has not been grasped by most theologians, however, is that as long as the
institutional church remains immersed in its *patriarchal forms,* such iconoclastic
insight on a sustained or widespread basis within its structures will continue to
be practically impossible. This being the case, what is happening is that
dimensions of eschatological truth which the institutional church fails to

proclaim under prevailing cultural conditions which screen its own vision are being proclaimed by counter cultural movements. The women's movement has the potential to function in this churchly way of proclaiming dimensions of human becoming which the oppressive forms of organized religion repudiate.

There are many ways of envisaging a church. One may visualize a space set apart from the rest of the world which has a special meaning for people and which is seen as a haven and a sanctuary. One may think of a charismatic community, like that of the early Christians, in which the gifts of healing and prophecy are manifested. Or one may stress the idea that the church is a people who have received a promise and who therefore leave home on an adventurous journey of discovery. Or one may think of it as a people sent forth with a mission and task assigned to them. In all of these senses the term "church" applies to the women's movement.

A space set apart. The religious mentality has tended to fix upon certain places as sacred and central in meaning. Even the frankly non-religious person in our culture tends to value certain "holy places" of his or her private universe. Often there is something regressive and escapist about this phenomenon. Frequently, it is a superstitious sense of specialness that attaches to "holy shrines," having nothing to do with individual growth and social change. Yet the image of a space set apart says something meaningful and points out a way of understanding the major liberation movements of our time. The women's movement provides a space—not simply in a physical sense, but rather a province of the mind—where it is possible to be oneself, freely, without the mendacious contortions of mind, will, feeling, and imagination demanded of women if they are to survive "out there." This space—which is wherever the community of liberation comes together—is sacred space, for it is where women can discover in their lives the power of self-actualization and transcendence.

When such a space set apart is discovered, there is danger of deteriorating into escapism and of absolutizing it in this particular form. At this point in history, however, the danger that women will succumb to accusations of escapism and monism far outweighs these possibilities themselves, especially when such accusations are couched in psychoanalytic jargon. Yet there is a point to be seen here. There is a kind of escapism, quite different from that usually meant by the movement's critics. That is, women are conditioned to "escape" seeing the fact of sexual caste and its full implications. For this reason the movement could deteriorate by fixation upon single limited issues (e.g. repeal of abortion laws) to the exclusion of others. This would involve a refusal to think through to deeper meanings, and would then be a kind of monism because it would imply failure to be consistent with the dynamic of women's liberation that opens out upon the whole society, pointing the way to human liberation. In that case, the transcendent aspect of the movement would be lost.

Charismatic community. The new sisterhood is a charismatic community. This is manifested in the freedom that is experienced and communicated.

Although there are organizations within the movement, for example NOW (National Organization for Women) and WEAL (Women's Equity Action League), it is not reducible to an organization. More properly it is a community that is non-hierarchical, without precise membership lists or rules. Its style is personal. It exists wherever women unite in mind, feeling, and will for liberation. One of the charismatic aspects of the community is its power of healing. The official instruments of modern sexist society for the "healing" of women are in large measure designed to blunt aspirations to humanity. The exceptional members of the religious or psychoanalytic priestly caste who actually use their situation in order to liberate are deviants who do not function according to their role specifications. It is the movement, however, that offers the non-institutional—in fact, counter-institutional—charismatic healing of liberation. Another charismatic aspect of the new sisterhood is prophecy. Whereas the priests of patriarchy function to sustain the delusion that what is, is right, the prophetic function is to point beyond what is to what has never been, but can become. Just by becoming themselves women are functioning as prophets of a new age.

Critics inevitably charge this charismatic community, as well as others, with fanaticism. Reduction of the movement to a mythical band of bra-burners as well as to the other alleged "extremist" behavior is a common tactic. Women are over-susceptible to this attack, having been conditioned to self-distrust. Although critics will urge "moderation" and separation from "extreme" elements, the most adequate response is deeper radicalization. Women can learn from such criticism the pitfalls of not being radical enough, of occasionally becoming fixated upon minor issues. To become radicalized is to think through to the interconnections among the phenomena associated with sexual caste so that energy is not deflected upon trivia.

Exodus community. As exodus community the new sisterhood has left home on the basis of a promise. The promise is within women's minds, in new-found potentialities that point toward future fulfillment. The journey which is begun on the basis of this promise involves leaving behind the false self imposed from without. In some cases this may literally mean walking out of an intolerable marriage or an oppressive job. Since one cannot ordinarily leave the whole society, however, the adequate exodus requires the development of a community in which freedom is fostered and which can exist in dialectic with the wider society. The movement functions in this way.

Critics of this idea will of course claim that women's liberation is not an exodus community in an authentic sense but rather that it is "disloyal" to Christian teaching and, when carried to "extremes" (i.e., when carried through to its logical conclusions), unorthodox and heretical. This charge is, of course, true if faith is taken to mean blind assent to dogmas rather than openness to experience and ultimate concern. The real danger is that the movement will be *merely* unorthodox and heretical, that is, reformist within pre-established structures and arguing from the unchallenged *a priori* assumptions of the past—whether religious or other assumptions. Insofar as it is true to itself, sisterhood points beyond mere unorthodoxy as well as beyond orthodoxy. Instead of simply refuting or reinterpreting the old, it reaches out to find and give expression to the really new. Rather than stopping at such goals as the ordination of women, for example, it is bringing about a transcendence of traditional sex role socialization and so has a dynamic which can transform the whole cultural climate in which such issues arise. As an exodus community which has "gone away" from tradition, the new sisterhood can incorporate the values of tradition, not in the sense of attempting to preserve the past, but rather in the sense of releasing the values that were suffocated by sexist symbols and power structures by reincarnating them in better symbols, language, societal forms and action.

Community with a mission. Because women are experiencing new promise in themselves there is growing awareness of a new task—or in theological terms, of a mission to spread the good news of liberation. Basically, this communication starts with living out the liberation process in one's own life. It extends to cooperating for a common purpose. The idea of task or mission is complementary to the exodus aspect of sisterhood. Whereas the latter means "going away" and living in creative tension with the dominant culture, the idea of task emphasizes the necessity of bringing back to the general consciousness— including consciousness within institutional churches—the insight made possible through withdrawal and freedom.

Critics will argue that "missionaries" usually try to force their interpretation of existence upon others. They will insist, for example, that if women who are "just housewives" are happy that way, then other women are elitist and intolerant in suggesting that this is inadequate. In responding to this, women have to realize that definitions of female existence have been imposed upon the female sex down through the millennia. It is completely disproportionate to accuse women of doing the "forcing" under these circumstances. Yet this criticism should be listened to, not because its sophistry deserves respect, but because the words do point to a real problem. The problem stems from the fact that women have been forced into restrictive modes of existence. Many are caught in situations which make "hearing the message" a threat to all security. The task or mission of sisterhood, then, includes building bridges, suggesting realistic alternatives, and aiding the efforts of those whose situation makes it impossible for them to adopt free and radical lifestyles.

RELATION OF SISTERHOOD AS CHURCH
TO THE INSTITUTIONAL CHURCH

By assuming roles which the institutional church's bias prohibits it from carrying out adequately, the women's movement is functioning as church ministering not only to the wider society but also to the institutional church, bringing to it the message of eschatological fulfillment which it itself should be proclaiming. In providing a space set apart from the sexist society it is creating a model for the institutional church as community of liberation. As charismatic community, it communicates its healing power to the sickness of the institutional church by giving hope to women. As exodus community, it is suggesting to organized religion that it also should "go away" from the culture in which it is immersed and from the traditions which hinder liberation. As community with a mission, the women's movement offers criticism of and resistance to the oppression carried on by organized religion, and offers it the possibility of discovering its own mission of liberation.

CONCLUSION: TOWARD HUMAN LIBERATION— THE SISTERHOOD OF MAN

The structures which limit us into sex roles are human products, and human beings support them, even though often we are not conscious of the processes involved. It would be unrealistic, then, to imagine that change can take place without conflict between persons—between women and men, and between persons of the same sex. Yet, although such risk is built into the very existence of a movement to bring about change, shattering sexual stereotypes at the expense of the more compassionate virtues is not the goal. It is nowhere written that we must pass from patriarchy through matriarchy in order to become humanized. To settle for reducing "the Other" to victimized status would be failure.

The change in consciousness which is being effected in some women is of course extending to some men. Granted the necessity for women to define ourselves independently, the fact is that some men are becoming sensitized to the problem. It was because she recognized this possibility that Simone de Beauvoir, at the end of her work, *The Second Sex,* wrote that "to gain the supreme victory, it is necessary, for one thing, that by and through their natural differentiation men and women unequivocally affirm their brotherhood." While it might appear to some as a kind of nitpicking to single out her choice of the word "brotherhood," the fact is that the choice is revealing. For "brotherhood" has generally signified the "us versus a third" relationship, that is, subject-object relationship that fails to extend itself to intersubjectivity. De Beauvoir's analysis does not have enough depth in this regard, perhaps because she is influenced by Sartre's view that to love each other simply means to hate the same enemy, that is, to have solidarity versus a third. An analysis which cannot get beyond such presuppositions would seem to lead us to a dead end as far as any possibility of deeply changing forms of consciousness and behavior is concerned. In Sartre's view, liberation means that the oppressed class rises up and by its "stare" reduces the oppressor class to objects. If this is true, then we are caught in the cycle of conflict and vindication. Although De Beauvoir obviously wants to extend "brotherhood" further than this, she does not go far enough in pointing the way beyond it, partly because the term itself is loaded with patriarchal bias. The more adequate conception of the new community is expressed by "sisterhood of man."

Just as the sisterhood of women signifies a bonding that never took place before, so the sisterhood of man is a new kind of bonding of people, men and women, for liberation from sexual stereotypes. This is its first meaning. Moreover, since the process of liberation points to a mode of relating between persons—between women and women, men and men, and women and men—which is qualitatively different from that which the sex role socialization of patriarchy would allow people to attain, the sisterhood of man also has a meaning that points beyond the limitations of the present situation and even beyond the demands of conflict and vindication toward a new mode of human community. That is, it signals the becoming of interpersonal relationships among whole human beings.

LIBERATION AS REVELATION

In modern society, technical controlling knowledge has reached the point of violating the privacy and rights of individuals and destroying the natural environment. In reaction against this, social critics sometimes call for awakening of interpersonal consciousness, that is, of intersubjectivity. I am suggesting that this cannot happen without the communal and creative refusal of victimization by sexual stereotypes which I am calling the sisterhood of man. This creative refusal involves conscious and frequently painful efforts to develop new lifestyles in which I-Thou becomes the dominant motif, replacing insofar as possible the often blind and semi-conscious mechanisms of I-It, which use the other as object. In the realm of knowledge, this means removing the impediments to that realm of knowing which is subjective, affective, intuitive, or what the scholastics called "connatural." It means breaking down the barriers between technical knowledge and that deep realm of intuitive knowledge which some theologians call ontological reason.[9]

Objective or technical knowledge is necessary for human survival and progress. It is the capacity for "reasoning." Clarity of thinking and the construction of language require its use. So also does the ability to control nature and society. However, by itself, cut off from the intuitive knowledge of ontological reason, technical knowledge is directionless and ultimately meaningless. When it dominates, life is deprived of an experience of depth, and it tends toward despair.

Technical knowledge of itself is detached. It depends upon a subject-object split between the thinker and that which is perceived. It is calculative, stripping that which is perceived of subjectivity. Technical knowledge, cut off from ontological reason, degrades its object and dehumanizes the knowing subject. Because it reduces both to less than their true reality, at a certain point it even ceases to be knowledge in any authentic sense. When it is thus divorced from ontological reason, the psychological and social sciences which it dominates become dogmatic, manipulative, and destructive. Under its dominion, theology and all of religion deteriorate into superstition.

Widening of experience so pathologically reduced can come through encounter with another subject, an I who refuses to be an It. If, however, the encounter is simply a struggle over who will be forced into the position of It, this will not be ultimately redemptive. It is only when the subject is brought to a recognition of the other's damaged but never totally destroyed subjectivity as equal to his/her own, having basically the same potential and aspiration to transcendence, that a qualitatively new way of looking at the world can begin to emerge. This is the meaning of women's liberation as revelation and as spiritual revolution.

NOTES

1. A documented historical study and criticism of this can be found in my book, *The Church and the Second Sex* (New York and London: Harper and Row, Publishers, 1968).

2. The language of male theologians continues to reveal unawareness of the problem:

"God is, of course masculine, but not in the sense of sexual distinction . . ." John L. McKenzie, S.J., *The Two Edged Sword* (New York: Bruce Publishing Co., 1956), pp. 93–94.

"To believe that God is Father is to become aware of oneself not as a stranger, not as an outsider or an alienated person, but as a son who belongs or a person appointed to a marvelous destiny, which he shares with the whole community. To believe that God is Father means to be able to say 'we' in regard to all men." Gregory Baum, *Man Becoming* (New York: Herder and Herder, 1970), p. 195.

A woman whose consciousness has been awakened can only say that such language makes her aware of herself as a stranger, as outsider, as alienated person, not as a daughter who belongs or is appointed to a marvelous destiny.

3. Images and conceptualizations used in God language which legitimate sexual hierarchy will have to be ruled out as grossly inadequate. Even conceptualizations which transcend this category are implicitly compatible with oppressiveness if they encourage detachment from the reality of the human struggle against oppression in its concrete manifestations. The lack of explicit relevance of intellection to the fact of oppression in its precise forms, such as sexual hierarchy, is itself oppressive. Tillich's theology is radically liberating, but the relevance of "power of being" to the problem of sexism must be spelled out. Just as his language about God is too "detached," so too is the rest of his systematic theology. His discussion of estrangement, for example, when he "breaks the myth" of the Fall, is too general, without taking into account the malignant view of the man-woman relationship which the androcentric myth itself inadvertently "reveals" and perpetuates. Since the residue of this specific content of the myth still deeply affects Western culture in its attitudes, customs, and laws (e.g., concerning prostitution and

abortion), it is not adequate to talk abstractly of estrangement while religion perpetuates its concrete manifestations.

4. It would be unrealistic to dismiss the fact that the instruments of communication, that is, the whole theological tradition in Western society, have been controlled by the superordinate group within the structure of patriarchy. The usual and accepted means of theological dissent have been restricted in such a way that only some questions have been allowed to arise. The time is rapidly approaching when it will be realized that the traditional "array of projections" (Berger's expression) can hardly function as "signals of transcendence" in an adequate way, since these are functioning to hamper self-transcendence.

5. My conviction of the present impossibility of drawing adequate models from the past because an irreparable break in consciousness has taken place is supported by Margaret Mead's theory that we have moved from a configurative culture (in which children and adults learn from their peers) to a prefigurative culture (in which adults learn also from their children). She writes that "today's elders have to treat their own past as incommunicable." *Culture and Commitment: A Study of the Generation Gap* (Garden City: Doubleday and Co., Inc., 1970), p. 61. "If we are to build a prefigurative culture in which the past is instrumental rather than coercive, we must change the location of the future . . . So, as the young say, 'The Future is Now.' " *Ibid.,* pp. 75–76.

6. For this reason the Black theology being written by such theologians as James Cone reveals an incapacity to go to the root of the problem. Cone's theology is full of vengeance, fiercely biblical and patriarchal. It transcends religion as a crutch but settles for being religion as a gun, and is tailored to fit only the situation of racial oppression. It inspires a will to vindication but leaves unexplored the possibility of self-transcendence which involves integration and transformation (of the self and of the fabric of society). Cone's Black God and Black Messiah are merely the same patriarchs after a pigmentation operation, their behavior unaltered.

7. See Thomas S. Szasz, *The Manufacture of Madness* (New York and London: Harper and Row, Publishers, 1970). In this work, which he subtitles "A Comparative Study of the Inquisition and the Mental Health Movement," Dr. Szasz shows the strong similarities between the belief in and punishment of witchcraft and the belief in and punishment of "mental illness." He has valuable insights regarding the use of women as society's scapegoats in both cases.

8. See, for example, Johannes Metz, *Theology of the World* (New York: Herder and Herder, 1969).

9. Tillich's insights on technical and ontological reason, developed especially in the first volume of his *Systematic Theology,* are very helpful, but of course his insight does not extend to the psychological implications of women's liberation. His work provides a theoretical basis which can be extended and applied.

9

OVERCOMING THE BIBLICAL AND TRADITIONAL SUBORDINATION OF WOMEN

Anne McGrew Bennett

All this century Protestantism has been stirred and inspired by the great leaders of the Social Gospel. There have been similar influences in Catholicism. This century has been one of many struggles, and some successes, for a measure of social justice: the eight-hour day; the right of labor to organize; massive legislation establishing social security, welfare rights, civil rights, human rights.

One of the strange characteristics of this movement for justice is that women, for the most part, have not been included or if included have been relegated to an inferior status. As an example of this exclusion, household workers (i.e., women) will be included, for the first time, under the protection of the minimum wage in California beginning March 4, 1974.

John Kenneth Galbraith, in his new book *Economics and the Public Purpose,* states that

> the modern economy . . . requires for its success a crypto-servant class . . . The conversion of [housewives] into a crypto-servant class [Galbraith here is speaking of middle-class and upper-middle-class housewives] was an economic accomplishment of the first importance . . . The servant role of woman is critical for the expansion of consumption in the modern economy. That it is so generally approved . . . is a formidable tribute to the power of the convenient social virtue.[1]

Betty and Theodore Roszak in *Masculine/Feminine* write of

> . . . the invidious use of sexual stereotyping over the last century. . . . The truth is that women are members of a caste, socially dispersed by the family system, but collectively victimized by a lifelong process of sexual stereotyping contrived to make the world safe for male supremacy.[2]

This statement was presented at a class on Foundations and Methods of Christian Ethics, Pacific School of Religion, 1973.

The church and seminaries are still largely blind to the way that woman is thought of as "not-quite-human"[3] and blind to the depth of their patriarchal structure and sexist theology.

Women, since about 1970, have been entering seminaries in large numbers. Women are now ordained in all but four major communions in the United States (Roman Catholic, Orthodox, Missouri Synod Lutheran, Episcopal), and those communions are hard pressed to maintain their discrimination. However, the deep issues are not getting attention—perhaps they are not comprehended, obviously they are fearsome.

An example of this blindness is the symbol which was used on the name tags and programs of the 1973 annual meeting of the American Academy of Religion in Chicago. The symbol was two white male hands firmly clasped under the words "The Annual Meeting." I wonder sometimes if the choice of this symbol was due to blindness or if it was a flaunting of male power saying to the few women who were there, "This is a male club, women are outsiders." There are many powerful forms of communication and control and exclusion.

In a study of anti-Semitism in contemporary America, *The Tenacity of Prejudice,* there is a section about social club discrimination against Jews by the college educated. If one substitutes "professional societies" for "social club" and "women" for "Jews," the far-reaching power of male-clergy associations, male theological societies, etc., in supporting sexism comes into clear focus:

> The educated are the guardians of the ideal values of our society. They constitute a cultural elite whose responsibility is to form and maintain standards of belief and behavior . . . tending to define for others what is respectable in the realm of belief and permissible in the realm of conduct . . . freedom of personal association is a democratic right. But in a society pervaded by ethnic and racial ["sexist"] prejudice this . . . has less than innocent consequences . . . social club ["professional societies"] discrimination helps to create and maintain the image of Jews ["women"] as socially ["profession-ally"] undesirable and to cast the Jew ["woman"] into the role of the outsider. It reduces the moral authority of the educated to speak out against prejudice, and it implicitly legitimates the virulent expressions of anti-Semitism ["sex-ism"] that the educated disavow for themselves. However unprejudiced they may be, the college educated who support social ["professional society"] discrimination condone one of the historic institutions of prejudice.[4]

In an ordination service for a woman which I attended recently, the official church representatives were men; the nouns and pronouns of the modern gospel songs were heavily masculine; when the prayer of Invocation began with the words "Mother-Father-God" there was an audible titter; in a charge to the soon-to-be-ordained woman that she give a central place to a prophetic ministry all the prophets, ancient and modern, who were held up as role models were men; the United Church of Christ Statement of Faith was read in unison—it is a short statement, but God is referred to in masculine pronouns twenty-one times; and, of course, humankind is referred to as "man," "men," "him" without comparable feminine words.

Why is it so easy, so "natural," to treat women as "other"—an "other" to exploit, or enjoy, or ignore with impunity?

Western culture, which is the dominant world culture today, has been largely molded by the Judeo-Christian faith. Therefore we must examine the religious myths and symbols and history which are the very fabric of our theology, of our worship and of our common life in order to begin to understand the root causes of discrimination which have given woman a certain "place" based on sex.

The most superficial examination of the scriptures reveals that it comes out of a male-dominated society. Dr. Phyllis Trible, professor of Old Testament at Andover Newton Seminary, describes biblical religion in these words:

> It is superfluous to document patriarchy in Scripture. Yahweh is the God of Abraham, Isaac, and Jacob as well as of Jesus and Paul. The legal codes of Israel treat women primarily as chattel. Qoheleth condemns her "whose heart is snares and nets and whose hands are fetters," concluding that although a few men may seek the meaning of existence, "a woman among all those I have not found." Paul considers women subordinate to their husbands, and, even worse, I Timothy makes woman responsible for sin in the world. Considerable evidence indicts the Bible as a document of male supremacy. Attempts to acquit it by tokens such as Deborah, Huldah, Ruth, or Mary and Martha only reinforce the case.[5]

If these statements are all, or the essence, of what biblical religion means, then women are in a very bad situation and have little hope of claiming whole personhood as long as the Judeo-Christian faith molds our understanding of God/man/woman.

There is another approach to the Bible. The Bible and biblical tradition can be reread keeping in mind the patriarchal bias of the writers and redactors and interpreters in an effort to understand our biblical faith without sexist blinders.

Begin with the myth of the creation of humankind: "So God created man in his own image; in the image of God he created him; male and female he created them" (Gen. 1:27). This verse has been interpreted quite differently for man than for woman. There is no question in the minds of men who follow the Judeo-Christian faith but that they are created in God's image with all the dignity and power that that means. As for women, it has been widely taught and believed that because they are not male they are an inferior creation.

Reread the myth. Begin with the previous verse: "Then God said, 'Let us make man in our image and likeness' . . ." (1:26). Notice that in this passage the writer does not have God say "Let us make man in my image," but "in our image." The Hebrew word for God in these passages is not *Yahweh* or *El*, which are masculine, singular nouns used to refer to God. The Hebrew word is *Elohim*. It is a plural word which is used in the Bible for a female or male God or Gods.

The goddess of the Sidonians is referred to in the Bible as *Elohim*. It is always translated masculine, singular.[6]

Scholars—most of them male, of course—have a great deal of trouble with this word. Some of them try to ignore the plural and dismiss it as the plural of majesty. However, the late Old Testament scholar and Dean of Christ Church Oxford, Cuthbert A. Simpson, who is the exegete in *The Interpreter's Bible* for these particular passages in the creation story in which *Elohim* is used, suggests that there is "here an attempt . . . to give expression to the feeling that God could not be adequately represented as just a bare unity."[7]

There is another problem for us in this passage as we think about woman because of the use of the word "man": "God created man." The word "man" can be used in the generic sense and include woman. It is so used here. The Hebrew word in this passage is a generic term, not a male term.[8] It should be translated "persons" or "humankind," not "man," which may mean "male" and always carries a male image.

How much difference would there be in our understanding of man/woman, woman's "place," if in the creation story the word *Elohim* were used throughout for the word "God" and the referent masculine pronouns; and if the generic term "persons" were used instead of "man"?

> Elohim said, "Let us create persons in our image and likeness . . ."
>   Elohim created persons in Elohim's own image; male and female Elohim created them.   (Gen. 1:26, 27)

This most ancient myth, in profound symbolism, describes God as inclusive being and all persons made in God's image. God's attributes are not limited and there are no inferior persons. Woman is portrayed the same as man. Both are persons; sex is secondary.

The second chapter of Genesis contains another creation myth. According to the usual interpretation of this story, woman was made after man to be a helper for him. It is best not to be too literal in interpreting myths; but it cannot be maintained that woman is inferior even if she was created after man without admitting that man is inferior to the creeping things because he was created after them. Neither man nor woman in this story is said to be made "in God's image." Furthermore, the word translated as "help meet" or "helper" is the Hebrew word used of divine, or superior, help. The word never refers to inferior help in the Bible.

Probably the story, myth, most often quoted to justify keeping woman inferior to man is the story of the Fall when Eve (whose name, by the way, means "Life," or "Mother of all living") and Adam are still in the Garden of Eden. They have eaten of the forbidden fruit and God says to Eve, according to the modern translators of this story: "I will increase your labour and your groaning, and in labour you shall bear children. You shall be eager for your husband, and he shall be your master" (Gen. 3:16).

The commentaries by the scholars on this passage are most interesting and very different from the common interpretation. Dean Simpson writes: "Most significant is the fact that [the writer] far in advance of his time sees that this domination of woman by man is an evil thing. The implication is that the relationship between husband and wife was intended by God to be a mutual and complementary relationship of love and respect, not a relationship in which one dominated the other."[9]

Professor Trible writes: "This statement is not license for male supremacy, but rather it is condemnation of that very pattern."[10]

A literal translation of this passage from the Septuagint reads quite differently from our translations:

> "Unto the woman [God] said, a snare hath increased thy sorrow and thy sighing; Thou art turning away [from God] to thy husband, and he will rule over thee."[11]

In this translation it is very clear that woman is being warned against depending on her husband rather than on God.

Surely the scholars know that the translation in our Bible implies a false interpretation and that only a few people have access to their commentaries. Many an article and sermon has extolled "woman's place" as helper to her husband, not to mention statements justifying treating women as inferior persons and second-class citizens. I've never read an article or heard a sermon on the subject "Man is evil when he dominates woman," have you?

Half the human race, men, grow up with an exalted ego because God and humankind are always referred to by their identification, masculine pronouns, and woman is referred to as their "help meet." What violence these interpretations have done to both women and men.

Sometimes when I raise questions about the interpretations of the old myths in the Bible or insist that women, as well as men, should be celebrated in liturgies, I am told: "Oh, don't bother with the past, let's get on with what needs to be done now." I want to explain why I think we must insist on rereading and reinterpreting the myths and history without sexist blinders or there will be little real change for women. If an easily identifiable group within the culture is portrayed as inferior, as never having made any general contributions to society—that is, if their contributions are always thought of as within one very limited area (with women this would be within the biological sphere, giving birth and nurturing the family)—then that group of persons is thought of as "other" and the dominant group in the culture continues to hold them in an inferior, usually a servant, role. The members of the oppressed group themselves accept the second-class, not-quite-human role because they know little or nothing about their past which would lead them to have any other opinion.

In the Judeo-Christian heritage the patriarchal culture has been so dominant, and still is, that women even though they have had a significant historical role are ignored, omitted, in history and the ritual celebrations. Thus their history is forgotten and without a past women are considered "other," not to be counted as full members of the community. A twentieth-century illustration of this is the way historians and social scientists continue to declare that Negroes got the vote after the Civil War and that all Americans have been equal under the law since the Fourteenth Amendment became law in 1868. Black women as well as white women waited until 1920 to get the vote; and women are still trying to get the Equal Rights Amendment passed which will, at long last, include them.

The bias of scholars is very evident in the way they interpret biblical myths or history. As an example I quote from three Old Testament scholars writing about Adam and Eve eating the apple in the Garden of Eden.

First, comments from Dr. Gottfried Quell in a book titled *Kittel's Bible Key Words*. Scholars in all parts of the world consider the articles in this book indispensable for a modern exposition of the truth of the Bible. In the section on Adam and Eve and their Fall, Dr. Quell describes the woman, Eve, as "naive," and says that she, Eve, is "already intrigued by the beauty of the forbidden fruit, listens like a fool to the words [of the serpent] about being clever, though she hardly understands them . . . and commits the act of disobedience." Dr. Quell attributes Adam's disobedience to his "passionate longing, shown in a thousand ways, to get knowledge and be clever. . . ." Then, in a footnote, Dr. Quell quotes two other biblical scholars, one of whom suggests "the creation of woman may have been the result of a sin, i.e., an act of divine anger"; the other scholar calls the suggestion "fairly certain."[12]

Now, comments from Dr. Phyllis Trible—try to remember that her comments are about the same people and the same story!

> Why does the serpent speak to the woman and not to the man? . . . the woman is more appealing . . . she is the more intelligent one . . . the one with greater sensibilities . . . . She contemplates the tree, taking into account all the possibilities. The tree is good for food. . . . Above all, it is coveted as the source of wisdom. . . . The woman is fully aware when she acts, her vision encompassing the gamut of life. She takes the fruit and she eats. The initiative and the decision are hers alone. There is no consultation with her husband. She seeks neither his advice nor his permission. [Eve] acts independently. By contrast [Adam] is a silent, passive and bland recipient . . . [Adam] does not theologize, he does not contemplate; he does not envision the full possibilities of the occasion. His one act is belly-oriented. . . . If the woman be intelligent, sensitive and ingenious, the man is passive, brutish, and inept. . . .[13]

Finally, comments from J. Edgar Bruns, director of the Institute of Christian Thought at St. Michael's College, Toronto. In a study of ancient mythologies Professor Bruns finds one theme dominant: "the equation of woman with intelligence and civilization." "In the book of Genesis, Adam and Eve are forbidden to eat of the tree of the knowledge of good and evil, a phrase that signifies *all* knowledge. The serpent . . . tells Eve that if she and Adam eat of the tree they will become as gods and that is why the Lord has forbidden them to partake of its fruit. Eve is tempted, to the point of yielding, but why? Because she sees that 'the tree was desirable for the purpose of knowing.' . . . She is over-eager for wisdom and disobeys. . . ."[14]

Reread the story and make up your own mind which scholar is closest to the actual character portrayals in the story. Notice when you read it that Eve admitted her guilt, but that Adam blamed God for his act. Notice also that the first great promise to humankind is to Eve: "her brood" will strike the serpent's head.

Reread the Old Testament and the New Testament; search for the references to women; keep in mind the statement of the British historian J. H. Plumb: "The past is always a created ideology with a purpose, designed to control individuals, or motivate societies, or inspire classes. Nothing has been so corruptly used as concepts of the past. . . ." A past without women is a "created ideology."

Sarah, Rebekah, and Rachel, whose husbands were Abraham, Isaac, and Jacob, are most independent, fascinating women. Sarah's name means "ruler." We always hear about God's promise to Abraham—we are called the "children" of Abraham. Actually the promise of God was to Sarah. The promise was through Isaac, Sarah's son. Abraham already had a son. It is Sarah who is the Mother of nations. Even the name of the Jews, Israelites, comes not from Abraham but from Sarah. Her name has the same root as Israel.[15] Abraham was Sarah's consort.

In an eight-volume work called *The Legends of the Jews,* a compilation of old Jewish traditions, there are many references to Sarah, Rebekah, and Rachel. They are called the Matriarchs, the prophetesses, the Mothers. *The Legends* tells about the "cloud of light" representing God's presence which was over Sarah's tent and later over the tent of Rebekah; about the ceremonial gifts at the dedication of the Tabernacle which honored the Mothers; there was no mention of any gifts honoring the Fathers. There is a listing of some twenty-two women called "women of valor" in *The Legends.*[16]

Reread the Exodus story. Notice that it is the women who are the leaders in the revolution. It was the women who refused to obey the Pharaoh. The Hebrew midwives disobey. Pharaoh's own daughter and her maidens scheme with female slaves (Miriam and her mother) to adopt a Hebrew child whom she names Moses. If Pharaoh had realized the power of women, he might have reversed his decree and had females killed rather than males. In the biblical story Miriam's role doesn't end when she was a young girl hiding her brother in the bulrushes. She was one of the leaders until her death. In the legends are stories that it was Miriam who taught the wandering Hebrews to dig for water, to till the ground, cultivate the tree; and that she restrained Moses from attacking and killing the people who lived in Canaan. Only after her death did the Hebrews make war against the tribes living in Canaan. Dr. Trible points out that the Exodus story teaches that liberation is a refusal of the oppressed to participate in an unjust society and that liberation begins in the home of the oppressor. She says: ". . . a patriarchal religion which creates and preserves such feminist traditions contains resources for overcoming patriarchy."[17]

Deborah, as reported in the book of Judges, was a judge, chief of the tribes of Israel, commander in chief of the army, queen. But when you read the modern commentaries, all these roles are combined under the terms "a charismatic leader" or "prophetess." Why, in the twentieth century, cannot the scholars report a woman's status as "head of state" correctly? Fortunately the story of Deborah has not been omitted from the Bible. It couldn't be, for the Song of Deborah is one of the oldest and most prized literary treasures of the Hebrew people.[18]

Huldah is another of our ancestors to celebrate. Huldah is the woman who was consulted when King Josiah heard about a book that had been found in the Temple and ordered the high priest to seek guidance from the Lord about the book's validity. In the biblical account, 2 Kings 22:11–14, the high priest and four high government officials went to Huldah the prophetess and consulted her. It is no wonder that most readers of the account pay little attention to her; she is identified as ". . . the wife of Shallum [who is] the son of Tikvah, son of Harhas, the keeper of the wardrobe." And they consulted her "at home in the second quarter of Jerusalem." It is interesting to read in *The Legends* that she was the head of an academy in Jerusalem.[19]

The extreme male-centeredness of biblical writers, especially editors, is shown in the hundreds of incidents throughout the Hebrew Bible in which feminine words have been changed to masculine in order to express reverence for the Holy. Feminine words referring to sacred objects or having to do with worship have been changed to masculine. For example, the golden dishes on the altar, the bread, curtains, rings, doorposts, candlesticks are feminine words, but they have been changed to masculine. Even the milk cows that brought back the Ark are referred to as masculine six times! As one research scholar writes, "We may formulate the following principle: whenever someone or something attained an unusual or elevated status, whether temporary or permanent, the Scribes used masculine . . . suffixes with reference to feminine words."[20]

However, the Hebrew people never limited God's attributes to the masculine. There are many passages in the Old Testament which liken Yahweh's relationship to Israel as that of a mother caring for her children. More specifically, God is described as being known and working in the world through *Shekinah,* which means the presence of God among the people, for example, in the cloud of light, burning bush, and in the Temple. God was in heaven, but Shekinah was God's presence on earth, according to the Jews. The word *Shekinah* is feminine gender. God is known through *Torah,* which means the guidance of God. The books of the law are *Torah,* but Torah is much more—*Torah* is the powerful "word" of God. This word is also of feminine gender. God is known and works through

Chokmah, which means wisdom. Wisdom was thought of as pre-cosmic, involved in creation along with *Torah. Chokmah*, too, is a feminine word. These Hebrew words—*Shekinah, Torah, Chokmah*—reflecting the feminine attributes of God, have never been changed into masculine gender, although biblical scholars will often use the pronoun "he" or "it" with them.[21]

Reread the Gospels and examine the record of the life and teachings of Jesus of Nazareth. Observe that Jesus nowhere distinguishes between men and women as children of God. On the contrary, he said and did things which indicated that he thought of women as the equal of men. In the male-centered Jewish world of his time, this was indeed revolutionary. The Gospels are filled with concrete examples of Jesus' feminist position—teaching women the meaning of the scriptures, including women in the group who went with him through towns and villages preaching the Good News, using the experiences of both women and men in the parables.[22]

The role of women in the church of early Christian times has become hidden history. Joan Morris, an English historian, has just published a book titled *The Lady Was a Bishop* that documents the fact that women in the early church "held a place in the hierarchical service of the Church that is now denied to them." They were ordained with episcopal jurisdiction. Women were abbesses independent of bishops and monarchs. One abbess in the fourth century had jurisdiction over as many as thirty towns where she supervised the clergy, who vowed obedience to her. From the seventh century until the Reformation there were twice as many nuns as monks. The Church Council in the eighth century was called by a woman, Empress Irene. Margaret of Scotland in the eleventh century not only called a Synod but was the chief speaker.[23]

The Reformation returned to a Hebrew and an Old Testament evaluation of women which allowed woman a position in the home but in subservience to her husband. In the witch craze of the sixteenth and seventeenth centuries, women were the chief victims. The Protestant churches which were born in this era still bear scars of its antifeminine sentiments. Neither Luther nor Calvin had a place for women as responsible religious colleagues.[24]

I've emphasized the biblical heritage, especially the Old Testament, and church history because it is this heritage—the heavily male-dominated thought and structure—which still largely influences our language, images, thought patterns, our understanding of sexuality and personhood, our common life. Scientific knowledge, economic and political systems have changed, but we are a patriarchal culture now as then. This patriarchal culture, from primitive times to the present, has so manipulated religion as to provide a rationale, in the name of religion, for holding women in an inferior, submissive place. If religious sanction is given for holding down those you love, and who love you, is it any wonder that there are no limits to rationalizing violence toward, and exploitation of others?

Women's liberation involves every facet of life and meaning. If—no, *when* it is admitted that over half of humankind, women, are considered and treated as not-quite-human and we look into the abyss which has resulted from our denial of God and creation, a long step will have been taken toward restoring wholeness to our understanding of God and persons, and full humanity to both oppressor and oppressed.

What is the role of the church and seminaries, and especially of those persons in the field of Christian ethics, to expose the distortions of myth and history, to be advocates for fact and truth in the interpretation of history and myth, and to be activists in the struggle for whole personhood for all?

NOTES

1. John Kenneth Galbraith, *Economics and the Public Purpose* (Houghton-Mifflin 1973), 233, 33.

2. Betty and Theodore Roszak, *Masculine/Feminine* (Harper 1969), xi.

3. Ibid., "The Human-Not-Quite—Human" (Dorothy Sayers), 116ff.

4. Gertrude J. Selznick and Stephen Steinberg, *The Tenacity of Prejudice* (Harper 1969), 187.

5. Phyllis Trible, "Depatriarchalizing in Biblical Interpretation," *Journal of the American Academy of Religion,* March 1973, 30.

6. Alan Richardson, ed., *A Theological Word Book of the Bible* (Macmillan 1950) "Elohim" (O. S. Rankin), 94; *Interpreter's Dictionary of the Bible* (Abingdon 1962), vol. E-J, 411ff. "Elohim" (B.W. Anderson); *Encyclopedia Judaica* 1971, vol. 7, 679, "Eloha, Elohim" (Louis F. Hartman); William Robertson Smith, *Religion of the Semites* (KTAV 1969 edition) 16, 52 et passim; William L. Reed, *The Asherah in the Old Testament* (Texas Christian University Press 1949) passim; Raphael Patai, *The Hebrew Goddess* (KTAV 1967) 16–35 et passim.

7. Cuthbert A. Simpson, "Genesis," *Interpreter's Bible* (Abingdon 1952) vol. I, 483.

8. Ibid., vol. I, 510.

9. [Ibid.]

10. Trible, loc. cit., 41.

11. Katherine C. Bushnell, *God's Word to Women* (1923) sections 114 to 145.

12. Gottfried Quell, *Kittel's Bible Key Words* (Harper 1951) "Sin in the Old Testament," "The Story of the Fall," 24, 25, 28, 30, et passim 1–32.

13. Trible, loc. cit., 40.

14. J. Edgar Bruns, *God as Woman, Woman as God* (Paulist Press 1973) 1, 20, 22, et passim.

15. *Interpreter's Dictionary of the Bible,* vol. IV, "Sarah" (S. J. DeVries) 219; Bushnell, op. cit., sections 277–8.

16. Louis Ginsberg, *The Legends of the Jews* (Philadelphia Jewish Publications Society 1909). Check index for innumerable references. See especially vol. III, 193, vol. V, 258, vol. I, 297, vol. III, 192–3, 206, 266, vol. I, 203, 287.

17. Trible, loc. cit., 34; Ginsberg, op. cit., vol. II, 262ff., vol. III, 317.

18. *Interpreter's Dictionary of the Bible,* vol. I "Deborah" (D. Harvey), 808–9. *Interpreter's Bible,* vol. 2, 712, 717ff.

19. Ginsberg, op. cit., vol. VI, 377.

20. Mayer G. Slonin, "The Substitution of the Masculine for the Feminine Hebrew Pronominal Suffixes to Express Reverence," *Jewish Quarterly Review,* vol. 29, 397–403.

21. Trible, loc. cit. 31–34; Bruns, op. cit., 35–40; W. D. Davies, *Invitation to the New Testament* (Doubleday 1968) 28–32; *Encyclopedia Judaica* (1971) vol. II, 1354; Theodore Reik, *Pagan Rites in Judaism* (Farrar, Straus, 1964), chap. 7, 74–75; W. D. Davies, *Paul and Rabbinic Judaism* (SPCK London 1948) 145, 163–8, 184–9, 211–14, 216–7 et passim.

22. Elsie Thomas Culver, *Women in the World of Religion* (Doubleday 1967) chaps. 3–4; Leonard Swidler, "Jesus Was a Feminist" (Woman Packet, Church Women United); Sister Albertus Magnus McGrath, O. P., *What a Modern Catholic Believes About Women* (Thomas More Press 1972) chaps. 2–3.

23. Joan Morris, *The Lady Was a Bishop* (Macmillan 1973) passim; Culver, op. cit., chaps. 4–8; McGrath, op. cit., chaps. 4–5.

24. Culver, op. cit., chaps. 9–10 et passim; McGrath, op. cit., chap. 6 et passim; Krister Stendhal, *The Bible and the Role of Women* (Fortress 1966) passim; Morris, op. cit., chap. 10 et passim.

10

AGAPE IN FEMINIST ETHICS

Barbara Hilkert Andolsen

THE TWENTIETH-CENTURY DISCUSSION

The contemporary Protestant discussion of *agape* has stressed the concept of other-regard often epitomized by self-sacrifice. Emphasis on other-regard has been accompanied by a suspicion toward, or outright condemnation of, self-love. Love defined as a sacrifice has been seen as a norm unambiguously appropriate only in private, not public, relationships. *Agape* as a self-sacrifice has been rooted in a Christology which concentrates upon Jesus' self-immolation upon the Cross. Some Catholic moral theologians have countered with themes of mutuality and Trinitarian grounding which many Protestant ethicists have been reluctant to adopt. Feminist ethicists are critical of the emphasis on sacrifice as the quintessence of *agape* and of the denigration of self-love.

The work which set the terms for the twentieth-century debate about the meaning of *agape* as a norm for Christian ethics was Anders Nygren's *Agape and Eros*. In this book Nygren (1932:97) defined *eros* as a "natural self-love, which extends its scope to embrace also benefactors of the self." Hence a love motivated in any way by concern for personal reward is an unchristian love.

For Nygren, self-love is always a morally negative quality. Human beings all have an innate tendency toward selfishness which is the root cause of their perversity of will. Nygren stated categorically: "Christianity does not recognise self-love as a legitimate form of love. Christian love moves in two directions, towards God and towards its neighbour; and in self-love it finds its chief adversary which must be fought and conquered" (1932:217).

In contrast to *eros, agape* is an absolutely disinterested love modeled upon God's love for unworthy human beings. Such love is unmotivated by any desire for personal gain. The neighbor who is loved is not loved because of her/his attractive qualities. Rather persons are enabled to love the unlovable neighbor as a result of God's love.

In Nygren's work sacrifice of self for the sake of others is the paradigm of Christian love. *Agape* is "a love that gives itself away, that sacrifices itself, even to the uttermost" (1932:118). *Agape* is utterly heedless of the self's own interests.

For Nygren, the sacrificial love for the neighbor displayed by Christians mirrors and is made possible by God's sacrificial love for human beings. Indeed Nygren's final words reminded the reader of "the sacrificial, self-giving majesty of Christ's love" (1932:741). This divine love is made known on the Cross. Hence Nygren rooted his ethical norm in the doctrine of the Atonement. The true Christian must attempt to emulate God's love as s/he pours her/himself out completely on behalf of the neighbor.

Reinhold Niebuhr followed in the footsteps of Nygren, condemning self-love and emphasizing sacrifice as the primary historical manifestation of *agape*. Nevertheless Niebuhr criticized Nygren for having drawn an absolute distinction between divine *agape* and human love. Niebuhr believed that human beings naturally long for a state of peace in which the self lives in harmony with her/his fellow human beings in obedience to God. However, human sin makes such lasting harmony impossible within history.

In this world human beings live lives at cross purposes. The human capacity for self-transcendence permits human beings to develop extravagant desires. Each person seeks to obtain an undue share of this life's rewards in a futile attempt to guarantee personal survival and self-sufficiency. In Niebuhr's work selfish concern for personal gain is the chief manifestation of human sin. According to him, "man's self-love and self-centeredness is inevitable" and is at the root of human evil (1941:263).

Just as Niebuhr followed Nygren in condemning self-love, he agreed with Nygren that sacrificial love represents the epitome of Christian love as manifest within history. Like Nygren, Niebuhr learned the importance of sacrificial love by reflecting on the life of Jesus. According to Niebuhr the love of Jesus is a completely disinterested love which "refuses to participate in the claims and counterclaims of historical existence" (1943:72). Jesus, acting out of love for others and heedless of his own claim even to life itself, allowed himself to be crucified for the sake of humankind. Thus the cross of Christ stands as a judgment against all egocentric self-assertion.

Niebuhr took for granted the split between the public world and the private home which characterizes advanced industrial society. Then he asserted that love is a norm more readily applied in intimate, personal relationships—often familial ones. The non-religious standard for personal behavior is *mutual* love, i.e., that state "in which the concern of one person for the interests of another prompts and elicits a reciprocal affection" (1943:69). Mutual love is based upon the reasonable expectation that one will receive return in proportion to what one gives to the other.

But paradoxically intimate, mutually loving relationships can be sustained only by a religious norm of *agape* (or *sacrificial* love). Only when each party acts on behalf of the other without excessive regard for personal return do loving relationships blossom. "Complete mutuality, with its advantages to each party to the relationship, is therefore most perfectly realised where it is not intended, but love is poured out without seeking return" (Niebuhr, 1932:265–266). Selfless love alone can overcome the innate human tendency toward excessive concern for personal reward.[1]

As soon as Niebuhr's focus shifted to the public world of government and business he found *agape* to be a problematic moral standard. Given his model of social life, Niebuhr could find no straightforward way to use Christian love as the measure of public action. Niebuhr conceived of society as a collectivity composed of competing subunits each pressing its own advantage as strongly as possible. A given unit's drive toward gain is checked only by force exerted by competing units. In a society which is a conflux of competing pressures there is no simple place for *agape*—a love which is characterized by total refusal to exert pressure on one's own behalf. Therefore, Christian love must remain "history's 'impossible possibility' " (1943:76).

As a working norm for public affairs Niebuhr substituted justice. The aim of justice is the promotion of equality and human freedom. The function of justice is the creation of a tolerable balance between the interests of competing groups. Operationally justice is achieved through the rational calculation of interests and rights. Because of Niebuhr's acute awareness of human selfishness, especially corporate selfishness, where economics and government are concerned, he reduced *agape* to a remote star. Christians can use *agape* as a reference point to get their moral bearings, but in the public world the total actualization of love will never be reached. Thus according to Niebuhr sacrificial love is the operating norm for personal life; justice, the standard for social life.

That distrust of self-love and self-assertion which typified the work of Nygren and Niebuhr is also found in Gene Outka's *Agape: An Ethical Analysis*.[2] For Outka self-love is not so much the primal sin as it is an innate human tendency. Outka seems to agree with Barth that it would be superfluous to regard self-love as a Christian duty, for "God will never think of blowing on this fire, which is bright enough already" (1972:221). The intrinsic human propensity for self-love can quickly become excessive. Hence the command to love the neighbor is a moral corrective "directed against an uncritical intensification of natural self-assertion" (1972:300).

Outka recognizes that self-regarding actions may be legitimate, especially if one is asserting one's own important interests against the less significant interests of another. However, Outka connects such self-regarding actions with justice—a public norm attractive to Christians and non-Christians alike. "In this way justice may have a limiting effect on agape qua radical other-regard. Justice may not only rule out the familiar move to the side of one's own interests. It may also rule out the less familiar move too far to the side of another's interests"

(1972:301). Note that the distinctively Christian *agape* remains, for Outka, exclusively other-regard.

Outka's primary definition of *agape* is equal-regard. By this he means an attitude of concern for all neighbors without regard for their social utility, personal attractiveness, or individual merit. Equal-regard is also unalterable. Even when love is never (or no longer) returned, the agent ought to remain consistent in her/his loving posture.

While Outka emphasizes other-regard as a crucial element in Christian love, he does not make other-regard and self-sacrifice synonymous. He notes that to act on behalf of the neighbor is often to enhance one's own happiness as well. Other-regard and self-interest are frequently compatible.

In this work, sacrifice is valued for its contribution to the welfare of the neighbor, not as a demonstration of moral purity. Self-sacrifice is "an often appropriate exemplification of neighbor-regard subordinate to such regard rather than the quintessence of it . . ." (1972:278). Nonetheless, in circumstances where the legitimate interests of the self and of others are in conflict, Outka seems to hold that *agape* always endorses the other's need. The Christian must ever be prepared to go the other mile.

While the three ethicists discussed above display varying degrees of uneasiness with self-regard, Martin D'Arcy views self-regard as a positive quality. In his work, Christian love is characterized by a balance between self-respect and self-giving. He insists that "the perfect correspondence between taking and giving, self-regard and self-surrender . . . is reached in Agape" (1956:274). Unfortunately under the influence of Jung, D'Arcy repeatedly connects self-regard with the masculine and self-surrender with the feminine. However, he does state clearly that a healthy person displays both masculine and feminine qualities.

D'Arcy unlike the others sees serious dangers in self-abnegation as well as self-aggrandizement. A person must be concerned for her/his own integrity as well as the other's good. Human beings can fail to establish life-enhancing relationships by erring in the direction of excessive self-surrender as well as excessive selfishness. One can completely lose oneself in the other and to do so is just as wrong as to remain totally self-centered. D'Arcy refuses to offer a simple formula for a balanced love. Instead he asserts that "there is an infinite variety of talent and character among men. Hence it would be ridiculous to try to prescribe any one mixture of self-love and disinterested love for all alike. But what no one can neglect is a sense of personal dignity" (1956:366).

D'Arcy differs from other ethicists in making self-regard a component of *agape*. He also differs from them in the warrant he provides for *agape* thus defined. D'Arcy grounds *agape* in a doctrine of the Trinity rather than a doctrine of the Atonement. In his view a human love which is characterized by both possession and surrender is analogous to the love within the Trinity: "in the mutual love of the Trinity all is given without loss, and all is taken without change, save that a new Person is

revealed in this wondrous intercommunion . . ." (1956:16). The total mutuality of
the Trinity is the model for a full human mutuality.

In the final analysis D'Arcy's emphasis on self-regard as a legitimate aspect of
agape and his interest in the Trinity remains a minority opinion in twentieth-
century American ethics.[3] Yet his work foreshadows the work of contemporary
feminist ethicists.

AGAPE AND FEMALE EXPERIENCE

At least among Protestant ethicists there has been a heavy emphasis on
other-regard and self-sacrifice as distinctive characteristics of an *agape* rooted in
the doctrine of the Atonement. Feminists contend that this view of *agape* is far
too narrow—reflecting largely male experience. Since until recently women have
been almost completely excluded from professional theological discussions, male
theologians have not realized the partiality of their perspective. Therefore men
have described their experience as universal human experience, when, in fact, it
is the experience of a limited portion of the human race.

In a groundbreaking 1960's article, theologian Valerie Saiving Goldstein
asserted that the contemporary theological understanding of *agape* was unsatis-
factory:

> Contemporary theological doctrines of love have, I believe, been constructed
> primarily upon the basis of masculine experience and thus view the human
> condition from the male standpoint. Consequently, these doctrines do not
> provide an adequate interpretation of the situation of women—nor for that
> matter, of men. . . . (1960:27)

Thus she leveled her revolutionary charge that the prevailing understanding of
agape was inadequate not on abstract intellectual grounds, but precisely because
it failed to take the distinctive experience of women as women into account.

Goldstein predicated significant psychological differences between women
and men. These psychological differences were rooted in turn in physiological
differences between the sexes. Men are born to and nurtured by women.
However, since they lack the same reproductive organs, boys cannot just emulate
their mothers. They must grow up to adopt a different life pattern than that of
their nurturers. Men must forge their own distinctive identities, and this process
of becoming men is fraught with anxiety. Goldstein agreed with Niebuhr that
men tend to respond to anxiety with a distorted self-love or pride. Moreover, she
concurred that self-sacrificial love is the appropriate corrective for pride.

However, Goldstein insisted that the experience of women is quite different.
Women can identify entirely with those who care for them as children. As
women mature they can find an identity by passively accepting the role of
biological mother. Such passive acceptance of biological destiny does not

engender anxiety, rather it fosters a sloth which causes women to neglect their own development as persons. Hence the sins to which women as women are prone are faults such as distractibility, sentimentality, violation of privacy, excessive dependence, and "lack of an organizing center" (1960:37).

Women have a tendency to give themselves over to others to such an extent that they lose themselves. Thus they squander their distinctive personal abilities. The virtues which theologians should be urging upon women as women are autonomy and self-realization. What many male theologians are offering instead is a one-sided call to a self-sacrifice which may ironically reinforce women's sins.

While many feminists would disagree with Goldstein's description of how female physiology shapes female destiny, they would concur that women (by nature and/or as a result of cultural conditioning) are often prone to destructive self-abnegation. Many women live for others to a damaging degree. Largely focused upon others, such women are unable to establish a satisfying self-definition. The danger facing women who define themselves exclusively in terms of their relationship to others is described by one widow:

> . . . I really did devote my life to Thurman—in every respect. And all of a sudden I have to make a life of my own. And I don't know where to start. You put yourself last all the time and all of a sudden the person that you banked on is gone. (S. Goldstein, 1980:16)

Some women are so concerned for others that they lose the ability to be centered selves.

Another example of women's temptation to excessive selflessness is the reluctance of a gifted community organizer to accept a fellowship to study rural development, because of her feeling of obligation toward a mother and adult brothers who have not yet escaped " 'the plantation mentality,' " and, hence, are overly dependent upon her (Steinem, 1980:40). Women often show insufficient regard for their own self-development and personal fulfillment when making such decisions.

Limitations of Self-sacrifice as a Norm for Women

Agape defined exclusively as other-regard or self-sacrifice is not an appropriate virtue for women who are prone to excessive selflessness. The latter insight may appear to be a unique realization of the modern feminist movement. But, in fact, nineteenth-century American feminists recognized the destructive effects of an overemphasis on self-sacrifice as the quintessential Christian virtue.[4]

One hundred years ago Elizabeth Cady Stanton, one of the chief theorists of the woman suffrage movement, criticized male religious figures for stressing self-sacrifice as the central virtue for women. She alleged that "men think that self-sacrifice is the most charming of all the cardinal virtues for women . . . and in order to keep it in healthy working order they make opportunities for its illustration as often as possible" (1895, I:84).

Anna Howard Shaw, Methodist minister turned suffragist orator, was also alarmed by the overemphasis on self-sacrifice in the moral teaching of the Christian churches to women: "The greatest defect in the religious teaching to and accepted by women is the dogma that self-abnegation, self-effacement, and excessive humility were ideal feminine virtues" (Shaw, n.d.: B22, F492).

In an 1893 sermon, Shaw suggested that women should be wary of situations in which they are asked to sacrifice their own self-development for the sake of a male relative. Shaw alleged that when a brother could be educated only if a sister was not; when a husband advanced because his wife set aside her own desires; or when a mother assisted her son at great personal cost; all too often "the sacrifice of the woman for the uplifting of the man seems to be the one thought, regardless of the principle of justice" (1960, II:56).

Seventy-five years later, Margaret Farley echoed the claim that women have too often found in practice that Christian self-sacrifice means the sacrifice of women for the sake of men: "Women . . . are painfully aware that for too long they have been primarily the servants of men, subject to the regulations of men, surrendered to the limitations imposed upon them by men" (Farley, 1975:58).

Perhaps feminist skepticism about self-sacrifice is most succinctly summarized by Mary Daly (1973:100) who alleged:

> There has been a *theoretical* one-sided emphasis upon charity, meekness, obedience, humility, self-abnegation, sacrifice, service. Part of the problem with this moral ideology is that it became accepted not by men, but by women, who hardly have been helped by an ethic which reinforces the abject female situation.

Men have espoused an ethic which they did not practice; women have practiced it to their detriment.

Industrialization and Feminine Sacrifice

It is no accident that women have been the ones to take the ethic of self-sacrifice most to heart, for women have been confined to the home—that arena where an ethic of self-giving seemed unambiguously appropriate. (See my discussion of Reinhold Niebuhr above.)

The contemporary overemphasis on self-sacrifice as the central Christian virtue is based upon an uncritical acceptance of the dichotomy between the private and public spheres of life. With industrialization the home and the workplace have become separated. One set of values including service and self-sacrifice are said to govern action within the home; another set, including rationality and assertiveness, to govern the workplace. Since women are identified primarily with the home, they become the persons called to a life of perpetual self-giving. Rosemary Ruether (1976:49–50) has accurately assessed the result for ethics of accepting a bifurcation of human experience into man's world and woman's place.

This split between the public realm or work as the sphere of material relations and functional rationality and the "home" as the feminine sphere of morality and sentiment had a devastating effect on both women and the quality of public culture.

As we have seen, women attempting to live lives ruled by *agape* defined as total self-giving lose the ability to act as responsible, centered selves. By contrast, men are condemned to spend a major portion of their lives in a public world where Christian values such as *agape* seem to have no place.[5]

Self-sacrifice as a Subordinate Virtue

While feminists have rejected an ethic which demands total self-giving of women as a means of promoting family stability within industrial society, some would concede that sacrificial acts can be legitimate. Anna Howard Shaw did not necessarily disapprove of women making sacrifices on behalf of others. What she criticized was an ethic shaped by men for women in which self-sacrifice was always the paramount virtue. Shaw asserted that when women compiled their own table of virtues they would retain self-sacrifice, but place by its side the complementary virtues of honesty, courage, and self-assertion. Women would insist upon the freedom to determine for themselves those situations in which they were morally obligated to assert their own claims for justice and those in which they would willingly sacrifice their own interests in order to benefit others.

Shaw was ill at ease with the notion that women should sacrifice their own self-development in order to smooth the way for men. However, she could accept the idea that self-determining women would make sacrifices for the sake of great moral causes, including, but not limited to, the cause of women's rights:

> It has been said that it is the greatest sacrifice one can make for a friend to give up one's life for one's love; . . . But how much richer, . . . is the praise of her who lays down her own good . . . for the good of another unknown, or for the good of a nation yet unborn. (1960, II:63–64)

Thus Shaw advocated that self-sacrifice be balanced by self-assertion and that sacrifice be made manifest by women in the public realm as well as in the domestic sphere.

Feminists know that loyalty to relationships or causes must sometimes be upheld at the cost of personal suffering. However, some are reluctant to label such sustained commitment sacrifice, because, for them, sacrifice connotes something destructive to the self. Mary Daly repudiates self-sacrifice. To her, that word implies both diminution of one's personal core and loss of contact with that Be-ing which women find/create deep within themselves.

Nonetheless, Daly's call for women to act with courage and discipline implicitly reveals that women must be prepared to accept suffering. However, the suffering which Daly accepts is suffering which results from a collective female struggle to end women's oppression, rather than from individual self-effacement on behalf of some man. It is the suffering endured in order to free creative female energies, not the pain which results from having such energy sapped by men (Daly, 1978).

Agape as Mutuality in Feminist Thought

While valuing courage and discipline in the struggle for justice, feminist thinkers have repudiated any notion of self-sacrifice as the quintessential feminine virtue. Contemporary feminist theologians have gone beyond a critique which questions the application of *agape* as a norm primarily in the case of women in domestic circumstances. Women's corrosive experience with *agape* defined as self-sacrifice has led them to articulate a different definition of *agape*. Feminists are gravitating toward a definition of love as mutuality which is in some ways similar to the definition offered by thinkers such as D'Arcy.

This trend in feminist ethics is typified by the work of Margaret Farley who defines *agape* as a full mutuality marked by equality between the sexes. For Farley, mutuality implies that all parties in a loving relationship display both active and receptive qualities. For women, receptivity is the stumbling block in Christian love, because receptivity has been distorted into demeaning passivity, submissiveness and self-surrender. Theologians have mistakenly asserted that God is totally active; the Christian, totally passive. They have assumed that the Christian is completely active on behalf of the neighbor; the neighbor, completely receptive. Such models for behavior leave no room for mutuality. Farley insists that both parties in a love relationship are active. The one who appears to be receptive is at the same time active. Receiving can be an active posture as for example when one "receives" a guest.

Love is the active affirmation of the goodness and beauty of the other. Theologians have failed to appreciate that "receiving and giving are but two sides of one reality which is other-centered love" (Farley, 1975:63). Beverly Wildung Harrison concurs that the love which is the Christian ideal has a rhythm involving taking as well as giving: "The love we want and need is mutual love. Love that sometimes has the quality of giving, but sometimes also the quality of receiving" (ms. in progress). Harrison insists that mutual love is so radical that most human beings are unable to maintain the openness and vulnerability which this love demands. It is not just self-giving which human beings find difficult, but also receptivity and dependence upon love from others. Christian ethicists are wrong to denigrate "mere mutuality," because true mutuality represents a demanding and precious enhancement of human life.

Friendship is an important paradigm of that mutuality which Farley and Harrison extol. Friendship is a relationship marked by mutual respect and regard. It is a reciprocal relationship in which all the parties are confirmed as having worth and hence all the parties are benefited. Eleanor Haney offers friendship as a key model of the good as feminists perceive it. Haney praises this human connection as one marked by respect, fidelity, trust, and affection, not competition, domination, or assertions of superiority. Friendship makes an excellent model for mutuality, because within a friendship, both the self and the other can be affirmed and enriched at one and the same time (Haney, 1980).

Grounding *Agape* as Mutuality

Christian ethicists who have stressed self-sacrifice as a central Christian virtue have frequently done so on Christological grounds. They assert that the life and especially the crucifixion of Jesus reveal him to be a person who pours himself out completely in service to others. Then they conclude that his followers should also live a life of complete self-giving.

Beverly Harrison has recently challenged an interpretation of the crucifixion of Christ as a sacrifice to the point of self-immolation *pursued for the sake of sacrifice*. She asserts that Jesus did not desire death on the Cross as a manifestation of total self-surrender. Rather he accepted death as the consequence of his unswerving commitment to mutual love. Jesus remained faithful to radical love even when his fidelity resulted in a life-endangering confrontation with the forces of loveless power—forces which threaten the dignity of persons. It is not suffering itself which Christians should seek. Rather we should emulate Jesus' absolute dedication to love which highlights human dignity.

Other feminists who stress mutuality, not sacrifice, turn to the Trinity, not the Atonement, for theological justification. Farley grounds *agape* as mutuality in Trinitarian, not Christological doctrines. She insists that a human love characterized by equality and mutuality best reflects the quality of relationship within the Trinity: "the First Person and the Second Person are infinitely active and infinitely receptive, infinitely giving and infinitely receiving, holding in infinite mutuality and reciprocity a totally shared life" (Farley, 1975:66–67).

But Farley knows that feminists are reluctant to turn to a Trinity symbolized in exclusively masculine terms for a vision of love. Therefore, she suggests that the traditional imagery used to portray the Trinity is not the only imagery suited to the task. Farley remarks that, in light of modern biology which reveals the active role of women in reproduction, God could be symbolized as Mother as well as Father. She proposes that the relationship between the First and Second Persons—a relationship marked by total mutuality—would better be conveyed in contemporary culture by the terms husband and wife than by the ancient Roman image of father and son. Thus Farley proposes new images of the Trinity to supplement the old.

CONCLUSIONS

Feminist work on the meaning of love presents a serious challenge to the dominant view among twentieth-century American ethicists. Women have demonstrated that excessive self-regard is not the sole root of human evil. Frequently for women the problem is too little self-assertion rather than too much. Neither self-sacrifice nor other-regard captures the total meaning of *agape*. The full expression of the Christian ideal is mutuality.

Agape redefined as mutuality cannot be a norm applicable within only one sphere of life. It must serve as a norm for political and economic life as well as family life. When mutuality is used as a norm for judging public life, it becomes apparent that the structures of society will have to undergo profound change.

The present division between the public and private has been possible largely because of women's sacrifice of themselves for the sake of other family members. Mutuality demands a reintegration of private and public life. There are two tasks which need to be done in order to move toward that goal. Ethicists need to imagine radically new ways of organizing social life so that work, politics, and personal life are meshed in a fashion which enhances the possibilities for mutuality.

At the same time that ethicists envision radically new structures, they must learn more about concrete conditions in the public world. This is necessary in order to develop specific strategies for the reintegration of life. In the split between the private and the public world, the humanities became allied with the private world of personal development. Thus ethicists have little actual experience with business which they scorn as an immoral enterprise. Given this recent history, ethicists will have to educate themselves about real world conditions in order to help evaluate options. Ethicists need to consider questions such as "How can we utilize new technologies like microcomputers to enhance life rather than to cause greater alienation?" Or "Should companies be urged to permit arrangements such as flextime as a contribution to the reintegration of public and private life?"

While Christians work to create structures which promote mutuality, they still face a world distorted by evil in which sacrifice of self-interest sometimes seems to be the more responsible course of action. However, according to feminist ethicists, sacrifice can no longer be considered the self-evident Christian solution to every moral conflict. Therefore, ethicists need to discuss criteria for discerning those situations in which sacrifice is legitimate.

As we have seen idealization of sacrifice has played a role in the victimization of women. This suggests that sacrifice is often inappropriate for the disadvantaged. Sacrifice by the privileged on behalf of the oppressed is much more likely to be justified.

Second, in situations in which the needs and desires of all parties cannot be satisfied, basic human needs (both physical and psychological) should be met first. The party in greater need has a *prima facie* claim on the other. Third, where the parties in the situation have a long-term relationship, they should attempt to balance the occasions of sacrifice. Most important, situations of sacrifice should be viewed as symptomatic of disruptions in the primordial harmony. Human beings should be dedicated to so providing for human needs and so diminishing oppression that situations calling for sacrifice are reduced to a minimum.

Farley's effort to resymbolize the Trinity in order to ground a feminist ethic of equality and mutuality demonstrates the problem of a Christian warrant for such a feminist ethic. She (1975:67) is unwilling to accept as adequate for women (and men) the traditional symbols of Father, Son and Spirit, if these are used exclusively. She rightly insists that "there be room in the process for women to know themselves . . . as able to be representatives of God as well as lovers of God." An equally important point is that men need to have the chastening experience of being unlike the Goddess.

It is, however, questionable whether any religion which unselfconsciously incorporates a female aspect of the Deity would remain Christianity. In the essay discussed here, Farley has been able to resymbolize the Trinity largely because she bracketed the incarnation. The Second Person of the Trinity can be imagined as logos or memory and still be Jesus of Nazareth. But can we really conceive of Jesus as wife? Can we truly accept as the Son of the Mother the one who came to do the will of the Father? The jarring character of the last two questions suggests that it will be extraordinarily difficult for Christianity to embody in its symbols a belief that women are full human beings and hence are equally capable of serving as symbols of divine power. Yet unless such fundamental changes in attitudes toward women and toward ultimate power come about it will not be possible to ground securely an ethic of mutuality in Christian religious dogmas.

NOTES

1. Niebuhr stressed the contrast between a mutual love prone to degenerate into less than love and *agape* or purely disinterested love. Daniel Day Williams (1968) challenged this sharp contrast. He attempted to show that there was a greater continuity between mutual love and *agape*. Nonetheless, Williams agreed that sacrificial love represented the pinnacle of Christian love. Therefore, Williams, along with Niebuhr and Nygren, is open to the feminist critique with respect to the role he accords sacrificial love.

2. Any analysis of Outka's own position based upon *agape* must remain tentative. Outka clearly states that his purpose is to examine religious treatments of *agape*, not to construct his own theory of love. Nonetheless, a careful reading of this book provides hints concerning the position on *agape* which Outka finds most cogent.

3. D'Arcy is, of course, a Catholic ethicist. This brief exploration of contemporary Christian ethics suggests that the Catholic tradition offers more useful material for a feminist articulation of the meaning of *agape*. However, such a judgment is premature. Further study would be required to investigate fully the relationship between the emerging feminist position and earlier Christian discussions.

4. In the first section of this article I confined my investigation to the work of twentieth century Christian ethicists. However, in this section I shall broaden my focus to include the work of nineteenth as well as twentieth century feminists. Since women have had few opportunities to reflect critically on theological matters, it is important to pay attention to all those who have spoken. Moreover, there is a remarkable agreement among nineteenth and twentieth century feminists about the dangers of self-abnegation. Such uniform testimony concerning women's moral experience deserves serious consideration.

5. For an extended investigation of this topic see Harrison (1974 and 1975) and Ruether (1976).

REFERENCES

Daly, Mary
   1973 *Beyond God the Father: Toward a Philosophy of Women's Liberation.* Boston: Beacon Press.
   1978 *Gyn/Ecology: the Metaethics of Radical Feminism.* Boston: Beacon Press.
D'Arcy, Martin C.
 - 1956 *The Mind and Heart of Love: Lion and Unicorn a Study in Eros and Agape.* New York: Meridian Books.
Farley, Margaret
   1975 "New patterns of relationship: beginnings of a moral revolution." Pp. 51–70 in Walter Burkhardt, ed., *Woman: New Dimensions,* New York: Paulist Press.
Goldstein, Steve
   1980 "A year to grow—and to remember," *New York Daily News,* July 20, pp. 14–16.
Goldstein, Valerie Saiving
   1960 "The human situation: a feminine view," *The Journal of Religion* (April). Reprinted in Carol P. Christ and Judith Plaskow, eds., *Womanspirit Rising,* New York: Harper and Row Publishers, 1980, pp. 25–42.
Haney, Eleanor Humes
   1980 "What is feminist ethics? a proposal for continuing discussion," *The Journal of Religious Ethics* 8/1 (Spring), 115–124.
Harrison, Beverly Wildung
   1981? "Anger as a work of love: Christian ethics for women and other strangers," *Union Theological Quarterly* (in progress).
   1975 "The new consciousness of women: a socio-political resource," *Cross Currents* 24 (Winter), 445–62.
   1974 "Sexism and the contemporary church: when evasion becomes complicity," in Alice L. Hageman, ed., *Women and Religion: Voices of Protest,* New York: Association Press, pp. 195–216.
Niebuhr, Reinhold
   1932 *Moral Man and Immoral Society.* New York: Charles Scribner's Sons.
   1941 *The Nature and Destiny of Man,* Volume 1. New York: Charles Scribner's Sons.
   1943 *The Nature and Destiny of Man,* Volume II. New York: Charles Scribner's Sons.
Nygren, Anders
   1932 *Agape and Eros.* Philadelphia: Westminster Press.

Outka, Gene
   1972 *Agape: An Ethical Analysis.* New Haven: Yale University Press.
Ruether, Rosemary Radford, and Eugene Bianchi
   1976 *From Machismo to Mutuality: Woman—Man Liberation.* New York: Paulist Press.
Shaw, Anna Howard
   n.d.   Manuscript, the Schlesinger Library, Radcliffe College. The Dillon Collection, the Shaw Series, Box 22, Folder 492.
   1960 *The Speeches of Anna Howard Shaw: Collected and Edited with Introduction and Notes.* Wilmer A. Linkugel, ed. Ann Arbor: University Microfilms.
Stanton, Elizabeth Cady, et al.
   1895 *The Woman's Bible.* New York: European Publishing Company.
Steinem, Gloria
   1980 "Getting off the plantation with Lorna, Bessie, Joyce and Bernadette," *Ms.,* August, pp. 39–40.
Williams, Daniel Day
   1968 *The Spirit and Forms of Love.* New York: Harper and Row.

11

MORAL VALUES AND BLACK WOMANISTS

Toinette M. Eugene

> I come out of a tradition where those things are valued; where you talk
> about a woman with big legs and big hips and black skin. I come out of a
> black community where it was all right to have hips and be heavy. You
> didn't feel that people didn't like you. The values that [imply] you must be
> skinny come from another culture. . . . Those are not the values that I was
> given by the women who served as my models. I refuse to be judged by the
> values of another culture. I am a Black woman, and I will stand as best as I
> can in that imagery.*

The values black women have derived for themselves and have offered as options
to the black community as well as to the members of a broader, dominant society
cannot be understood or adequately explained apart from the historical context
in which black women have found themselves as moral agents. Moreover, the
moral values that black women have provided as a legacy to the black
community as well as to the feminist movement in American society suggest a
distinctive religious consciousness and documentable religious traditions which
have been irrepressible in redeeming and transforming an entire human
environment.

The central theses of this essay, which traces specific moral values and black
feminism to their root causality within black religious traditions, are also theses
derived in part from the highest expressions of moral and faith development as
described particularly in the theoretical research and publications of Carol
Gilligan and James Fowler.[1]

By drawing upon this psychological research and by reviewing black religious
history, this essay asserts that public activism and private endurance are
paradigmatic of black women's value indicators in both the black religious
traditions and in feminist communities. Social activism, self-sacrifice, and other
similar value indicators may be verified in the lives of Mary McLeod Bethune
and Nannie Helen Burroughs, to name but two exemplary models. Nevertheless, these value measures and these valuable models represent more than unusual
courage and strength; they also represent realistic responses to economic
deprivation and political and social inequality. Black women have been forced to

---

*Bernice Reagon, *Black Women and Liberation Movements.*

perform labor and to take risks that few white women have been called upon to do, either in the name of religious traditions or in behalf of the survival of their race.

Black women, however, are not special specimens of womanhood; rather, they are women who have been given less protected and more burdensome positions in society. As Michelle Wallace has so poignantly pointed out, this has resulted in the "myth of the superwoman," which is not a description of black women but, rather, a measure of the difference between what is regularly expected of white women and what is essentially required of black women.[2]

It is obvious that black women have experienced oppressive structures of racism, class bias, and male supremacy in both religion and society in this country. What is not always so obvious to a dominant white-world view, and even to feminist theological understandings, is that Afro-American culture and religion have generated alternative interrelated notions of womanhood contradictory to those of mainstream American economics, society, and theology.[3] These alternative experiences, visions, and images of womanhood have been forged out of the furnace of a moral value system endemic to the black church.

This essay will explore aspects of the moral consciousness and value system that guides black women in their ongoing struggle for survival through a commentary on black religious traditions in which black women share. Within this commentary some reflections will also be offered regarding black women's perspectives on feminism as a white women's movement and on feminist theologies.

BLACK WOMEN AND
MORAL VALUES DURING SLAVERY

Historically, the black church has been the fiery furnace through which systematic faith affirmations and liberating principles for biblical interpretation have been developed by black people. Within this "invisible institution," hidden from the observation of slave masters, black women, along with black men, developed an extensive moral value system and religious life of their own. In the language of moral-development theorist Carol Gilligan, they established and operated out of a web or network of relationships and intimacy with others in community.[4] The moral values of care, compassion, and cooperation with other black and oppressed persons served as criteria for decisions and actions intended to lay hold of the good, the true, and the beautiful.

The biblical interpretations of the antebellum black church which provided black people with webs of relationships centering on the God of justice and of liberation made slaves incontestably discontented with their servile condition. In the case of black women whose bodies and spirits were wantonly violated by the immoral sexual advances of white masters, the moral value system of black people in this period encouraged slave women to eliminate the sources of their oppression in order to maintain and sustain their fragile nexus with God, community, and self as valued and trusted friends. Paula Giddings, in her text, *When and Where I Enter: The Impact of Black Women on Race and Sex in America,* reports on the moral resistance black slave women offered:

> So, by the early eighteenth century an incredible social, legal, racial structure was put in place. Women were firmly stratified in the roles that Plato envisioned. Blacks were chattel, White men could impregnate a Black woman with impunity, and she alone could give birth to a slave. Blacks constituted a permanent labor force and metaphor that were perpetuated through the Black woman's womb. And all of this was done within the context of the Church, the operating laws of capitalism, and the psychological needs of White males. Subsequent history would be a variation on the same theme.
>
> In its infancy slavery was particularly harsh. Physical abuse, dismemberment, and torture were common. . . . Partly as a result, in the eighteenth century, slave masters did not underestimate the will of their slaves to rebel, even their female slaves. Black women proved especially adept at poisoning their masters, a skill undoubtedly imported from Africa. Incendiarism was another favorite method; it required neither brute physical strength nor direct confrontation. But Black women used every means available to resist slavery— as men did—and if caught, they were punished just as harshly.[5]

In the midst of this dehumanizing slave environment, black families survived. They overcame the slaveholders' attempts to reduce them to so many subhuman labor units, managing to create an ongoing system of family arrangements and kin networks. Domestic life became critically important, for it was the only place where slaves had any equality and autonomy as human beings in relation to one another.[6]

Regarding domestic life and labor, Angela Davis, in *Women, Race and Class,* has observed a paradox of great significance for black women and men:

> The salient theme emerging from domestic life in the slave quarters is one of sexual equality. The labor that slaves performed for their own sake and not for the aggrandizement of their masters was carried out on terms of equality. Within the confines of their family and community life, therefore, Black people managed to accomplish a magnificent feat. They transformed that negative equality which emanated from the equal oppression they suffered as slaves into a positive quality: the egalitarianism characterizing their social relations.[7]

Harriet Tubman and countless others provided egalitarian images of slave women as strong, self-reliant, proud of their roots and of their ability to survive, convinced of their right to a place in society through the liberation of all black people. Equally oppressed as laborers, equal to their men in the domestic sphere, they were also equal in their moral resistance to slavery, participating in work stoppages and revolts, fleeing north and helping others to flee.

The ability of black people to cope in a hostile society has endured into the twentieth century; studies of black women in urban situations show that the means by which black families survived slavery still enable black women and their families to survive today.

Within this historical framework of past and present hostility black women have always perceived networks of relationality in the liberation struggle differently from white women. Domesticity has never been seen as entirely oppressive but rather as a vehicle for building family life under slavery; male/female relationships have always been more egalitarian; there has been less emphasis on women's work as different from and inferior to men's; slaves and freed persons, male and female, have consistently tended to rebel against the sexual oppression of black women as well as the emasculation of black men. It is easy to understand why many black people today see the white feminist movement as an attempt to divide black people. Contemporary black feminists caution against espousing the more "radical" white feminist stances because they leave out, as irrelevant, black men, black children, black families. Consequently, a primary moral value for black people is articulated in this overarching and enduring black feminist position: solidarity among black people is essential for survival.

A dramatic statement of black women's unique attitude toward solidarity with black men is found in the 1977 statement of the Combahee River Collective, a black lesbian feminist group from Boston.

> Although we are feminists and lesbians we feel solidarity with progressive Black men and do not advocate the fractionalization that white women who are separatists demand. Our situation as Black people necessitates that we have solidarity around the fact of race. . . . We struggle together with Black men against racism, while we also struggle with Black men about sexism.[8]

These black lesbian feminists explicitly rejected a feminist separatism that equates all oppression with sexual oppression and fails fully to comprehend the reality that black women *and men* are victims of shared racial oppression. Feminist separatism is not a viable political philosophy for most black women. Ethicist Barbara Hilkert Andolsen, in her remarkable assessment of racism and American feminism, *Daughters of Jefferson, Daughters of Bootblacks,* issues a strong caveat to white women who are desirous of understanding the black feminist experience:

> Those of us who are white feminists need to be careful that we do not articulate limited strategies for dealing with sexism as if they were the only legitimate feminist strategies. White feminist separatist theories or strategies that ignore the strong bond forged between many black women and men in a shared struggle against racism do not speak to all women's experience.[9]

White feminists have a responsibility to learn about black women's perspectives on women's issues, to analyze how racist social structures may distort the impact of white feminist proposals, and to support black women in their self-defined struggle for liberation. Black feminists are creating their own analyses of sexism and of the interconnections between racism and sexism. White feminist theologians who are seeking to contribute to an inclusive feminist theology that respects and reflects the diversity of women's experience need to learn from the experiences, moral values, and feminist theology articulated by black women.

There is ample material to draw upon from the insights of the distinctive theological consciousness of black women during slavery. For example, the biblical exegetical abilities of Maria Stewart coupled with her assumptions (what would later be known as modernist thinking) gave black women in 1832 a freer rein to express and act upon ideas that liberated them from the oppression of both sexism and racism.[10] For Stewart, simple logic demanded that in light of the role of women in the past, "God at this eventful period should raise up your females to strive . . . both in public and private, to assist those who are endeavoring to stop the strong current of prejudice that flows so profusely against us at present."[11] Maria Stewart was sure enough of her moral values to admonish others not to doubt the mission of her gender. "No longer ridicule their efforts," she counseled. "It will be counted as sin."[12]

At a women's rights convention in Akron, Ohio, in 1851, several of the most celebrated examples of early black feminist theological perspectives were rendered by the legendary abolitionist and mystic, Sojourner Truth, in her famous "Ain't I a Woman?" speech. From the very beginning of the conference, the white women were overwhelmed by the jeering ridicule of men who had come to disrupt the meeting. Their most effective antagonist was a clergyman who used both the gender of Jesus and the helplessness of the women to counter their feminist arguments. Sojourner squelched the heckler by correcting his theology first, noting that Jesus came from "God and a woman—man had nothing to do with Him."[13] Second, Truth asserted that women were not inherently weak and helpless.

Raising herself to her full height of six feet, flexing a muscled arm, and bellowing with a voice one observer likened to the apocalyptic thunders, Truth informed the audience that she could outwork, outeat, and outlast any man. Then she challenged, "Ain't I a Woman?"[14] She spoke of women's strength and moral abilities to set things aright: "If the first woman God ever made was strong enough to turn the world upside down all alone, these women together ought to be able to turn it back, and get it right side up again. And now they are asking to do it, the men better let them."[15] Moral values asserted by black women who give credence to the black Judeo-Christian tradition honor reconciliation as highly as liberation.

The accumulated experiences and expressions of black women during slavery were greatly influenced and nurtured by their webs of relationship with the black church and its biblical interpretations of the salvific power of God. These women who toiled under the lash for their masters, worked for and protected their families, fought against slavery and who were beaten, raped, but never subdued passed on to their nominally free female descendants a rich legacy of their own moral value system. It was a legacy of hard work so decidedly different from a White Anglo-Saxon Protestant (WASP) work ethic; it was a legacy of perseverance and self-reliance, a legacy of tenacity, resistance, and insistence on sexual equality—in short, a legacy of love spelling out standards for a new womanhood.[16]

FEMINIST MORAL VALUES AND
BLACK RELIGIOUS TRADITIONS

The institution of chattel slavery in America was destroyed by the most momentous national event of the nineteenth century, the Civil War. Emancipation removed the legal and political slave status from approximately four million black people in the United States, which meant that, in principle, these blacks owned their persons and their labor for the first time. Unfortunately for the vast majority of Afro-Americans, the traditional practices of racial and gender subordination subjected them to incredible suffering after that war.

The black woman began her life of freedom with no vote, no protection, and no equity of any sort. Black women, young and old, were basically on their own. The patterns of exploitation of the black woman as laborer and breeder were only shaken by the Civil War; by no means were they destroyed. Throughout the late nineteenth and early twentieth centuries, black women were severely restricted to the most unskilled, poorly paid, menial work. Virtually no black woman held a job beyond that of a domestic servant or field hand. Keeping house, farming, and bearing and rearing children continued to dominate all aspects of the black woman's life. The systematic oppression and routinized exclusion of black females from other areas of employment served as confirmations for the continuation of the servile status of black women. As Jeanne Noble describes it, "While freedom brought new opportunities for black men, for most women it augmented old problems."[17] After emancipation, racism and male supremacy continued to intersect patriarchal and capitalist structures in definitive ways.

The religious consciousness of the black freedwoman in the latter nineteenth century focused on "uplifting the black community." The black female was taught that her education was meant not only to uplift her but also to prepare her for a life of service in the overall community. There was a general attitude, says Noble, that "Negro women should be trained to teach in order to uplift the masses."[18] This attitude provided an additional impetus for black women, such as Nannie Helen Burroughs, Charlotte Hawkins Brown, and Mary McLeod Bethune, to found schools. Although the curricula of these schools included academic subjects, there were large doses of industrial arts courses, particularly homemaking, and an environment that enforced codes of morality and thrift. It was biblical faith grounded in the prophetic tradition that helped black women devise strategies and tactics to make black people less susceptible to the indignities and proscriptions of an oppressive white social order.

Understanding the prophetic tradition of the Bible and of the black church has empowered black women to fashion a set of moral values on their own terms, as well as mastering, radicalizing, and sometimes destroying the pervasive negative orientations imposed by the values of the larger society. Also, they articulate possibilities for decisions and action which address forthrightly the circumstances that inescapably shape black life.

Flowing from black women's biblical faith grounded in the prophetic tradition, many black women have been inspired by the Bethune and Burroughs models to hold in high regard a diaconal model of black feminist theology which is extremely consistent with their experience and identity. Without necessarily rejecting white feminist models of theology that focus principally or only on mutuality and equality as essential components of liberation, the preferential choice made by many black feminists is for a theology of servant leadership that was espoused by Christ. This biblical model of feminist liberation theology is principally focused on solidarity with those who suffer or who are marginalized in any way. A much greater examination, integration, and expression of this black feminist perspective and alternative to "mainstream" models of feminist liberation theology is needed.[19]

Rosemary Ruether has been in the forefront among feminist theologians who have insisted that the eradication of racism must be a major priority. She has produced particularly illuminating analyses of the interconnections between racism and sexism.[20] When discussing the future of feminist theory in the academic world, Ruether acknowledges that she speaks from a "white western Christian context," and she calls for an inclusive feminist theology that must emerge out of "a network of solidarity" existing among many feminist communities "engaged in the critique of patriarchalism in distinct cultural and religious contexts," rather than "one dominant form of feminism that claims to speak for the whole of womankind."[21]

In contrast, black theologian Delores Williams has observed that although Ruether rightly emphasizes the increasing numbers of women students in theological schools and lauds the "enormous amount of solid work in all fields of feminist theology that has been accomplished in these past fifteen years," Ruether does not remind her audience that the work has been done by and on behalf of white women.[22] Black women are a tiny percentage among the graduate students in religion; they are an even smaller percentage of the faculties in departments of religion and seminaries. As of yet, there is no "enormous amount" of published work on black feminist theology to offset, or to dialogue with, the claims Ruether cavalierly makes about feminist theology as if black perspectives on feminist theologies were abundantly or equally included.

During the mass migration of southern blacks to the North (1910–1925), tens of thousands of black women and men left home, seeking social democracy and economic opportunity. During this colossal movement of black people, the black church continued to serve as the focal point and center for maintaining the moral value system and the network of relationships which sustained community life.

Not surprisingly, this accelerated movement of blacks out of the South impinged on the black woman's reality in very definite ways. Black women migrated north in greater numbers than black men. Economic necessity dictated that most black women who immigrated to the urban centers find work immediately. In order to survive themselves and to provide for their families, black women once again found only drudge work available to them.

The interaction of race and sex on the labor market exacted a heavy toll on the black woman, making all aspects of migration a problem of paramount religious significance. Her experience as a wife and a mother, responsible for transmitting the moral values, culture, and customs of the black community to her children, served as a decisive factor in determining how the Bible was read and understood. Simultaneously while the black woman was trying to organize family life according to black traditional roles, the white male-dominated industrial society required that she serve as a catalyst in their labor transition process. Her own unfamiliarities and adaptation difficulties had to be repressed because she was responsible for making a home in crowded substandard housing, finding inner-city schools that propagated literacy for her children, and earning enough income for her family to cover the most elementary needs.

The moral and religious value system of the black church served as a sustaining force and as an interpretive principle that guided migrant black women in facing life squarely, in acknowledging its raw coarseness. The white elitist attributes of passive gentleness and an enervative delicacy, considered particularly appropriate to womanhood, proved nonfunctional in the pragmatic survival of black women. Cultivating conventional amenities was not a luxury afforded them. Instead, black women are aware that their very lives depended upon their being able to decipher the various sounds in the larger world, to hold in check the nightmare figures of terror, to fight for basic freedoms against the sadistic law enforcement agencies in their communities, to resist the temptation to capitulate to the demands of the *status quo*, to find meaning in the most despotic circumstances, and to create something where nothing existed before. The expression of a moral value system for black women meant and required a "sheroic" self-sacrifice and self-giving that could not ever afford shyness, silence, softness, or diffidence as a response indicating subservience.

From the period of black urban migration through World Wars I and II, black women who were rooted in the strong moral values and prophetic traditions of the black church became religious crusaders for justice. Mary McLeod Bethune and her associates recorded and talked about the grimness of struggle among the least visible people in the society. Bethune was adamant about the unheralded achievements of black women, always encouraging them to "go to the front and take our rightful place; fight our battles and claim our victories."[23] She believed in black women's "possibilities," moral values, and their place on this earth. "Next to God," she once said, "we are indebted to women, first for life itself, and then for making it worth having."[24]

In response to the hostile environment, deteriorating conditions, and the enduring humiliation of the social ostracism experienced by black people especially during these war years, Bethune and company exposed the most serious and unyielding problem of the twentieth century—the single most determining factor of black existence in America—the question of color. In their strategic attacks against the ideological supremacy of racist practices and values, they appealed to the religious traditions of black people that began in their invisible church during slavery.

From the period of urbanization of World War II to the present, black women still find that their situation is a struggle to survive collectively and individually against the harsh historical realities and pervasive adversities of today's world. Federal government programs, civil rights movements, and voter-education programs have all had a positive impact on the black woman's situation, but they have not been able to offset the negative effects of inherent inequities that are inextricably tied to the history and ideological hegemony of racism, sexism, and class privilege.[25]

Precisely because of this reality and overwhelmingly oppressive national ideology, Rosemary Ruether warns white feminists to give explicit attention to the ways in which they are involved in race and class privilege. If they do not, she says, they risk social encapsulation.

> Any woman's movement which is only concerned about sexism and not other forms of oppression, must remain a woman's movement of the white upper class, for it is only this group of women whose only problem is the problem of being women, since in every other way, they belong to the ruling class.[26]

Moreover, both black and white feminist groups that do not give explicit attention to the realities yoking racism and sexism will find that they can be easily manipulated by dominant males who appeal to unexamined class and race interests to achieve economic exploitation of all women. Work and dialogue between feminists of color and white feminists in this essential area is, in some sense, just beginning. Meanwhile, black women and their families continue to be enslaved to hunger, disease, and the highest rate of unemployment since the Depression years. Advances in education, housing, health care, and other necessities are deteriorating faster now than ever before.[27]

Both in informal day-to-day life and in the formal organizations and institutions of society, black women are still the victims of the aggravated inequities of the tridimensional phenomenon of race/class/gender oppression. It is in this context that the moral values of black women and the emergence of black feminist consciousness shaped by black biblical and religious traditions must continue to make a decisive difference for a debilitated and nearly dysfunctional human environment.

WOMANIST RELATIONSHIPS, MORAL VALUES AND BIBLICAL TRADITIONS

Because of a social reality, which is so totally demoralizing, and because of the religious traditions from which most black women have come, the Bible has been the highest source of authority in developing and delivering a black moral praxis and a moral theology that is usable in all circumstances. By selectively utilizing the pages of revered Old Testament books, black women have learned how to refute the stereotypes that have depicted black people as ignorant minstrels or vindictive militants. Remembering and retelling the Jesus stories of the New Testament has helped black women to deal with the overwhelming difficulties of overworked and widowed mothers, or underworked and anxious fathers, of sexually exploited and anguished daughters, or prodigal sons, and of dead or dying brothers whose networks of relationality are rooted deeply in the black community. Black feminist consciousness and moral values grow out of and expand upon black, biblical experience and hermeneutics.

Black feminist consciousness may be more accurately identified as black womanist consciousness, to use Alice Walker's concept and definition. In the introduction to *In Search of Our Mothers' Gardens*, Walker proposes several descriptions of the term "womanist," indicating that the word refers primarily to a black feminist and is derived from "womanish," that is, outrageous, audacious, courageous, or willful behavior.[28] To be a faithful womanist, then, or to operate out of this system of black moral value indicators which flow from biblical understandings based on justice and love, is to express in word and deed an alternative ontology or way of living in the world that is endemic to many black women. It is precisely womanist religious responses of endurance, resistance, and resiliency offered in the face of all attempts at personal and institutional domination that may provide a renewed theological legacy of liberation for everyone concerned.

In exploring the implications contained in Walker's richly descriptive prose, it is possible to make some concluding reflections on black moral values and on the contribution of black women's life experiences as they interface with white feminist liberation theologies.

Womanist responses and black moral values are meant to be alternative standards of womanhood and contradictory and paradoxical to those of mainstream American society. Womanist images and black moral values are meant to be paradigmatic of an authentic Christian community of the oppressed that embraces not only the story of the resurrection, but is moreover a referent for the redemptive tribulations through which Jesus as Suffering Servant has come. Womanist moral values are expressed through radical healing and empowering actions with those who are considered as the very least in the reign of God.

Walker adds that a womanist is "committed to the survival and wholeness of entire people, male *and* female. Not a separatist . . . [she] is traditionally capable."[29] The practical implications of such meanings for interaction and dialogue between black women's moral values and the diverse tenets of white feminist ethics are obvious and challenging. Black womanist moral values can redeem us from naivete regarding the nature and function of liberation as well as deliver us from a simplistic, black pseudo expression of providence, that "de Lawd will provide." Nonetheless, a womanist religious tradition does subscribe to the black folk wisdom that God can make a way out of no way for those, like Zora Neale Hurston and others, who just refuse to resign from the human race.

Womanist moral values of "appreciation for the struggle, a love of the folk, and a love of self—*regardless*"[30] offer to all black people and to all others a continual and open means of interaction between those who claim diverse womanist and feminist identities and experiences, and among all those who have a significant agenda for more authentic theologies of liberation.

NOTES

1. Carol Gilligan, *In a Different Voice: Psychological Theory and Women's Development* (Cambridge: Harvard University Press, 1982), and James W. Fowler, *Stages of Faith: The Psychology of Human Development and the Quest for Meaning* (San Francisco: Harper and Row, 1981).

2. Michelle Wallace, *Black Macho and the Myth of the Superwoman* (New York: Dial Press, 1979).

3. Toinette M. Eugene, "Black Women Contribute Strong Alternate Images," *National Catholic Reporter,* April 13, 1984, p. 4.

4. Carol Gilligan as described in James W. Fowler, *Becoming Adult, Becoming Christian* (San Francisco: Harper and Row, 1984), pp. 39–40.

5. Paula Giddings, *When and Where I Enter: The Impact of Black Women on Race and Sex in America* (Toronto: Bantam Books, 1984), p. 39.

6. Herbert Gutman, *The Black Family in Slavery and Freedom, 1750–1925* (New York: Pantheon Books, 1976), pp. 356–357.

7. Angela Y. Davis, *Women, Race and Class* (New York: Random House, 1981), p. 18.

8. Combahee River Collective, "A Black Feminist Statement," in *This Bridge Called My Back: Writings by Radical Women of Color,* eds. Cherrie Moraga and Gloria Anzaldua (Watertown, MA: Persephone Press, 1981), p. 213.

9. Barbara Hilkert Andolsen, *Daughters of Jefferson, Daughters of Bootblacks: Racism and American Feminism* (Macon, GA: Mercer University Press, 1986), p. 98.

10. Paula Giddings, *When and Where I Enter,* p. 52.

11. Bert James Lowenberg and Ruth Bogin, eds., *Black Women in Nineteenth Century*

American Life: Their Words, Their Thoughts, Their Feelings (University Park and London: The Pennsylvania State University Press, 1976), p. 149.

12. Ibid.

13. Ibid., p. 236.

14. Ibid., p. 235.

15. Ibid., p. 236.

16. Angela Davis, *Women, Race and Class,* p. 29.

17. Jeanne L. Noble, *Beautiful, Also Are the Souls of My Black Sisters: A History of the Black Woman in America* (New York: Prentice Hall, 1978), p. 63.

18. Jeanne L. Noble, as discussed in Paula Giddings, *When and Where I Enter,* p. 101.

19. Toinette M. Eugene, "Black Women Contribute . . ."

20. Rosemary Ruether has written about racism many times. Two of her more detailed treatments of the topic are "Between the Sons of Whites and the Sons of Blackness: Racism and Sexism in America," in *New Woman/New Earth: Sexist Ideologies and Human Liberation* (New York: Seabury Press, 1975), pp. 115–33, and "Crisis in Sex and Race: Black Theology vs Feminist Theology," *Christianity and Crisis* 34 (15 April 1985): 67–73.

21. Rosemary Ruether, "Feminist Theology: On Becoming the Tradition," *Christianity and Crisis* 45 (4 March 1985): 58.

22. Delores Williams, "The Color of Feminism," *Christianity and Crisis* 45 (29 April 1985): 164–165.

23. Elaine M. Smith, "Mary McLeod Bethune and the National Youth Administration," *Clio Was a Woman: Studies in the History of American Women,* Mabel E. Deutrich and Virginia C. Purdy, eds. (Washington, D.C.: Howard University Press, 1980), p. 152.

24. Ibid.

25. Angela Davis, *Women, Race and Class,* pp. 231–232.

26. Rosemary Ruether, *New Woman/New Earth,* p. 116.

27. *Facts on U.S. Working Women,* U.S. Department of Labor Women's Bureau, Fact Sheet No. 85–6, July 1985.

28. Alice Walker, *In Search of Our Mothers' Gardens: Womanist Prose* (San Diego: Harcourt Brace Jovanovich, 1983), pp. xi–xii.

29. Ibid., p. xi.

30. Ibid.

12

HETEROSEXIST THEOLOGY

Being Above It All

Carter Heyward

HETEROSEXISM

Sexism is the foundation of heterosexism. Heterosexist theology is constructed on the assumption that male domination of female lives is compatible with the will of God. The rightness of compulsory heterosexuality is predicated on the belief in a natural order or process that alone is good—so that any deviation from it is sinful. Basing contemporary moral theory on medieval concepts of natural law necessitates projecting an image or fantasy of "good order" onto human social relations—thereby denying altogether the role of human agency in determining moral good.[1]

While belief in natural law may not strike us as necessarily heterosexist, in a sexist situation like the praxis of the church the assumption of a natural order is infused with corollary presuppositions about gender and sexuality.[2] It is in this social praxis, historical and contemporary, that the image of heterosexual marriage emerges as the prototype for the Right—i.e., the Natural and Moral—Relation not only between male and female, but also between Christ and his church. Compulsory heterosexuality safeguards this divinely willed Right Relation. To coerce heterosexual bonding is simply to affirm what is natural. And what is natural reflects the good order of the cosmos, thereby revealing the divine purpose. The Be-ing of God involves being heterosexual.

In the church, individualistic psychology is often drawn on for support in upholding the sanctity of compulsory heterosexual relations. Thus church bodies often commission psychiatrists to make clinical judgments of the "maturity" of

This essay is from a panel presentation on Lesbian Feminist Issues in Religion (Women and Religion Section) at the American Academy of Religion, Anaheim, Calif., Nov. 25, 1985. It was expanded into a book, *A Sacred Contempt: Heterosexism and the Liberal God* (New York: Harper and Row, 1989).

individual candidates for the ordained ministry. More often than not, "maturity" is understood by the ecclesiastical authority (and often by the psychiatrist) as synonymous with heterosexual marriage or, at least, with the candidate's willingness to abstain from any sexual activity outside such marriage. On this basis, church authorities frequently will deny that they are against homosexuality per se, but rather will insist that they are opposed to all sexual activity outside of marriage, heterosexual as well as homosexual. To the rejoinder that *homosexual* marriages are not permitted in the church, the typical response is, "Of course not," as if the very notion were unintelligible to Christian sensibilities of what is both natural and moral.[3]

It should not be surprising that the church would consecrate psychology as its Great High Priest. Psychology, in large part, remains the most highly individualistic of the modern sciences, and liberals have strong investment in the interior life and yearnings of individuals as the locus of sin and grace, problems and transformation.[4] Moreover, what is psychologically "normal" provides the content for the theologian's understanding of the natural and moral. What is specifically lacking is a *critical* analysis of the ways in which unjust power relations between men and women shape the lens through which we view the natural/moral order. Liberal proponents of natural law fail to enter into serious engagement with those whose lives are marginalized by its truth-claims.

My thesis in this essay is that liberal Christianity is morally bankrupt in relation to women and all homosexual persons. In fact, the liberal church damages these people because, as a theo-political ideology, liberalism is not only set against collective advocacy as a primary mode of Christian witness; it is also contemptuous of the particular claims of feminist and all openly gay/lesbian people. In what follows I attempt to illustrate why.

Specifically I shall contend that Paul Tillich, as a paradigmatic modern liberal, presents an amoral, individualistic God-Man as constitutive of Being itself. Moreover, the contemporary liberal church, as represented by the praxis of mainline denominations, operates on the same nonrelational and irresponsible assumptions about divine and human life. Most important, the individual's experience of *normative* Christian life is steeped historically in heterosexism.

GOD ABOVE GOD

Hannah Tillich, Paul's widow, tells of a conversation between "the old woman and the old man":

> "Why do you always remain on the borderline?" asked the old woman. "Why can't you decide between Yin and Yang, between the mountains and the deep blue sea? . . ."
>
> "Why should I decide?" retorted the old man nastily. "I don't know where I belong. Besides, indecision allows for freedom."[5]

Paul Tillich went beyond the romantic reductionism of natural law into a more complex theological reasoning which took some account of the ambiguities of human existence. Still, Tillich's theology suffered from problems classic to liberal philosophy. First, he did not have an adequate understanding of the social, relational basis of either human or divine Being. "Being" is constitutive of the inner life of the individual agent. Second, for this reason, Tillich did not see the *theological* significance of the material, embodied, and economic grounds of human being. His specific focus was on the ability of the well-educated Euroamerican male to cope spiritually within the "structures of existence." His concept of God, a logical companion piece to his anthropology, floats free of the contingencies of relationality, physicality, and material need—and, thus, as Alison Jaggar would suggest, from our actual "ground of being."[6]

Tillich recognizes his own "estrangement" as constitutive of his "existence." He notes a problem with the extent to which Christian theologians traditionally have rendered estrangement—or sin—as rooted in "concupiscence," defined narrowly as sexual desire. Of the church's "ambiguous" attitude toward sex, Tillich writes, "The church has never been able to deal adequately with this central ethical and religious problem."[7]

Interestingly, Tillich seems puzzled by this lingering "devaluation of sex" in Christian tradition. He evidently fails to notice a connection in Christian history between the devaluation of sex and the devaluation of women. This failure itself reflects the bias in Tillich's perspective on the meaning of estrangement, creation, existence, and essence. In other words, his world view—grounded in his experience and articulated in his theology—reveals much about the "actualized creation and estranged existence" of a white male German academic failing to acknowledge (or perhaps even to notice) that the limits of this theological epistemology are set not only by his "finitude" as "man" but more particularly by his experience as one white German male.

Writing on behalf of all men (and I leave intact the linguistic ambiguity of Tillich's theology), Tillich subsumes the conditions of human existence under a series of ontological polarities. Every man lives in tension between the angst of his existence and the divine essence from which he has fallen into this alienated situation. Tillich's fundamental image of human life reflects the [his] experience of existing between death/dying and life/living. While Tillich's academic concern is not, basically, a moral one, and while he does not reduce death to evil or life to good, his theology suggests that human existence is synonymous with a moral struggle against Nonbeing and that, in the struggle, justice is actualized as a moral good. Still, this existential process is located in the life of the individual man.[8] As Norene M. Carter has demonstrated, since Tillich fails to present alienation as a social, material condition, his ontology does not address responsibly the moral issues involved in human alienation from other humans, the rest of creation, or the Creator.[9] For human angst originates not in the individual's psychospiritual ontology but rather in the historical structures of alienated social relations which render each person victor or vanquished in a myriad of relational configurations which are beyond her or his individual capacity to alter.

To those who cannot accept the traditional God of theism, Tillich offers the image of a "God above God" who is eternally beyond the structures of existence.[10] It is from this God above God that we have fallen into alienated existence. And it is with this God that we can reunite in New Being, through participation and transformation by Christ, the Essential God-Man.[11] In refusing to confuse essence with existence, God with man—even in Christ— Tillich misleads us, drawing us away from realizing the part we may play in the drama of salvation.

Tillich does not deny the importance of human "acceptance" of the New Being.[12] He also does not, however, stress the role of human agency in salvation. This is probably because he does not recognize the corporate character of being—either human or divine—and thus, is stuck both epistemologically and soteriologically in his perception that "man" (the individual white male) must be "grasped" by an ontological force (Being, or the Christ) outside himself, before he can participate in the drama of salvation. Ironically, while Tillich is attempting to present a theology that cuts through the individualism of human existence, he fails to grasp the power of human subjectivity when "humanity" is understood as an *essentially corporate reality:*

> The objective reality of the New Being precedes subjective participation in it. . . . Regeneration [and conversion], understood in this way, have little in common with the attempt to create emotional reactions in appealing to an individual in his subjectivity.[13]

Tillich draws us beyond the structures of our existence—however dehuman- izing, and oppressive—toward an "essence" that should not be confused with our daily human experiences of love and work, pain and struggle, confusion and play. But does it suffice to suggest that our alienation originates in our fall from God, in the spiritual malaise of individual men and women? It may be small comfort to imagine that the solution to our predicament is to bear up courageously on the basis of whatever mental gymnastics enable us to leap high enough to probe deep enough to be grasped by New Being.

Despite his insistence that it is entirely at the initiative of the "divine Spirit" that "man" is "grasped" by the "New Being," the bulk of Tillich's work reflects his efforts to seek, find, and be open to the "essential Godman."[14] Again, the problem is that Tillich did not acknowledge the collective, relational, sensual and embodied ground on which he stood with others, a "ground of being" on which justice-making has more to do with one's acceptance of social, relational responsibility than with one's actualization of "as many potentialities as possible without losing oneself in disruption and chaos."[15]

Tillich takes little account of the social, political, historical character of each individual, thus little account of the limits of the individual's spiritual aspirations. Neither Tillich nor other liberal Christians comprehend deeply creative power—at once human and divine—as historically and ontologically embodied among us, transacted between and among ourselves daily as co-creative agents upon whom the Power of Love in history depends. The liberal deity may, in some anthropomorphic sense, "love" us, but it is likely to tax our understandings of what actual loving involves, because a God above God (or an Essential God-Man) remains eternally unaffected by the clamor and clutter of human struggle, including the passions, problems, and confusions of human sexuality.

On the surface, Tillich's theology has nothing to do with sexism, heterosexism, racism, or any other "ism." That is precisely the point of liberal philosophy. God is simply above the fray. This, more than any other, is the grievance of Latin American, Afro-American, Asian American, and feminist liberation theologians against the "objectivity" espoused by liberal theological scholars. This "objectivity" presupposes the subject's ability to manufacture a critical distance between himself and his object of study (such as "God") in order to produce a theology free of bias or ideology.

A more perceptive hermeneutic suggests, however, that Tillich's theology, his portrait of God, has *everything* to do with holding traditional power arrangements in place. For his God above God is finally indifferent to the details of how we live together on the earth. The Prince of Wales and the prisoner on death row, the murdered gay activist Harvey Milk and his murderer Dan White, have the same ontological constitution and live under the same conditions of existence. Their salvation histories involve, essentially, the same angst. A liberal disposition fails to notice its own moral bankruptcy.

Unlike the traditional GodFather, whose anthropomorphic antagonism toward uppity women and wanton sexual behavior is well documented in Christian history, the liberal God of self-consciousness, human potential, and science controls women and homosexual people not because he is hostile to us (God forbid!), but rather because he is neutral in relation to us. Liberal morality is a basically individualistic realm, in which the subject determines right from wrong. In Friedrich Schleiermacher's words,

> In the sinful nature the bad exists only correlatively with the good, and no moment is occupied exclusively by sin. . . . Insofar as the consciousness of our sin is a true element of our being, *and sin therefore a reality,* it is ordained by God as that which makes redemption necessary. (italics mine)[16]

Not only are good and evil, grace and sin, necessary correlates in the work of redemption in liberal Protestantism, but the reality of sin is predicated upon our noticing it! And we are first and finally moral monads, accountable to the pangs of our own God-*consciousness,* not to a God whose justice may be calling us to account *regardless* of how we feel about it or what we think.

To believe that we can discern our own ethics, choose from many options, and act on the basis of individual "conscience" is, in effect, to admit defeat in the struggle against the structures of our alienation. It is to give *explicit* assent to the immoral proposition that whether one rapes or not, pays taxes or not, drops the bomb or not are decisions that only the responsible individual or individuals can make. It is furthermore to give implicit assent to the dualistic assumption that such matters, in historical fact, are none of God's business. In the realm of God, the opinions of a Jerry Falwell and a John McNeill are of equal consequence—none at all. For the liberal deity has turned over to us the realm of human affairs. What we do, each of us, about racism, sexism, heterosexism or any other human problem is our business.

To their peril, many women as well as male homosexual Christians draw upon the moral neutrality of Christian liberalism in arguing for their right to live and let live.[17] This is finally a self-defeating argument, for the problems of injustice cannot be solved by appeals to "freedom" as a value-free "right."[18] From a moral perspective, freedom is not value-free; it is the power of personal agency in the context of *just* social relations—that is, relations in which the positive value of all persons has been established as a given. Of course, it is indeed logical that, pleading for "neutrality" and "freedom" in matters of morality, liberal Christians should have no reason to believe that God cares whether people are feminists, lesbians, or gay men. It would seem truer to its own ethical heritage if the liberal church were to say to its members who do not conform to traditional gender roles or sexual practices: "God doesn't care whether you are gay or straight, or whether you are a feminist or an adherent to traditional gender roles. God wants you to be true to yourself and faithful in relation to God and God's people." But this is not what most liberal churches have said.

In one sense, the implications of theological liberalism for gay men, lesbians and feminists are identical with those for all women, racial/ethnic minority peoples, the poor and others whose oppression should be of more immediate moral concern to church leaders than the spiritual pilgrimages of individuals. There is another sense, however, in which gender and sexual injustice occupy a special place at the hallowed table of Christian fellowship. Sexism and heterosexism receive a particular "blessing" from the liberal philosophical tradition's *trivialization* of the female gender and human sexuality as embodied, material, "lower" phenomena. The "normative dualism" of Christian liberalism has been shaped by sexism and sealed in heterosexism.[19] I need not elaborate here examples from the works of Christian Fathers who have located created, spiritual power in the hypothetically disembodied male mind.[20] Thus, today, while the material concerns of *men* of color and poor *men* can be subsumed *idealistically* into the liberal vision of a nonracist, nonclassist world, women and openly homosexual persons *embody and represent* the specific material phenomena which, in Christian idealism, came early to its full expression in the contributions of Augustine. From the standpoint of Christian idealism, then, to press seriously for women's liberation or for the affirmation of gay and lesbian sexual activity is to fly in the face of the idealistic tradition itself, in which femaleness and sexual activity are, de facto, ungodly and thus singularly undeserving of the justice that constitutes the liberal vision of the divinely ordained world.[21] Thus does liberal Christianity embody its own contradiction between its ideal of one, inclusive world and its sacred contempt for femaleness and sexual passion.[22]

While many liberal churches appear to have attended to the problem of sexism, they fail utterly to take heterosexism seriously and thus, in fact, fail to do justice to any women's lives, whether lesbian, heterosexual, bisexual, genitally active, genitally inactive, or celibate. It is important to note that the liberal churches have always displayed some measure of tolerance toward those women and those homosexual people whose *public* presence has been strictly in conformity with patriarchal social relations.[23] Passive, self-deprecating women, and men and women who have kept their homosexual activities "closeted" from public knowledge have been well received on the whole throughout Christian history. I would even conjecture that such women and men have comprised the larger part of the church. Women and homosexual people pose no practical problem to the church unless they *publicly challenge* the church's sexism and heterosexism. This is exactly what is happening today. Many feminists, gay men, and lesbians have begun to "come out" of concealment and put themselves visibly on the ecclesial line as representative of those women and men who, throughout Christian history and the ecumenical church today, have seen that the liberal Christian emperor has no clothes—no sense of the misogynist, erotophobic, and oppressive character of his realm.

Thus, it is true that from the standpoint of advanced patriarchal capitalist social relations, the liberal deity has begun to incorporate, superficially, the "rights" of women and of racial/ethnic minorities and the poor into his divine agenda, as *idealistic* moral claims which need not disrupt the harmony of life as it is meant to be lived in the realm of God. However, the feminist and gay/lesbian demand (not request) that women and homosexual persons be affirmed (not tolerated) poses a challenge not only to the good ordering of liberal social relations, but also a threat to the essence of liberal religion. For the liberal deity is, above all, a noncontroversial gentleman—the antithesis of much that is embodied by feminists and by openly gay and lesbian people who dare to challenge the moral deficit of liberal Christianity. At stake this time, from a feminist liberation perspective, are not the bodies of witches and faggots, but the nature and destiny of God.

NOTES

1. For constructive moral epistemologies which build on creative insights from natural law tradition, see Beverly Wildung Harrison, *Making the Connections: Essays in Feminist Social Ethics* (Boston: Beacon, 1985), especially the introduction by Carol S. Robb and 3–21, 115–34, and 235–63; Anthony Battaglia, *Toward a Reformulation of*

Natural Law (New York: Seabury, 1981); Daniel C. Maguire, *The Moral Choice* (New York: Doubleday, 1978); Margaret Farley, "New Patterns of Relationship: Beginnings of a Moral Revolution," in *Woman: New Dimensions,* ed. Walter J. Burghardt (New York: Paulist, 1976); and B. Andolsen, C. Gudorf, and M. Pellauer, eds., *Women's Conscious-ness, Women's Conscience* (Minneapolis: Winston Press), esp. 211ff.

2. See Samuel Laeuchli, *Power and Sexuality: The Emergence of Canon Law at the Synod of Elvira* (Philadelphia: Temple University Press, 1972); Anne Llewellyn Barstow, *On Studying Witchcraft as Women's History* (forthcoming); and the classic, infamous, *Malleus Maleficarum* (Hammer of Witches), by monks Sprenger and Kraemer, for the extent to which Christian assumptions about the natural as moral are steeped in misogyny. See also Harrison on the relation between hatred of women and fear of homosexuality, "Misogyny and Homophobia: The Unexplored Connections," in *Making the Connec-tions,* 135–51.

3. At least one seminary (The Episcopal Seminary in Alexandria, Virginia) requires all of its students to sign a pledge that they will not engage in sexual activity outside of marriage while they are students at the Seminary. And at least one psychiatrist who screens candidates for ordination in a liberal Episcopal diocese has indicated to those whom he interviews that their sexual behavior is *the* critical factor in his judging their fitness for ordination. While he expresses interest in hearing details of *heterosexual* lives, he makes no secret of his special disdain for gay men and lesbians, who are, in his judgment, "immature" and unfit for ordained ministry.

4. For attention to interiorized spirituality as a moral problem, see Dorothee Sölle (with Shirley Cloyes), *To Work and to Love: A Theology of Creation* (Philadelphia: Fortress, 1984), as well as other pieces by Sölle. This same theme is explored in the Amanecida Collective's *Revolutionary Forgiveness: Feminist Reflections on Nicaragua* (Maryknoll, N.Y.: Orbis, 1986), as well as throughout the growing corpus of liberation theologies. See, for example, Ernesto Cardenal, *The Gospel in Solentiname,* 4 vols., trans. Donald Walsh (Maryknoll, N.Y.: Orbis, 1976–82); Gustavo Gutiérrez, *The Power of the Poor in History,* trans. Robert Barr (Maryknoll, N.Y.: Orbis, 1983), and Phillip Berryman, *The Religious Roots of Rebellion: Christians in Central American Revolution* (Maryknoll, N.Y.: Orbis, 1984). In her essay, "While Love is Unfashionable: An Exploration of Black Spirituality and Sexuality," in *Women's Consciousness, Women's Conscience,* Toinette M. Eugene examines connections between justice, sexuality, and spirituality in Black experience.

5. Hannah Tillich, *From Time to Time* (New York: Stein and Day, 1973), 15. I am grateful to Tom F. Driver for reminding me how vividly Hannah Tillich writes of her husband's liberal disposition.

6. See Paul Tillich, *Systematic Theology,* 3 vols. (Chicago: University of Chicago Press), 2: esp. 155–58.

7. ST, 2:52.

8. See ST, 1:182–86 on "freedom and destiny"; and 1:255–56 and 2:29ff on "the Fall." Also *The Courage to Be* (New Haven: Yale University Press, 1952) and *Love, Power and Justice* (New York: Oxford University Press, 1954).

9. Norene M. Carter, a feminist ethicist who lives and works in the Boston area, discusses Marx's and Tillich's different understandings of alienation in an unpublished essay she wrote for Elisabeth Schüssler Fiorenza's and Carter Heyward's class on The Bible and Feminist Hermeneutics, Episcopal Divinity School, spring semester, 1985.

10. Tillich discusses "God above God" in *The Courage to Be.*

11. See ST, 2, esp. part 2.B:118–24.

12. ST, 2, esp. 2.E:165–79.

13. ST, 2:177.

14. ST, 2:178.

15. *Love, Power and Justice,* 70.

16. Friedrich Schleiermacher, *The Christian Faith,* ed. H. R. Mackintosh and J. S. Stewart, English trans. of 2nd German ed. (Philadelphia: Fortress, 1976), 332, 335.

17. This is the position of many gay advocacy groups in religion. Alternatives to this theology are being given voice by such gay/lesbian activists as David Fernbach, *The Spiral Path: A Gay Contribution to Human Survival* (Boston: Alyson, 1981), Mary E. Hunt, *Fierce Tenderness: Toward a Feminist Theology of Friendship* (San Francisco: Harper and Row, 1987), and Cherríe Moraga, *Loving in the War Years* (Boston: South End Press, 1983).

18. See James Luther Adams, *On Being Human Religiously,* ed. Max L. Stackhouse (Boston: Beacon Press, 1976), esp. 1–88, and Harrison, 81–190, for interpretations of "freedom" and "rights" on the normative basis of justice.

19. See Alison M. Jaggar, *Feminist Politics and Human Nature* (Totowa, NJ: Rowman & Allanheld, 1983), esp. 27–50 and 173–206.

20. Important resources for grasping the extent of misogyny—and women's courage and creativity—in Christian tradition include Kari Børreson, *Subordination and Equivalence: The Nature and Role of Women in Augustine and Thomas Aquinas* (Washington, D.C.: University Press of America, 1981); Rosemary R. Ruether and Eleanor McLaughlin, *Women of Spirit: Female Leadership in the Jewish and Christian Traditions* (New York: Simon and Schuster, 1979); Elizabeth A. Clark, *Jerome, Chrysostom, and Friends: Essays and Translations* (New York: Edwin Mellen Press, 1979); Elisabeth Schüssler Fiorenza, *In Memory of Her: A Feminist Reconstruction of Christian Origins* (New York: Crossroad, 1983); Phyllis Trible, *Texts of Terror: Literary-Feminist Readings of Biblical Narratives* (Philadelphia: Fortress, 1984). See Clarissa W. Atkinson, Constance H. Buchanan, and Margaret R. Miles, eds., *Immaculate and Powerful: The Female in Sacred Image and Social Reality* (Boston: Beacon Press, 1985), for similar themes within and beyond Jewish and Christian religions.

21. It is interesting to me that, in Thomist theology (in which the spiritual is the *super*natural and the "male principle" is in its image), femaleness is cast as "natural." But in modern liberalism's equation of the natural with divine process, the construct of female "nature" (receptive, passive) is set as different from that male "nature" which is normative for a fully human life. Femaleness is, thus, "unnatural" in liberal theology as are sexual acts which run contrary to human (and divine) "nature." Whether "natural" (beneath the super-natural God-man) or "unnatural" (beneath the natural God-man), women are objects rather than subjects of moral agency in Christian history. Liberalism thus has changed nothing with regard to classical Christianity's sacred contempt for women. Homosexual men, of course, have a very different history. As long as they have been "discreet," they have maintained heterosexist benefits of male privilege and domination. *Openly* gay men—not closeted homosexuals—receive scorn and contempt in Christian history.

22. For help in understanding the politics of this dynamic, see Zillah R. Eisenstein, *The Radical Future of Liberal Feminism* (New York and London: Longman, 1981), Beverly Wildung Harrison, *Our Right to Choose: Toward a New Ethic of Abortion* (Boston: Beacon Press, 1983), and Jaggar, *Feminist Politics and Human Nature.*

23. John Boswell explores this in *Christianity, Social Tolerance and Homosexuality: Gay People in Western Europe from the Beginning of the Christian Era to the Fourteenth Century* (Chicago: University of Chicago Press, 1980).

PART 3

Exploring Our Lives Together

13
LET HER WORKS PRAISE HER

Clare Benedicks Fischer

The title of this chapter, taken from the song in praise of the hardworking woman of Proverbs 31, echoes the scriptural call to honor woman's work. In antiquity, the community affirmed "in the gates" the labors of the persevering Hebrew wife, thus symbolically reconciling the private and public spheres of work. It is this vision of unity, with its recognition of the dignity and value of womanpower, which I wish to underscore in my assessment of the contemporary work ethic.

Until comparatively modern times, home and workplace were not separated, and the imagery we have today of gender and place was unknown. There is no doubt that the sexual division of labor spans centuries, but the merger of masculine identity with the idea of going from the hearth, and of feminine identity with staying at home is less than three hundred years old. Yet, this association has proven to be tenacious and, perhaps, the greatest obstacle to an authentically egalitarian society. Despite the fact that the utilization of women in the labor force has increased rapidly in the last three decades, the prescriptive authority of "a woman's place" has not dramatically changed. In a recent economic analysis of job satisfaction[1] one author notes that with the erosion of the traditional sexual division of labor by shifts in the work population, he fears that male work motivation may be in jeopardy. Masculinity and successful providing reinforce one another, both requiring that the woman assume material dependence upon her spouse. This relationship of male responsibility and female dependence implies that the wife remain at home and be looked after.

While research in the ethics of work reveals the persistence of the traditional dichotomy between home and work, it identifies the growing reality of the "working woman." Economists cannot disregard the rapid rise of the female labor force since the end of the Second World War. However, they fret about the postindustrial society in which resources are no longer inexhaustible and

183

progress is not infinite. Is it not absurd that the potential of woman's energy continues to go unrecognized?

Although the social scientist leaves us with some unsettling conclusions about contemporary trends, we would hope that the theologian would readily identify the positive aspects of woman's changing role. In the past twenty years a new theology, known under the rubric of "theology of work" has emerged.[2] Contributors to this theological discussion talk about the humanization of life and about the realization of self through work. But they write as if woman's activity in economic and cultural terms is either nonexistent or limited to the reproductive and nurturing functions. They ignore the role of women in building the earth, implying that the implementation of equality in the work force might effectively disrupt family life and jeopardize human purpose.

A theology of work must include an account of woman's contribution and potential. It must discover and lay to rest those powerful myths which perpetuate the idea of woman's secondary role. It must inform and educate everyone about woman's share in the creation of a progressively better life. Traditional approaches cannot illuminate our present circumstances. We are too far removed from the expectations and life-styles of antiquity to subscribe to a purely scriptural view of human activity. Three analytical approaches are here suggested which can provide orientation and guide us toward a more humane condition: the penitential, the creationist, and the eschatological.

THE GARDEN: WORK AS PENANCE

The memory of the lost garden, that paradise where all goods were harvested effortlessly, infuses what we are calling the "penitential" theology of work with a mood of remorse. Based upon the Genesis myth, work—on this view—is understood as a curse, a consequence of the primal act of disobedience. To redeem the conditions of the garden, thistles and thorns must be uprooted with great pain and frustration in order to make way for the consumable. The necessities for human survival are to be gleaned only through incessant toil. Human history after the Fall is a restless record of an irksome coping with the resistant; a confrontation with the unruly weeds which glut the garden and detract from order. Until elusive nature succumbs to human governance work will not end.

The justification for a separation of human work roles on the basis of divine ordinance, however, cannot be derived from either of the creation narratives of Genesis; both point to the unitary nature of the obligation to tend the garden. In Genesis 1:28–31 male and female are enjoined to "be fruitful," to "subdue" and "have dominion" over the earth together, and the woman of Genesis 2:15–23 is man's partner in Eden. Only with the breach of authority, with the symbolic ingestion of the forbidden fruit, does a division of labor emerge. But even in the discharge of the curse (Gen.3:16–18) no authority is given for a separation of capacities according to sexual identity. A rigid formulation of distinctive spheres of activity emerges, rather, with a penitential theology of work. With its compulsion to order, to secure mastery over an elusive nature, it sets about dispelling ambiguities and disharmonies. It understands a distinction in function—productive and reproductive—to be an application of a natural law grounded on biological difference. Accordingly, any deviance from this bipolar organization of work represents a reenactment of the original sin. So men *must* go forth from the hearth, and women *must* remain at home with the children. Despite this theological attempt to regulate the domains of human effort in order to prevent cosmic disharmonies, human history has not kept the work roles of men and women that neatly separated; innumerable women have also worked for their bread by the sweat of their brows.

Two myths, which represent obstacles to women's right to gainful employment today, reflect this penitential theology of work. Both lose credence in face of the social facts.

The first myth asserts, ostensibly on a biological basis, that women have a singular purpose—the care and maintenance of their families. But one need only refer to the Old Testament to disprove this myth. The woman of Proverbs 31, whose "works praise her," engages in a number of tasks that take her away from the home, including marketing and real estate; she performs these tasks clothed in "strength and dignity."

In a comprehensive study of women and work[3] we find ample evidence that women were involved in productive work throughout history, until the time of the Industrial Revolution. Many of the tasks which had been women's responsibilities in an earlier age, tasks such as spinning and soap-making, were then assumed by men in a factory setting. Only gradually have women, in their struggle for employment opportunities, begun to secure these work tasks again.

The current effort of women is to demonstrate the viability of combining work and home commitments. A glance at the statistical record indicates that the female labor force has doubled since 1940, with more than 33 million women in the work force as of 1972. This number represents 42 percent of the adult female population of the United States, and 38 percent of the total labor force. The most dramatic change has come with the eightfold increase of working mothers in less than thirty years. Over 50 percent of the female labor force have responsibility for children between the ages of six and seventeen. Twenty-nine percent of all white women workers, and 47 percent of all minority women workers, have children under six.

A more recent myth is that of homemaking as a "career." In our culture the activity of running a home is clothed in an illusive professionalism. It requires, according to Myrdal and Klein, that the housewife integrate in her person an "unholy alliance" between Eden's work ethic of productivity and its imagery of leisure. She must be continuously busy, expending up to as much as sixty hours a week on household duties but, buttressed by the media's vision of the lady of leisure, she must work just as hard to be sleek, beautiful, and glamorous. In short, the career homemaker is superwoman—she overcomes all the contradictions between drudgery and efficiency, routine and adventure. Her education comes from popular culture—magazines, television advertisements, and soap opera role models provide innumerable examples of successful women and their "tips." In this breathless world of the professional housewife we glimpse the penitential imagery of work as "keeping order"—her career triumphs are the dissolution of all dirt and the overcoming of physical and familial disarray.

Theologians writing about work usually distinguish the Hebrew from the Greek view, emphasizing the elitism and competitiveness of the latter. To be sure, the ancient Greeks looked upon manual labor with disdain and gladly delegated onerous responsibilities in order to free themselves to be citizens of the polis. The modern housewife similarly frees her family to function outside the home without trivial distractions. However, the Greeks did not originate competitive activity. Hebrew sources, according to one biblical scholar,[4] indicate that competition is a consequence of fratricide. The narrative of Cain and Abel (Gen. 4:2–9) offers a symbolic account of the jealousy and rivalry which lead to sibling murder. The implications of this act, paralleling the Fall of man, are an accursed condition and a history of strife between brothers and sisters. For women in a patriarchal culture, the results of original sin and of Cain's homicide have been domination and division.

The penitential theology of work instructs us that redemption is dependent upon remedial activity. Our work is to repair our relationships with others and with the earth. One imperative for constructive change is to right the imbalances which have reigned throughout history. Male sovereignty in the productive spheres of human life must be countered with enhanced female participation—not dominance but equality according to Charlotte Perkins Gilman: "There is before us no overturning, no attempt at a new domination of women over men. . . . It is not a contest between them, but a recognition of a common hope, a common power, a common duty."[5]

THE COMMUNITY: CREATION AND WORK

The optimism of a "creationist" approach to the theology of work contrasts dramatically with the disciplined assertiveness of the penitential view. Whereas the penitential view stressed the brokenness and lostness that characterizes the disobedient nature of humans, the creationist or "incarnational" perspective, deriving also from the Genesis myth, focuses instead upon the wholeness of creation and the proclivity to share and tend. Humankind is made in God's image (Gen. 1:27) and its authentic expression is symbolized in the divine magnanimity and cooperative spirit of the garden (Gen. 1:28). To participate in the creative order, humans work, and this work is an expression of solidarity and service. We find this idea reiterated in the Gospel parables (especially Matt. 25) and Pauline epistles (Gal. 6:2) of the New Testament.

On this creationist view, work is "right and proper." Human identity is inseparable from it and correlates with the effort expended, in community, in the ongoing, progressive, collaborative construction of the earthly city. The example of the female ant (Prov. 6:6–8) provides a model of productivity; she requires no external authority or motivation: "consider her ways and be wise." Failure, then, is idleness, or such work as derives from negative motivation rather than positive desire. Paul warns the Thessalonians that the new covenant does not imply abandonment of earthly endeavors—to shirk self-responsibility for the tasks of this world is to lose sight of human purpose (2 Thess. 3:7–12).

The creationist approach again suggests two highly debilitating myths about women's work. Both myths deny the seriousness of purpose or the significance of meaning which might otherwise be embraced in the divine scheme. Female labor is regarded as derivative and trivial. At the core of the argument is disbelief in woman's capacity to be motivated, or to make commitments on her own. Women are assumed to be lacking a zest for building the earth, except when authority directs or supports their endeavors.

The first of these two myths offers the stereotype of the woman worker who labors in the job market only to *supplement* her family's income. Supposedly, her motivation is entirely dependent upon others' needs, and her own commitment is partial, insignificant, and unreliable. But the motivation of the working woman needs to be assessed in the light of the facts.

It has been estimated that nearly nine out of ten American women will seek work for a wage at some point in their lives. On the average they will work for twenty-five years and their reasons for doing so are not for "pin money" or incidental motives. "The majority of women do not have the option of working solely for personal fulfillment."[6] This includes, as of 1972: 7.5 million single women; 6.2 million widowed, divorced, and separated women who are raising children; and more than 7 million women whose husbands did not earn adequate incomes to provide for their families.

Approximately one-third of the women workers in the United States work because they *must*—they are *not* derivative, they do *not* supplement, they *provide*. A recent survey of European women workers, reported in the American press, indicated that one-half of those interviewed identified economic necessity as the reason for employment.[7]

The other myth, a corollary one, is that housewifery is preferred by modern women because it makes so few demands upon their time. It posits the idle wife and mother who, thanks to technology, has little to do, but visit with her friends, watch television, and indulge her natural predisposition to be passive and lazy.

John Galbraith's thesis, however, that the modern housewife is a "crypto-servant," an unpaid domestic who manages the home and generates a progressively expanding rate of consumption, dispels the idea of indolence. Arguing from an expertise in economics, he describes how the housewife performs her menial labors without wages because she has been deluded by the notion of "convenient social virtue." Her tireless, though uncompensated housework is valued at more than $13,000 a year. Her most important function, however, is that of wisely buying in the marketplace, managing the goods of capitalist production, no small task for the indolent.

> ". . . in their crypto-servant role of administrators [they] make an indefinitely increasing consumption possible. As matters now stand (and for as long as they so stand), it is their supreme contribution to the modern economy."[8]

The creationist understanding of work is, after all, companionship in service. Neither the myth of deficient motivation nor the myth of prevailing indolence communicate the isolation and alienation of the woman worker. If she is responsible for the support of her family as well as its management (housework), she has little time or energy for sociability. On the other hand, her sense of performing *only* household labor often keeps her in a frenzied state. Ms. Myrdal and Ms. Klein note:

> . . . there is sufficient evidence to justify the suspicion that housewives often unconsciously expand it [housework] in order to allay their feelings of frustration by providing evidence that they are fully occupied and indispensable.[9]

Woman's feeling of being an accessory rather than a principal in the creation of human history can be dispelled only at that juncture in time and place where recognition is open, and the myopia of cultural vision is corrected by "work-humanship." "The closeness of that sort of community grows to the extent that labor not only demands mutual respect and care, but also the combination of each one's contribution to the same teamwork."[10]

PROMISE: WORK AS FULFILLMENT

Besides the penitential approach and the creationist view, a third—an eschatological—perspective is offered. Theologians who speak of the subject of work from this perspective give it a christocentric emphasis. The reference is not to the experience of the man Jesus, but to the mystery of Christ's mission on earth—that ambiguity of presence and otherness. The disjunction of human experience and transcendent purpose is overcome by an act of faith. Ultimate significance and authentic completion must await the Second Coming, but humans cannot defer their personal quest for meaning to an indefinite tomorrow. So, in sharing in that mystery of the "end," and fathoming its permeation into all things and events present, persons are able to take comfort in, and secure assurance from, their earthly endeavors. Both the message of John 4:34, where Jesus' nourishment is obtained in fulfillment of the divine work, and of Paul ("in him all things hold together," [Col. 1:17]) inform this approach.

From the point of view of women's experience, the eschatological perspective is the most promising, assuring an integration of persons such as heretofore has never been realized in human history. The low self-esteem of working women is well known. Their ability to escape the fetters of role assignment is only beginning to be put to the test.

> Work is more than a bread-and-butter issue. Our self-esteem and dignity are functions of the work we perform. Sexual or role stereotyping has not only inhibited the development of women's economic power, but has robbed women of the self-esteem, dignity, confidence in their innate abilities.[11]

The motif of fulfillment on this eschatological view stands in opposition to two more myths about female labor. Both represent ways of seeing woman as non-self-determining. And again their credibility is shaken by the facts. The first myth focuses on female aptitudes and the distortion in occupational aspiration and actual work assignment. The woman worker is said to be intellectually inept for, or physically incapable of, certain jobs. Her talents and capacities are defined by traditional stereotypes about the workplace.

Statistical analysis of occupational categories, of course, demonstrates the obvious—that most women who work for a wage are employed in repetitious, low-skilled positions requiring only minimal education or training. In brief, the female "employment ghetto" is composed of women whose individuality is at a low premium; they can be easily replaced and they function in service positions. One and a half million women work as domestics, earning less than $2,000 a year; 34 percent of the employed female labor force expends its energy on tedious clerical jobs, another 17 percent on factory assembly lines, and at least 8 percent on their feet as sales personnel.

What these facts patently indicate is simply the tremendous waste of women's abilities as persons. There is something askew when 20 percent of the women who have completed four years of college are employed in clerical positions and only 16 percent of the female labor force is classified as being professional (a category which includes traditional service jobs such as nursing, teaching, and librarianship).

The second myth assumes an inherent unreliability among women workers. It focuses on their presumably high rate of job turnover and absenteeism, and regards them as poor risks in the employment market. Women are said to be indifferent and to lack commitment to their work. This myth of unreliability argues that women's biological "vulnerabilities" and familial responsibilities augment these disabilities. Although the facts of women's home distractions cannot be denied, there is considerable evidence that women work with as much consistency as men when job inducements are equal.

Perhaps the most jarring aspect of this myth is its implicit support of the statistical reality of unequal pay scales. Despite the move for "equal pay for equal work," the gap widens. Eli Ginzberg reports that women earn approximately less than three-fifths as much as men.[12]

Obviously, inequitable remuneration and minimal inducements contribute substantially to job abandonment and absenteeism. At the same time, these factors reinforce the woman worker's depressed view of her own economic value.

The theological implications of this waste are apparent when we turn again to the eschatological notion of completion, fulfillment. Feelings of futility in employment, and in unemployment, negate one's sense of sharing in the "becoming" of the earth. To the extent that women are locked out of responsible positions, and undervalued in the ones which they have, their sense of participation in the ultimate task—creation—remains one-sided. This seems especially true when the figures of black unemployed women and the poverty levels of minority families are considered. Ginzberg notes, "Of the families with female heads who worked year-round, full-time, Negroes were four times more likely than whites to be caught in poverty!"[13]

Society is deprived of an immeasurable potential when it closes the doors to female participation in all facets of its work. Every woman is deprived when from her earliest years she is prevented from aspiring to and striving for what she could become, prevented by prescribed stereotypes, restraints of behavior, and limitations of education and occupation. When woman's work one day unfolds into the creative expression it must become if it is to contribute authentically to the fulfillment and wholeness of the human endeavor, then suspicions about intellect and reliability will be dispelled in the knowledge that all humankind thrives "for the sake of doing well a thing that is well worth doing."[14]

Among the countless approaches to the question of work, and the examination of woman's role in the modern economy, there is a valuable perspective emerging from the theological view of women's work. Theologically, we may perceive three relationships derived from the three approaches (penitential, creationist, and eschatological) taken here. These relationships define our presence and purpose in the world in terms of the "garden," the "community," and the "future." The first refers to natural resources; the second, to human resources; and the last, to our mutual responsibility for human history. They offer a simple guide to a more holistic existence:

1. we are persons who in reverence must tend and care for all nature;

2. we are persons in a relationship with one another, which demands loving community;

3. we are persons in a relationship with one another, which calls for attentiveness.

These three relationships necessarily lead to concrete programs of action—to vocational and continuing education, child-care services, modifications in maternity and pregnancy policies; and encouragement to participate and take leadership in unions—programs which will effect the changes needed to bring about an attentive, caring humanity. Both the material and psychological circumstances of women's work must be transformed to assure humankind that human history is really worth it.

> Something must be wrong in a social organization in which men may die a premature death from coronary thrombosis, as a result of overwork and worry, while their wives and widows organize themselves to protest their lack of opportunities to work.[15]

NOTES

1. Daniel Yankelovich, "The Meaning of Work," *The Worker and the Job,* ed. Jerome Rosow (New Jersey: Prentice-Hall, 1974).

2. Among the titles are: M.D. Chenu, *The Theology of Work* (Chicago: H. Regnery and Co., 1963); Louis Savary, *Man, His World and His Work* (New York: Paulist Press, 1967); J.H. Oldham, *Work in Modern Society* (Richmond: John Knox Press, 1961).

3. Alva Myrdal and Viola Klein, *Women's Two Roles, Home and Work* (London: Routledge and Kegan Paul, 1956).

4. Alan Richardson, *The Biblical Doctrine of Work* (London: SCM Press, 1952).

5. Charlotte Perkins Gilman, *His Religion and Hers* (New York: Century Co., 1923), 279–80.

6. Data from "Why Women Work," Women's Bureau, Employment Standards Administration, U.S. Dept. of Labor, Washington, D.C., 1973.

7. *Women Today* 4 (15 April 1973): 51.

8. John Kenneth Galbraith, *Economics and the Public Purpose* (Boston: Houghton Mifflin Co., 1973), 37.

9. Myrdal and Klein, *Women's Two Roles,* 37.

10. Peter Schoonenberg, *God's World in the Making* (Pittsburgh: Duquesne University Press, 1964), 156.

11. Lucille Rose, in *Report of Proceedings,* "Women's Work" conference, The New School, New York, September 1973.

12. Eli Ginzberg, "Introduction," in Robert Smuts, *Women and Work in America* (New York: Schocken, 1971), ix.

13. Ibid., x.

14. Dorothy Sayers, quoted in Oldham, *Work in Modern Society,* 52.

15. Myrdal and Klein, *Women's Two Roles,* 186.

14

FEMINIST THEOLOGY AND BIOETHICS

Margaret A. Farley

The aim of this essay is to explore the connections between feminist theology and issues in the field of bioethics. I have construed the task largely as a descriptive one; that is, I shall try to indicate some basic contours of feminist theology and some ways in which the values it emphasizes bear on the vast network of ethical issues related to the biological sciences, technology, and medicine. In addition, and in order to press the question of possible contributions by feminist theology to bioethics, I shall focus on the particular implications of feminist theology for the development and use of reproductive technology.

To some extent, the connection between the concerns of feminist theology and bioethics is obvious. Whatever else feminist theology does, it proceeds from a methodological focus on the experience of women, and whatever feminist ethics does, it begins with a central concern for the well-being of women. Medical ethics (as a part of bioethics) can be expected to share in some important way this focus and this concern, if for no other reason than that women constitute the majority of those who receive and provide health care ([46], pp. 119, 125; [33]). Beyond this, however, traditional religious views of women associate them symbolically and literally with nature, with the body, with human relationships, with reproduction—all themes for feminist theological critique and reconstruction, all foci for major concerns of bioethics in its broadest dimensions. The obviousness of the connection between these two disciplines, however, does not in itself give us the present and potential lines of mutual influence.

Before beginning a closer look at the relation between feminist theology and bioethics, three caveats are perhaps in order. That is, it is helpful to identify some forms of relation which we should *not* expect to find.

First, we should not expect to find feminist theology articulating for bioethics fundamental values or moral principles which are in every way unique to a feminist theological perspective. Few contemporary theological ethicists who take seriously the task of making explicit the connection between religious beliefs and ethical action claim for their theologies exclusive access to moral insight in the formulation of commonly held norms ([19], p. 9; [18], p. 119; [14], pp. 84–90; [13], p. 26).[1] It is not only religious belief, or theology, or a particular theology that can ground, for example, a requirement to respect persons, or a principle of equality, or a rational system of distributive justice. Likewise, it is not only feminist theology that can ground a view of human persons as fundamentally interpersonal and social, or that can formulate a view of nature that requires human stewardship rather than exploitation. Still, theologies do yield ethical perspectives that are unique in some respects, moral points of view that claim hermeneutically privileged insights, even particular moral action-guides that chart frontiers for human decision. Feminist theology is no exception in this regard. Indeed, it may have a more explicit ethical entailment than many other theologies. Moreover, its critical function may provide an essentially new perspective on some issues in bioethics.

Second, there is no one definitive form of feminist theology which can be looked to as representing all of its possible implications for bioethics. Theology in general is pluralistic on many levels. Feminist theology is not just one among many options in theology; it is itself pluralistic on many of the same levels as is theology generally. Thus, there are feminist theologies that are centered in ancient forms of goddess worship, and others that locate themselves, with important distinctions, in the Jewish or Christian biblical traditions, and still others that move beyond any historical traditions at all. There are diverse perspectives within particular traditions, too—perspectives that vary as much as process theology varies from medieval scholasticism. So clear have the differences in feminist theologies become that typologies abound in a growing effort to compare and contrast them ([36], pp. 214–234; [10], pp. 7–36; [31]). This wide divergence must be kept carefully in mind while we, nonetheless, explore a rather remarkable convergence of basic ethical concerns, values, and to some extent, norms for action.

Third, while it is not difficult to identify some parameters of an ethic which derives from and/or is reinforced by feminist theology, the kind of systematic development necessary to bring basic values to bear on very specific bioethical issues remains in important respects still to be undertaken. Indeed, feminist theology as such is at beginning points in its systematic formulation. While monumental strides have been taken by feminist biblical scholars, theologians, and historians ([4], [36], [39], [10], [42]), sustained theological synthesis is new on the horizon, at least for the Christian tradition [36]. Even newer is a systematic comprehensiveness and depth on the ethical side of feminist theology [14]. The import of the still limited development of feminist theology and ethics lies in the general conviction of most theologians that there is no easy route from the sources of religious faith to the specific insights needed for many of the radically new questions generated by scientific and medical capabilities. This conviction is mirrored in the reservations, though not final condemnation or approval, which many feminist theologians and ethicists express regarding, for example, some technologies of reproduction ([14], p. 37; [36], p. 226). It is also mirrored in the recognition of the necessity of collaboration with disciplines other than theology and ethics for the gradual forging of moral perspectives on the multitude of issues which a comprehensive bioethics may address.

There are limits, then, to the connections presently discernible between feminist theology and bioethics. Within those limits, however, lie meeting points, challenges, resources, of potential critical importance to both disciplines. We turn first to the methods, sources, and relevant themes of feminist theology.

FEMINIST THEOLOGY

Of all the themes in feminist theology which have direct bearing on issues in bioethics, three can be raised up for central consideration. These are the themes of (1) relational patterns among human persons, (2) human embodiment, and (3) human assessment of the meaning and value of the world of 'nature'. Feminist theology's development of these themes includes an articulation of basic ethical perceptions and leads to the formulation of some ethical action-guides. Moreover, attention to the emergence and treatment of these themes illuminates important methodological decisions which, as we shall see, constitute not only central commitments for feminist theology but possible warrants for ethical arguments in bioethics.

Patterns of Relation

Feminism, in its most fundamental sense, is opposed to discrimination on the basis of sex. It opposes, therefore, any ideology, belief, attitude, or behavior which establishes or represents such discrimination. In terms of social structure, feminism is opposed, then, to patriarchy. This opposition has the ultimate aim of equality among persons regardless of gender. To achieve this aim, however, feminism is necessarily pro-woman. Since discrimination on the basis of sex—or sexism—has been and remains pervasively discrimination against women, feminism aims to correct this bias by a bias for women, however temporary or prolonged that bias must be. A bias for women includes a focal concern for the well-being of women and a taking account of women's experience in coming to understand what well-being demands for women and men.

Feminist theology perceives profound discrimination against women in traditions of religious patriarchy. The major work of feminist theologians to date has been the unmasking of beliefs, symbols, and religious practices which establish and foster this discrimination. What they have found are massive tendencies in religious traditions to justify patterns of relationship in which men dominate women. Within the history of Christianity, for example, the major pattern of relationship between women and men has been one of dominance and subjugation. This has been sustained through a variety of beliefs about the essential inferiority of women to men and the need for a hierarchical order in social arrangements. Theological assessments of woman's nature, like many philosophical assessments, were based on views of a fundamental dualism within humanity. In these views, women and men are distinguished as polar opposites, representing body or mind, emotion or reason, passivity or activity, dependence or autonomy. The female-identified pole is always inferior to the male. Even when men and women are considered complementary in their duality, complementarity never means equality when it comes to role-differentiation. Thus, for example, men are to be primary agents, leaders, initiators; women are helpers, followers, supporters. More than this, women are often symbolically associated with evil. They are perceived as temptresses, to be feared as the threat of chaos to order, carnality to spirituality, weakness to strength. Even when women are exalted as symbols of virtue rather than vice, they bear the liabilities of impossible expectations and the burden of mediating 'femininity' to men [35].

Feminist theology's critique of religious traditions goes further, however, to the central symbols of faith. Feminists argue, for example, that Christianity's traditional formulation of a doctrine of God is itself a sexist warrant for discrimination against women. Though the Christian God transcends gender identification, personal metaphors for God are strongly masculine. This is true in the biblical tradition as well as in theological formulations of the doctrine of the Trinity. Moreover, Christian faith is centered in a savior who is male. Hence, there is a strong tendency in this tradition to consider men more appropriate as representatives of God in the human family, society, and the church. Indeed, traditional Christian theology has often granted the fullness of the *imago Dei* to men, yielding it only derivatively and partially to women. Thus is sealed the primary role of men in the human community. But more than this, feminist theologians point to the character of the Christian God as it is frequently drawn ([2]; [4]). That is, God is portrayed as sovereign, transcendent, requiring submission from human persons. It is on this model of relationship (dominance and submission) that human relationships are then patterned. Hence, as God is to God's people, so man is to woman, husband to wife, pastor to congregation, and on and on through the many forms of human life.

Some feminists have argued that the Christian view of the human self and its ideal development is also determined by the submissive role of persons in relation to God. That is, the height of Christian virtue is thought to be often portrayed as patient suffering and self-sacrificial love, and the mode of Christian action as humble servanthood. Women are socialized into these ideals in a way that men are not, for men can imitate the autonomy and agency of God in their role as God's representatives. Doctrines of sin which stress the evil of prideful self-assertion serve as a caution to men, but they only reinforce the submissiveness which already characterizes women [25]. Nietzsche's critique of Christianity as a religion for weaklings and victims can then be applied to the effect of Christian faith on women if not on men [5].

What emerges in feminist theology (in relation to Christianity, but here a harbinger of systematic developments in relation to other historical religions as well) is an analysis of what are judged to be oppressive patterns of relationship and ideologies which foster them. These patterns of oppression are identified not only in relations between men and women but in every human relation where the pattern is one of domination and subjugation on the basis of sex or race or class or any other aspect of persons which is used to deny full humanity to all. Given the radical nature of the feminist critique of Christianity (a critique which ultimately reaches to every major doctrine—of God, creation, redemption, the human person, sin and grace, the church, eschatology), feminist theologians either move away from Christianity altogether, or they take up the task of critical reconstruction of Christian theology. In either case, they have by and large moved to develop a view of human relations characterized by equality and mutuality, in which both autonomy and relationality are respected.

Feminist theologians who take up the task of restoring and reconstructing Christian theology 'beyond the feminist critique' argue that there are fundamental resources within the tradition which are not ultimately sexist and which can be brought to bear precisely as a challenge to sexism. With feminist hermeneutical methods, for example, biblical resources are available which reveal a God who does not need to compete with human beings for sovereignty, who comes forth from freedom in order to call forth freedom from human persons; a God who is able to be imagined in feminine as well as masculine terms [42], for whom 'friend' or 'partner' are more apt metaphors than 'king' or 'logos' ([20]; [39]). Reformulations of gender-assignment within the doctrine of the Trinity free a male-identified God from some of the limits of the human imagination and, indeed, from some of the problems which parent/child metaphors retain both for the life of God in itself and the relation of God to human persons. The prophetic traditions in the Old and New Testaments provide biblical grounds for challenging religious as well as secular institutions, or in other words, 'every elevation of one social group against others as image or agent of God, every use of God to justify social domination and subjugation' ([36], p. 23). Biblical and historical studies using a feminist hermeneutic yield evidence of Christian community organized not on the model of sexist hierarchy but on bases of equality and reciprocity [10].

It might be argued that what feminist theology is doing offers no new insights regarding patterns of human relationships. When it argues for equality between women and men, it simply extends to women the insights of liberalism. When it concerns itself with economic structures as well as political, it only blends a form of Marxism with liberalism. When it raises up the importance of mutuality, it follows the theorists of sociality—George Herbert Mead, Martin Buber, John MacMurray. When it criticizes notions of Christian love as self-sacrifice, it just gets clear on what has been taught all along. When it analyzes claims for self-determination and active participation in all the spheres of human life, it only repeats the agenda of liberation theology.

Feminist theologians are drawing on all of these sources of insight. Like feminists in general, however, they conclude that none of these other traditions or movements adequately address the oppression of women. This is not just a failure of extension. Rather, it represents a fundamental need for deeper analysis of the contexts of human life, concepts of the human self, and categories of human relation. From the hermeneutical vantage point of the experience of women—of their oppression and their achievements, their needs and contributions, their freedom and their responsibilities—feminist theology assumes groundbreaking work on questions of human relationships.

It has not been open to feminist theology, for example, simply to appropriate a view of the human person which makes autonomy paramount as the ground of respect or the primary principle to be protected in social relations. The issue of relationality as equiprimordial with autonomy as a feature of human personhood has pressed itself on feminist theologians from the experience of women. It is this that has demanded continued analysis of the nature of human relations and has led to historical and biblical studies of, for example, Christian communities, and to theological studies of the very nature of God (as relational). But if feminist theology cannot ignore relationality, neither has it been able to let go of autonomy as an essential feature of personhood [40]. Romantic returns to organic notions of society where relation is all, each in her place, without regard for free agency or for personal identity and worth which transcends roles—these are options that feminists judge can only repeat forms of oppression for women. It is this conviction that prompts continued biblical and theological studies of the compatibility of autonomy with dependence on God, the coincidence of activity and receptivity in peak experiences of relation, and social models which both protect individuality and promote the common good.

In another example, feminist theology has not been able to critique and then ignore interpretations of the differences between women and men. The whole enterprise of feminist theology still has something to do with demythologizing and de-ontologizing these differences, yet taking persons seriously as woman-persons and man-persons. Faced with these issues, feminist theology has had to take account of insights from the biological and behavioral sciences, and from philosophy. It has also had to maintain a focus on the concrete experience of women in systems where roles and spheres of human life are gender-specific. Refusal to defer these issues prompts unique probing of the fundamental possibilities and requirements of human relations, whether intimate or public. There is potential universal relevance for all human relationships in a move, for example, from traditional ideas of gender 'opposites', or even gender opposite 'complements', to ideas of gender 'analogies', where the primary focus is on similarity rather than difference [45].

Pluralism in feminist theology, of course, leads to some profoundly different choices regarding historical forms of human relationships. As in feminism generally, disagreements can be on the level of strategy (is there any possibility of radically transforming existing religious traditions?); or on the analysis of the cause of oppression (whether it is most fundamentally religion, or culture in a more general sense, or the conspiracy of men, or economics, etc.); or even on important characteristics of the model of relation to be advocated (do exclusivity and separatism contradict the values of equality and mutality?). Such disagreements are extremely serious, and it would be a mistake to underestimate them. Still, there is basic unanimity among feminist theologians on the values that are essential for nonoppressive human relationships—the values of equality, mutuality, and freedom.[2] The depth of significance given to these values is testified to, not denied, in the disagreements they entail. For feminist theologians who finally reject traditional religious traditions as irretrievably sexist, the alternative is a 'women's culture' which can incorporate these values despite the impossibility of transforming existing religions or society at large. For feminist theologians who continue to stand within their traditions, the alternative is a radical restructuring of institutions and a radical revision of religious doctrine and practice.

Embodiment

The second theme in feminist theology which has particular bearing on issues of bioethics is the theme of human embodiment. Less needs to be said about this theme, since an understanding of it follows directly upon many of the concerns we have already explored regarding patterns of human relationships. There is, however, a clear history of association of ideas that we must trace if we are to see the import of this theme both for feminist theology and bioethics.

Body/spirit is in many ways the basic dualism with which historical religions have struggled since late antiquity. Women, as we have already noted, have been associated with body, men with mind. Those who have speculated on the reasons for this have generally noted the tendency to locate the essence of woman in her childbearing capabilities. Women's physiology has been interpreted as 'closer to nature' than men's in that many areas and functions of a woman's body seem to serve the human species as much as or more than they serve the individual woman [24]. Moreover, women's bodies, in this interpretation, are subject to a kind of fate—more so than men's. Women are immersed in 'matter', in an inertness which has not its own agency. This is manifest not only in the determined rhythms of their bodily functions, but in a tendency to act from emotion rather than from reason, and in women's 'natural' work which is the caring for the bodies of children and men.

Whatever the reasons women have been associated with the body, they have thereby also been associated with the going evaluations of human bodyliness and matter in general. Historical religions which have made this connection have frequently devalued the body in relation to the spirit. Despite resistance from basically world-affirming attitudes in Judaism, and despite an ongoing conflict with positive Christian doctrines of creation and incarnation, both of these traditions incorporated negative views of the human body (and especially women's bodies). In late antiquity, Judaism was influenced by world-denying attitudes of Near Eastern gnosticism and mysticism. Christianity absorbed these same influences in its very foundations, along with Greek philosophical distrust of the transitoriness of bodily being.

Integral to views of the human body have been views of human sexuality. Once again, despite traditional influences toward positive valuation (of sexuality as a part of creation, as implicated in the very covenant with God, etc.), strongly negative judgments have been brought in. From ancient blood taboos, to Stoic prescriptions for the control of sexual desire by reason, to Christian doctrines of the consequences of original sin, fear and suspicion regarding the evil potentialities of sex have reigned strong in the Western conscience. So great, in fact, has been the symbolic power of sex in relation to evil that there seems to have been 'from time immemorial', as Paul Ricoeur puts it, 'an indissoluble complicity between sexuality and defilement' ([30], p. 28).

Central to the association of women with bodyliness has been the interpretation of their sexuality as more 'carnal' than men's, again 'closer to nature', more animal-like, less subject to rational control. Disclosure of this historical view of women's sexuality came as a surprise to many feminists whose direct learning from religious traditions had tended to be the opposite—that is, that women are less passionate than men, and hence more responsible for setting limits to sexual activity. The reversal in this regard has its roots, too, in religious traditions, and reflects the tendency we have seen before to identify women with evil, on one hand, and place them on a pedestal, on the other [3]. In either case, women's identity remains closely tied to the way they relate to their bodies, and in either case, women have learned to devalue their bodies. For women themselves, Freud's comment on beliefs about menstruation, pregnancy, and childbirth held true: '. . . it might almost be said that women are altogether taboo' ([12], p. 75).

With the rise of feminist consciousness, all past interpretations of the meaning of women's bodies were called into question. Women's turn to their own experience for new interpretations of embodiment was not a simple process, however. Feminist theology, like feminism in general, has continually modified original insights, not settling once and for all a meaning for every woman's experience. Thus, a beginning feminist response to past religious and cultural associations of women with their bodies was a rejection of this association. Anatomy was *not* destiny; women were not to be identified with their bodies any more than were men; women could transcend their bodies through rational choices. Such a response paradoxically freed women, however, to take their bodies more seriously. Rather than abstract from bodyliness, reinforcing a dichotomy between body and mind, women soon moved to 'reclaim' their bodies—to claim them as their own, as integral to their selfhood and their womanhood. This entailed new practical and theoretical approaches. Reflecting on their experiences, women shared insights and interpretation, formulated new symbols, expanded and revised understandings of human embodiment as such [43].

Struggling to move beyond the dualism of body and self that had limited them for so long, feminist philosophers and theologians used a phenomenological method to describe what it means to *be* a body as well as *have* a body, to understand their own bodies as ways of being inserted into the world, as structured centers of personal activity, as body-subjects not just body-objects [28]. From an understanding of themselves as embodied subjects, women 'reclaim' their bodies not just by taking them seriously and 'living' them integrally, but by refusing to yield control of them to men. New intimate self-understandings and new philosophical and theological anthropologies yield new personal and political decisions.

The World of Nature

The third theme in feminist theology which is potentially relevant to issues in bioethics is the meaning and value of the world of nature. Feminist theologians' concern for this theme is directly influenced by their concern for patterns of human relations and for the world as the place of human embodiment.

Just as women have been thought of in religious and cultural traditions as 'close to nature', so the world of nature has been symbolized as female. This is a clue to the difficulties which feminist theologians have with past beliefs and attitudes regarding nature. They find, in fact, a correlation between patterns of domination over women and efforts at domination over nature ([36], pp. 72–85; [37], pp. 57–70).

Perceptions of nature change through history, of course, and its symbolism is always to some extent ambivalent. Nature has been exalted in importance beyond the being and culture of humans, or reduced to a tool for humans; it has been viewed as the cosmic source of life and goodness, or a mysterious force to be feared and fled or controlled. All of these interpretations of nature mirror similar identifications of the essence of woman. However, especially in the history of Christian thought, a pattern emerges which raises serious questions for feminist theology.

Despite the fact that a Christian world-view and specific Christian teachings have supported 'sacramental' views of the whole of creation, sometimes especially of nature (as revelatory of the fidelity, the presence, the grandeur and the graciousness of the living God), Christianity has nonetheless also tended to trivialize the value of nature. Ascetic theologies sometimes reduced nature to a transitory illusion, a distraction from 'higher things', in the manner of some Hellenistic philosophies. Christian leaders sometimes forbade the study of nature as dangerous or a waste of time. When nature and culture were paired among traditional dualisms, nature was assigned the value of the negative pole.

Similarly, while there is a strong tradition in Christian thought requiring reverence for and stewardship of nature, there is also strong support for a way of relating to nature which sees it only as something to be used, dominated, controlled by human persons ([19], p. 7). In this latter view, because nature has no value of its own, it can be treated as the private property of humanity (or of individuals), with no limits on its exploitation or manipulation short of the limits of human persons' own self-interest. Where total possession is permitted, the concept of 'rape' does not apply.

Rosemary Ruether traces a history of Western attitudes toward nature which moves from an early ascetical 'flight' from nature to a modern 'return' to nature ([36], p. 82). The rise of scientific research in the seventeenth century helped secularize a view of nature, fostered a perception of it as intrinsically rational, penetrable, manageable. Unintended negative consequences of scientific and technological development, visible from the nineteenth century on, produced romantic reactions calling for a different sort of return to nature—a restoration of 'pure' nature, uncontaminated and unalienated by human intervention. All of these attitudes toward nature, however, represented pieces of the pattern of hierarchical domination and subjugation—domination through possession and control, whether through denigration, or exploitation, or the expectation of mediated happiness and identity through 'keeping' nature as a haven for some (despite the suffering this in turn might cause for others) ([36], p. 85; [37]).

Feminist theology argues, alternatively, for a view of nature consonant with a view of a God who takes the whole of creation seriously, and a view of creation which does not see predatory hierarchy as the basis of order. Nature, in this view, is valuable according to its own concrete reality, which includes an interdependence with embodied humanity. It is limited in its possibilities, which precludes its moral use as the battleground for the ultimate challenge to human freedom. Human intelligence and freedom are not barred from addressing nature, but measures for understanding and just use are lodged both in nature itself and in ethical requirements for relations among persons.

FEMINIST THEOLOGICAL ETHICS

Given this overview of themes in feminist theology, it may be possible to identify some characteristics of a feminist theological ethic, moving still closer to connections with issues in bioethics. We have, for example, seen enough of feminist theology to draw some conclusions regarding the *methods* likely to characterize any ethics that derives from it. First in this regard is a sense in which feminist theology and ethics can be said to be concerned with objective reality, and hence to presuppose methodologically some access to an intelligible reality. The work of these disciplines began, after all, as a result of what was at base a new understanding of the reality of women. Like feminism in general, feminist theology had its origins in women's growing awareness of the disparity between received traditional interpretations of their identity and function within the human community and their own experience of themselves and their lives. The corresponding claim that gender role-differentiation and gender-specific limitations on opportunities for education, political participation, economic parity, etc., are discriminatory was based on the argument that past interpretations of women's reality were simply wrong. That is, past theories failed to discover the concrete reality of women and represented, in fact, distorted perceptions of that reality. Moreover, the attitudes and policies they fostered often did violence to that reality.

It would be a mistake to label feminist theology and ethics in any simple sense 'naturalistic', though the term is not wholly inappropriate. Feminist theology does not, obviously, reduce to a natural or behavioral science. Nor does it rely for its access to reality on human reason alone. And while feminist theological ethics searches for and proposes universally valid norms, it does so in a way that acknowledges the historical nature of human knowledge and the social nature of the interpretation of human experience. The fact that present insights may be superseded by future ones, and that present formulations of specific principles may change, does not contradict either the methodological requirement of attending to concrete reality or the methodological presupposition that the accuracy and adequacy of theories can be tested against that reality.

Closely aligned with all of this is the methodological commitment to begin with and continue a primary focus on the experience of women ([25]; [36], pp. 12–13). This is often coupled with the qualification that no claims are made for the universality of women's experience in relation to human experience. There is a claim made, however, that until a theology based on women's experience is developed, traditionally assumed universal claims for a theology based on men's experience will continue to render inadequate if not inaccurate the major formulations of religious belief.

A methodological commitment to the primacy of women's experience as a source for theology and ethics goes significantly beyond a simple focusing of attention, however. It yields, in addition, a feminist hermeneutical principle which functions in the selection and interpretation of all other sources. While not every feminist theologian articulates this principle in exactly the same way, it can be expressed as strongly as, 'Whatever diminishes or denies the full humanity of women must be presumed not to reflect the divine or an authentic relation to the divine, or to reflect the authentic nature of things, or to be the message or work of an authentic redeemer or a community of redemption' ([36], p. 19). As is to be expected, this principle functions in importantly different ways in different feminist theologies. In some, for example, it leads to the rejection of the authority of the Bible altogether [41]; in others it allows the relativization of the authority of some texts [10]; in still others it leaves all texts standing as a part of an authoritative revelation, but renders their meaning transformed under a new feminist paradigm [42]. The same is true for theological doctrines, historical events, and for sources of theology and ethics which can range from the comparative study of religions to philosophical and scientific writings and schools of thought.

A focus on women's experience, the use of a feminist hermeneutical principle, and a concern for the lived experience of women precisely as disadvantaged, can constitute for feminist theological ethics the bias for women which is the earmark of feminism in general. If this is chosen as a strategic priority, feminist theological ethics can be methodologically oriented ultimately as an ethic whose concerns include the well-being of both women and men, both humanity and the world of nature. Its theological center will depend on its ultimate warrants for these concerns.

Finally, in regard to method, feminist theological ethics has been open to both deontological and teleological patterns of reasoning ([14], pp. 12–13). On the one hand, for example, the very notion of 'strategic priority', as well as a strongly 'ecological' view of reality, implies a concern for consequences, an ethical evaluation of means in relation to ends and parts in relation to wholes, a relativization of values in situations of conflict. On the other hand, demands of the concrete reality of persons are such that some attitudes and actions can be judged unethical precisely because they contradict values intrinsic to that reality. The sorting out of what ultimately determines a specific obligation is the task of ethics, but neither of these modes of reasoning is ruled out for feminist theological ethics.

When we turn from method to *substance* in feminist theological ethics, we perhaps need only summarize the ethical import of what we have seen in regard to feminist theological themes. Thus, an ethic derived from feminist theology understands the well-being of persons in a way that takes account of their reality as embodied subjects (and hence includes considerations of persons as historical beings, living in social and cultural contexts, identified with yet transcending systems and institutions; as beings whose actuality includes potentiality for development as well as vulnerability to diminishment; beings constituted by complex structures of freedom, physiology, intelligence, affectivity, etc.; beings which are essentially interpersonal and social; beings which are unique as well as common sharers in humanity). It is an ethic which gives important status to principles of equality and mutuality. It holds together principles of autonomy and relationality. It gives ethical priority to models of relationship characterized by collaboration rather than competition or hierarchical gradation. Finally, it does not isolate an ethic of human relations from ethical obligations to the whole of nature. These sound like a list of ideals, high rhetoric which any ethic may incorporate somehow. Some test of it can be made by turning now to issues in bioethics.

FEMINIST THEOLOGY AND BIOETHICS

Feminist theology offers something of a distinctive perspective on many issues that we today include under the general rubric of bioethics. This is because women's lives are deeply implicated in areas of personal medical care, public health, and the development and use of biomedical technologies. Feminist theology also gains from analyses of issues arising in these areas, for here the lived experience of women reveals some of the central opportunities and limitations of the human condition. Here it is that 'reflection upon the goals, practices, and theories of medicine validates philosophical reflection upon many issues that have traditionally been of concern to women,' but ignored by the traditional disciplines of philosophy and theology ([46], p. 120).

We can explore the interrelation between feminist theology and bioethics in a number of ways. Thus, we can examine the perspective offered by feminist theology on the principles usually considered central to bioethics—principles of, for example, nonmaleficence and beneficence, veracity and fidelity, as well as autonomy, mutuality, and justice. We can also look to numerous specific issues for which feminist theology and ethics can be expected to have special relevance—issues such as abortion and sterilization, medical care of the elderly, psychiatric treatment of women, medical settings for childbirthing, conflict between nursing roles and moral rules, the use of amniocentesis for gender selection, models of doctor/patient relationships in a culture and in relation to a profession marked by sexism. Among these and other possibilities, however, let me select for consideration the issue of the development and use of reproductive technologies.[3] A feminist theological approach to this issue may, in even a brief attempt, show some of the implications of feminist theology for understanding both context and principles in the area of bioethics.

The potentialities of reproductive technology have for some time caught the attention of feminists. It raises issues, however, on which unanimity of view does not exist. Some feminists have argued that the ultimate source of women's oppression is their physiological capability of bearing children. While physical motherhood can constitute individual and social power, it also renders women powerless—before nature, before men, before their children, before society (which judges them, and which determines the conditions under which their children must grow). In the face of this powerlessness, and the suffering it entails, technology offers a solution. Indeed, in an extreme view, women's liberation can only be achieved with a revolution not only against forms of society, but against nature itself. Thus, Shulamith Firestone argued for the 'freeing of women from the tyranny of their reproductive biology by every means available', including technology which could separate women once and for all from a gender-identified responsibility for reproduction ([11], p. 238).

This was a relatively early position, however, and strong disagreement has come from other feminists on a variety of grounds. Many consider the analysis of the causes of oppression to be wrong ([21], pp. 87–91). Others see in the development of reproductive technologies a new means of devaluing women, rendering them "expendable in the procreative process" ([14], p. 37). Still others argue that some uses of technology, such as amniocentesis for the purpose of gender selection, will pit women against themselves [26].

Feminists agree on at least two things with regard to these questions. First, the history of women's experience in relation to the power and process of reproduction is, indeed, a history of great pain. While fertility, pregnancy, and childbirth have been a source of women's happiness and fulfillment, and an occasion for powerful expressions of great human love and enduring fidelity to duty, they have also been the locus of a cumulative burden of immense oppression and suffering. The twentieth century incursion of technology into reproduction (the 'medicalization' of pregnancy and childbirth) has often added to this suffering, extended this oppression.

Second, and closely following, feminists are in agreement that the development and use of reproductive technology cannot be evaluated apart from its concrete, socio-cultural context. This context has been, and remains, an "historically specific social order in which positions of power and privilege are disproportionately occupied by men" ([7], p. 41). As long as sexism continues to characterize the lived world which women know, technology will have different consequences for women and for men. Far from freeing women from unnecessary burdens in reproduction, further technological development may result in greater bondage.

Given these agreements, however, neither feminism in general nor feminist theology renders wholly negative judgments on reproductive technology. One obvious reason for this is that such technology can take many forms. Evaluations of developments of contraceptives, childbirth procedures, methods of abortion, artificial insemination, *in vitro* fertilization, fetal diagnosis, cloning, and many other technologies can hardly be lumped together in a single comprehensive judgment. Only a total anti-technology approach could yield that. Generally, despite deep ambivalence toward reproductive technologies, feminists can affirm that

> natural-scientific breakthroughs represent genuine gains in human self-understanding. The widespread social irresponsibility of medical practice, exacerbated by male monopoly of the medical profession that is only now changing, must not be confused with the value of scientific discoveries ([14], pp. 169–170).

Science and technology have, in fact, been instruments of reform at times, even in regard to almost intractable problems of sexism ([32], pp. 22, 83, 136).

But if a single ethical judgment cannot be made for all forms of reproductive technology, then it will be helpful here to narrow our focus still more to one form. Once again, this will have implications beyond itself for reproductive technology more generally, but we cannot expect thereby to have resolved all questions. The form of technology that I will consider is *in vitro* fertilization for the purpose of producing a child (that is, not just as a procedure for the purpose of scientific research with no intention of bringing a child 'to term'). As a technology, it raises the issue of profound change in human modes of reproduction, not just the issue of improving present modes.

One place to begin a feminist analysis of *in vitro* fertilization (with embryo transfer or some other form of providing for gestation) is with women's experience to date of technology in the area of pregnancy and birth. As we have already noted, this is in many respects not a happy experience. Recent studies have helped to make visible the difficulties women have had in this regard ([44]; [22]; [29]; [17]; [5]). Recalling these difficulties can help us to formulate the questions that need to be asked of *in vitro* fertilization. If, for example, the use of medical technology in relation to childbirth has been oppressive to women, or to their children, in what way has it been so? One response to this question is that it has contributed to the alienation of women from their bodies, their partners, and their children (by, for example, moving childbirth into settings appropriate primarily for the treatment of disease, isolating mothers both from 'women's culture' and their spouses, regimenting the presence of mothers with their babies, etc.);[4] and that it has placed women in a network of professional relations which unjustifiably limit their autonomy (in the manner of a 'patient'). Does the development and use of *in vitro* fertilization hold this same potential for alienation, albeit in different ways? From a feminist theological perspective, the question can be: Does *in vitro* fertilization violate (or is it in accord with) feminist understandings of embodiment, norms for relationships, and concerns for the common good? The following considerations hold this question as their backdrop.

For many feminists the sundering of the power and process of reproduction from the bodies of women would constitute a loss of major proportions. Hence, the notion of moving the whole process to the laboratory (using not only *in vitro* fertilization but artificial placentas, *et al.*) is not one that receives much enthusiasm. On the other hand, *in vitro* fertilization is not perceived as a procedure which necessarily violates the essential embodying of reproduction. If its purpose is primarily to enable women who would otherwise be infertile to conceive a child, it becomes a means precisely to mediate embodiment. Feminists generally oppose the kind of sacralization of women's reproductive organs and functions that would prohibit all technological intervention. In fact, a desacralization in this regard is seen as a necessary step in the breaking of feminine stereotypes and the falsification of anatomy as destiny. Moreover, feminist interpretations of sexuality are very clear on the validity of separating sexuality from reproduction. Without contradiction, however, they also affirm reproduction as a significant potential dimension of separating sexuality from reproduction. Without contradiction, however, they also affirm reproduction as a significant potential dimension of series of 'natural' physical connections between sexual intercourse and the fertilization of an ovum by male sperm. Indeed, it is a failure of imagination which sees this as the only way in which integrated sexuality can be related to reproduction. All in all, then while human embodiment remains a central concern in a feminist analysis of *in vitro* fertilization, it does not thereby rule out the ethical use of this technology.

Feminists are generally clear on the need to understand and experience childbearing in an active way. Pregnancy and childbirth are not events in relation to which women should be wholly passive ([14], pp. 169, 246–247). Part of taking active control and responsibility regarding their reproductive power can include a willingness to use technology insofar as it makes childbearing more responsible, less painful, and more safe. Sometimes discernment of just these consequences for technology is difficult, but the fact that it is called for indicates, again, that *in vitro* fertilization is not ruled out in principle.

Perhaps the most troubling aspect of *in vitro* fertilization, and of other technologies which actually empower reproduction, is the question of primary agency and responsibility. This question in itself has many sides. For example, women's previous experience with reproductive technology suggests that (at least in the concrete context of present societies) women's own agency is likely to be submerged in the network of multiple experts needed to achieve *in vitro* fertilization. Far from this accomplishing a liberation of women from childbearing responsibilities, it can entail 'further alienation of our life processes' ([36], p. 227). Moreover, efforts to restrict and share the agency of professionals often move only in the direction of what some feminists fear as collectivism or state control, the 'total alienation of one's life to institutions external to one's own control and governed by a managerial elite' ([36], p. 226]). In any case, without a drastic change in the composition of society and the professions, widespread use of *in vitro* fertilization could, it seems, make it difficult for women to achieve or sustain control of human reproduction.

But does it matter whether women or men, parents or scientists, control reproduction? Feminists argue that those who will bear the responsibility for childrearing should have primary agency in decisions about childbearing—not just because it is their right if they are to bear the burden of such responsibility, but because this is required for the well-being of offspring. 'Only those who are deeply realistic about what it takes to nourish human life *from birth onward* have the wisdom to evaluate procreative choice' ([14], p. 173).[5] Reproductive technologies that divorce decisions for childbearing from childrearing fail to take seriously the basic needs of children for not only material resources but personal relation and support, in contexts that allow the awakening of basic trust and the development of fundamental autonomy ([34], p. 258; [27], p. 65).[6] It is not only women who, in principle, can make these choices ([34], p. 262),[7] but it is 'parents', not just 'scientific facilitators' or society at large or any persons who are unprepared to take responsibility at an intimate as well as comprehensive level for our children. Such problems of agency are complex and sobering in the face of technological capabilities such as *in vitro* fertilization. They are not, in principle, intractable, perhaps not even in practice. They need not rule out the ethical use of *in vitro* fertilization, but they occasion grave moral caution.

Yet another consideration prompted by *in vitro* fertilization (and other reproductive technologies) regards the developing capability for 'selection' of offspring—from among many candidates (differentiated by gender, bodily health, intellectual capacity, etc.). The problem of 'discards' in *in vitro* fertilization is larger than the discernment of grave embryonic anomalies. For some feminists this capability can erode moral and religious obligation to accept all sorts of persons into the human community. In so doing, it undermines basic feminist principles of equality, inclusiveness, mutuality, and toleration of difference and of 'imperfection' ([7], p. 42). *In vitro* fertilization need not, of course, be used in this way. But once again, a voice of caution is raised.

Underlying all of these considerations is what might be called the need to measure *in vitro* fertilization according to norms of justice. If justice in its deepest sense can be understood as treating persons in truthful accordance with their concrete reality (a concrete reality which must be interpreted as best we can), then all the issues of embodiment, nondiscrimination, agency, responsibility, inclusive care, are issues of justice. They are not focused only on individuals, but on the human community. They converge in the fundamental question, 'How are we to reproduce ourselves as human persons?' They press us to new theories of justice which extend a requirement for 'just parenting' in relation to all human children. They include, then, too, questions of the meaning and value of *in vitro* fertilization in a world threatened by overpopulation, in countries where not every existing child is yet cared for, in communities where grave needs of children require the resources of science and technology. Questions of macroallocation of scarce goods and services may finally be unresolvable, but they cannot be ignored. At the very least, in this instance, they preclude justifications of *in vitro* fertilization on the basis of any absolute right to procreate.

A feminist analysis of *in vitro* fertilization remains provisional. It yields, however, the following position: Negatively there are not grounds for an absolute prohibition of the development and use of technology such as *in vitro* fertilization; positively, such technology may aid just and responsible human reproduction. The presence of certain circumstances, or certain conditions, sets limits to its ethical development and use—circumstances such as (a) high risk of injury to the well-being of either parent or child; (b) a context unconducive to the growth and development of any child produced (unconducive because, for example, no one is prepared to offer the child basic human personal relationship); (c) an intention to produce a child to be used as means only in relation to the producers' ends (as, for example, if the child is produced merely for the sake of the advance of scientific research, or for the duplication of one's own self without regard for the child's development into an autonomic self); (d) failure to meet criteria of distributive justice (when it is determined that other basic human needs place legitimate prior claims on the resources involved). Such conditions rule out spectres of human laboratory 'farms'. They also tell us something about the conditions for *any* ethical decisions regarding human reproduction, not just decisions made in the context of reproductive technology.

With this, then, we have one example of the relation between feminist theology and an issue in bioethics. My development of the issue must remain more suggestive than exhaustive of the particular ethical values and ultimate theological warrants that feminist theologians may offer. My suspicion is that future work in the area of bioethics will bring careful reflection on questions that I have not, within the limits of this essay, addressed at all; questions, for example, of women's interpretation not only of birth but of death, and women's evaluation of the strength of 'quality of life' claims in relation to sanctity-of-life principles. Whatever lines along which a feminist bioethics may develop, however, it will never be far from central concerns for human embodiment, for the well-being of women-persons on a par with the well-being of men-persons, for newly just patterns of relationship among all persons, and for the balanced care of the whole world of both nonpersonal and personal beings.

The Divinity School
Yale University
New Haven, Connecticut, U.S.A.

NOTES

1. For a contrary emphasis, see ([15], 48).

2. To the argument that separatist feminist movements do indeed contradict these values (by affirming a new form of elitism, by simply 'reversing' the order in the hierarchy of men and women, etc.), the response is sometimes given that separation does not entail domination, and that elitism is no more a necessarily substantial charge against separatist feminism than it is against any religious sectarianism. It is more difficult for some separatists to answer the criticism that they are duplicating oppressive patterns of 'identifying an enemy'.

3. Reproductive technologies include all those technologies which relate to human reproduction. They are sometimes differentiated from technologies of genetic engineering, though I do not in this essay maintain a sharp separation. For some helpful distinctions, see ([27], 8–10).

4. 'Tales of horror' are told more and more in recent sociological studies in this regard. However, it should be noted that very recently there have come significant changes—changes, for example, such as an increase in home birthing, the provision of

birthing rooms in hospitals, the rise once again of the profession of midwifery, etc. Some feminists express concern that some new movements, such as natural childbirth, incorporate an alienating technology just as previous methods did ([44], 183–198; [22], 628–630).

5. I am not, here, focusing on the grounds for women's right to procreative choice which are often central to feminist arguments—that is, a right to bodily integrity or a right to privacy. One reason I am not focusing on those grounds is that *in vitro* fertilization *can* be understood to prescind from women's bodies in a way that, for example, abortion cannot.

6. This can be maintained without conflicting with contemporary concerns for 'too much mothering', etc.

7. Nor should it be the exclusive prerogative of women. When it is this, it justifies a male dismissal of obligation regarding childbearing—something feminists have long been concerned to oppose.

BIBLIOGRAPHY

[1] Carr, A.: 1982, 'Is A Christian Feminist Theology Possible?' *Theological Studies* 43, 279–297.
[2] Christ, C. P.: 1977, 'The New Feminist Theology: A Review of the Literature', *Religious Studies Review* 3, 203–212.
[3] Cott, N. F.: 1978, 'Passionlessness', *Signs* 4, 227–228.
[4] Daly, M.: 1973, *Beyond God the Father*, Beacon, Boston.
[5] Daly, M.: 1978, *Gyn/Ecology: The Metaethics of Radical Feminism*, Beacon, Boston.
[6] Donegan, J. B.: 1978, *Women and Men Midwives: Medicine, Morality, and Misogyny in Early America*, Greenwood Press, Westport, Connecticut.
[7] Elshtain, J. B.: 1982, 'A Feminist Agenda on Reproductive Technology', *Hastings Center Report* 12, 40–43.
[8] Farley, M. A.: 1975, 'New Patterns of Relationship: The Beginnings of a Moral Revolution', *Theological Studies* 36, 627–646.
[9] Farley, M. A.: 1976, 'Sources of Sexual Inequality in the History of Christian Thought', *The Journal of Religion* 56, 162–176.
[10] Fiorenza, E. S.: 1983, *In Memory of Her: A Feminist Reconstruction of Christian Origins,* Crossroad, New York.
[11] Firestone, S.: 1971, *The Dialectic of Sex: The Case for Feminist Revolution,* Bantam, New York.
[12] Freud, S.: 1918, 'The Taboo of Virginity', *Collected Papers,* Vol. 8, 70–86.
[13] Gustafson, J. M.: 1975, *The Contributions of Theology to Medical Ethics,* Marquette University Press, Milwaukee.
[14] Harrison, B. W.: 1983, *Our Right to Choose: Toward A New Ethic of Abortion,* Beacon, Boston.
[15] Hauerwas, S.: 1978, 'Can Ethics Be Theological?' *The Hastings Center Report* 8, 47–49.
[16] Heyward, C.: 1979, 'Ruether and Daly: Theologians Speaking and Sparking, Building and Burning', *Christianity and Crisis* 39, 66–72.
[17] Lebacqz, K.: 1975, 'Reproductive Research and the Image of Woman', in Fischer, C. B. *et al., Women in A Strange Land,* Fortress, Philadelphia.

[18] McCormick, R. A.: 1983, 'Bioethics in the Public Forum', *Milbank Memorial Fund Quarterly* 61, 113–126.
[19] McCormick, R. A.: 1981, *How Brave A New World? Dilemmas in Bioethics,* Doubleday, Garden City, New York.
[20] McFague, S.: 1982, *Metaphorical Theology,* Fortress, Philadelphia.
[21] Mitchell, J.: 1971, *Woman's Estate,* Vintage, New York.
[22] Oakley, A.: 1979, 'A Case of Maternity', *Signs* 4, 606–631.
[23] O'Brien, M.: 1981, *The Politics of Reproduction,* Routledge and Kegan Paul, London.
[24] Ortner, S. B.: 1974, 'Is Female to Male as Nature Is to Culture?' in M. Z. Rosaldo and L. Lamphere (eds.), *Woman, Culture, and Society,* Stanford University Press, Stanford, 67–87.
[25] Plaskow, J.: 1980, *Sex, Sin, and Grace,* University Press of America, Washington, D.C.
[26] Powledge, T. M.: 1981, 'Unnatural Selection: On Choosing Children's Sex', in H. B. Holmes *et al.* (eds.), *The Custom-Made Child? Women-Centered Perspectives,* Humana Press, Clifton, New Jersey, 193–199.
[27] President's Commission for the Study of Ethical Problems in Medicine and Biomedical and Behavioral Research: 1982, *Splicing Life,* U.S. Government Printing Office, Washington, D.C.
[28] Rawlinson, M. C.: 1982, 'Psychiatric Discourse and the Feminine Voice', *The Journal of Medicine and Philosophy* 7, 153–177.
[29] Rich, A.: 1976, *Of Woman Born: Motherhood as Experience and Institution,* Prometheus, Buffalo.
[30] Ricoeur, P.: 1967, *The Symbolism of Evil,* Harper, New York.
[31] Robb, C. S.: 1981, 'A Framework for Feminist Ethics', *The Journal of Religious Ethics* 9, 48–68.
[32] Rosenberg, R.: 1982, *Beyond Separate Spheres: Intellectual Roots of Modern Feminism,* Yale University Press, New Haven.
[33] Rothman, B. K.: 1979, 'Women, Health, and Medicine', in J. Freeman (ed.), *Women: A Feminist Perspective,* Mayfield, Palo Alto, 27–40.
[34] Ruddick, S.: 1980, 'Maternal Thinking', *Signs* 6, 342–367.
[35] Ruether, R. R. (ed.): 1974, *Religion and Sexism: Images of Women in the Jewish and Christian Traditions,* Simon and Schuster, New York.
[36] Ruether, R. R.: 1983, *Sexism and God-Talk: Toward a Feminist Theology,* Beacon, Boston.
[37] Ruether, R. R.: 1981, *To Change the World,* Crossroad, New York.
[38] Russell, L.: 1982, *Becoming Human,* Westminster, Philadelphia.
[39] Russell, L.: 1979, *The Future of Partnership,* Westminster, Philadelphia.
[40] Saiving, V.: 1981, 'Androgynous Life: A Feminist Appropriation of Process Thought', in S. G. Davaney (ed.), *Feminism and Process Thought,* Edwin Mellen Press, New York, pp. 11–31.
[41] Stanton, E. C. (ed.): 1974, *The Original Feminist Attack on the Bible: The Woman's Bible,* Arno, New York.
[42] Trible, P.: 1978, *God and the Rhetoric of Sexuality,* Fortress, Philadelphia.
[43] Washbourn, P.: 1979, *Becoming Woman: The Quest for Spiritual Wholeness in Female Experience,* Harper, New York.
[44] Wertz, R. W., and Wertz, D. C.: 1977, *Lying-In: A History of Childbirth in America,* Free Press, New York.

[45] Whitbeck, C.: 1984, 'A Different Reality: Feminist Ontology', in: C. Gould (ed.), *Beyond Domination: New Perspectives on Women and Philosophy,* Rowman and Allanheld, Totowa, N.J., pp. 64–85.
[46] Whitbeck, C.: 1983, 'Women and Medicine: An Introduction', *The Journal of Medicine and Philosophy* 7, 119–133.

15

THEOLOGY AND MORALITY
OF PROCREATIVE CHOICE

Beverly Wildung Harrison
with Shirley Cloyes

Much discussion of abortion betrays the heavy hand of misogyny, the hatred of women. We all have a responsibility to recognize this bias—sometimes subtle—when ancient negative attitudes toward women intrude into the abortion debate. It is morally incumbent on us to convert the Christian position to a teaching more respectful of women's concrete history and experience.

My professional peers who are my opponents on this question feel they own the Christian tradition in this matter and recognize no need to rethink their positions in the light of this claim. As a feminist, I cannot sit in silence when women's right to shape the use of our procreative power is denied. Women's competence as moral decision makers is once again challenged by the state even before the moral basis of women's right to procreative choice has been fully elaborated and recognized. Those who deny women control of procreative power claim that they do so in defense of moral sensibility, in the name of the sanctity of human life. We have a long way to go before the sanctity of human life will include genuine regard and concern for every female already born, and no social policy discussion that obscures this fact deserves to be called moral. We hope the day will come when it will not be called "Christian" either, for the Christian ethos is the generating source of the current moral crusade to prevent women from gaining control over the most life-shaping power we possess.

Although I am a Protestant, my own "moral theology"[1] has more in common

This essay was adapted from articles appearing in the July and September 1981 issues of *The Witness* (vol. 64, nos. 7 and 9) and in Edward Batchelor, ed., *Abortion: The Moral Issues* (New York: Pilgrim Press, 1982). The reluctant author could not face a further revision of this essay, so its greater clarity is a result of Shirley Cloyes's collaboration. For a fuller discussion of these issues, see Beverly Wildung Harrison, *Our Right to Choose: Toward a New Ethic of Abortion* (Boston: Beacon Press, 1983).

with a Catholic approach than with much neoorthodox ethics of my own tradition. I want to stress this at the outset because in what follows I am highly critical of the reigning Roman Catholic social teaching on procreation and abortion. I believe that on most other issues of social justice, the Catholic tradition is often more substantive, morally serious, and less imbued with the dominant economic ideology than the brand of Protestant theological ethics that claims biblical warrants for its moral norms. I am no biblicist; I believe that the human wisdom that informs our ethics derives not from using the Bible alone but from reflecting in a manner that earlier Catholic moral theologians referred to as consonant with "natural law."[2] Unfortunately, however, all major strands of natural law reflection have been every bit as awful as Protestant biblicism on any matter involving human sexuality, including discussion of women's nature and women's divine vocation in relation to procreative power. And it is precisely because I recognize Catholic natural law tradition as having produced the most sophisticated type of moral reflection among Christians that I believe it must be challenged where it intersects negatively with women's lives.

Given the depth of my dissatisfaction with Protestant moral tradition, I take no pleasure in singling out Roman Catholic moral theology and the activity of the Catholic hierarchy on the abortion issue. The problem nevertheless remains that there is really only one set of moral claims involved in the Christian antiabortion argument. Protestants who oppose procreative choice[3] either tend to follow official Catholic moral theology on these matters or ground their positions in biblicist anti-intellectualism, claiming that God's "word" requires no justification other than their attestation that divine utterance says what it says. Against such irrationalism, no rational objections have a chance. When, however, Protestant fundamentalists actually specify the reasons why they believe abortion is evil, they invariably revert to traditional natural law assumptions about women, sexuality, and procreation. Hence, direct objection must be registered to the traditional natural law framework if we are serious about transforming Christian moral teaching on abortion.

To do a methodologically adequate analysis of any moral problem in religious social ethics it is necessary to (1) situate the problem in the context of various religious communities' theologies or "generative" stories, (2) do a critical historical review of the problem as it appears in our religious traditions and in the concrete lives of human agents (so that we do not confuse the past and the present), (3) scrutinize the problem from the standpoint of various moral theories, and (4) analyze existing social policy and potential alternatives to determine our "normative moral sense" or best judgment of what ought to be done in contemporary society. Although these methodological basepoints must be addressed in any socioethical analysis, their treatment is crucial when abortion is under discussion because unexamined theological presumptions and misrepresentations of Christian history figure heavily in the current public policy debate. Given the brevity of this essay, I will address the theological,

Christian historical, and moral theoretical problematics first and analyze the social policy dimensions of the abortion issue only at the end, even though optimum ethical methodology would reverse this procedure.

ABORTION IN THEOLOGICAL CONTEXT

In the history of Christian theology, a central metaphor for understanding life, including human life, is as a gift of God. Creation itself has been interpreted primarily under this metaphor. It follows that in this creational context procreation itself took on special significance as the central image for the divine blessing of human life. The elevation of procreation as the central symbol of divine benevolence happened over time, however. It did not, for instance, typify the very early, primitive Christian community. The synoptic gospels provide ample evidence that procreation played no such metaphorical role in early Christianity.[4] In later Christian history, an emergent powerful antisexual bias within Christianity made asceticism the primary spiritual ideal, although this ideal usually stood in tension with procreative power as a second sacred expression of divine blessing. But by the time of the Protestant Reformation, there was clear reaffirmation of the early Israelite theme of procreative blessing, and procreation has since become all but synonymous among Christians with the theological theme of creation as divine gift. It is important to observe that Roman Catholic theology actually followed on and adapted to Protestant teaching on this point.[5] Only in the last century, with the recognition of the danger of dramatic population growth in a world of finite resources, has any question been raised about the appropriateness of this unqualified theological sacralization of procreation.

The elevation of procreation as the central image for divine blessing is intimately connected to the rise of patriarchy. In patriarchal societies it is the male's power that is enhanced by the gift of new life. Throughout history, women's power of procreation has stood in definite tension with this male social control. In fact, what we feminists call patriarchy—that is, patterned or institutionalized legitimations of male superiority—derives from the need of men, through male-dominated political institutions such as tribes, states, and religious systems, to control women's power to procreate the species. We must assume, then, that many of these efforts at social control of procreation, including some church teaching on contraception and abortion, were part of this institutional system. The perpetuation of patriarchal control itself depended on wresting the power of procreation from women and shaping women's lives accordingly.

In the past four centuries, the entire Christian story has had to undergo dramatic accommodation to new and emergent world conditions and to the scientific revolution. As the older theological metaphors for creation encountered the rising power of science, a new self-understanding including our human capacity to affect nature had to be incorporated into Christian theology or its central theological story would have become obscurantist. Human agency had to be introjected into a dialectical understanding of creation.

The range of human freedom to shape and enhance creation is now celebrated theologically, but only up to the point of changes in our understanding of what is natural for women. Here a barrier has been drawn that declares No Radical Freedom! The only difference between mainstream Protestant and Roman Catholic theologians on these matters is at the point of contraception, which Protestants more readily accept. However, Protestants like Karl Barth and Helmut Thielicke exhibit a subtle shift of mood when they turn to discussing issues regarding women. They follow the typical Protestant pattern: They have accepted contraception or family planning as part of the new freedom, granted by God, but both draw back from the idea that abortion could be morally acceptable. In *The Ethics of Sex,* Thielicke offers a romantic, ecstatic celebration of family planning on one page and then elaborates a total denunciation of abortion as unthinkable on the next.[6] Most Christian theological opinion draws the line between contraception and abortion, whereas the *official* Catholic teaching still anathematizes contraception.

The problem, then, is that Christian theology celebrates the power of human freedom to shape and determine the quality of human life except when the issue of procreative choice arises. Abortion is anathema, while widespread sterilization abuse goes unnoticed. The power of man to shape creation radically is never rejected. When one stops to consider the awesome power over nature that males take for granted and celebrate, including the power to alter the conditions of human life in myriad ways, the suspicion dawns that the near hysteria that prevails about the immorality of women's right to choose abortion derives its force from the ancient power of misogyny rather than from any passion for the sacredness of human life. An index of the continuing misogyny in Christian tradition is male theologians' refusal to recognize the full range of human power to shape creation in those matters that pertain to women's power to affect the quality of our lives.

In contrast, a feminist theological approach recognizes that nothing is more urgent, in light of the changing circumstances of human beings on planet Earth, than to recognize that the entire natural-historical context of human procreative power has shifted.[7] We desperately need a desacralization of our biological power to reproduce[8] and at the same time a real concern for human dignity and the social conditions for personhood and the values of human relationship.[9] And note that desacralization does not mean complete devaluation of the worth of procreation. It means we must shift away from the notion that the central metaphors for divine blessing are expressed at the biological level to the recognition that our social relations bear the image of what is most holy. An excellent expression of this point comes from Marie Augusta Neal, a Roman Catholic feminist and a distinguished sociologist of religion:

As long as the central human need called for was continued motivation to propagate the race, it was essential that religious symbols idealize that process above all others. Given the vicissitudes of life in a hostile environment, women had to be encouraged to bear children and men to support them: childbearing was central to the struggle for existence. Today, however, the size of the base population, together with knowledge already accumulated about artificial insemination, sperm banking, cloning, make more certain a peopled world.

The more serious human problems now are who will live, who will die and who will decide.[10]

A CRITICAL HISTORICAL REVIEW OF ABORTION:
AN ALTERNATIVE PERSPECTIVE

Between persons who oppose all abortions on moral grounds and those who believe abortion is sometimes or frequently morally justifiable, there is no difference of moral principle. Pro-choice advocates and anti-abortion advocates share the ethical principle of respect for human life, which is probably why the debate is so acrimonious. I have already indicated that one major source of disagreement is the way in which the theological story is appropriated in relation to the changing circumstances of history. In addition, we should recognize that whenever strong moral disagreement is encountered, we simultaneously confront different readings of the history of a moral issue. The way we interpret the past is already laden with and shaped by our present sense of what the moral problem is.

For example, professional male Christian ethicists tend to assume that Christianity has an unbroken history of "all but absolute" prohibition of abortion and that the history of morality of abortion can best be traced by studying the teaching of the now best-remembered theologians. Looking at the matter this way, one can find numerous proof-texts to show that some of the "church fathers" condemned abortion and equated abortion with either homicide or murder. Whenever a "leading" churchman equated abortion with homicide or murder, he also *and simultaneously* equated *contraception* with homicide or murder. This reflects not only male chauvinist biology but also the then almost phobic antisexual bias of the Christian tradition. Claims that one can separate abortion teaching into an ethic of killing separate from an antisexual and antifemale ethic in the history of Christianity do not withstand critical scrutiny.[11]

The history of Christian natural law ethics is totally conditioned by the equation of any effort to control procreation with homicide. However, this antisexual, antiabortion tradition is not universal, even among theologians and canon lawyers. On the subject of sexuality and its abuse, many well-known theologians had nothing to say; abortion was not even mentioned in most moral theology. An important, untold chapter in Christian history is the great struggle that took place in the medieval period when clerical celibacy came to be imposed and the rules of sexual behavior rigidified.

My thesis is that there is a relative disinterest in the question of abortion overall in Christian history. Occasionally, Christian theologians picked up the issue, especially when these theologians were state-related, that is, were articulating policy not only for the church but for political authority. Demographer Jean Meyer, himself a Catholic, insists that the Christian tradition took over "expansion by population growth" from the Roman Empire.[12] Christians opposed abortion strongly only when Christianity was closely identified with imperial state policy or when theologians were inveighing against women and any sexuality except that expressed in the reluctant service of procreation.

The Holy Crusade quality of present teaching on abortion is quite new in Christianity and is related to cultural shifts that are requiring the Christian tradition to choose sides in the present ideological struggle under pressure to rethink its entire attitude toward women and sexuality. My research has led me to the tentative conclusion that, in Protestant cultures, except where Protestantism is the "established religion," merging church and state, one does not find a strong antiabortion theological-ethical teaching at all. At least in the United States, this is beyond historical debate.[13] No Protestant clergy or theologian gave early support for proposed nineteenth-century laws banning abortion in the United States. It is my impression that Protestant clergy, usually married and often poor, were aware that romanticizing nature's bounty with respect to procreation resulted in a great deal of human suffering. The Protestant clergy who finally did join the anti-abortion crusade were racist, classist white clergy, who feared America's strength was being threatened because white, middle-class, respectable women had a lower birth rate than black and ethnic women. Such arguments are still with us.

One other historical point must be stressed. Until the late nineteenth century the natural law tradition, and biblicism following it, tended to define the act of abortion as interruption of pregnancy after ensoulment, which was understood to be the point at which the breath of God entered the fetus. The point at which ensoulment was said to occur varied, but most typically it was marked by quickening, when fetal movement began. Knowledge about embryology was primitive until the past half-century, so this commonsense understanding prevailed. As a result, when abortion was condemned in earlier Christian teaching it was understood to refer to the termination of a pregnancy well into the process of the pregnancy, after ensoulment. Until the late nineteenth century, when Pope Pius IX, intrigued with the new embryonic discoveries, brought the natural law tradition into consonance with "modern science," abortion in ecclesiastical teaching often applied only to termination of prenatal life in more advanced stages of pregnancy.

Another distortion in the male-generated history of this issue derives from failure to note that, until the development of safe, surgical, elective abortion, the act of abortion commonly referred to something done to the woman, with or without her consent (see Exodus 22), either as a wrong done a husband or for the better moral reasons that abortion was an act of violence against both a pregnant woman and fetal life. In recent discussion it is the woman who does the wrongful act. No one would deny that abortion, if it terminates a pregnancy against the woman's wishes, is morally wrong. And until recent decades, abortion endangered the woman's life as much as it did the prenatal life in her womb. Hence, one premodern moral reason for opposing abortion was that it threatened the life and well-being of the mother more than did carrying the pregnancy to term. Today abortion is statistically safer than childbearing. Consequently, no one has a right to discuss the morality of abortion today without recognizing that one of the traditional and appropriate moral reasons for objecting to abortion— concern for women's well-being—now inheres in the pro-choice side of the debate. Anti-abortion proponents who accord the fetus full human standing without also assigning positive value to women's lives and well-being are not really pressing the full sense of Christian moral tradition in the abortion debate.

Beyond all this, the deepest moral flaw in the "pro-life" position's historical view is that none of its proponents has attempted to reconstruct the concrete, lived-world context in which the abortion discussion belongs: the all but desperate struggle by sexually active women to gain some proximate control over nature's profligacy in conception. Under the most adverse conditions, women have had to try to control our fertility—everywhere, always. Women's relation to procreation irrevocably marks and shapes our lives. Even those of us who do not have sexual contact with males, because we are celibate or lesbian, have been potential, even probable, victims of male sexual violence or have had to bear heavy social stigma for refusing the centrality of dependence on men and of procreation in our lives. The lives of infertile women, too, are shaped by our failure to meet procreative expectations. Women's lack of social power, in all recorded history, has made this struggle to control procreation a life-bending, often life-destroying one for a large percentage of females.

So most women have had to do whatever we could to prevent too-numerous pregnancies. In societies and cultures, except the most patriarchal, the processes of procreation have been transmitted through women's culture. Birth control techniques have been widely practiced, and some primitive ones have proved effective. Increasingly, anthropologists are gaining hints of how procreative control occurred in some premodern societies. Frequently women have had to choose to risk their lives in order not to have that extra child that would destroy the family's ability to cope or bring about an unmanageable crisis.

We have to concede that modern medicine, for all its misogyny, has replaced some dangerous contraceptive practices still widely used where surgical abortion is unavailable. In light of these gains, more privileged western women must not lose the ability to imagine the real-life pressures that lead women in other cultures to resort to ground-glass douches, reeds inserted in the uterus, and so on, to induce labor. The radical nature of methods women use bespeaks the desperation involved in unwanted pregnancy and reveals the real character of our struggle.

Nor should we suppress the fact that a major means of birth control now is, as it was in earlier times, infanticide. And let no one imagine that women have made decisions to expose or kill newborn infants casually. Women understand what many men cannot seem to grasp—that the birth of a child requires that some person must be prepared to care, without interruption, for this infant, provide material resources and energy-draining amounts of time and attention for it. The human infant is the most needy and dependent of all newborn creatures. It seems to me that men, especially celibate men, romanticize this total and uncompromising dependency of the infant on the already existing human community. Women bear the brunt of this reality and know its full implications. And this dependency is even greater in a fragmented, centralized urban-industrial modern culture than in a rural culture, where another pair of hands often increased an extended family unit's productive power. No historical interpretation of abortion as a moral issue that ignores these matters deserves moral standing in the present debate.

A treatment of any moral problem is inadequate if it fails to analyze the morality of a given act in a way that represents the concrete experience of the agent who faces a decision with respect to that act. Misogyny in Christian discussions of abortion is evidenced clearly in that the abortion decision is never treated in the way it arises as part of the female agent's life process. The decision at issue when the dilemma of choice arises for women is whether or not to be pregnant. In most discussions of the morality of abortion it is treated as an abstract act[14] rather than as a possible way to deal with a pregnancy that frequently is the result of circumstances beyond the woman's control. John Noonan, for instance, evades this fact by referring to the pregnant woman almost exclusively as "the gravida" (a Latin term meaning "pregnant one") or "the carrier" in his *A Private Choice: Abortion in America in the Seventies*.[15] In any pregnancy a woman's life is deeply, irrevocably affected. Those such as Noonan who uphold the unexceptional immorality of abortion are probably wise to obscure the fact that an unwanted pregnancy always involves a life-shaping consequence for a woman, because suppressing the identity of the moral agent and the reality of her dilemma greatly reduces the ability to recognize the moral complexity of abortion. When the question of abortion arises it is usually because a woman finds herself facing an unwanted pregnancy. Consider the actual circumstances that may precipitate this. One is the situation in which a woman did not intend to be sexually active or did not enter into a sexual act voluntarily. Since women are frequently victims of sexual violence, numerous cases of this type arise because of rape, incest, or forced marital coitus. Many morally sensitive opponents of abortion concede that in such cases abortion may be morally justifiable. I insist that in such cases it is a moral good because it is not rational to treat a newly fertilized ovum as though it had the same value as the existent, pregnant female person and because it is morally wrong to make the victim of sexual violence suffer the further agonies of unwanted pregnancy and childbearing against her will. Enforced pregnancy would be viewed as a morally reprehensible violation of bodily integrity if women were recognized as fully human moral agents.

Another more frequent case results when a woman—or usually a young girl—participates in heterosexual activity without clear knowledge of how pregnancy occurs and without intention to conceive a child. A girl who became pregnant in this manner would, by traditional natural law morality, be held in a state of invincible ignorance and therefore not morally culpable. One scholarly Roman Catholic nun I met argued—quite appropriately, I believe—that her church should not consider the abortions of young Catholic girls as morally culpable because the Church overprotected them, which contributed to their lack of understanding of procreation and to their inability to cope with the sexual pressures girls experience in contemporary society. A social policy that pressures the sexually ill-informed child or young woman into unintended or unaware motherhood would be morally dubious indeed.

A related type of pregnancy happens when a woman runs risks by not using contraceptives, perhaps because taking precaution in romantic affairs is not perceived as ladylike or requires her to be too unspontaneous about sex. Our society resents women's sexuality unless it is "innocent" and male-mediated, so many women, lest they be censured as "loose" and "promiscuous," are slow to assume adult responsibility for contraception. However, when pregnancies occur because women are skirting the edges of responsibility and running risks out of immaturity, is enforced motherhood a desirable solution? Such pregnancies could be minimized only by challenging precisely those childish myths of female socialization embedded in natural law teaching about female sexuality.

It is likely that most decisions about abortion arise because mature women who are sexually active with men and who understand the risk of pregnancy nevertheless experience contraceptive failure. Our moral schizophrenia in this matter is exhibited in that many people believe women have more responsibility than men to practice contraception and that family planning is always a moral good, but even so rule out abortion altogether. Such a split consciousness ignores the fact that no inexorable biological line exists between prevention of conception and abortion.[16] More important, such reasoning ignores the genuine risks involved in female contraceptive methods. Some women are at higher risk than others in using the most reliable means of birth control. Furthermore, the reason we do not have more concern for safer contraceptive methods for men and women is that matters relating to women's health and well-being are never urgent in this society. Moreover, many contraceptive failures are due to the irresponsibility of the producers of contraceptives rather than to bad luck.[17] Given these facts, should a woman who actively attempts to avoid pregnancy be punished for contraceptive failure when it occurs?

In concluding this historical section, I must stress that if present efforts to criminalize abortion succeed, we will need a state apparatus of massive proportions to enforce compulsory childbearing. In addition, withdrawal of legal abortion will create one more massively profitable underworld economy in which the Mafia and other sections of quasi-legal capitalism may and will profitably invest. The radical right promises to get the state out of regulation of people's lives, but what they really mean is that they will let economic activity go unrestrained. What their agenda signifies for the personal lives of women is quite another matter.

An adequate historical perspective on abortion recognizes the long struggle women have waged for some degree of control over fertility and their efforts to regain control of procreative power from patriarchal and state-imperial culture and institutions. Such a perspective also takes into account that more nearly adequate contraceptive methods and the existence of safe, surgical, elective abortion represent positive historic steps toward full human freedom and dignity for women. While the same gains in medical knowledge also open the way to new forms of sterilization abuse and to social pressures against some women's use of their power of procreation, I know of no women who would choose to return to a state of lesser knowledge about these matters.

There has been an objective gain in the quality of women's lives for those fortunate enough to have access to procreative choice. That millions upon millions of women as yet do not possess even the rudimentary conditions—moral or physical—for such choice is obvious. Our moral goal should be to struggle against those real barriers—poverty, racism, and antifemale cultural oppression—that prevent authentic choice from being a reality for every woman. In this process we will be able to minimize the need for abortions only insofar as we place the abortion debate in the real lived-world context of women's lives.

ABORTION AND MORAL THEORY

The greatest strategic problem of pro-choice advocates is the widespread assumption that pro-lifers have a monopoly on the moral factors that ought to enter into decisions about abortion. *Moral* here is defined as that which makes for the self-respect and well-being of human persons and their environment. Moral legitimacy seems to adhere to their position in part because traditionalists have an array of religiomoral terminology at their command that the sometimes more secular proponents of choice lack. But those who would displace women's power of choice by the power of the state and/or the medical profession do not deserve the aura of moral sanctity. We must do our homework if we are to dispel this myth of moral superiority. A major way in which Christian moral theologians and moral philosophers contribute to this monopoly of moral sanctity is by equating fetal or prenatal life with human personhood in a simplistic way and by failing to acknowledge changes regarding this issue in the history of Christianity.

We need to remember that even in Roman Catholic natural law ethics, the definition of the status of fetal life has shifted over time and in all cases the status of prenatal life involves a moral judgment, not a scientific one. The question is properly posed this way: What status are we morally wise to predicate to prenatal human life, given that the fetus is not yet a fully existent human being? Those constrained under Catholic teaching have been required for the past ninety years to believe a human being exists from conception, when the ovum and sperm merge.[18] This answer from one tradition has had far wider impact on our culture than most people recognize. Other Christians come from traditions that do not offer (and could not offer, given their conception of the structure of the church as moral community) a definitive answer to this question.

Even so, some contemporary Protestant medical ethicists, fascinated by recent genetic discoveries and experiments with deoxyribonucleic acid (DNA), have all but sacralized the moment in which the genetic code is implanted as the moment of humanization, which leaves them close to the traditional Roman Catholic position. Protestant male theologians have long let their enthrallment with science lead to a sacralization of specific scientific discoveries, usually to the detriment of theological and moral clarity. In any case, there are two responses that must be made to the claim that the fetus in early stages of development is a human life or, more dubiously, a human person.

First, the historical struggle for women's personhood is far from won, owing chiefly to the opposition of organized religious groups to full equality for women. Those who proclaim that a zygote at the moment of conception is a person worthy of citizenship continue to deny full social and political rights to women. Whatever one's judgment about the moral status of the fetus, it cannot be argued that that assessment deserves greater moral standing in analysis than does the position of the pregnant woman. This matter of evaluating the meaning of prenatal life is where morally sensitive people's judgments diverge. I cannot believe that any morally sensitive person would fail to value the woman's full, existent life less than they value early fetal life. Most women can become pregnant and carry fetal life to term many, many times in their lifetimes. The distinctly human power is not our biologic capacity to bear children, but our power to actively love, nurture, care for one another and shape one another's existence in cultural and social interaction.[19] To equate a biologic process with full normative humanity is crass biologic reductionism, and such reductionism is never practiced in religious ethics except where women's lives and well-being are involved.

Second, even though prenatal life, as it moves toward biologic individuation of human form, has value, the equation of abortion with murder is dubious. And the equation of abortion with homicide—the taking of human life—should be carefully weighed. We should also remember that we live in a world where men extend other men wide moral range in relation to justifiable homicide. For example, the just-war tradition has legitimated widespread forms of killing in war, and Christian ethicists have often extended great latitude to rulers and those in power in making choices about killing human beings.[20] Would that such moralists extended equal benefit of a doubt to women facing life-crushing psychological and politicoeconomic pressures in the face of childbearing! Men, daily, make life-determining decisions concerning nuclear power or chemical use in the environment, for example, that affect the well-being of fetuses, and our society expresses no significant opposition, even when such decisions do widespread genetic damage. When we argue for the appropriateness of legal abortion, moral outrage rises.

The so-called pro-life position also gains support by invoking the general principle of respect for human life as foundational to its morality in a way that suggests that the pro-choice advocates are unprincipled. I have already noted that pro-choice advocates have every right to claim the same moral principle, and that this debate, like most debates that are morally acrimonious, is in no sense about basic moral principles. I do not believe there is any clear-cut conflict of principle in this very deep, very bitter controversy.

It needs to be stressed that we all have an absolute obligation to honor any moral principle that seems, after rational deliberation, to be sound. This is the one absolutism appropriate to ethics. There are often several moral principles relevant to a decision and many ways to relate a given principle to a decisional context. For most right-to-lifers only one principle has moral standing in this argument. Admitting only one principle to one's process of moral reasoning means that a range of other moral values is slighted. Right-to-lifers are also moral absolutists in the sense that they admit only one possible meaning or application of the principle they invoke. Both these types of absolutism obscure moral debate and lead to less, not more, rational deliberation. The principle of respect for human life is one we should all honor, but we must also recognize that this principle often comes into conflict with other valid moral principles in the process of making real, lived-world decisions. Understood in an adequate way, this principle can be restated to mean that we should treat what falls under a reasonable definition of human life as having sanctity or intrinsic moral value. But even when this is clear, other principles are needed to help us choose between two intrinsic values, in this case between the prenatal life and the pregnant woman's life.

Another general moral principle from which we cannot exempt our actions is the principle of justice, or right relations between persons and between groups of persons and communities. Another relevant principle is respect for all that supports human life, namely, the natural environment. As any person knows who thinks deeply about morality, genuine moral conflicts, as often as not, are due not to ignoring moral principles but to the fact that different principles lead to conflicting implications for action or are selectively related to decisions. For example, we live in a time when the principle of justice for women, aimed at transforming the social relations that damage women's lives, is historically urgent. For many of us this principle has greater moral urgency than the extension of the principle of respect for human life to include early fetal life, even though respect for fetal life is also a positive moral good. We should resist approaches to ethics that claim that one overriding principle always deserves to control morality. Clarification of principle, for that matter, is only a small part of moral reasoning. When we weigh moral principles and their potential application, we must also consider the implications of a given act for our present historical context and envision its long-term consequences.

One further proviso on this issue of principles in moral reasoning: There are several distinct theories among religious ethicists and moral philosophers as to what the function of principles ought to be. One group believes moral principles are for the purpose of terminating the process of moral reasoning. Hence, if this sort of moralist tells you always to honor the principle of respect for human life, what he or she means is for you to stop reflection and act in a certain way—in this case to accept one's pregnancy regardless of consequences. Others believe that it is better to refer to principles (broad, generalized moral criteria) than to apply rules (narrower, specific moral prescriptions) because principles function to open up processes of reasoning rather than close them off. The principle of respect for life, on this reading, is not invoked to prescribe action but to help locate and weigh values, to illuminate a range of values that always inhere in significant human decisions. A major difference in the moral debate on abortion, then, is that some believe that to invoke the principle of respect for human life settles the matter, stops debate, and precludes the single, simple act of abortion. By contrast, many of us believe the breadth of the principle opens up to reconsideration the question of what the essential moral quality of human life is all about and to increase moral seriousness about choosing whether or when to bear children.

Two other concerns related to our efforts to make a strong moral case for women's right to procreative choice need to be touched on. The first has to do with the problems our Christian tradition creates for any attempt to make clear why women's right to control our bodies is an urgent and substantive moral claim. One of Christianity's greatest weaknesses is its spiritualizing neglect of respect for the physical body and physical well-being. Tragically, women, more than men, are expected in Christian teaching never to honor their own well-being as a moral consideration. I want to stress, then, that we have no moral tradition in Christianity that starts with body-space, or body-right, as a basic condition of moral relations. (Judaism is far better in this regard, for it acknowledges that we all have a moral right to be concerned for our life and our survival.) Hence, many Christian ethicists simply do not get the point when we speak of women's right to bodily integrity. They blithely denounce such reasons as women's disguised self-indulgence or hysterical rhetoric.[21]

We must articulate our view that body-right is a basic moral claim and also remind our hearers that there is no unchallengeable analogy among other human activities to women's procreative power. Pregnancy is a distinctive human experience. In any social relation, body-space must be respected or nothing deeply human or moral can be created. The social institutions most similar to compulsory pregnancy in their moral violations of body-space are chattel slavery and peonage. These institutions distort the moral relations of a community and deform a community over time. (Witness racism in the United States.) Coercion of women, through enforced sterilization or enforced pregnancy, legitimates unjust power in intimate human relationships and cuts to the heart of our capacity for moral social relations. As we should recognize, given our violence-prone society, people learn violence at home and at an early age when women's lives are violated!

Even so, we must be careful, when we make the case for our right to bodily integrity, not to confuse moral rights with mere liberties.[22] To claim that we have a moral right to procreative choice does not mean we believe women can exercise this right free of all moral claims from the community. For example, we need to teach female children that childbearing is not a purely capricious, individualistic matter, and we need to challenge the assumption that a woman who enjoys motherhood should have as many children as she and her mate wish, regardless of its effects on others. Population self-control is a moral issue, although more so in high-consuming, affluent societies like our own than in nations where a modest, simple, and less wasteful lifestyle obtains.

A second point is the need, as we work politically for a pro-choice social policy, to avoid the use of morally objectionable arguments to mobilize support for our side of the issue. One can get a lot of political mileage in U.S. society by using covert racist and classist appeals ("abortion lowers the cost of welfare rolls or reduces illegitimacy" or "paying for abortions saves the taxpayers money in the long run"). Sometimes it is argued that good politics is more important than good morality and that one should use whatever arguments work to gain political support. I do not believe that these crassly utilitarian[23] arguments turn out, in the long run, to be good politics for they are costly to our sense of polis and of community. But even if they were effective in the short run, I am doubly sure that on the issue of the right to choose abortion, good morality doth a good political struggle make. I believe, deeply, that moral right is on the side of the struggle for the freedom and self-respect of women, especially poor and nonwhite women, and on the side of developing social policy that ensures that every child born can be certain to be a wanted child. Issues of justice are those that deserve the deepest moral caretaking as we develop a political strategy.

Only when people see that they cannot prohibit safe, legal, elective surgical abortion without violating the conditions of well-being for the vast majority of women—especially those most socially vulnerable because of historic patterns of oppression—will the effort to impose a selective, abstract morality of the sanctity of human life on all of us cease. This is a moral battle par excellence, and whenever we forget that we make it harder to reach the group most important to the cause of procreative choice—those women who have never suffered from childbearing pressures, who have not yet put this issue into a larger historical context, and who reverence women's historical commitment to childbearing. We will surely not reach them with pragmatic appeals to the taxpayer's wallet! To be sure, we cannot let such women go unchallenged as they support ruling-class ideology that the state should control procreation. But they will not change their politics until they see that pro-choice is grounded in a deeper, tougher, more caring moral vision than the political option they now endorse.

THE SOCIAL POLICY DIMENSIONS OF THE DEBATE

Most people fail to understand that in ethics we need, provisionally, to separate our reflection on the morality of specific acts from questions about how we express our moral values within our social institutions and systems (that is, social policy). When we do this, the morality of abortion appears in a different light. Focusing attention away from the single act of abortion to the larger historical context thrusts into relief what "respect for human life" means in the pro-choice position. It also illuminates the common core of moral concern that unites pro-choice advocates to pro-lifers who have genuine concern for expanding the circle of who really counts as human in this society. Finally, placing abortion in a larger historical context enables proponents of pro-choice to clarify where we most differ from the pro-lifers, that is, in our total skepticism that a state-enforced antiabortion policy could ever have the intended "pro-life" consequences they claim.

We must always insist that the objective social conditions that make women and children already born highly vulnerable can only be worsened by a social policy of compulsory pregnancy. However one judges the moral quality of the individual act of abortion (and here, differences among us do exist that are morally justifiable), it is still necessary to distinguish between how one judges the act of abortion morally and what one believes a societywide policy on abortion should be. We must not let those who have moral scruples against the personal act ignore the fact that a just social policy must also include active concern for enhancement of women's well-being and, for that, policies that would in fact make abortions less necessary. To anathematize abortion when the social and material conditions for control of procreation do not exist is to blame the victim, not to address the deep dilemmas of female existence in this society.

Even so, there is no reason for those of us who celebrate procreative choice as a great moral good to pretend that resort to abortion is ever a desirable means of expressing this choice. I know of no one on the pro-choice side who has confused the desirability of the availability of abortion with the celebration of the act itself.

We all have every reason to hope that safer, more reliable means of contraception may be found and that violence against women will be reduced. Furthermore, we should be emphatic that our social policy demands include opposition to sterilization abuse, insistence on higher standards of health care for women and children, better prenatal care, reduction of unnecessary surgery on women's reproductive systems, increased research to improve contraception, and so on. Nor should we draw back from criticizing a health care delivery system that exploits women. An abortion industry thrives on the profitability of abortion, but women are not to blame for this.

A feminist position demands social conditions that support women's full, self-respecting right to procreative choice, including the right not to be sterilized against our wills, the right to choose abortion as a birth control means of last resort, and the right to a prenatal and postnatal health care system that will also reduce the now widespread trauma of having to deliver babies in rigid, impersonal health care settings. Pro-lifers do best politically when we allow them to keep the discussion narrowly focused on the morality of the act of abortion and on the moral value of the fetus. We do best politically when we make the deep connections between the full context of this issue in women's lives, including this society's systemic or patterned injustice toward women.

It is well to remember that it has been traditional Catholic natural law ethics that most clarified and stressed this distinction between the morality of an individual act on the one hand and the policies that produce the optional social morality on the other. The strength of this tradition is probably reflected in the fact that even now most polls show that slightly more Catholics than Protestants believe it unwise for the state to attempt to regulate abortion. In the past, Catholics, more than Protestants, have been wary of using the state as an instrument of moral crusade. Tragically, by taking their present approach to abortion, the Roman Catholic hierarchy may be risking the loss of the deepest wisdom of its own ethical tradition. By failing to acknowledge a distinction between the church's moral teaching on the act of abortion and the question of what is a desirable social policy to minimize abortion, as well as overemphasizing it to the neglect of other social justice concerns, the Roman Catholic church may well be dissipating the best of its moral tradition.[24]

The frenzy of the current pope and many Roman Catholic bishops in the United States on this issue has reached startling proportions. The United States bishops have equated nuclear war and the social practice of abortion as the most heinous social evils of our time.[25] While this appallingly misguided analogy has gained credibility because of the welcome if modest opposition of the bishops to nuclear escalation, I predict that the long-term result will be to further discredit Roman Catholic moral wisdom in the culture.

If we are to be a society genuinely concerned with enhancing women's well-being and minimizing the necessity of abortions, thereby avoiding the danger over time of becoming an abortion culture,[26] what kind of a society must we become? It is here that the moral clarity of the feminist analysis becomes most obvious. How can we reduce the number of abortions due to contraceptive failure? By placing greater emphasis on medical research in this area, by requiring producers of contraceptives to behave more responsibly, and by developing patterns of institutional life that place as much emphasis on male responsibility for procreation and long-term care and nurturance of children as on female responsibility.

How can we reduce the number of abortions due to childish ignorance about sexuality among female children or adult women and our mates? By adopting a widespread program of sex education and by supporting institutional policies that teach male and female children alike that a girl is as fully capable as a boy of enjoying sex and that both must share moral responsibility for preventing pregnancy except when they have decided, as a deliberative moral act, to have a child.

How would we reduce the necessity of abortion due to sexual violence against women in and out of marriage? By challenging vicious male-generated myths that women exist primarily to meet the sexual needs of men, that women are, by nature, those who are really fulfilled only through our procreative powers. We would teach feminist history as the truthful history of the race, stressing that historic patterns of patriarchy were morally wrong and that a humane or moral society would be a fully nonsexist society.

Technological developments that may reduce the need for abortions are not entirely within our control, but the sociomoral ethos that makes abortion common is within our power to change. And we would begin to create such conditions by adopting a thoroughgoing feminist program for society. Nothing less, I submit, expresses genuine respect for all human life.

NOTES

1. I use the traditional Roman Catholic term intentionally because my ethical method has greater affinity with the Roman Catholic model.

2. The Christian natural law tradition developed because many Christians understood that the power of moral reason inhered in human beings qua human beings, not merely in the understanding that comes from being Christian. Those who follow natural law methods address moral issues from the consideration of what options appear rationally compelling, given present reflection, rather than from theological claims alone. My own moral theological method is congenial to certain of these natural law assumptions. Roman Catholic natural law teaching, however, has become internally incoherent by its insistence that in some matters of morality the teaching authority of the hierarchy must be taken as the proper definition of what is rational. This replacement of reasoned reflection by ecclesiastical authority seems to me to offend against what we must mean by moral reasoning on best understanding. I would argue that a moral theology cannot forfeit final judgment or even penultimate judgment on moral matters to anything except fully deliberated communal consensus. On the abortion issue, this of course would mean women would be consulted in a degree that reflects their numbers in

the Catholic church. No a priori claims to authoritative moral reason are ever possible, and if those affected are not consulted, the teaching cannot claim rationality.

3. For a critique of these positions, see Paul D. Simmons, "A Theological Response to Fundamentalism on the Abortion Issue," in *Abortion: The Moral Issues,* ed. Edward Batchelor, Jr. (New York: Pilgrim Press, 1982), 175–187.

4. Most biblical scholars agree that either the early Christians expected an imminent end to history and therefore had only an "interim ethic," or that Jesus' teaching, in its radical support for "the outcasts" of his society, did not aim to justify existing social institutions. See, for example, Luke 4 and 12; Mark 7, 9, 13, and 14; Matthew 25. See also Elisabeth Schüssler Fiorenza, "You Are Not to be Called Father," *Cross Currents* (Fall 1979), 301–323. See also her *Bread Not Stone: The Challenge of Feminist Biblical Interpretation* (Boston: Beacon Press, 1985).

5. Few Roman Catholic theologians seem to appreciate how much the recent enthusiastic endorsement of traditional family values implicates Catholicism in Protestant Reformational spirituality. Rosemary Ruether is an exception; she has stressed this point in her writings.

6. Helmut Thielicke, *The Ethics of Sex* (New York: Harper and Row, 1964), 199–247. Compare pp. 210 and 226ff. Barth's position on abortion is a bit more complicated than I can elaborate here, which is why one will find him quoted on both sides of the debate. Barth's method allows him to argue that any given radical human act could turn out to be "the will of God" in a given context or setting. We may at any time be given "permission" by God's radical freedom to do what was not before permissible. My point here is that Barth exposits this possible exception in such a traditional prohibitory context that I do not believe it appropriate to cite him on the pro-choice side of the debate. In my opinion, no woman could ever accept the convoluted way in which Barth's biblical exegesis opens the door (a slight crack) to woman's full humanity. His reasoning on these questions simply demonstrates what deep difficulty the Christian tradition's exegetical tradition is in with respect to the full humanity and moral agency of women. See Karl Barth, "The Protection of Life," in *Church Dogmatics,* part 3, vol. 4 (Edinburgh: T. and T. Clark, 1961), 415–22.

7. Compare Beverly Wildung Harrison, "When Fruitfulness and Blessedness Diverge," *Religion and Life* (1972), vol. 41, no. 4, 480–496. My views on the seriousness of misogyny as a historical force have deepened since I wrote this essay.

8. Marie Augusta Neal, "Sociology and Sexuality: A Feminist Perspective," *Christianity and Crisis* 39, no. 8 (14 May 1979), 118–122.

9. For a feminist theology of relationship, see Carter Heyward, *Toward the Redemption of God: A Theology of Mutual Relation* (Washington, D.C.: University Press of America, 1982).

10. Neal, "Sociology and Sexuality." This article is of critical importance in discussions of the theology and morality of abortion.

11. Susan Teft Nicholson, *Abortion and the Roman Catholic Church,* JRE Studies in Religious Ethics II (Knoxville: Religious Ethics Inc., University of Tennessee, 1978). This carefully crafted study assumes that there has been a clear "antikilling" ethic separable from any antisexual ethic in Christian abortion teaching. This is an assumption that my historical research does not sustain.

12. Jean Meyer, "Toward a Non-Malthusian Population Policy," in *The American Population Debate,* ed. Daniel Callahan (Garden City, N.Y.: Doubleday, 1971).

13. See James C. Mohr, *Abortion in America* (New York: Oxford University Press,

1978), and James Nelson, "Abortion: Protestant Perspectives," in *Encyclopedia of Bioethics,* vol. 1, ed. Warren T. Reich (New York: Free Press, 1978), 13–17.

14. H. Richard Niebuhr often warned his theological compatriots about abstracting acts from the life project in which they are embedded, but this warning is much neglected in the writings of Christian moralists. See "The Christian Church in the World Crises," *Christianity and Society* 6 (1941).

15. John T. Noonan, Jr., *A Private Choice: Abortion in America in the Seventies* (New York: Free Press, 1979). Noonan denies that the history of abortion is related to the history of male oppression of women.

16. We know now that the birth control pill does not always work by preventing fertilization of the ovum by the sperm. Frequently, the pill causes the wall of the uterus to expel the newly fertilized ovum. From a biological point of view, there is no point in the procreative process that can be taken as a clear dividing line on which to pin neat moral distinctions.

17. The most conspicuous example of corporate involvement in contraceptive failure was the famous Dalkan Shield scandal. Note also that the manufacturer of the Dalkan Shield dumped its dangerous and ineffective product on family planning programs of third-world (overexploited) countries.

18. Catholic moral theology opens up several ways for faithful Catholics to challenge the teaching office of the church on moral questions. However, I remain unsatisfied that these qualifications of inerrancy in moral matters stand up in situations of moral controversy. If freedom of conscience does not function *de jure,* should it be claimed as existent in principle?

19. I elaborate this point in greater detail in "The Power of Anger in the Work of Love" in this book [*Making the Connections* (Boston: Beacon, 1985)].

20. For example, Paul Ramsey gave unqualified support to U.S. military involvement in Southeast Asia in light of just-war considerations but finds abortion to be an unexceptional moral wrong.

21. See Richard A. McCormick, S.J., "Rules for Abortion Debate," in Batchelor, *Abortion: The Moral Issues,* pp. 27–37.

22. One of the reasons why abortion-on-demand rhetoric—even when it is politically effective in the immediate moment—has had a backlash effect is that it seems to many to imply a lack of reciprocity between women's needs and society's needs. While I would not deny, in principle, a possible conflict of interest between women's well-being and the community's needs for reproduction, there is little or no historical evidence that suggests women are less responsible to the well-being of the community than are men. We need not fall into a liberal, individualistic trap in arguing the central importance of procreative choice to issues of women's well-being in society. The right in question is body-right, or freedom from coercion in childbearing. It is careless to say that the right in question is the right to an abortion. Morally, the right is bodily self-determination, a fundamental condition of personhood and a foundational moral right. See Beverly Wildung Harrison, *Our Right to Choose: Toward a New Ethic of Abortion* (Boston: Beacon Press, 1983).

23. A theory is crassly utilitarian only if it fails to grant equal moral worth to all persons in the calculation of social consequences—as, for example, when some people's financial well-being is weighted more than someone else's basic physical existence. I do not mean to criticize any type of utilitarian moral theory that weighs the actual consequences of actions. In fact, I believe no moral theory is adequate if it does not have a strong utilitarian component.

24. For a perceptive discussion of this danger by a distinguished Catholic priest, read George C. Higgins, "The Prolife Movement and the New Right," *America,* 13 Sept. 1980, 107–110.

25. Philip J. Murnion, ed., *Catholics and Nuclear War: A Commentary on the Challenge of the U.S. Catholic Bishops' Pastoral Letter on War and Peace* (New York: Crossroads, 1983), 326.

26. I believe the single most valid concern raised by opponents of abortion is that the frequent practice of abortion, over time, may contribute to a cultural ethos of insensitivity to the value of human life, not because fetuses are being "murdered" but because surgical termination of pregnancy may further "technologize" our sensibilities about procreation. I trust that all of the foregoing makes clear my adamant objection to allowing this insight to justify yet more violence against women. However, I do believe we should be very clear that we stand ready to support—emphatically—any social policies that would lessen the need for abortion *without* jeopardizing women's right to control our own procreative power.

16

REPRODUCTIVE GIFTS AND GIFT GIVING

The Altruistic Woman

Janice G. Raymond

In the aftermath of the "Baby M" case, the surrogacy debate has mostly left the media forum and entered the state legislatures. Many of these legislatures are now debating the legal status of surrogate contracts. Where legislative committees have opposed commercial contracts, they have tended to view alternative noncommercial surrogate parenting arrangements as ethically and legally permissible. An underlying theme here is that noncommercial arrangements are seen as altruistic. This article examines the implications of an altruistic ethic, particularly in reference to surrogacy, and highlights its problems for women in the reproductive realm.

GIFTS AND GIFT GIVING

In his well-known study, *The Gift Relationship: From Human Blood to Social Policy,* Richard Titmuss opposed commercial systems of blood supply to noncommercial and altruistic systems of blood giving. Titmuss's concern was to shore up the spirit of altruism and voluntarism which he saw declining in western societies. His analysis is, in the main, a positive assessment of the possibilities of altruistic blood donation. But Titmuss also understood that giving was influenced by "the relationships set up, social and economic, between the system and the donor," and that these relationships are "strongly determined by the values and cultural orientations permeating the donor system and the society in general."[1] The dialectic between values and structural factors emerges strongly in his work. We must ask, he wrote, if there is truly "no contract of custom, no legal bond, no functional determinism, no situations of discriminatory power, domination, constraint or compulsion, no sense of shame or guilt, no gratitude imperative and no need for the penitence of a Chrysostom" (239).

The role of cultural values and constraints in shaping gift-giving arrangements is vital.

In the case of many new reproductive practices, and surrogacy especially, "the donor system" mainly depends on women as the gift givers—women who donate the use of their bodies and the fruit of their wombs. Those who endorse altruistic surrogacy as an alternative to commercial surrogacy accept, without comment or criticism, that it is primarily women who constitute the altruistic population called upon to contribute gestating capacities.[2] The questions that Titmuss raised about "contract of custom," "functional determinism," "situations of discriminatory power," "domination, constraint or compulsion," as well as possible "shame or guilt" and a "gratitude imperative" form part of the unexamined hallowing of altruistic surrogacy.

This unexamined acceptance of women as reproductive gift givers is very much related to a longstanding patriarchal tradition of giving women away in other cultural contexts—for sex and in marriage, for example. Following Titmuss, we must continually in these discussions of altruism ask: who gives and why? But further, who has been given away historically and why? In this sense, women are not only the gift givers but the gift as well. The pervasiveness of women's personal and social obligation to give shapes the contexts of reproductive gifts and gift giving. We see this most clearly in the situation of so-called altruistic surrogacy.

ALTRUISM VERSUS COMMERCIALISM

Those critical of commercial surrogacy often contrast it to noncommercial or altruistic surrogacy. The New Jersey Supreme Court, in its appellate judgment, *In the Matter of Baby M,* found surrogate contracts contrary to the law and public policy of the state. Nonetheless, it concluded that there were no legal impediments to arrangements "when the surrogate mother volunteers, without any payment, to act as a surrogate."[3] Many state legislative committees are taking action to prohibit commercial surrogacy but are leaving untouched the whole area of noncommercial surrogate practices. Altruism and voluntarism emerge as moral virtues in opposition to commercialism. George Annas, who has opposed commercial surrogacy, is sympathetic to the view that "one can distinguish between doing something out of love and doing it for money. As long as existing adoption laws are followed, voluntary relinquishment of a child to a close relative (such as an infertile sister) seems acceptable."[4] Such a scenario has in fact already been played out.

In this country, one publicized case of altruistic surrogacy occurred in 1985 when Sherry King offered to become pregnant for her sister, Carole, who had undergone a hysterectomy eighteen years before. Sherry King provided both egg and womb. "I know I couldn't be a surrogate mother for money . . . I'm doing this for love and for my sister."[5]

Such agreements have not been confined only to sisters. In 1987, a forty-eight-year-old woman, Pat Anthony, acted as a surrogate mother for her daughter and gave birth to triplets in South Africa. The attending obstetrician, Dr. Bernstein, commented: "We feel that what Pat Anthony has done for Karen is the acceptable face of surrogacy . . . There was no payment, no commercialism. It was an act of pure love."[6] Thus altruism becomes the ethical standard for an affirmative assessment of noncommercial surrogacy.

Altruism also is invoked to soften the pecuniary image of commercial surrogacy. Noel Keane, the well-known surrogate broker, has made an educational video called "A Special Lady," which is often shown to teenage girls in high schools and other contexts, encouraging them to consider "careers" as surrogates. The video promotes the idea that it takes a special kind of woman to bear babies for others, and that women who engage in surrogacy do so not mainly for the money but for the special joy it brings to the lives of those who can't have children themselves. A 1986 article in *The Australian* used exactly the same "special" appeal to argue "Why rent-a-uterus is a noble calling." Sonia Humphrey, the author, stated:

> It does take a special kind of woman to conceive, carry under her heart and bear a child which she knows she won't see grow and develop. It also takes a special kind of woman to take a baby which is not hers by blood and rear it with all the commitment of a biological mother without the hormonal hit which nature so kindly provides . . . But those special women do exist, both kinds. Why shouldn't both be honored?[7]

Altruism holds sway. Part of its dominance as an ethical norm derives from its accepted opposition to commercialism. Particularly in the current debate about legalizing surrogate contracts, opponents contend that these contracts make children into commodities to be bought and sold. They allege that this is tantamount to baby selling, and some have renamed the practice commercialized childbearing. Many have focused on the economic exploitation of the women who enter surrogate contracts, women who are in need of money or are financially dead-ended. In these perspectives, the ethical objection is restricted to the fact that a price tag is attached to that which should have no price. The corollary is often that surrogacy "for free" is morally and legally appropriate.

More significant for the dominance of altruism in the reproductive context, however, is the moral celebration of women's altruism. As Caroline Whitbeck has stated in a different context, "the moral expectation upon women is that they be nurturant, that is, that they ought to go beyond respecting rights and meet the needs of others."[8]

THE MORAL CELEBRATION
OF WOMEN'S ALTRUISM

The cultural norm of the altruistic woman who is infinitely giving and eternally accessible derives from a social context in which women give and are given away, and from a moral tradition that celebrates women's duty to meet and satisfy the needs of others. The cultural expectation of altruism has fallen most heavily on pregnant women, so that one could say they are imaged as the archetypal altruists. As Beverly Harrison notes:

> Many philosophers and theologians, although decrying gender inequality, still unconsciously assume that women's lives should express a different moral norm than men's, that women should exemplify moral purity and self-sacrifice, whereas men may live by the more minimal rational standards of moral obligations . . . perfection and self-sacrifice are never taken to be a day-to-day moral requirement for any moral agent except, it would seem, a pregnant woman.[9]

Harrison calls this a "supererogatory morality," acts that are expected to go beyond the accepted standards of obligation. Although traditionally women have been exhorted to be passive, simultaneously they are expected to be more responsible than men for meeting the needs of others. "We live in a world where many, perhaps most, of the voluntary sacrifices on behalf of human well-being are made by women, but the assumption of a special obligation to self-giving or sacrifice . . . is male-generated ideology" (62). The other side of this altruistic coin is male self-interest. A man is allowed to be more self-seeking, to go to great lengths to fulfill his self-interests, and this has been rationalized, in the case of surrogacy, as genetic continuity and "biological fulfillment."[10]

This is not merely an ideological pronouncement about female self-giving and male self-seeking. It raises complex questions about moral double standards in a cultural context where men as a class set the standards and women live them out, where inequality is systemic, and where women have an investment in their own subordination. This does not mean that every man is self-interested and every woman is altruistic. Were that the case, surely the biological determinists would be right!

There is, moreover, a distinct moral language that is part of this tradition that celebrates women's altruism. It is the language of selflessness and responsibility toward others in which women's very possibilities are framed. It is the discourse of maternalism, which traditionally has been the discourse of devotion and dedication in which women turn away from their own needs. It is also the discourse of maternal destiny in which a real woman is a mother, or one who acts like a mother, or more specifically, like the self-sacrificing, nurturant, and care-taking mothers women are supposed to be. If a woman chooses a different destiny and directs her self elsewhere, she risks placing herself outside female nature and culture. This language also encases women's activities in mothering metaphors, framing many of the creative endeavors that women undertake. Motherhood becomes an inspirational metaphor or symbol for the caring, the nurturing, and the sensitivity that women bring to a world ravaged by conflict.

A body of recent feminist literature, exemplified in the work of Carol Gilligan, has valorized women's altruistic development as the morality of responsibility, emphasizing that this is morality "in a different voice" from men. Formerly a mainstay of separate but equal ideology—as in "vive la différence"— this same discourse is now being transformed by some feminists into an endorsement of women's difference in human and moral development. Yet as Catharine MacKinnon notes,

> For women to affirm difference, when difference means dominance, as it does with gender, means to affirm the qualities and characteristics of powerlessness . . . So I am critical of affirming what we have been, which necessarily is what we have been permitted . . . Women value care because men have valued us according to the care we give them.[11]

Altruism has been one of the most effective blocks to women's self-awareness and demand for self-determination. It has been an instrument structuring social organization and patterns of relationship in women's lives. The social relations set up by altruism and the giving of self have been among the most powerful forces that bind women to cultural roles and expectations.

The issue is not whether altruism can have any positive content in the lives of women, but rather that we cannot abstract this question from the gender-specific and gender-unequal situation of cultural values and structures in which new reproductive practices are arranged. This is not to claim that voluntary and genuine magnanimity does not exist among women. It is to say that more is at stake than the womb, the egg, or the child as gift—and the woman as gift giver.

CREATING WOMEN IN THE
IMAGE OF VICTIM

Altruism is not crudely obligatory. The more complex issue is what kind of choices women make within the context of a culture and tradition that orients them to give and give of themselves. To paraphrase Marx, women make their own choices, but they often do not make them just as they please. They often do not make them under conditions they create but under constraints they are powerless to change. The social construction of women's altruism should not reduce to creating women in the victim image.

Yet when feminists stress how women's choices are influenced by the social system and how women are channeled into giving, for example, they are reproached for portraying women as passive victims. Lori Andrews in her essay

"Alternative Modes of Reproduction" for the Rutgers *Reproductive Laws for the 1990s* project faults feminist critics of the new reproductive technologies for embracing arguments based on "a presumed incapacity of women to make decisions."[12] For such detractors, pressure seems to exist only at the barrel of a gun.[13]

For women gifts play many roles. They generate identity, they protect status, and they often regulate guilt. Women who don't give—time, energy, care, sex—are often exposed to disapproval or penalty. But the more important element here is that on a cultural level women *are expected* to donate themselves in the form of time, energy, and body.

Emile Durkheim, in his classic work *Suicide,* maintained that suicide, seemingly the most individual of acts, must be viewed as the result of certain facts of the social milieu, what he called *courants suicidogènes.* One of these social currents was altruism. Durkheim discussed altruistic suicide as the manifestation of a *conscience collective*—the capacity of group values and forces to supersede the claims of individuality and, in the case of soldiers and widows, for example, to influence a tendency to suicide. Durkheim observed that altruistic suicide involved a group attachment of great strength, such that individual assertion and fulfillment and even life itself became secondary. The ego was given over to and eventually absorbed in another, having been stripped of its individuality. Altruism resulted when social integration was strong, so binding that the individual became not only absorbed in the group but in the group's expectations.[14]

Durkheim's analysis of social integration is especially applicable to the social construction of women's altruism of which I speak. For women, family expectations often generate this kind of social integration, with family values and inducements overriding a women's individuality. This is especially evident in the context of family surrogacy arrangements.

FAMILY TIES, GIFTS, AND THE INDUCEMENT OF ALTRUISM

The potential for women's exploitation is not necessarily less because no money is involved and reproductive arrangements may take place within a family setting. The family has not always been a safe place for women. And there are unique affective "inducements" in familial contexts that do not exist elsewhere. Although there is no "coercion of contract" or "inducement" of money, there could be the coercion of family ties in which having a baby for a sister or another family member may be rationalized as the "greatest gift" one woman can give to another.

Thus we must also examine the power and role of gifts in shaping social life. In *The Gift: Forms and Functions of Exchange in Archaic Societies,* Marcel Mauss contends that gifts fulfill certain obligations. These obligations vary, but in all these instances—whether gifts are used to maintain social affection or to promote unity or loyalty within the group—they are experienced as prescriptive and exacting.[15] This is true on a cultural level, as Mauss has pointed out, but it is even more true on a family level, the context most often cited as the desirable site of altruistic reproductive exchanges.

Family opinion may not force a woman, in the sense of being outrightly coercive, to become pregnant for another family member. However, where family integration is strong, the nature of family opinion may be so engulfing that, for all practical purposes, it exacts a reproductive donation from a female source. And representing the surrogate arrangement as a gift holds the woman in tutelage to the norms of family duty, represented as giving to a family member in need.

Within family situations, it may also be considered selfish, uncaring, even dishonorable for a woman to deprive a relative of eggs or her gestation abilities. The category of altruism itself is *broadened* in family contexts to include all sorts of nontraditional reproductive "duties" that would be frowned on if women undertook them for money. Within families, it may be considered selfish for a woman to deprive her husband of children by not allowing the reproductive use of another female family member, especially *because* the arrangements will be kept within the family.

It is also highly likely that those with less power in the family will be expected to be more altruistic. Indeed they may be coerced to be so, as happened to Alejandra Muñoz. Muñoz, a poor, illiterate Mexican woman, was brought across the U. S. border illegally to bear a child for relatives at the urging of many family members. Muñoz was deceived about her role, having been told by family members that when she became pregnant, the embryo would be flushed out and transferred to the womb of her infertile cousin, Nattie. When this did not happen, she vowed to end the pregnancy but was beleaguered and thwarted by family members. Her relatives kept her under house confinement until the delivery. When she fought to keep her child, she was threatened with exposure as an illegal alien.[16]

In 1989, a New Jersey State Task Force on New Reproductive Practices recommended that unpaid surrogate arrangements between friends, relatives, or others be made legally unenforceable. One task force member specifically directed her criticism of noncommercial surrogacy to the family context. Arguing that surrogate arrangements between family members portend the same "disastrous implications" as the Baby M contract, Emily Arnow Alman said that she could foresee the "not-so-bright cousin" being exploited to bear a child for a relative.[17]

We might ask further what is suitable matter for exchange. When we speak of reproductive gifts and donations, but more especially in the case of surrogacy, where the gift and donation is the woman's body and ultimately the child who may be born of such a practice, we put the donation of persons side by side with the exchange of objects and things. The director of the New Jersey task force stated: "The task force feels that the state shouldn't confer any imprimatur of legitimacy on the practice of surrogacy in any form," and that "treating women and children and limiting their liberty by contracts enforceable by the state makes them less than human beings."[18]

GENDER-SPECIFIC ETHICS, PUBLIC POLICY, AND LEGISLATION

While the altruistic woman may be at the center of noncommercial reproductive exchanges, so too is a portrait of science and technology as altruistic. A feature story on the mapping of the human genome in *The Economist* in May 1986 emphasized that "science's reputation—after *Challenger* and Chernobyl—could do with an altruistic megaplan."[19] The new reproductive technologies provide science with one part of this image: *in vitro* fertilization is represented as offering "new hope for the infertile"; surrogacy gives infertile couples the gift of a child; egg donation is helping others to have children. But it is not the technologies that are the sources of these reproductive gifts. It is women, and the historical medicalization of women's bodies in the reproductive context. Women are taken for granted in the name of reproductive research, the advancement of reproductive science, and, of course, the giving of life.

Altruism cannot be separated from the history, the values, and the political structures reinforcing women's reproductive inequality in our society. Questions such as, Who is my stranger? which Titmuss designates as the altruistic question with respect to blood donation, cannot be asked within the context of reproductive donations without asking the prior question of Who is my Samaritan?

Reproductive gift relationships must be seen in their totality, not just as helping someone to have a child. Noncommercial surrogacy cannot be treated as a mere act of altruism, for more is at issue than the ethics of altruism. Any valorizing of altruistic surrogacy and reproductive gift giving for women must be assessed within a context of political inequality, lest it help dignify inequality. Moral meaning and public policy should not be governed by the mere absence of market values. Moral meaning and public policy should be guided by the presence of gender specificity.

What does this mean? For one thing, it means that any assessment of reproductive exchanges, whether they involve commerce or not, takes as its ethical starting point the question of women's status and how the exchange enhances or diminishes gender inequality. Gender-specific ethics devotes primary attention to the consequences to women. It recognizes not only the harm but the devaluation that happens to all women when some are used for reproductive exchanges.

In *Feminism Unmodified: Discourses on Life and Law,* Catharine MacKinnon develops this notion of gender specificity as a foundation for legislation. Gender specificity recognizes "the most sex-differential abuses of women as a gender" and the reality that this is not a mere sex "difference" but "a socially situated subjection of women."[20] It also recognizes that treating women and men as the same in law, as if all things are equal at the starting point, is gender neutrality.

A gender-specific ethics and public policy confronts the degradation of women in the "private" sphere of reproduction and recognizes the gender inequality that exists as a result, for example, of women's expected altruism. Validating altruistic surrogacy on the level of public policy leaves intact the image and reality of a woman as a *reproductive conduit*—someone through whom someone passes. The woman used as a conduit for someone else's procreative purposes, most evident in the case of surrogacy, becomes a mere instrument in reproductive exchanges, an incidental incubator detached from the total fabric of social, affective, and moral meanings associated with procreation. Thus the terminology of "donor" is inaccurate; women are more appropriately "sources" of eggs, wombs, and babies in the context of reproductive exchanges. Further, we are not really talking about "donations" here but about "procurement."

Surrogacy, situated within the larger context of gender inequality, is not simply the commercialization of women and children. On a political level, it reinforces the perception and use of women as a breeder class and reinforces the gender inequality of women as a group. This is not symbolic or intangible but strikes at the core of what a society allows women to be and become. Taking the commerce out of surrogacy but leaving the practice intact on a noncommercial and contractual basis glosses over that essential violation.

Proposals that the law keep clear of reproductive exchanges where no money changes hands are based on gender-neutral assumptions. If the harm of surrogacy, for example, is based only on the commercialization and commodification of reproduction, then the reality that *women* are always used in systems of surrogacy gets no fundamental legal notice. We must note that babies are not always born of surrogate contracts, but women are always encumbered.

As a matter of public policy, the violation of a woman's person, dignity, and integrity have received no legal standing in most legislation opposed to surrogacy other than as mere allusion (the New Jersey Task Force recommendations are a notable exception). By not giving the violation of women primary standing in legislation opposing commercial surrogacy, women's systematic inequality is made invisible and kept in place. That inequality can then be romanticized as noble in so-called altruistic arrangements.

Gender-specific ethics and public policy raise serious doubt about the concept and reality of altruism and the ways it is used to dignify women's inequality. The focus on altruism sentimentalizes and thus obscures the ways women are medicalized and devalued by the new reproductive technologies and practices.

An uncritical affirmation of reproductive gifts and gift givers—of egg donations, of "special ladies" who serve as so-called surrogate mothers for others who go to such lengths to have their own biological children, and of reproductive technology itself as a great gift to humanity—fails to examine the institutions of reproductive science, technology, and brokering that increasingly structure reproductive exchanges.

Women give their bodies over to painful and invasive IVF treatments when it is often their husbands who are infertile. Women are encouraged to offer their bodies in a myriad of ways so that others may have babies, health, and life. These noble-calling and gift-giving arguments reinforce women as self-sacrificing and ontological donors of wombs and what issues from them.

Altruistic reproductive exchanges leave intact the status of women as a breeder class. Women's bodies are still the raw material for other's needs, desires, and purposes. The normalization of altruistic exchanges may have, in fact, the effect of promoting the view that women *should* engage in reproductive exchanges free of charge. In the surrogacy context, altruism reinforces the role of women as *mothers for others* and creates a new version of *relinquishing motherhood.*

The new reproductive altruism is very old in that it depends almost entirely upon women as the givers of these reproductive gifts. This is not to say that women cannot give freely. It is to say that things are not all that simple. It is also to say that this emphasis on giving has become an integral part of the technological propaganda performance. And finally, it is to say that the altruistic pedestal on which women are placed by these reproductive practices is one more way of glorifying women's inequality.

NOTES

1. Richard M. Titmuss, *The Gift Relationship: From Human Blood to Social Policy* (New York: Pantheon Books, 1971), 73.

2. Men donate sperm, of course, but sperm donation is simple and short-lived. As one commentator put it, comparing the donation of eggs and wombs to the donation of sperm is like comparing the giving of an eye to the shedding of a tear.

3. *Matter of Baby M,* 537 A2d 1265 (N. J. 1988).

4. George J. Annas, "Death Without Dignity for Commercial Surrogacy: The Case of Baby M," *Hastings Center Report* 18:2 (1988), 21–24, at 23.

5. "Florida Woman to Be Surrogate Mother for Sister," *Greenfield Recorder,* 12 November 1985.

6. Eric Levin, "Motherly Love Works a Miracle," *People,* 19 October 1987, 43.

7. Sonia Humphrey, "Why Rent-a-Uterus Is a Noble Calling." *The Australian,* 19 December 1986.

8. Caroline Whitbeck, "The Moral Implications of Regarding Women as People: New Perspectives on Pregnancy and Personhood" in *Abortion and the Status of the Fetus,* William Bondeson et al., eds. (Dordrecht: D. Reidel Publishing Co., 1983), 249.

9. Beverly Wildung Harrison, *Our Right to Choose: Toward a New Ethic of Abortion* (Boston: Beacon Press, 1983), 39–40.

10. *Matter of Baby M,* 217 N. J. Super, 313.

11. Catharine A. MacKinnon, *Feminism Unmodified: Discourses on Life and Law* (Cambridge: Harvard University Press, 1987), 39.

12. Lori B. Andrews, "Alternative Modes of Reproduction," in *Reproductive Laws for the 1990s: A Briefing Handbook,* Nadine Taub and Sherril Cohen, eds. (Newark, N. J.: The State University, Rutgers, 1989), 269.

13. This reductionistic view has been challenged by many, including the New Jersey Supreme Court, which reversed the trial court's decision in the Whitehead-Stern surrogacy case. To its credit, the court recognized the complexity of consent in its assessment that for the so-called surrogate, money is an "inducement," as is the "coercion of contract."

14. Emile Durkheim, *Suicide: A Study in Sociology,* trans. John A. Spaulding and George Simpson (New York: The Free Press, 1951), 217–40.

15. Marcel Mauss, *The Gift: Forms and Functions of Exchange in Archaic Societies,* trans. Ian Cunnison (New York: W. W. Norton & Co., 1967), see especially chap. 1.

16. Alejandra Muñoz, press conference on the founding of the National Coalition against Surrogacy. Washington, D. C., August 31, 1987.

17. Robert Hanley, "Limits on Unpaid Surrogacy Backed," *New York Times,* 12 March 1989.

18. Hanley, "Limits."

19. "How to Build a Human Being," *The Economist,* 24 May 1986, 87.

20. MacKinnon, *Feminism Unmodified,* 40–41.

17

LOVE YOUR ENEMY

Sex, Power, and Christian Ethics

Karen Lebacqz

> Dear Abby: A friend of mine was picked up and arrested for raping a 24-year-old woman he had dated twice. He had sex with her the first time he took her out. He said she was easy. The second time . . . she gave him the high-and-mighty act and refused to have sex with him. He got angry, and I guess you could say he overpowered her. Now he's got a rape charge against him, which I don't think is fair. It seems to me that if she was willing to have sex with him on the first date, there is no way she could be raped by him after that. Am I right or wrong?   —A Friend of His[1]

This letter to "Dear Abby" highlights two problems. First, a young man has "overpowered" his date, forcing sexual contact on her. Second, the "friend" who writes this query is confused about whether such forced sex constitutes rape or whether it simply constitutes sex.

These two problems represent two dimensions of sexuality and violence in women's experience. First, violence in the sexual arena is a commonplace occurrence. Women are raped and experience forced sex with considerable frequency. Second, "normal" patterns of male-female sexual relating in this culture are defined by patterns of male dominance over women. Hence, "our earliest socialization," argues Marie Fortune, "teaches us to confuse sexual activity with sexual violence."[2]

In this essay I argue that an adequate Christian sexual ethic must attend to the realities of the links between violence and sexuality in the experiences of women. It must attend to male power and to the eroticizing of domination in this culture. Because domination is eroticized, and because violence and sexuality are linked in the experiences of women, the search for loving heterosexual intimacy is for many women an exercise in irony: women must seek intimacy precisely in an arena that is culturally and experientially unsafe, fraught with sexual violence and power struggles.

Typical approaches to sexual ethics are therefore inadequate because they presume an equality, intimacy, and safety that does not exist for women. Rather, heterosexual women need to operate out of a "hermeneutic of suspicion" that does not ignore the role conditioning or status of men and women in this culture. I will use the term "enemy" as a role-relational term to highlight the need to be attentive to the dangers built into heterosexual sexuality. The attempt to form a heterosexual relationship can then be seen as an exercise in "loving

244

your enemy." From African-American reflections on living with the enemy, I then draw two norms for a heterosexual ethic: forgiveness and survival.

WOMEN'S EXPERIENCE: SEXUALITY AND VIOLENCE

Statistics on rape are notoriously unreliable, but most observers now agree that a conservative estimate suggests that at least one out of three women will be raped or will be the victim of attempted rape in her lifetime.[3] Rape and fear of rape are realities for many if not most women. Violence is directly linked with sexuality in the experience of many women.

What is particularly troubling is the *context* in which rape occurs. Popular images of the rapist perpetuate the myth that rape is an attack by a stranger. Indeed, the myth that rape is only committed by strangers may encourage men to attack the women with whom they are intimate, since—like the "friend" from "Dear Abby"—they do not believe that they can be charged with rape for forcing sexual intercourse on someone they know.

Rape is not committed only by strangers. In a study of nearly one thousand women, Diana Russell found that only 11 percent had been raped (or had been the victims of attempted rape) by strangers, while 12 percent had been raped by "dates," 14 percent by "acquaintances," and 14 percent by their husbands.[4] Thus, while roughly one woman in ten had been attacked by a stranger, more than one woman in three had been attacked by someone she knew. Rape or attempted rape does not happen just between strangers. It happens in intimate contexts, and in those intimate contexts it happens to more than one third of women. In a study of six thousand college students, 84 percent of the women who reported being attacked knew their attackers, and more than 50 percent of the rapes occurred on dates.[5] Moreover, these rapes are often the most violent: Menachem Amir found that the closer the relationship between the attacker and the victim, the greater was the use of physical force; neighbors and acquaintances were the most likely to engage in brutal rape.[6] Thus, not only are women not safe on the streets, they are not safe in presumably "intimate" contexts with trusted friends, neighbors, acquaintances, and even spouses.

The picture is even more complicated. If we look not at the *number of women* who experience rape or attempted rape but at the *number of attacks,* the picture changes dramatically. Of the total number of rapes reported by Diana Russell, *wife rape accounted for 38 percent of all attacks.* Nearly two fifths of rape crimes are perpetrated within the presumed intimacy of heterosexual marriage.[7] Thus, it is not only in *public* places that women must fear for our safety: the nuclear, heterosexual family is not a "safe space" for many women. Moreover, while violent rape by a stranger is something that most women will not experience more than once in their lives, violent rape by a spouse is clearly a repeated crime.

Some women live with the daily threat of a repeated experience of rape within the most "intimate" of contexts: marriage.

The net result is that sexuality and violence are linked in the experience, memory,[8] and anticipation of many women. Those who have experienced rape or who live with a realistic appraisal of it as a constant threat may eventually come to live with "a fear of men which pervades all of life."[9]

Beverly Harrison charges that "a treatment of any moral problem is inadequate if it fails to analyze the morality of a given act in a way that represents the concrete experience of the agent who faces a decision with respect to that act."[10] If the concrete experience of so many women facing the realities of heterosexual sexuality is an experience of violence and fear, then any adequate Christian sexual ethic must account for the realities of rape, violence, and fear in women's lives.[11] Heterosexual women must formulate our sexual ethics within the context of understanding the ironies of searching for intimacy in an unsafe environment.

EROTICIZING DOMINANCE:
THE SOCIAL CONSTRUCTION OF SEXUALITY

The problem is not just that rape occurs or that women experience violence and fear in the arena of sexuality. A treatment of any moral problem must not only represent the concrete experience of the agent(s) involved, but must also *understand that experience in its social construction.*[12]

The problem is not just that a man raped his twenty-four-year-old date, though this is serious enough. The problem is not only that rape is common, though it is. The problem is that the rapist's friend, like many others in this culture, does not think that what happened was rape and does not understand the difference between sexual violence and ordinary heterosexual sexuality.[13] The "friend" who writes to "Dear Abby" is not alone. Of the college women whose experiences of attack fit the legal definition of rape, 73 percent did not call it rape because they knew the attacker. Only 1 percent of the men involved were willing to admit that they had raped a woman. In another survey, over 50 percent of male teenagers and nearly 50 percent of female teenagers deemed it acceptable for a teenage boy to force sexual contact on a girl if he had dated her several times or if she said she was willing to have sex and then changed her mind.[14] Thus, in circumstances similar to those reported to "Dear Abby," a large number of young people would not consider forced sex to constitute rape.

Nor is it only teenagers who think it acceptable for men to force sexual contact on women. In another study, nearly 60 percent of "normal" American men said that if they could get away with it, they would force a woman to "commit sexual acts against her will." When the vague phrase "commit sexual acts against her will" was changed to the more specific term "rape," 20 percent still said they would do it if they could get away with it.[15]

In fact, men *do* get away with rape. Forcible rape has a lower conviction rate than any other crime listed in the Uniform Crime Reports.[16] A few years ago, a jury acquitted a man of the charge of rape even though the woman's jaw was fractured in two places as a result of her resistance; the acquittal rested on the finding that "there may have been sexual relations on previous occasions."[17] The confusion as to whether it is possible to rape a woman once she has consented to sexual relations therefore seems to be reflected in the law.[18] Given the attitude "I would do it if I could get away with it" and the fact that people do get away with it, it is no wonder that one out of three women will be raped or will be the victim of attempted rape.

Thus, violence has been structured into the system itself, structured into the very ways that we experience and think about heterosexual sexuality. Sexuality is not a mere "biological" phenomenon. It is socially constructed.[19] Sexual arousal may follow biological patterns, but *what* we find sexually arousing is culturally influenced and socially constructed. In short, there is a social dimension to even this most "intimate" of experiences, and in this culture sexuality, imbalances of power, and violence are linked. As Marie Fortune so pointedly puts it, "the tendency of this society to equate or confuse sexual activity with sexual violence is a predominant reality in our socialization, attitudes, beliefs, and behavior."[20] Thus, it is not only the actual experiences of violence and fear that we must address in order to have an adequate sexual ethic. We must also address the social construction of sexuality that creates the climate of violence and fear that permeates women's lives and confuses sexuality and violence.

Why is sexuality linked with violence in our socialization and experience? *The social construction of heterosexual sexuality in this culture has been largely based on patterns of dominance and submission in which men are expected to be dominant and women are expected to be submissive.* Men are expected to disregard women's protests and overcome their resistance. When a man "overpowers" a woman, is he raping her or is he simply being a man in both his eyes and hers?

Social domination is linked to cultural patterns in which men in general have more power than women do. Men are not only physically larger in general, but they also possess power to control social, legal, financial, educational, and other important institutions. We are accustomed to male power because it surrounds us. However, the point of interest is not simply that men *have* power. Rather, the key factor is that male power has become *eroticized*. Men and women alike are socialized not only to think that being a man means being in control but also to find male domination sexually arousing. The overpowering of a woman is a paradigm for "normal" heterosexual relations, at least among young people and in segments of popular literature.

Studies of pornography demonstrate the eroticizing of domination in this culture.[21] Andrea Dworkin, Nancy Hartsock, and others argue that pornography is a window into one of the primary dynamics of the social construction of sexuality in this culture: "we can treat commercial pornography as . . . expressing what our culture has defined as sexually exciting."[22] Pornography would suggest that men are socialized to find both male power and female powerlessness sexually arousing.[23] In pornography, domination of women by men is portrayed as sexy. It is the power of the man or men[24] to make the woman do what she does not want to do—to make her do something humiliating, degrading, or antithetical to her character—that creates the sexual tension and excitement. Dworkin puts it bluntly: the major theme of pornography is male power, and the means to achieve it is the degradation of the female.[25] Since power-as-domination always has at least an indirect link with violence, this means that there is at least an indirect link between sexual arousal and violence in this culture.[26] In pornography, women are raped, tied up, beaten, humiliated—*and* are portrayed as initially resisting and ultimately enjoying their degradation. No wonder many real-life rapists actually believe that women enjoy sado-masochistic sex or "like" to be forced;[27] this is the constant message of pornography.

Pornography is big business.[28] While pornography may not reflect the active *choices* of all men in this culture, it reflects a significant dimension of the *socialization* of both men and women.

However, it is not only men in this culture who find male power or female powerlessness sexy. Women in this culture (even feminist women, as Marianna Valverde so devastatingly demonstrates)[29] are attracted to powerful men, whether that power is defined in macho, beer-can-crushing terms or in the more subtle dynamics of social, economic, and political power.[30] Women also link violence and sexuality. In Nancy Friday's classic study of women's sexual fantasies, "Julietta" gives voice to this pattern: "[W]hile I enjoy going to bed with some guy I dig almost any time, I especially like it if there's something in the air that lets me think I'm doing it against my will. That I'm forced by the man's overwhelming physical strength."[31] Julietta is sexually aroused, at least in fantasy, by the thought of being overpowered. Nor is she alone. In *Shared Intimacies: Women's Sexual Experiences,* Lonnie Barbach and Linda Levine report that women's most frequent fantasies are "variations on the theme of being dominant and submissive."[32] Not all women link domination and eroticism, but the pattern is there.

Since men and women alike are socialized both to expect men to overpower women and to find the exercise of power sexually arousing, it is no wonder that the boundary between acceptable "normal" sexual exchange and rape has been blurred. The letter to "Dear Abby" exposes the confusion that arises in a culture that links dominance with eroticism and implies that sexual arousal and satisfaction involve a man overpowering a woman. The "friend" assumes that the woman secretly likes to be forced and that rape is acceptable on some level because on some level it cannot be distinguished from regular sexual contact.

CRITERIA FOR AN ADEQUATE ETHICS

It is plain, then, that to be adequate, Christian sexual ethics must deal not only with the realities of rape and fear in women's lives, but also with socialization patterns in which both men and women are socialized to find male power and female powerlessness sexually arousing. It must deal with the realities of the link between violence and sexuality in this culture, and it must understand the ways in which the social construction of sexuality contributes to the lived experiences of women and men. Only in this way will we truly link the personal with the political; only in this way can we bring moral reflection on sexual behavior into line with the fact that sexual relations are political and not merely personal.

To be adequate, Christian moral reflection must begin with real experience, not with romantic fantasies about love, marriage, and the family. We must name the realities of sexual violence in women's lives. We must take account of the fact that women often experience their sexuality in a context of rape, date rape, acquaintance rape, forced sexual contact, and spousal rape. If nearly 40 percent of rapes happen within heterosexual marriage, then a sexual ethic for heterosexuals must account for this real, lived, concrete experience of women. A Christian sexual ethic must have something to say to the man who raped his twenty-four-year-old date, to the woman who was raped, and to the "friend" and everyone else who is confused about what constitutes acceptable sexual contact between men and women.

To be adequate, Christian sexual ethics must carry out cultural analysis and mount a cultural critique. We must attend not only to the differences in power between men and women in a sexist culture, but also to the distortions that such differences in power have brought to the experience of sexuality itself. An ethic based on assumptions of mutuality and consent falls short of dealing with the social construction of sexuality in terms of the eroticizing of dominance and submission.

To be adequate, Christian sexual ethics must develop a role-based model of personal sexual relations because only a role-based model is adequate to the moral complexities that are exposed when we begin to take seriously the degree to which our sexuality and our sexual interactions are socially constructed. Women are not respected in the sexual arena, but are raped, attacked, and treated as objects. At the same time, heterosexual women seek to trust, love, and be intimate with those who have the power to rape, attack, and be disrespectful.[33] The twenty-four-year-old woman who was raped by her date must now struggle to find intimacy with those who will represent for her the violence in her memory and life. Other heterosexual women will "make love" to spouses who have raped them before and will rape them again. All heterosexual women seek partners from among those who represent the power of male domination in this culture. There are ambiguities and ironies in the search for intimacy in all these contexts. An adequate Christian sexual ethics must attend to these ambiguities and ironies.

A HERMENEUTICS OF SUSPICION

The first step for such an ethic will certainly be a "hermeneutics of suspicion." The distortions of culture must be exposed for what they are. This means that we ask first whether patterns of sexual arousal based on male domination and female submission are trustworthy patterns.

To say that women eroticize domination in fantasy is not to say what happens when women actually experience sexual domination. Since the issue of forced sex came up repeatedly in her interviews, Shere Hite finally asked women whether they were afraid to say no to a man's overtures, and if so, how they felt during and after the act of intercourse. Uniformly, the women indicated that they did *not* find sex pleasurable under such circumstances and that they experienced anger and feelings of powerlessness.[34] Whatever their fantasies may be, women do not in fact like being forced and do not enjoy sex when it happens against their will. Barbach and Levine put it bluntly: "what women enjoy in fantasy and what they actually find arousing in reality are two very different things."[35]

The famous "Hite report" on women's sexuality surfaced evidence that many women who are fully capable of orgasm and frequently do achieve orgasm during masturbation do not in fact have orgasms during heterosexual intercourse. Why, Hite asked, "do women so habitually satisfy men's needs during sex and ignore their own?"[36] Her answer is that "sexual slavery has been an almost unconscious way of life for most women." One of Hite's subjects put it bluntly: "sex can be political in the sense that it can involve a power structure where the woman is unwilling or unable to get what she really needs for her fullest amount of pleasure, but the man is getting what he wants."[37] Hite concludes that lack of sexual satisfaction (perhaps better: lack of joy, pleasure, the erotic) is another sign of the oppression of women.

The first step toward an adequate Christian sexual ethics for heterosexual people, then, is to expose cultural patterns in which sexuality becomes a political struggle and in which domination is eroticized. The first step is an active hermeneutics of suspicion.

POWER AND SEX: THE NEED FOR A
ROLE-BASED MORALITY

If the first step for such an ethic is a hermeneutic of suspicion, I believe that the second step is a recovery of the significance of role and status.

In other arenas of ethical inquiry, the significance of role or status would not be questioned. For example, in their role as pastor, ministers hold professional power. They also represent ministry, the church, and even God in the eyes of parishioners. Based on their role or status, there is a power gap between pastor and parishioner. Because of this power gap, pastor and parishioner do not come into sexual arenas as "equals,"[38] and sexual approaches by a pastor to a parishioner are problematic at best.[39] In short, the power that attaches to the pastoral role is morally relevant for determining what is ethically acceptable for a pastor to do in the sexual arena. If the power that attaches to the pastoral role/status is morally relevant in determining an appropriate sexual ethic, then the power that attaches to any role/status is *also* morally relevant. This means that the power of men in a sexist culture is morally relevant for determining an appropriate sexual ethic for men and women. If sexual contact between people is ethically problematic when one has more power than the other, then all heterosexual sexual contact is ethically problematic in a sexist society.

What we need is an approach to sexual ethics that can take seriously the power that attaches to a man in this culture simply because he is a man (no matter how powerless he may feel), the power that he has as representative of other men, and the power that he has for women as representative of the politics of dominance and submission and as representative of the threat of violence in women's lives.

I believe that many heterosexual women know this and live it in our everyday lives. Yet we have been reluctant to deal with its implications on the theoretical level. We have been leery of a sexual morality that pays attention to roles or status—with good reason: too often, paying attention to roles has meant that it is "woman's place" to please or serve the man. However, in our efforts to reject inappropriate roles for women, we are in danger of assuming that all attention to role or status in sexual morality should be taboo. Because the traditional roles assigned to men and women were sexist, there is a tendency, even among feminists, to seek a role-less or role-free morality. Thus, feminists speak of "intimacy," "mutuality," "reciprocity," and "sharing" as central to sexual ethics. Such terms assume an equality of the partners involved. This assumption may be valid in lesbian or gay circles.[40] Nonetheless, it is precisely my argument that *the partners involved in heterosexual sexuality are not equal in power or status in this culture* and that therefore a sexual ethics that assumes their equality and ignores differences in power will be an inherently flawed sexual ethics.

In a sexist culture, women do not have equal freedom, knowledge, and power with men. Their "consent" to engage in heterosexual sexual exchange is therefore circumscribed by cultural distributions of power. Until these distributions are attended to, we will not have an adequate sexual ethics.

I propose that *the man's status or role as representative of those who have power in the culture is important in the development of a sexual ethic.* The representative nature of men as people with power in this culture needs to be kept before us. Even when the individual man works hard not to be an oppressor, his representative role should not be ignored any more than the pastor's representative role and its attendant power should be ignored. In other words, we need to keep the political dimensions before us, rather than retreating to a private language of mutuality, relationality, and sharing.

I use the term "enemy" to indicate the man's role as representative of those who have power in this culture. I am aware of the dangers of labeling anyone as the "enemy." In her recent book, *Women and Evil,* Nel Noddings argues that when we label someone as the enemy, we devalue that person's moral worth.[41] It is not my purpose to return to a labeling and condemnation of men that often characterized the feminist movement a number of years ago; neither do I wish to devalue the worth of men.[42] Many men today are working hard to divest themselves of the vestiges of sexism that affect them. Not all men experience their sexual arousal along patterns defined by traditional pornography with its degradation of women. "Enemy" is a strong term, and to suggest that it can be used to designate the role of men because of the power of men in a sexist society is to run the risk of misunderstanding. Nonetheless, in the situation of the young woman who was raped, it is not unwarranted to suggest that her date has proven himself to be her "enemy," to be one who will vent his anger and use his power against her by using her for his own ends without regard for her person, her feelings, or her needs. Similarly, for the 25 percent of college women who also experience rape or attempted rape, we need a strong word. Precisely because the term "enemy" is strong, and even problematic, it will force us to take seriously the issues involved.

"LOVE YOUR ENEMY": TOWARD A CHRISTIAN SEXUAL ETHIC

If we understand men and women to be in power positions that can be characterized by the role designation "enemy," then an examination of the meaning of "love of enemies" may contribute something to an ethic for heterosexual sexuality. While I believe that the meaning of love of enemies can usefully illumine the moral situation from both the man's and the woman's side, I will focus here on the woman's plight and on what love of enemy might mean for her.

I will frame this discussion with two words drawn from reflections of black Christian ethicists. African-Americans in this country have had reason to struggle with what it is to be in relationship with those who stand in the role of enemy and to explore the meaning of "love of enemies." I will therefore take the words of a black man and the words of a black woman as each offering insight into the meaning of ethics in a context of "enemies."[43] These two words set boundaries within which a new approach to heterosexual sexual ethics as an exercise in "loving your enemy" might take place.

The first word is *forgiveness*. For the explication of this term I turn to Martin Luther King, Jr. King situates forgiveness at the heart of love of enemies: "The degree to which we are able to forgive determines the degree to which we are able to love our enemies."[44] One cannot even begin the act of loving the enemy, he argues, without prior acceptance of the necessity of forgiving, over and over again, those who inflict evil and injury upon us.

Forgiveness is a difficult word for many women to hear. What would it mean to tell the young woman who has been raped to forgive? Significantly, forgiveness does *not* mean ignoring the past or moving prematurely to reconciliation. On this, King is clear: "forgiveness does not mean ignoring what has been done or putting a false label on an evil act."[45] The Amanencida Collective puts it even more strongly: "to grant pardon, those on the receiving end must recognize their actions as being wrong, in need of pardon."[46] Hence, recognition of the injustices in the situation is part and parcel of forgiveness and hence part and parcel of love of enemies.

According to King, forgiveness means that the evil act no longer serves as a barrier to relationship. Forgiveness is the establishment of an atmosphere that makes possible a fresh start. The woman who has been raped and who then begins to date again—taking the risk that she will be able to find a safe space with a man, even though he represents the power of men and the very violence that she has experienced—is exercising "forgiveness." She is declaring her willingness to enter relationship.

In short, while forgiveness means that "the evil deed is no longer a mental block impeding a new relationship,"[47] the stress here needs to be on *new* relationship. To forgive does not mean going back to the relationship the way it was or accepting the evils perpetrated within it. Love of enemies, for King, begins in forgiveness, but forgiveness itself begins in the recognition of something that needs to be forgiven and, therefore, in the recognition of injustices that need to be redressed. Love of enemies requires justice.[48] Indeed, Paul Lauritzen argues that, in the absence of repentance, forgiveness may even be "morally objectionable" because it can involve "an unjustifiable abandonment of the appropriate retributive response to wrongdoing."[49] The stress in forgiveness is on recognition of the evil. The evil must be named for what it is, and the participants must be willing to establish a new relationship that does not incorporate that evil. Forgiveness means that we must be willing to set things right so that there can be a fresh start. Forgiveness is essentially restorative.[50] Where there is a concrete evil fact such as rape, forgiveness may require repentance; where the man is not himself one who rapes but simply one who represents the power of men in sexist society, forgiveness requires a willingness to establish a relationship based on justice.

Forgiveness, then, is not sentimentality; it requires recognition of injustice and redress of injustice. It is based on truth. Forgiveness means that the relationship is changed, but that the enemy remains the enemy.[51] Forgiveness does not mean that we recognize no one as enemy; rather, forgiveness means that we recognize that though an individual or group stands in the role of enemy, yet we can seek a relationship with that person or group that is a relationship free of injustice. While love of enemies requires forgiveness, the link between forgiveness and justice must be remembered.

This brings me to the second word, *survival*. Women who have been raped often speak of themselves as "survivors." This word then seems appropriate for a heterosexual ethics directed to women who are aware of the dynamics of male dominance and violence in their lives.

For an explication of survival, I draw on Katie Cannon's work. "Throughout the history of the United States," declares Cannon, "the interrelationship of white supremacy and male superiority has characterized the Black woman's moral situation as a situation of struggle—a struggle to survive."[52] Being sexually and socially exploited by both white and black males, black women developed skills to "prevail against the odds with integrity."[53] In a situation where freedom and choice and consent "have proven to be false in the real-lived texture of Black life,"[54] and where sex is experienced both as an act of love *and* as an act of terror,[55] ethics cannot be based on assumptions that grow out of control, power, or freedom—the prerequisites of consent or mutuality. Instead, a different ethic (and by extension, I would argue, a different sexual ethic) emerges.

Black female protagonists, argues Cannon, are portrayed in black women's literature as women for whom survival is an overriding ethical perspective. They are "women with hard-boiled honesty, a malaise of dual allegiance, down-to-earth thinking, the ones who are forced to see through shallowness, hypocrisy and phoniness in their continual struggle for survival."[56] There were things that the black woman had to tell her children even though she did not want to (e.g., to say "Sir" or "Ma'am" to those who were their sworn enemies) so that they would survive. And there were things that she wanted to tell her husband (e.g., that a white man had leered at her) but did not dare, lest it provoke her husband to an action that might cost his life. Survival was the test for how one dealt with one's sexuality and how one handled being black and female in the midst of an oppressive culture.

These qualities of hard-boiled honesty, dual allegiance, down-to-earth thinking, and seeing through hypocrisy are important for heterosexual women of all colors. We need to learn a hard-boiled honesty and a down-to-earth thinking that debunks the romantic myths that link our sexuality with dominance and submission. We need to listen to our dual allegiance that makes us both love this enemy and yet fear (justifiably) for our well-being in a sexist culture. We need to see through the hypocrisy of a culture and a religion that neglects the violence against women and urges women toward premature reconciliation or toward a "love" of men not based on justice. Perhaps above all, those of us who are white as well as female and who therefore benefit as well as suffer from the current social construction of sexuality need to learn to "face life squarely, front and center, without reverence or protection by the dominant powers in society."[57] In short, we need skills oriented toward survival.

Cannon's perspective seems important to me because it does not postulate what Hartsock calls "an artificial community of formal equals"[58] whose sexual relations can be described in terms of consent and mutuality. Rather, Cannon recognizes that all people do not have equal power and that issues of unequal power are central to ethical decision-making. Ethics must be done with attention to the social construction of experience and to the ongoing history of a community.

As forgiveness, with its implicit recognition of injustices that need rectification, is the first word to illumine love of enemies, so survival with its hard-nosed realism is the second.

The twenty-four-year-old woman who has been raped should forgive her attacker (enemy) only if he acknowledges wrong-doing, repents, and seeks a new relationship free of power, domination, and violence. She should seek relationship with those men who are actively struggling to combat the legacy of a sexist culture. She should love her enemies, both specific and representative, but she should not lose sight of the fact that she is dealing with "enemies," understood in a role-relational sense.[59] Her survival should be central to the meaning of love of enemies.

I would therefore argue that feminist analyses of culture that intend to expose injustices are themselves an act of love for the enemy and should remain part and parcel of any heterosexual sexual relationship. Those analyses intend to help men as well as women move to the point where we can redress injustices, set things right, and have the possibility for that joyful eroticism we want to develop. Women who are heterosexual should neither give up their feminism nor mute the power of the feminist critique of the culture.

Is it possible to love the person and yet recognize and hold this feminist stance? Retaining perspective and critique is often one of the hardest things to do. Too often, we have taken love to mean putting oneself aside. Stephen Mott comes dangerously close to this when he urges that the minimal statement of Christian love is looking to the other's well-being and not to our own self-benefit and that the highest expression of love is self-sacrifice.[60] Similarly, Sam Keen argues that the first step in love of enemies is what he calls *metanoia*, the perceptual movement away from what we consider to be the center.[61]

Like most feminists, I am very uneasy about any understanding of love or forgiveness that urges a losing of the self or of the self's perspective, for this contradicts the value of survival. One of the things that happens all too often to women, particularly in abusive situations, is a tendency to lose their own perspective. The story of Alice will illustrate. When first visited in the hospital where she had nearly died from severe damage to her kidneys following a beating by her husband, Alice described being pushed into the stove and "stomped on" by her husband Mike. A week later, after Mike had brought her flowers, made apologies, and promised to mend his ways, Alice changed her description of the incident: "perhaps it was my fault. Mike says he didn't really throw me against the stove. He just pushed at me, and I fell. . . ."[62] Alice gives up her own testimony that she was in fact pushed and beaten in the face of pressure from her spouse to change her story ("Mike says. . . .") and because of her own desire to keep her relationship with him intact ("How could someone so kind and gentle like Mike, someone that I could love so much and who could love me so much, do this to me?"). Here, Alice lost her perspective; she exchanged it for Mike's perspective in the effort to retain relationship.

I would argue that Alice cannot genuinely love Mike if she gives up her own perspective or moves too quickly to reconciliation. Fortunately, we have also come to a better understanding of the need for self-love as a part of *agape*. There can be no *agape* if the agent loses herself; without a self, love is impossible. The agent's own integrity and "endeavor to stay with his or her own considered insights and commitments" are central to the ability to love, as Gene Outka notes.[63] Alice cannot really love Mike if she ignores the fact that he *is* her "enemy," understood in role-relational terms. "Love of enemies" cannot mean a forgiveness that ignores injustices or loses the perspective that there *are* enemies. This is probably the most important task for women. A role-based morality never ignores the fact that the other by whom I am confronted is historically conditioned by a specific culture and will represent and carry the scars of that culture, just as I do.

It is partly for this reason that I am less sanguine than some of my feminist colleagues about relational ethics. Minimally, I would argue that all of our relationships are mediated to a certain extent through roles and status and that our roles and status are culturally conditioned and socially constructed. Even as we are in the midst of attempting to change those roles, it is still important that we attend to them. We need a heterosexual sexual ethic that neither permits nor encourages loss of perspective and of self. To speak only the language of relationality, intimacy, or mutuality is to offer Alice no clues as to how to deal with the "enemy" in her own household. As much as we may love the individual, it is important to deal with that individual as standing in a role and therefore representing the cultural conditioning that attaches to that role.

Noddings argues that it is when we deal with others as representatives, rather than as concrete others, that we can do evil to them.[64] I recognize the dangers in dealing with others as representatives rather than as concrete persons, and I would not suggest that we ever ignore the concrete reality of the other. As Martin Luther King, Jr., puts it, "we must recognize that the evil deed of the enemy-neighbor, the thing that hurts, never quite expresses all that he is."[65] The man who is representative of domination and violence toward women, who stands in the role of "enemy" in that sense, is nonetheless a person with his own pains and history. By suggesting that "love of enemies" may be a helpful category for looking at heterosexual ethics, it is not my purpose to ignore the personal histories and pains of individual men, but rather to recognize the significance of social constructions and historical contingencies in ethics.

I seek a sexual ethics that does not abstract men and women from the concrete historical realities that have shaped us. Given the historical and cultural link between heterosexual sexuality and the pattern of dominance and submission, I think that an adequate sexual ethic for heterosexuals must be informed by a recognition of the representative nature of men and women and therefore by the meaning of "love of enemies."[66]

To recognize the other whom one loves as "enemy" and to deal with the enemy in terms of roles means to remember that each of us represents what Gustavo Gutiérrez would call a "class"—a group that is socialized differently and has different understandings and perspectives because of that socialization. Women's and men's experiences of the world are different. To remember that the one we love is in the role of "enemy" is to remember this fact. To recognize the one whom one loves as "enemy" is to accept the implications of the social construction of sexuality and to understand that the task is not simply to create a private haven into which one can retreat, but is to work for a new social construction of sexuality that will undo the injustices that permeate the present culture.

Heterosexual love is a very difficult task for a woman who is also a feminist. The heterosexual woman must love a concrete other who is a distinct individual with his own history. He is also a man and therefore represents the socialization of heterosexuality into patterns of domination and submission. Sexuality is not only God's marvellous gift to the human race, it is also a social construction fraught with the problems of human power relations. To love the concrete other who is also the enemy is to walk between forgiveness and survival.

NOTES

1. *San Francisco Chronicle,* January 7, 1990, Sunday Punch section.

2. Marie Marshall Fortune, *Sexual Violence: The Unmentionable Sin* (New York: Pilgrim Press, 1983), 22.

3. The National Institutes of Health and *Ms.* magazine recently conducted a study of six thousand college students; their findings are reported in the videotape *Against Her Will: Rape on Campus,* narrated by Kelly McGillis. The study established that one out of four women had been raped or had been the victim of attempted rape on campus. These statistics reflect only those who experienced attack on campus and do not reflect child sexual abuse, marital rape, or other attacks that raise the average.

4. Diana Russell, *Rape in Marriage* (New York: Collier Books, 1962), reported in Linda A. Moody, "In Search of Sacred Spaces," *American Baptist Quarterly* 8/2 (June 1989): 109–10.

5. *Against Her Will: Rape on Campus.*

6. Menachem Amir, "Forcible Rape," *Federal Probation* 31/1 (1967): 51, reported in Diane Herman, "The Rape Culture," in *Women: A Feminist Perspective,* ed. Jo Freeman (Palo Alto, Calif.: Mayfield, 1979), 50.

7. Indeed, Andre Guindon notes that half the crimes in North America are perpetrated within the heterosexual family and suggests that images of man as the violent one contribute not only to these crimes but also to those perpetrated outside the heterosexual family. See *The Sexual Creators: An Ethical Proposal for Concerned Christians* (New York: University Press of America, 1986), 173.

8. It is hard to overestimate the long-term effects of rape, especially when the victim is a young child or girl or when the rape is the victim's first sexual experience. Most rapes are in fact perpetrated on very young victims.

9. Carole R. Bohn, "Dominion to Rule: The Roots and Consequences of a Theology of Ownership," in *Christianity, Patriarchy and Abuse: A Feminist Critique,* ed. Joanne Carlson Brown and Carole R. Bohn (New York: Pilgrim Press, 1989), 109.

10. Beverly Wildung Harrison, "Theology and Morality of Procreative Choice," in *Making the Connections: Essays in Feminist Social Ethics,* ed. Carol S. Robb (Boston: Beacon Press, 1985), 123.

11. Indeed, I am convinced that the treatment of sexual ethics is inadequate because it fails to represent the concrete experience of women, including both our experiences of pain and our experiences of erotic joy. The feminist literature has begun to reflect both of these concerns.

12. While this is not explicit in the quotation above, it is both implicit and explicit elsewhere in Harrison's work.

13. Legal definitions of rape vary from state to state. In the past, in some jurisdictions rape has been defined in such a way that attack of one's spouse would *not* have fit the definition of rape. Most states today have definitions along the lines of that proposed by Fortune (*Sexual Violence,* 7): "forced penetration by the penis or any object of the vagina, mouth, or anus against the will of the victim."

14. These statistics are reported in Fortune, *Sexual Violence,* 2. They are taken from Laurel Fingler, "Teenagers in Survey Condone Forced Sex," *Ms.,* February 1981, 23.

15. Carol Turkington, "Sexual Aggression Widespread," *APA Monitor* 18/13 (1987): 15, quoted in Polly Young-Eisendrath and Demaris Wehr, "The Fallacy of Individualism and Reasonable Violence against Women," in *Christianity, Patriarchy and Abuse,* ed. Brown and Bohn, 136.

16. Camille E. LeGrand, "Rape and Rape Laws: Sexism in Society and Law," *California Law Review* 61/3 (1973): 927, reported in Herman, "The Rape Culture," in *Women: A Feminist Perspective,* ed. Freeman, 57.

17. Herman, "The Rape Culture," in *Women: A Feminist Perspective,* ed. Freeman, 57.

18. Herman argues that this attitude reflects the clear understanding of women as the property of men. In this regard, L. William Countryman's *Dirt, Greed, and Sex: Sexual Ethics in the New Testament and Their Implications for Today* (Philadelphia: Fortress Press, 1988) is instructive.

19. It is often difficult to see this, because we think of the erotic dimension as personal, private, or biological. In *Intimate Matters: A History of Sexuality in America* (New York: Harper and Row, 1988), John D'Emilio and Estelle B. Freedman demonstrate that the assumption that sexuality is oriented toward erotic and personal pleasure is itself a modern development.

20. Fortune, *Sexual Violence,* 16.

21. While there is no single definition of pornography, I take Marianna Valverde's to be consonant with that of most other feminist thinkers. Valverde proposes that pornography is characterized by (1) the portrayal of men's social and physical power over

women as sexy, (2) the depiction of aggression as the inevitable result of power imbalances, such that we expect the rape of the powerless by the powerful, and (3) the idea of sex as having a relentless power to cut across social barriers and conventions, so that people will do things to others that would not normally be expected (e.g., rape a nun). See Marianna Valverde, *Sex, Power and Pleasure* (Philadelphia: New Society Publishers, 1987), 129f. Particularly important in Valverde's analysis, however, is her recognition that pornography cannot be defined solely by the content of the material, but must also be defined by its *use*—e.g., the commercialization of sex. See also Mary Hunt, "Theological Pornography: From Corporate to Communal Ethics," in *Christianity, Patriarchy and Abuse,* ed. Brown and Bohn.

22. Nancy C. M. Hartsock, *Money, Sex and Power: Toward a Feminist Historical Materialism* (Boston: Northeastern University Press, 1985), 168.

23. The Professional Ethics Group of the Center for Ethics and Social Policy at the Graduate Theological Union has had a grant from the Lilly Endowment to conduct studies of pastors. These studies suggest that many men find a woman's tears or other signs of vulnerability very sexually arousing. We had one pastor in our study who claimed that he was addicted to pornography.

24. Pornography often depicts group attacks on a woman. Similarly, rape itself is often done by gangs or in the presence of other men. See Herman, "The Rape Culture," in *Women: A Feminist Perspective,* ed. Freeman, 47.

25. Andrea Dworkin, *Pornography: Men Possessing Women* (London: The Women's Press, 1981), 24–25. Dworkin argues (69) that pornography reveals an inextricable link between male pleasure and the victimizing, hurting, and exploitation of women: "sexual fun and sexual passion in the privacy of the male imagination are inseparable from the brutality of male history." I think that to claim that male pleasure is "inextricably" tied to hurting the other is too strong. Nonetheless, the prevalence and power of pornography in our midst demonstrates that much pleasure for both men and women has been tied to having power to make another person do what is humiliating.

26. The roots of violence need further exploration. In *Touching Our Strength* (San Francisco: Harper and Row, 1989), 13–15, Carter Heyward notes that the recent work of the Stone Center for Developmental Services and Studies at Wellesley College, Massachusetts, suggests that the roots of violent abuse lie in socialization for separation, in which we are cut off from the possibilities of mutuality and joy in our most important relationships.

27. Herman, "The Rape Culture," in *Women: A Feminist Perspective,* ed. Freeman, 47.

28. Hunt, "Theological Pornography," in *Christianity, Patriarchy and Abuse,* ed. Brown and Bohn, 95.

29. Valverde, *Sex, Power and Pleasure,* 62.

30. In *Office Romance: Love, Power, and Sex in the Workplace* (New York: Rawson Associates, 1989), 159, Lisa A. Mainiero quotes one executive woman as saying, "The combination of power and business judgment can be a real turn-on. It's sexy as hell."

31. Nancy Friday, *My Secret Garden: Women's Sexual Fantasies* (New York: Pocket Books, 1973), 110.

32. Lonnie Barbach and Linda Levine, *Shared Intimacies: Women's Sexual Experiences* (New York: Bantam Books, 1980), 123.

33. Two caveats need to be entered here. First, Mariana Valverde (*Sex, Power and Pleasure,* 47) charges that, due to the wide range of heterosexual experiences, we cannot speak confidently about heterosexuality in general. Second, Harrison and Heyward

("Pain and Pleasure," 148) charge that in the sexual arena more than in any other, feminists tend to impose their own morality on others. My intention is neither to label all heterosexual men or women, nor to impose an ethic on them, but rather to lift up dimensions of experience that have been neglected, in hopes that those dimensions might assist at least some women in the effort to create a Christian sexual ethic that takes their experience seriously. I am also keenly aware that what I will describe here is culture-bound and may not speak as helpfully to those from different backgrounds.

34. Shere Hite, *The Hite Report* (New York: Dell Publishing Co., 1976), 461–62. One woman said, "I felt like hell—angry and unhappy." Another "hated" herself for being afraid to say no. Another thought she was not "supposed" to say no since she was married; she "faked orgasms."

35. Barbach and Levine, *Shared Intimacies,* 125. The responses also make clear that women do not always feel that they can say no and that women will tend to blame themselves instead of the man—hating their own passivity or "weakness." They further make clear that women will fake orgasm rather than confront their partner with the truth of their dislike. Deception is a technique commonly used by those with little power against their oppressors.

36. Hite, *The Hite Report,* 419.

37. Ibid., 420. Whether men are in fact getting what they want is, of course, also an issue. My own interpretation would be that in an oppressive society, most men also do not get what they really want.

38. Karen Lebacqz, "Pastor-Parishioner Sexuality: An Ethical Analysis," *Explor 9* (Spring 1988): 67–81.

39. See Marie Marshall Fortune, *Is Nothing Sacred? When Sex Invades the Pastoral Relationship* (San Francisco: Harper and Row, 1989), and Peter Rutter, *Sex in the Forbidden Zone: When Men in Power—Therapists, Doctors, Clergy, Teachers, and Others—Betray Women's Trust* (Los Angeles: Jeremy P. Tarcher, Inc., 1989).

40. Indeed, I am personally convinced that those in the "straight" community have much to learn from those who have not been confined by male-female patterns of relating.

41. Nel Noddings, *Women and Evil* (Berkeley: University of California Press, 1989), 198.

42. In *Talking Back: Thinking Feminist, Thinking Black* (Boston: South End Press, 1989), 127, Bell Hooks argues that labeling men "the enemy" in the early stages of the feminist movement was an effective way to begin the critical separation that women needed in order to effect rebellion, but that as the movement has matured, we have seen the error in such separation and have come to appreciate the need for the transformation of masculinity as part of the feminist movement.

43. In so doing, I will no doubt stretch and possibly misuse their insights; if so, I offer my most genuine apologies. Nothing could prove better how socially constructed all of our realities are than the difficulties experienced by a white person of some privilege in trying to utilize insights drawn from black experience.

44. Martin Luther King, Jr., *Strength to Love* (London: Hodder and Stoughton, 1963), 43.

45. Ibid., 35. Similarly, Paul Tillich argues that in accepting someone into the unity of forgiveness, *"love exposes . . . the acknowledged break with justice"* (*Love, Power, and Justice* [New York: Oxford University Press, 1954], 86).

46. Carter Heyward et al., *Revolutionary Forgiveness: Feminist Reflections on Nicaragua* (Maryknoll: Orbis Press, 1987), 93.

47. King, *Strength to Love*, 35.

48. Ibid.

49. Paul Lauritzen, "Forgiveness: Moral Prerogative or Religious Duty?" *Journal of Religious Ethics* 15/2 (Fall 1987): 150. Lauritzen does argue (151), however, that in the context of religious belief, forgiveness *can* be given without repentance on the other's part because the forgiveness itself takes away the character of the sin.

50. Ibid., 143. Forgiveness is then akin to "jubilee justice"; see Karen Lebacqz, *Justice in an Unjust World: Foundations for a Christian Approach to Justice* (Minneapolis: Augsburg Press, 1987).

51. Victor Furnish, *The Love Command in the New Testament*, 67, quoted in Lauritzen, "Forgiveness," 150.

52. Katie G. Cannon, *Black Womanist Ethics* (Atlanta: Scholars Press, 1988), 6–7.

53. Ibid., 7.

54. Ibid., 75.

55. Ibid., 85.

56. Ibid., 89.

57. Ibid., 125.

58. Hartsock, *Money, Sex and Power*, 177.

59. In this regard, I have not found the literature on love of enemies as helpful as I wished. Most of it is focused on instances where we clearly recognize our enemy, whereas I am trying to deal with a situation where we do not recognize that we are in fact dealing with an enemy and where re-cognition is the first step (see Lebacqz, *Justice in an Unjust World*, 108f.). Also, the literature focuses on attitudes rather than roles; its primary concern is reducing enmity (cf. Stephen C. Mott, *Biblical Ethics and Social Change* [New York: Oxford University Press, 1982], 37). If "enemy" is understood as a culturally constructed role, then the task is not to reduce hatred but to ask how one loves the person who stands in a particular role, just as one might ask about love of mother, sister, teacher, etc.

60. Mott, *Biblical Ethics and Social Change*, 42.

61. Sam Keen, *Faces of the Enemy: Reflections of the Hostile Imagination* (San Francisco: Harper and Row, 1986).

62. This story is reported in Polly Young-Eisendrath and Demaris Wehr, "The Fallacy of Individualism and Reasonable Violence against Women," in *Christianity, Patriarchy and Abuse*, ed. Brown and Bohn, 127–28.

63. Gene Outka, *Agape: An Ethical Analysis* (New Haven: Yale University Press, 1972), 35.

64. Noddings, *Women and Evil*, 211. Note, though, that *agape* itself appears to be tied to status/role issues, not to questions of personal attitude. Outka says that *agape* is regard for the neighbor that in crucial respects is independent and unalterable, implying that it is indeed given to the other not because of personal likes or tastes but because of the status of the other as person. *Agape* deals with putting others into the role of "neighbor." It is a role-relational term.

65. King, *Strength to Love*, 36.

66. The analogy may be particularly apt since there is evidence to suggest that the term *echthros* in Matt. 5:43–48 and Luke 6:27–28, 32–36 refers to a local enemy, even a member of the household. See W. F. Arndt and F. W. Gingrich, *Greek-English Lexicon of the New Testament* (Chicago: University of Chicago Press, 1957), 331, and Richard Horsley, "Ethics and Exegesis: 'Love Your Enemies' and the Doctrine of Non-Violence." *JAAR* 59/1 (Spring 1986): 17. Horsley suggests, "the phrase surely means those with whom one is in personal, local interaction."

18

THE MORAL LANDSCAPES OF EMBODIMENT

Elizabeth Bettenhausen

I

"Ah, yes! Do we deserve this or do we *deserve* this?" Audrey settled against the tree and into a satisfied grin. "One whole week all to ourselves."

The women watched the lake and pines and sky become a deep, glowing blue. "We should turn fifty more often," Mary said. Their laughter was a mixture of ease and concern, full of sparks like the campfire. "Or at least we should get together more often."

"Now there's an idea," Verda agreed. "Do you remember that trip back after spring break when we were sophomores? I thought we'd never get past that icy stretch of road near St. Louis. I could just see the headline: *Females Slide into Mississippi.*"

"You were all so worried and helpful," Mary said. "And I was just scared spitless."

"Of course you were." The old soothing confidence was still in Rosemary's voice. "It's not every day you end up in Student Health with appendicitis."

Mary laughed. "But I didn't know it was appendicitis. I thought some horrible natural law was dishing out a punishment for all the times I let my body distract me from 'The Life of the Mind.' Can't you still hear old Professor Smith intoning: 'Ladies and Gentlemen, we are here to live The Life of the Mind'?"

"Yes, and he sure was consistent. No evidence of the body was allowed in *his* classes. Do you remember when he flew into that rage when Jane broke into tears? 'Young lady, if you insist on acting like a female, you will have to remove yourself from my lecture.' If he had known what she was crying about, he would have exploded like Rumpelstiltskin."

"Did Rumpelstiltskin explode?"

"Or grind himself away or whatever."

Poking at the fire with a branch, Mary said, "When Andrea came home for

262

Thanksgiving, that all came back to me. She was talking about topics covered in her philosophy course, and I thought to myself, 'Most of these problems are anti-body or no-body.' I asked whether having a body was talked about as a good thing, and she laughed. 'Mom, why mess up the body by putting it into the curriculum?' That's a far cry from my worries about physical feelings in the middle of a lecture on existentialism."

"But," Rosemary said, "this generation is just as dualistic as we were. Keeping the body out of the classroom in order to maintain the fun of nights and weekends isn't a great improvement over worrying about getting pregnant from sitting in the wrong chair!"

They alternated laughter and a litany of other notions they'd held about bodies and sex.

Then Verda's intensity surprised them. "But, Mary. At least you knew you had physical feelings."

"Sure. Didn't everybody?"

"I didn't," Verda said. "I mean I didn't feel like I had a body or any self at all. I remember one time in that course on contemporary ethics. That monotone faculty guy—remember him?—was going on and on about self-sacrifice being the be-all and end-all. All of a sudden it dawned on me that I never really had a self. Not having a self was the only way to keep the pain away when I was a girl. And I never really learned how to get one." The low flickering fire almost made her invisible against the lake.

"You always seemed to me to have a self," Audrey said. "You painted, you loved soccer, and you got *A's* in every single course. What are you talking about, not having a self?"

"Oh, I could do what others wanted me to do and say what the professors wanted to hear. But it wasn't like it was me saying it. I couldn't think up my own ideas. If the ethics prof said all horses are purple, I'd think, 'Well, he's probably right. He probably knows something I don't know about horses. I must be wrong.' And in a couple of days I'd be saying to someone, 'All horses are purple, you know.' I didn't really believe it and didn't even care about it. But I didn't want any conflict." Verda stopped and seemed to be absorbed into her own silence.

But Audrey was ready to talk. "I *never* believed half of what they said! And the other half was so obviously mental masturbating that I figured I wasn't expected to take it personally! But I certainly would never have thought to connect my body with the course material. And I must admit, I was more than a little embarrassed when Jane burst into tears! I can still hear the teaching assistant in the discussion section the next day: 'You girls should not be here in the first place. This is hard mental work, and if you can't take it, stay in the kitchen!' "

"I remember once when one of the women cried in a university council meeting," Mary said. "And that's *exactly* what the provost said to her!"

"What was she crying about?"

"One of the fourteen hundred vice presidents had just made a report trying to justify closing the rape crisis center on campus the month before. This woman had spent the better part of two days listening to a student who was pregnant after three seniors raped her at a drunken frat party. The young woman was frantic with fear and totally misplaced guilt. When the VP said that rape is no longer a problem on the campus, the faculty woman lost it."

"Thank goodness!" said Rosemary.

"Well, thank goodness and goodbye promotion. The provost literally yelled at her, 'If you can't take it, stay in the kitchen,' and went into this tirade about feminine weakness. 'No wonder you all get raped!' was the end of his fury."

"And somebody straightened him out, I hope," said Rosemary.

"Oh, no, not at all. A dean moved that we receive the report, some junior faculty twerp seconded the motion, and it passed easily. It was enough to drive several of us to weep, but we didn't give them the pleasure. We controlled our bodies, as they say."

Hearing that, Verda rejoined the conversation. "Learning how to hold in the tears was one of the worst parts of being abused. And then after I left home, sometimes the tears would just start flowing and I'd never know why."

"The shortest verse in the Bible is 'Jesus wept.'" Sometimes Audrey's comments seemed to come from some other conversation.

But Verda's comment surprised them all. "That's the verse that kept me going," she said. "In Sunday School I always liked that verse."

"Well, you never heard much about that verse in 'Intro to Christian Theology.'"

"You never heard about child abuse in that course either. And maybe for the same reasons."

"Actually we didn't even hear about it in ethics classes—"

"Except the feminist ones—"

"And not always there either."

"Jesus weeping and child abuse. Well, they both have to do with the body. And the body doesn't show up in the curriculum."

"Oh, I don't know. Some professors pay a lot of attention to body!"

"Yeh, but not as part of the syllabus!"

"Not an *explicit* part of the syllabus, you mean."

"I never thought of my body as a good thing until after I got out of there," Mary said. "Andrea told me that one of her male professors actually said the other day in class, 'My body is here for your convenience, so you can interact with me. If my body disappeared, I'd still be here, but you would not know it.'"

"You're kidding!"

"Nope. I wrote it down as evidence that mind/body splits are still around."

"Well, if it's the prof I'm thinking of, Andrea should watch out. If she questions him about it, he'll kiss that 'A' she earned goodbye."

"Oh, kissing is not allowed in—"

"It is too. That's one of the benefits of their mind-body split: Their body gets to kiss, but their mind holds the endowed chair."

"This is getting pretty heavy. We keep this up and I'm going to urge Andrea to study for a different profession."

"Which one was it again where women's and girl's bodies are treated with respect and delight?"

"This is too depressing. Let's get back to Mary's confusion of appendicitis and eros!"

"That's what *started* all this!"

"Whatever happened to Jane anyway? Anybody know?"

Rosemary hesitated and then said, "I heard she . . . no, that's only rumor."

"I wouldn't be surprised if she killed herself," Verda said. "In many ways not acknowledging the body is easier than facing what happened. Often it takes years before a woman and her body are on good terms. Sometimes the pain is so deep she never does get there. And it's just as bad when what she can't face is a great big pleasure that she thinks shouldn't be named."

Prodding the embers, she continued. "But easier isn't necessarily better. I'd like to think that my body is a student too. Then I can become more than a victim. I can become a self, an embodied self. But male colleagues don't think having a body is important professionally. Or it's just a drag in their career goals. Writing papers about body is dealing with 'trivia,' one of them said the other day."

"If you don't want to deal with dirty diapers, dirty floors, dirty laundry, just call it 'trivia' and pay someone sub-minimum wage to take care of it."

"But that makes it sound like the body is dirty."

"My floors may be dirty, but my body isn't dirty."

"Yes," Verda agreed. "But for most of my life I did think my body was dirty. Ever since I was twelve and realized that what happened to me for six years was rape."

After a long silence, Muriel spoke for the first time. "Just don't mention that at the office or at school." They had almost forgotten she was there. "Words are weapons," she said. "Silence is the best way. That way they'll ignore you and you can be safe. That's what Jane forgot, to keep silent."

II

The women burst out laughing at my question. We had been engrossed in discussing whether other-than-human animals, plants, and things have—well, for lack of a better word—consciousness or souls. The conversation had begun with Georgia O'Keeffe's comment, "When I paint I *am* the trees," and with Mary Oliver's poem, "Some Questions You Might Ask," The poem begins,

Is the soul solid, like iron?
Or is it tender and breakable, like
the wings of a moth in the beak of the owl?
Who has it, and who doesn't?
I keep looking around me.
The face of the moose is as sad
as the face of Jesus.[1]

We had asked the poet's question: "Why should I have it and not the camel?" "What about all the little stones, sitting alone in the moonlight?"

Our varied experiences of interacting with the Earth sounded variations on the main theme. Two women said being encountered by a rock or an animal was made possible by the divinity present in each and all. Others chose not to draw on the concept of divinity to name an intrinsic value and energy in all things. The variations took the form of new questions. Was consciousness or soul in all its manifestations identical to divinity? Is the molecular exchange among all things at the base of the apprehension of the unity of all rich difference? Is being sighted a disadvantage in knowing this unity by touching? Is the human body a firmly finite boundary, even barrier, or is it more extended in space than an individualistic model of autonomy would permit us to know?

We voiced that main theme: a mutuality of meeting, a reciprocity of awareness can and does happen between human beings and other aspects of Earth, animate and inanimate. Conversations with trees and rabbits were our experience, as were apprehending spirit embodied in a stone on the beach; deep befriending between a woman and a German shepherd dog or a Persian cat; being empowered by the energy of an antique mirror; being loved by a rock.

When the silence of a thinking pause began to stir, I asked, "Now, how much does all of this fit with your understanding of Christianity?" That's when we all burst out laughing! All of us are members of the church, and several are ordained ministers, yet our laughter was immediate and hearty and multivalent. Laughing meant first that this mutuality of meeting with other-than-human earthly reality does not fit at all with traditional Protestantism. Our laughing signaled how great the separation is between Earth and church. The laughing also carried strong overtones of regret and anger. The regret is sorrow that such an invigorating aspect of our experience is usually excluded from the church and the academy. The anger, literally "being in these straits," is against the injustice of having to choose daily between being faithful in the church's official terms and being faithful to Earth's integrity. The laughing was also the laughing of power. None of us is about to leave anthropocentric Christianity unchallenged.

The laughing of power is also because none of us has left androcentric Christianity unchallenged. Separating justice for girls and women from justice for plants, animals, and ore-rich hills is no more possible for us than it has been for masculinist theologians. However, we know the effects in our minded bodies when they relegate our well-being and the Earth's to a "lower" level of value. We have learned from the disseminated seminal ideas of seminaries. In the fifth century the theologians debated whether female human beings had souls. Today masculinist theologians smirk at what they call "pagan" or "romanticist" or "soft" eco-theology. Attending to Mary Oliver's questions is "unscholarly" and heterodox theology. When old power Protestant denominations grow impotent, officials fling accusations of heresy instead of the seeds of constructive change.

After our conversations I was reading Alice Walker's essays, "Everything Is a Human Being" and "The Universe Responds." Walker writes, "The Earth holds us responsible for our crimes against it, not as individuals, but as a species—this was the message of the trees."[2] At that point the thought crossed my mind that too little attention has been paid in Christian interpretations of crucifixon to the suffering of the trees used to make crosses. And my friendship with individual trees over the years would not pardon my species-complicity in the unthanking destruction of forests, rivers, prairies. Original sin is larger than individual repentance.

Untangling and reweaving this web toward truth, I grant that solidarity in suffering does not necessarily exonerate. The justice we women desire and demand is neither more nor less than the justice due GrandMother Earth. If the well-being of girls and the well-being of the environment seem to be mutually exclusive, that is a sign that superficial analysis has set in. If violence against women and violence against the Earth have to compete for political attention, that is a sign that reductionism is at work. Fortunately, many women have realized this interdependence, giving rise to the need for new words: ecofeminism and ecowomanism.

The choice between justice for human beings and justice for the "natural" world is a false choice, part of a tangled web woven to give illusory advantage to late-arriving *Homo* allegedly *sapiens*. Economic justice is no less an aesthetic matter and no more a moral matter than ecological justice is. The destruction of earthly beauty is a sign of moral danger. Or perhaps conspicuous consumption has already brought many beyond the point described by Czeslaw Milosz:

> And when people cease to believe that there is good and evil
> Only beauty will call them and save them
> So that they still know how to say: this is true and that is false.[3]

When the beauty of Earth is relegated to "general, non-salvific revelation" by the theologians, truth has already been tangled. When divinity is restricted to incarnation in one isolated body, deceit weaves more and more bonds of alienation.

Whether the church in its denominational expressions will take ecological justice more seriously is directly and inextricably tied to its teaching and actions for sexual and racial justice. Domineering dominion which batters the wife is like the dominion that pollutes the air and poisons the rivers. Incestuous abuse of the child is like the abuse that pours garbage into the land. Racist subjugation of entire nations is like the subjugation which destroys plant and animal species. The other in human body is the other of the Earth. And so when the women burst out laughing, the Earth did too.[4]

III

"Why not have them make a list of good things about having a body?" Ann suggested. "It is nice to have a body if you want to ride a bicycle. It is nice to have a body if you want to eat double chocolate ice cream. It is nice to have a body if you like being hugged or like to run through puddles barefoot."

"I never thought of that! That's a very good idea!" Corrine was, as usual, enthusiastic. "I'll try it in the next group session."

Ann was completely taken aback. She had been assuming in the discussion that by now all women would have absorbed the feminist dictum that being embodied is good. Habits of universalizing die hard. Corrine had been describing young women in a drug-abuse program. Most of them had been physically and often sexually abused as children. Every single one of them thought very negatively about her body. "I'm so ugly," was a common complaint. "Too fat, too thin, too dark, too light, too flabby." The list went on and on. Everyone thought of the body as a problem. None thought of the body as making pleasure possible or as valuable in itself. "Our bodies, our selves" had been absorbed, but negatively: "I'm so ugly." The embodied self was not a powerful and positive agent, but rather a problem.

Ann's wandering attention returned to the conversation. Angela was talking. "But you are all assuming that having a body is good because you all assume it will be healthy and whole. For some people body means dying or constant memories of torture. What good is a body then?"

"But that doesn't mean the body itself is bad. Body isn't only dying or only torture." Jackie was intense in trying to hold on to a new conviction.

"I'm not saying it's only that or even that for everybody. I am saying it's hard to be completely enthusiastic about having a body when you are dying from cancer or when you've never known your body except as it was beaten by your uncle."

"Oh, Angela! I didn't know you were dying! Why didn't you tell us?!"

"Who said I was dying?"

"You did. You just said you have cancer."

"I did not."

"Didn't you? You just said . . ."

"She said it's hard to get happy about having a body when you are dying from cancer. She didn't say *she* had cancer."

Jackie was persistent. "I just assumed that anyone with that much negative passion about a condition must have experienced it."

"Jackie! You don't really believe that, do you?"

"Whether she does or not, lots of people do." Molly had been waiting for an opening in the rush of words. "People tend to operate on the assumption of self-interest. If you take the part of people with AIDS, you must have AIDS. If you advocate lesbian rights, you must be a lesbian. If you are really active for African-American empowerment but look Norwegian, somewhere you must have had a Zulu great-great-grandparent."

"But that assumes that everybody is this neat little self with borders like barriers: Norwegian is not Zulu, lesbian is not straight, AIDS is not social. Being self-interested refers then to this little autonomous slice of the human species called Jackie or Samuel or Angela and excluding every thing or one else."

"Right! and the assumption is that everyone is motivated first and foremost and maybe exclusively by self-interest. So if you speak out passionately against child abuse, people assume you were abused as a child."

"But what if 'self' really refers to 'all human beings' or 'all animals' or even to Gaia, as Lovelock and Margulis claim?"

"What do you mean, *really* refers?"

"Well, like a category mistake. If someone called C-sharp the whole of Bach's motet, *Jesu, Meine Freude,* that would be an error. And maybe the mistake is not self-interest but a too narrow scope for 'self.' One person cannot be the whole of self, just as C-sharp cannot be the whole of a motet."

"Try that out with the editor when your article is late!"

"Or when the IRS comes to put you in jail for non-payment. 'Please, Mr. IRS man, you are making a category mistake. I am only part of the human self.' "

"Well, it might be for institutional convenience that we locate moral agency in individual persons. Maybe it parallels historical developments in notions of private property."

"But what does this have to do with the body?" Jackie sounded more than a bit impatient. "I thought we were talking about the body being good, which suits me just fine. I like having control of my body. Now you're telling me it's not mine and it's a whole lot bigger than I thought. Thanks a lot!"

Angela began smiling a wickedly subversive smile. "If the self encompasses more than any one person, then dualisms are out. Or rather, difference is inescapable. That means part of every so-called straight male is lesbian!"

"Yes," Jackie pointed out, "but then part of every lesbian is Jesse Helms!"

"Oh, shit! So much for that anthropology."

"This all sounds so abstract, just like old boys' seminars. What difference does it make where the boundaries of the self are?"

"It would make a difference for the little child beaten by her father. If he thinks she is just an extension of his own ego or just some of his property, she can kiss safety goodbye."

"But does her safety have to depend on being a separate, autonomous agent? Couldn't the doors of the self always be open? Or the doors *to* the whole self?"

"Sure, *if* we could start over without racism and without sexism and—"
"And without violence."
"And *with* everybody having two feet for running through puddles."
"And enough money to buy a bicycle and double chocolate ice cream."
"And—"

NOTES

1. Mary Oliver, *House of Light* (Boston: Beacon, 1990), 1.
2. Alice Walker, *Living by the Word* (San Diego: Harcourt Brace Jovanovich, 1988), 142.
3. Czeslaw Milosz, "One More Day," in Czeslaw Milosz, *The Collected Poems* (New York: Ecco Press, 1988), 408.
4. A somewhat different version of section II appeared as "Earth, Women, Church," in *Sequoia: News of Religion and Society* 10/4 (October/November 1990).

19

ON HEALING THE NATURE/HISTORY
SPLIT IN FEMINIST THOUGHT

Joan L. Griscom

As I have considered the increasing discussion of the relation between women and nature, two important trends stand out, trends which appear to me strangely and seriously contradictory. This essay is an effort to help in healing this split in our thought.

The first trend involves the perception that there are four major systems of oppression in our patriarchal world: not only the domination of nature and women, but also domination by race and class. All four are thematically and historically interwoven. Sheila Collins echoed other feminist theorists when she wrote: "Racism, sexism, class exploitation, and ecological destruction are four interlocking pillars upon which the structure of the patriarchal rests."[1] Feminists are now exploring the nature of this interlocking, or, as Rosemary Ruether calls it, interstructuring.[2] What are the similarities and differences between these four forms of oppression? To what extent are they the same?

I pause for a note on terminology. *Sexism* and *racism* are fairly clear: each consists in regarding a group—for example, males or whites—as superior to another group—females or nonwhites—on the basis of sex or race. *Classism* makes the same distinction on the basis of socioeconomic level; it operates nationally and, as in the relationship between the so-called developed and underdeveloped nations, globally. There is no one word that expresses the oppression of nature, but in accordance with these other terms, I would propose *naturism:* regarding humanity, one's own group, on the basis of nature, as superior to other groups, nonhuman nature. Admittedly, *nature* is a confusing word with many meanings. By *naturism*, I refer to humanity's domination of

The author would like to thank Lucy Lippard for her creative editing, which improved both the clarity and the substance of this essay.

nature, which has resulted in the ecological crisis. It includes *speciesism,* the belief that humans are superior to other animals. There are other, subtler manifestations. For example, since *mind* is associated with human superiority and since *body* is associated with *animal,* naturism includes the belief that mind is superior to body.

The second trend which concerns me contradicts the first one. While feminists mostly agree that these four forms of oppression are analogous expressions of the patriarchy, there is a severe split between feminists who are primarily concerned with nonhuman nature and those who are primarily concerned with human history (race, class, sex). This seems to me a fundamental issue underlying what has been described as the split between "spiritual" (or "cultural" or "countercultural") and "political" or "political/economic" feminists.[3] So I use the terms *nature feminists* and *social feminists.* Nature feminists customarily derive their norms from nature, whereas social feminists derive them from history. Celebrating the close connections between women and nature, nature feminists affirm their biology; social feminists, intent on exploring social interconnections, are often deeply suspicious of biological explanations. Nature feminists, on the other hand, pay limited attention to social structures. At best, they are profoundly aware of racism and classism, and Third World and working-class women are part of the sisterhood, but nevertheless their journals normally lack analysis of such matters as race and class. Similarly, social feminists have paid limited attention to nature. For example, while they may discuss the ecological crisis, few incorporate it into their full social analysis, and some do not discuss it at all.

In general, the two groups have been far more hostile to each other than their common concerns might suggest. Social feminists may accuse nature feminists of avoiding resistance to the dominant culture and pulling together for comfort in a way that lacks political rewards. In their abhorrence of patriarchal social structures, many nature feminists assume a separatist lifestyle. In defense, some respond that they are not simply involved in personal liberation, that it is necessary to change the symbol system of a society as well as to develop social/political strategies for change.[4] Those working to further a religion of ecology, such as feminist Wicca, are seeking symbols that can transform our consciousness and thus our culture. Social feminists point out that conditions of survival in other countries are worsening, and to siphon energy away from direct action to work on transformation of consciousness may bypass the need for human liberation.

The condescension implicit and often explicit in such attacks does not assuage feelings. The nature feminist seeks to preserve the planet as well as the species in the face of destructive naturism and calls on women's power to further the struggle. Elizabeth Dodson Gray refers to naturism as "the most 'ruthless' mastering of all,"[5] for if the planetary ecology is destroyed, all sexes, races, and classes will also be destroyed. The historical bias of the social feminist all too often bypasses this fundamental consideration. Social feminists are clear that a historical materialism which omits the oppression of women is defective. But similarly, a social ethic which does not fully include nature in its analysis is defective.

As I observe this split between social and nature feminists, I find that each has hold of something the other lacks. Social feminists emphasize history and often disregard nature and biology; nature feminists emphasize nature and often disregard history and social structures. This is the nature/history split; and it is, of course, a false split, a false dualism. In actuality, one can derive norms from history and still include nature, for our relation to nature is *part of* our history. And one can derive norms from nature and still include history, for human history is *part of* nature.

One reason for this split is the traditional separation, observable in many disciplines, between history (human society) and nature (anything other than human). It seems especially acute within the behavioral sciences.[6] This is a type of subject/object split that considerably antedates Descartes; the relation of humanity and nature is perhaps the central question of all western philosophy.[7] One problem is the puzzling fact that we are at once part of nature and yet somehow separate. On the one hand, humanity is part of the total ecology, the total interlocking systems of the planet, and beyond; and, on the other hand, we are able to use and exploit our environment, to mold and shape its systems to our own purposes. In some sense, our biology and our culture are in conflict with each other; but, paradoxically, without our biology, we would have no culture.

In the rest of this essay, I will set out steps that seem necessary if feminists are to heal this split in our theory. We need to build conceptual connections between the four forms of oppression, and it is particularly important to build them between sexism, racism, classism—the three modes of human oppression—and naturism. I will then sketch some special insights which nature and social feminists offer each other, and briefly discuss an important issue: whether women are closer to nature than men.

THE CONNECTIONS BETWEEN
THE FOUR MODES OF OPPRESSION

The philosophical roots of this oppression are found in the western version of dualism, a mode of thought that divides reality, or aspects of reality, in halves. Patriarchal western thought is pervaded with "hierarchical dualism,"[8] the tendency not only to divide reality but to assign higher value to one half. Simone de Beauvoir traces this to be the primordial duality of Self and Other;[9] she shares Hegel's view that every consciousness is fundamentally hostile to another consciousness, a curiously individual and ahistorical perception for so social a feminist. Many others argue that dualistic thought develops out of sexism; some assign it to social domination in general. Whatever its source, it is the most powerful conceptual link between the four modes of oppression.[10]

In this value hierarchy, the first half of the dualism understands itself as intrinsically better than the second. Women have been seen as defective males throughout history, e.g., in Christian thought and psychological theory. Treatises are still written to defend the proposition that blacks are biologically inferior to whites. Human neocortical development, and the culture it enables, is understood as a clear sign of human superiority to animals. Since the first group is seen as intrinsically better, it is entitled to a larger share of whatever is divided. The higher socioeconomic classes are entitled to a greater share of wealth; and the myth persists that the poor are poor because they are either lazy or stupid. On a global basis, better food is reserved for men, for they are considered more valuable than women, and malnutrition is appreciably higher for Third World women. Nature is seen as so inferior to humanity that we have freely despoiled the environment for centuries.

Thus the superior half is entitled to more power than the inferior—power over, needless to say, not power for. The inferior groups become utilitarian objects, resources to be exploited and possessions to be enjoyed, a vast resource of profit and pleasure. Profit is reaped from the cheap labor of women segregated in pink-collar work or unpaid housework and child-rearing: pleasure is provided by woman as sexual object. Nature is also a convenient resource to be exploited for profit, as a source of energy or raw materials, or for pleasure, as a source of recreation. Since some humans think it unethical to conduct medical experimentation on themselves, they displace the inconvenience and pain onto animals.

Interestingly, the lower part of each social dualism is associated with nature and regarded as somehow more "physical" than the higher part. Women are seen as physically weaker, more vulnerable to their physiology, and dangerously sexual, seducing men from higher pursuits. Actually, women, blacks, and the lower classes all appear more sexual. The lower classes supposedly have less sexual control and hence have more children. The myth of the sexual "Negro" has caused great violence between the races in American history. Nature herself, sheer physicality, personified as woman, must be transcended through culture, personified as male.[11] Elizabeth Dodson Gray, whose insistence on the centrality of nature sometimes gives her special insights, notes that nature is in turn demeaned by its association with women.[12] Environmentalism reflects sentimental femininity, whereas anti-environmental politics are seen as masculine, realistic, efficient, and tough.

One difficulty with sketching parallels between the four modes of oppression is the inadvertent suggestion that they are identical. It is important to be aware that, while there are fundamental similarities, there are also all kinds of intermediate contradictions; they are interstructured in complex ways, both as historical and contemporary processes. As Rosemary Ruether says:

. . . they have not been exactly parallel. Rather, we should recognize them as interstructural elements of oppression within the overarching system of white male domination. . . . This intermediate interstructuring of oppression by sex, race, and also class creates intermediate tensions and alienations.[13]

Among these intermediate alienations are tensions between nonwhite and white working-class persons, between black women and black men, between working-class and middle-class women, etc. Historically, the black liberation movement has been male-dominated; until recently the tension between female and male has been suppressed. Similarly, feminism has been basically a white middle-class movement and has denied or suppressed the experience of poor, nonwhite women, both in the nineteenth and twentieth centuries. Each liberation movement, it seems, has tended to gloss over the particular type of oppression within its own ranks. Thus we have the spectacle of a black movement that has been sexist and a feminist movement that has been both racist and classist.

THE INTERSTRUCTURING OF NATURISM
AND THE THREE MODES OF SOCIAL OPPRESSION

This interstructuring is equally complex. Social and ecological domination are inextricably fused not only in theory but also in practice, as William Leiss had made clear; the exploitation of the earth is used to enhance the power of the already powerful.[14] While Leiss speaks solely in terms of classism, the same points hold true for racism and sexism. In general, the oppression of nature has gained resources for the ruling class so that they have been able to perpetuate their exploitation of women, nonwhites, the poor and the Third World in general. And similarly, of course, the exploitation of persons enables greater exploitation of resources; the four oppressions feed off each other to benefit those on top. Naturism flourishes in a context of social injustice.

However, the ecological movement, supposedly the antithesis of naturism, is itself a movement associated with the oppressors. The attack on naturism is frequently perceived by the oppressed as simply another means of preserving the elite's status and affluence. Many in the Third World perceive environmentalism as a conspiracy to deprive them of the technology they need so desperately for development; pollution controls, for example, both impede development and cost them money. Closer to home, the global problem is mirrored small in controversies like that around the Kaiparowitz project in Utah. To conservationists, the project meant pollution and infringement on precious wilderness; to local people, it meant jobs and survival, and the Sierra Club became their enemy. Bumper stickers which proclaim "Eat an Environmentalist" suggest great anger and alienation.

It is quite possible for ecology to be thoroughly co-opted by industrial capitalism, in the short run if not in the long run. This is part of Andre Gorz's thesis in *Ecology and Politics*.[15] As he explains, problems such as pollution and limited resources may be seen simply as technical constraints on capitalism. Technology can adapt; ecological costs can be absorbed; and the process of exploitation can continue unchecked. Gorz describes chillingly how, under western capitalism, world leaders willing to use hunger as a weapon in the service of sociopolitical domination are developing a kind of ecofascism. Such weaponry was proposed by Secretary of Agriculture John Block in his first public statement.

Nevertheless, ecology, although co-optable, remains a potentially subversive science. Its conceptual underpinnings of interdependence and balance clearly confront the hierarchical dualism underlying the systems of oppression. At a social level, it provides a critique of the greed and waste implicit in industrial progress and the dangers of unlimited growth. But it has to make common cause with feminists and those seeking to liberate us from the oppressions of race and class. As Rosemary Ruether says: "The ethic of reconciliation with the earth has yet to break out of its snug corners of affluence and find meaningful cohesion with the revolutions of insurgent people."[16] Some social feminists and various science-for-the-people groups have been working together on economic systems that can simultaneously benefit all persons and care for the earth. Both social and nature feminists have been working on the development of appropriate or alternative technology. Such cooperations are altogether vital if we are to avoid the catastrophic scene envisioned by Gorz.

WHAT DO SOCIAL FEMINISTS
HAVE TO TEACH US?

The question of what the four modes of oppression have in common includes the question of what societal mechanisms or structures keep them going. This is the kind of discussion lacking in works by nature feminists, such as Susan Griffin's passionate book *Woman and Nature*,[17] and it is a discussion to which social feminists have much to contribute. Social structures are, after all, just as imprisoning as individual consciousness. To a large extent, social structures condition our individual consciousness, and the transformation of consciousness is mediated by them. Nature feminists, of course, do not deny their existence, but in general they restrict their social analysis to sexism.

Social feminists teach us to add analyses of classism and racism to our attack on sexism. While it is possible to discuss women and nature without reference to class and race, such discussion risks remaining white and elite. Too much of the suffragist movement of the last century became a struggle of white women for white privileges. And nowadays, what do discussions of women and nature mean to working-class women whose daily necessities include welfare reform, abortion, daycare, decent working conditions, and the like? To study sexism without reference to racism or classism is really the privilege of white women in higher socioeconomic classes. Only for this group is sexism the only problem.[18]

Gorz's analysis of the potential co-optation of ecology by capitalism suggests the need for women to make common cause with other oppressed groups and incorporate those experiences into their analyses and strategies. He suggests the possibility that before naturism destroys planetary ecology, and humanity with it, human suffering may increase greatly beyond its present dimensions. In the face of such an enemy, human liberation movements need to work together.

WHAT DO NATURE FEMINISTS HAVE TO TEACH US?

In poetry, art, dance, and ritual, as well as in expository prose, nature feminists repeatedly remind us that we are part of the Earth and the universe, part of a great interdependent community of both animate and inanimate beings. Mary Daly invites us to rediscover "the cosmic covenant, the deep harmony in the community of being in which we participate."[19] In 1978, at a feminist conference on social ethics, a substantial number of participants—persons very sensitive to modes of social oppression—nevertheless took for granted that nonhuman nature is here for our use. In general, social feminists have been slow to perceive the parallels of naturism with the social dominations. To understand nature as a utilitarian object not only ignores the fact that we are part of nature but also sets up a false dichotomy between human and nonhuman nature. The ecological symbol of the Goddess, advanced primarily by nature feminists, has become a powerful symbol of the community of being for many feminists of different persuasions.[20] At best, rather than returning to pretechnological primitivism, nature feminists can assist us to live within ecological limits, regulating our wasteful consumption and not polluting our resources.

In addition, nature feminists can teach us to celebrate our bodies. It is only very recently that social feminists have started to say much about the body; and concepts are sadly lacking to help us link our individual embodiment with our social relations. Alice Rossi is the sociologist most responsible for introducing biology into her field,[21] and her pioneering efforts have been more attacked than facilitated. Traditionally, social feminists have been very suspicious of biology, in part because it has been used in reactionary ways against blacks and women. Further, our biology is in large part the reason we have been confined to the domestic sphere throughout history.[22] "Anatomy is destiny" are fighting words in the sisterhood. Nevertheless, in our efforts to reclaim our bodies and affirm our sexuality, there is room for bridge-building.

Nature feminists could help to save social feminists from certain excesses. Some have responded to the misuse of biology by denying its realities: the final chapter of Shulamith Firestone's *The Dialectic of Sex* is an extreme example. She asserts flatly that we must "free humanity from the tyranny of its biology."

Humanity can no longer afford to remain in the transitional stage between simple animal existence and *full control of nature.* And we are much closer to a major evolutionary jump, indeed, to direction of our own evolution, than we are to a return to the animal kingdom from which we came.[23]

So instead of succumbing to the "tyranny" of our biology, we will overthrow it and take total control. While Firestone traces most social domination to sexism, she does not extend this model to the relation of humanity and nature; indeed, she reverses it. In high contrast is Mary Daly's statement that we need to move "from a culture of rapism to a culture of reciprocity" with nature.[24]

ARE WOMEN CLOSER TO NATURE THAN MEN?

In a seminal article, Sherry Ortner argues that the universal devaluation of women (trans-historical and cross-cultural) has resulted from the association of women and nature.[25] Men, on the other hand, are customarily associated with culture. Nature feminists are now reversing the logic and invoking women's closeness to nature in order to heighten our value. A powerful theme in their work is the idea that women are closer to nature than men. It is a short step, though not all take it, to the affirmation that women are therefore in important ways superior to men.

The topic deserves an article in itself. It is both deeply complex and deeply emotional, and it may well be one of the greatest stumbling blocks to an alliance between social and nature feminists. So I shall simply sketch out a few issues. Much depends on the meaning of the word "closer," whether it applies to biological or social-psychological matters.

Those who believe that women's biology allies us more closely with nature cite processes such as menstruation and childbirth. These relate us to Mother or Sister Earth, the rhythms and processes of life, the flow of future generations, in a way that men's biology cannot replicate. Some argue that menstruation brings women a knowledge of our limits early in life, which may assist us to live within ecological limits. Others take the whole argument further and say that the very possession of a penis—an organ they perceive as intrinsically dominating and patriarchal—limits male perceptions and capacities.

I have several difficulties with such arguments. First, simply because women are *able* to bear children does not mean that doing so is *essential* to our nature. Contraception clarifies this distinction: the ability to give birth can now be suppressed, and there are powerful ecological pressures in favor of this. In this context, it is important that our biology *not* be our destiny. Second, I find it difficult to assert that men are "further" from nature because they neither menstruate nor bear children. They also eat, breathe, excrete, sleep, and die; and all of these, like menstruation, are experiences of bodily limits. Like any organism, they are involved in constant biological exchange with their environment and they have built-in biological clocks complete with cycles. They also play a role in childbearing; I do not share the perception that the removal of semen from a man's body and its implantation in a woman's somehow turns fatherhood into an adjunct role. In reproduction, men's genes are as important as women's.

I find that Elizabeth Dodson Gray's argument for the limitations of "penis-bound bodily experience" is a contradiction of her central theme, her powerful affirmation of ecological interconnectedness. Consider her beautiful description of body-in-connection-with-the-world: ". . . who-we-are is rooted in our kinship with the natural. The water of life flows through our tissues, and we are nourished, watered, fed, sustained, and ultimately return everything in our bodies to the world around us."[26] Surely this is as true of men as of women. Besides, her vision of the penis as intrinsically dominating is contradicted by her own moving description of heterosexual intercourse, which indicates that a penis can be an organ of profound interconnection.[27] A culture may indeed condition men to use their penises as organs of domination, but they are not innately bound to do so.

There is a serious problem in freezing biological differences into a theory of two natures in which women are relatively "good" (closer to nature) and men relatively "bad" (farther from nature). This sets up a new hierarchical dualism, as much the reverse of male sexism as Firestone's analysis. Since black is beautiful, white must be bad? Since Aryans are pure, Jews must be a danger to the race? Ultimately, the problem is ecological. In a true ecological vision, all participate equally, rocks as much as persons, males as much as females. All are part of the great community of being.

If the question is social-psychological, there may be more truth in the assertion that women are "closer" to nature: we may be potentially more sensitive to it. Certainly our social roles have largely been defined in terms of bodily functions, and differing sex roles and psychologies have developed. Conditioned to greater emotionality and nurturance, possibly we are more likely than men to respond to the idea of sisterhood and nonhuman nature.

But finally, and most importantly, the question itself is flawed. Only the nature/history split allows us even to formulate the question of whether women are closer to nature than men. The very idea of one group of persons being "closer to nature" than another is a "construct of culture," as Ortner puts it.[28] Since we are all part of nature, and since all of us, biology and culture alike, is part of nature, the question ultimately makes no sense.

CONCLUSION

As I contemplate the nature/history split, as it is manifested in the division and struggle between nature and social feminists, it becomes a Zen koan. Suddenly it becomes clear that our history is inseparably part of our nature, our social structures are inseparably part of our biology. As William Leiss wrote:

". . . once the illusion of the separation between nature and society is abandoned, the true character of social development as a series of increasingly complex states of nature becomes apparent."[29] These are strange paradoxes, these seeming divisions between nature and culture, which dissolve into nothingness when one tries to take hold of them.

As has long been recognized, such either/or choices, such false divisions, are the curse of our patriarchal culture. When nature feminists assert that women are biologically superior to men, I think they are setting up a false split between men and women. When social feminists say that nature feminists are siphoning energy away from direct action if they choose to work on transforming consciousness, I think they are setting up a false either/or. A good ecological rule, when confronted with such a choice, is to ask if both/and is a possible response. This is in keeping with the ecological ethical imperative: "Maximize interconnectedness."

Certainly there is little point in choosing up sides between nature and social feminists since, as I have tried to show, we have much to give each other. I therefore share Charlotte Bunch's wish for a "nonaligned feminism" which refuses to attach automatically to an either/or choice.[30] The feminist ethic spurs us to seek the truths in each other's positions rather than to assail each other's errors. This is easier said than done, of course, for we are all corrupted by the patriarchy; and *ad feminem* attacks, to coin a phrase, will remain in our literature. When such violence occurs between sisters it is doubtless well to look closely, for the issues that arouse the deepest emotions may be the most fertile to explore.

Social and nature feminists are part of each other. We have only just begun to study out the interstructuring of sex, race, and class. We need to work on understanding the interstructuring of naturism with the three modes of social domination. In working to heal the nature/history split, we may yet turn back the tide of ecofascism and advance our revolution.

NOTES

1. Sheila D. Collins, *A Different Heaven and Earth* (Valley Forge: Judson Press, 1974), 161.

2. Rosemary Radford Ruether, *New Woman/New Earth: Sexist Ideologies and Human Liberation* (New York: Seabury, 1975).

3. Charlotte Bunch, "Beyond Either/Or Feminist Options," *Quest* 3 (1976), 2–17; and Hallie Iglehart, "Unnatural Divorce of Spirituality and Politics," *Quest* 4 (1978), 12–24.

4. Starhawk, *The Spiral Dance: A Rebirth of the Ancient Religion of the Great Goddess* (San Francisco: Harper and Row, 1979).

5. Elizabeth Dodson Gray, *Why the Green Nigger? Remything Genesis* (Wellesley, MA: Roundtable Press, 1979), 6.

6. History itself, as commonly taught and written, is chiefly human history. Rare

indeed are books which set human history in an ecological context, such as Edward Hyams' *Soil and Civilization* (New York: Harper and Row, 1976).

7. Thomas B. Colwell, Jr., "Some Implications of the Ecological Revolution for the Construction of Value," *Human Values and Natural Science,* ed. E. Laszlo and J. B. Wilbur (New York: Gordon, 1970), 245–58.

8. Ruether, *New Woman/New Earth.*

9. Simone de Beauvoir, *The Second Sex,* ed. and trans. H. M. Parshley (New York: Knopf, 1953; original publication 1949).

10. Most social feminists critique this dualism from a dialectical point of view, whereas many nature feminists are monist.

11. Sherry B. Ortner, "Is Female to Male as Nature Is to Culture?" *Woman, Culture, and Society,* ed. Michelle Zimbalist Rosaldo and Louise Lamphere (Stanford: Stanford University Press, 1974), 67–87.

12. Gray, *Why the Green Nigger?*

13. Ruether, *New Woman/New Earth,* 116.

14. William Leiss, *The Domination of Nature* (New York: Braziller, 1972).

15. Andre Gorz, *Ecology and Politics,* trans. P. Vigderman and J. Cloud (Boston: South End Press, 1980; original publication 1975).

16. Rosemary Radford Ruether, "Motherearth and the Megamachine," *Womanspirit Rising: A Feminist Reader in Religion,* ed. Carol P. Christ and Judith Plaskow (San Francisco: Harper and Row, 1970), 43–52.

17. Susan Griffin, *Woman and Nature: The Roaring inside Her* (New York: Harper and Row, 1978).

18. Ruether, *New Woman/New Earth.*

19. Mary Daly, *Beyond God the Father: Toward a Philosophy of Women's Liberation* (Boston: Beacon, 1973), 177.

20. Starhawk, *The Spiral Dance.*

21. Alice Rossi, "A Biosocial Perspective on Parenting," *Daedalus* 106 (1977), 3–24.

22. Ortner, "Is Female to Male as Nature Is to Culture?"

23. Shulamith Firestone, *The Dialectic of Sex: The Case for Feminist Revolution* (New York: Morrow, 1970), 193. Italics mine.

24. Daly, *Beyond God the Father, 178.*

25. Ortner, "Is Female to Male as Nature Is to Culture?"

26. Gray, *Why the Green Nigger?* 83.

27. Ibid., 97.

28. Ortner, "Is Female to Male as Nature Is to Culture?"

29. Leiss, *The Domination of Nature,* xii.

30. Bunch, "Beyond Either/Or Feminist Options."

20

WOMEN AGAINST
WASTING THE WORLD

Notes on Eschatology and Ecology

Catherine Keller

to waste: v.t. 1. to lay waste; devastate   2. to use up; consume; to wear out
3. to emaciate; to cause to be consumed or weakened, as by overuse, disease,
or the like; to enfeeble   4. to expend needlessly, carelessly, or without
valuable result; to squander . . . see RAVAGE   —Merriam-Webster

Time is short, since the deterioration of some life-support systems appears
to be accelerating.   —State of the World 1988

Then I saw a new heaven and a new earth, for the first heaven and the first
earth had vanished, and there was no longer any sea. I saw the holy city, new
Jerusalem, coming down out of heaven from God, made ready like a bride
adorned for her husband.   —Rev. 21:1

The Earth is being wasted—devastated, with a violence echoed by the crude
contemporary idiom of "waste the sucker"; it's being used up, its profound
resources squandered, its lush abundance consumed, its complex surfaces worn
out. Yet this apocalyptic sort of message would not be worth repeating if it
weren't also the case that there is still great life and responsiveness in the Earth as
well. This is no time for despair—and there is no time for despair. Yet something
in us readily succumbs to a sense of futility, something perhaps more than, yet
related to, the objective configuration of economic and political forces laying
waste our planet. So I want to begin to ask: What is the connection between the
flagrant, accelerating waste of our world and the contemporary recrudescence of
the myth of the Apocalypse? Do women have, as women, a specific response to
make? I will not try here to offer any definitive answers; at present I am more
interested in getting these questions formulated, in feeling a way into their
tensions and possibilities.

Here is how the melodramatic voice of the connection sounds to me: "Waste
her! Go ahead, use 'er up! Devastate, consume, expend, squander, ravage, Daddy
will give us a new one. The final rapture is almost here!"

This is not the voice of any single belief: it is a voice uttered from the
whirlwind symbiosis of born-again Christian apocalypticism and military/
industrial consumerism, from an unprecedented alliance of reactionary premod-
ernism with hypermodern greed that reared its gleaming head during the decade
of the 1980s. Listen to what it says: "Waste not want not? Haste makes waste?
Old wives' tales—make way for the new bride! Who needs the warnings of

ecofreaks, antinuclear fanatics, and witch women who don't understand that the Lord has made all good things for our use: to use up before the millennium. Not to waste is to waste—make haste, Jesus is coming! Fill the Earth and subdue 'er!—that was God's command at the beginning. Now, at the end, let's dispose of that which was created to be at man's disposal."

Let me be clear: such a caricature does not reproduce the sincere faith of many born-again Christians, or any evangelical doctrines. I mean to evoke something more pervasive, more systemic, than the influence of the U.S. right-wing Christian movement, than even of its televangelists, those dispensationalist apocalypticists preaching the imminent demise of the world, preceded by their own rapture before the tribulations.[1] The power of the televangelists has been interrupted by the revelation that, at least in the realm of personal morality, they do not live by the absolutes they preach; and the rightest momentum of the 1980s may not sustain itself through another presidency. But regardless of the next moves of the religiopolitical right, the apocalyptic myth has been influencing and will continue to influence the course of planetary history. That is, the expectation of an end-time and of an end of time has, I believe, defined the limits of Western patriarchal consciousness, Christian, Jewish, and secular. Perhaps all the more effectively because largely unconsciously, the imagery that concludes the Bible has conveyed a formative framework for the end of history.

To the extent that this is true, it should come as no surprise that the paths of Western technological and political development have led us to the threshold of annihilation. Nor is it an accident that the masses of middle-class White humanity—including at this moment White middle-class women—who unlike people of color and the poor usually have no urgent matters of social survival facing them, do not rise up and make this end-of-the-world scenario *stop*. Of course, the most concrete reason that we as a class let it continue is because of our dependence upon ecological and military exploitation to sustain anything even vaguely resembling our middle-class life-styles. Our helplessness before the modern state generates both a widespread lack of belief in truly sustainable options and a sense of the futility of resistance.

I am claiming, however, that this economic dependency itself reflects artificial limits upon the imagination. Participants in Christian civilization, which extends far beyond the bounds of belief, have been preprogrammed by ancient visions to expect that when the going gets rough, the world will go. Apocalypticism leads some to a fervent hope for the end, which promises a new beginning, and others to a gloomy resignation to global destruction. These have always been the two sides of the apocalyptic consciousness: hope and despair.[2] Because of the literally apocalyptic situation of this late modern period, both of these attitudes side with omnicide.

Nuclear annihilation continues to be an option, one preferred by many for its impressive capacity to fulfill "God's" prophecy in such passages as Rev. 16:17f:

Then the seventh angel poured his bowl on the air; and out of the sanctuary came a loud voice from the throne, which said, "It is over!" And there followed flashes of lightning and peals of thunder, and a violent earthquake, like none before it in human history, so violent it was.[3]

But the nuclear and ecological threats are twin manifestations of the same source: the unchecked power of the military/industrial establishment, subliminally inspired and justified by apocalyptic assumptions of an end of history.

Within this textual context I will focus more on that form of doomsday annihilation that is already well under way: in the moment-by-moment "end of the world" proceeding through the tangible, cumulative, daily destruction of the physical environment. This we feel now all the time, this doom, this dread, this rage, quite apart from the pervasive nuclear anxiety. For instance, let's talk about the weather. It is again today, as I write, too hot for this time of year. I have winced each time native New Jerseyans (I haven't lived here long) shook their heads and said, "It just doesn't seem right. Maybe my memory mistakes me, but June was always more pleasant than this." "Springs have been getting shorter and shorter." I have felt a wretched gratitude if someone indicated that this is just a variation within a normal pattern. Maybe we still have time . . . But, of course, the information is now suddenly everywhere and unavoidable: that the warming pattern of the greenhouse effect, based especially on the burning of fossil fuels and the accumulation of now a century of industrial waste gases, has almost certainly begun, much sooner than scientists expected. I notice that sometimes I choose not to mention these things, as though it is impolite in the course of a simple discussion of the heat; at other times, a kind of apocalyptic rudeness overtakes me, and I say, "Well, unless we do something it is only going to get worse." This morning even that bastion of establishment "balance," the *New York Times,* took on the issue as its leading editorial: "The Greenhouse Effect? Real Enough." The editorial pointed out that, in the face of a disastrous drought unlike any this country had known, and the fact that "four of the last eight years—1980, 1981, 1983 and 1987—have been the warmest since measurements of global surface temperatures began a century ago, and 1988 may be another record hot year," measures should be taken and suggested a set of crucial means for slowing the greenhouse warming (including encouragement of nuclear energy development).[4]

Quite apart from moments of political consciousness, these end-time winces, semiconscious mixes of acknowledgment and denial, fill our days with nagging little apocalyptic tensions. We wonder whether to use bottled water even for making coffee and then wonder how to find out whether the bottled water comes from a nontoxic water source. Habits and plans shift, to outings that do not center around prolonged exposure to the sun. In this summer of 1988, people who previously didn't think about skin cancer, now, with a certain ruefulness, mention the ozone layer and wear a hat to play tennis, wear #35 sun block even for an hour in the sun.

It is good news that the news is finally getting around. We may get to widespread action. This end-time is not irreversible, yet, though some of the damage may be. But the prospect of a permanently scarred planet, like that of a person who comes out of a mugging with some scars, is no reason to shut down hope—yet isn't there something within all of us that seems to give up the future with each new wave of ecological bad news? To sustain action may require naming the apocalyptic element that has embedded world destruction within a vision of Divine providence moving history from creation to conclusion. The mythic miasma of a few apocalyptic texts, operating out of context and unconsciously, seems to preform our sense of time and history.

As you read the following two passages, remember recent heat waves, droughts, and media attention to the greenhouse effect, and consider the effects of the passages' juxtaposition on you:

> By 1987, what had become known as the ozone "hole" was twice the size of the continental United States. Though the hole involves a series of as yet poorly understood chemical reactions, it could portend an unexpectedly rapid ozone depletion globally and translate into lowered crop output and rising skin cancer and eye damage as more ultraviolet radiation reaches the earth.[5]

> The fourth angel poured his bowl on the sun; and it was allowed to burn men with its flames. They were fearfully burned; but they only cursed the God of heaven for their sores and pains, and would not repent of what they had done. (Rev. 16:8ff)

Obviously there is a certain fit—and fundamentalists are far more expert than I at matching biblical "prophecies" to current events. They read (and always have) these parallels as evidence of the imminence of the last days. Others, taking a staunchly secularist view, may write off such parallels as coincidence. Let me say that if these are the only two options, I suspect the fundamentalists are closer to the truth. Close enough to succumb to a frightening distortion, a distortion already infecting the apocalyptic writers themselves. It is hard to miss the patriarchal, militarist dualism in the book of Revelation. There may be a profound intuition at work in the vision of the oppressed community for which "John" wrote—that *if* civilization continues along the route of the gross and violent imperial materialism symbolized by the "whore of Babylon" (and Rome), *then* globally scaled destruction, involving not only society but the cosmos, becomes inevitable. But even the critique of imperialism is couched in the terms of both religious and male chauvinism; a literalist mindset seems to turn the outcome into a vindictively foregone conclusion. There is a voice that even in me—who has a background quite the opposite of any Christian fundamentalism—whispers, "Maybe it is inevitable. Maybe there is no other way than the way of regeneration through destruction." This voice, in myself, does not feel authentic; it has a derivative, superstitious, despairing ring. But, for millions of persons in this country, this voice has become dominant, militantly evangelical, and committed to the belief that ecological and/or nuclear disaster, along with increasing political injustice and violence, are more or less inevitable signs of the times: that is, of the end of time.

For this reason it is best not to simply and angrily discount them, but to try to hear. It is not only that as the prophecies of Revelation seem to approach realization, we have reason to think they were on target; rather, this is a formative text deeply enough inscribed in Western consciousness to have found the means of its self-fulfillment. That is, as the early Christian movement became increasingly institutionalized, patriarchal, and, finally, with Constantine, the bearer of imperial power, such mythic imagery became part of the understanding of time, nature, and history that has shaped the course of Western development. So it is not that the text of the bowl and the burning sun literally predicted the hole in the ozone layer, but that the text may be the *sine qua non* for the hole. But the text could have been—and has been—realized in many other ways as well.

If this hypothesis—that the end-time myth serves as *sine qua non* of the present end-time threat—has any validity, then it behooves us to examine the connection between ecology and eschatology. *Ecology:* the study of the relationships among things. *Eschatology:* the study of end things. Is it as simple as this—that because the relationships among things, among everything—animal, vegetable, and mineral—have been neglected and violated and because patriarchal humanity has exploited rather than nurtured its relationships to its environments that the literal "end" seems so imminent? That the degradation of relationships to means to ends in fact leads to end things? What relation does such degradation bear to Christian eschatology? Is eschatology a cause of the literal end? Is it also a resource against it?

Eschatology has traditionally referred to the final judgment and resurrection of the dead, to the inbreaking at any moment of the Divine realm, or to life after death. Early Christians as well as the Jews of the same period lived in high expectations, born of the classic prophecies, of a new heaven and earth, a new Jerusalem, envisioned originally as a just and harmonious world order in which humanity has ceased its wars and its exploitations and lives in harmony with a renewed ecosphere. Apocalyptic eschatology is a radical development of that hope, taking the form of mythopoeic visions of end-times involving a catastrophic end of history, a rapture of the saved, the sons of light, who are installed in triumphant glory along with the Messiah at the Second Coming, and a Final Judgment in which the sons of darkness receive, after gruesome tribulations during which they do not repent, the justice of eternal corporal punishment.

Of course, mainline Christianity quickly veered away from the early charismatic hope for an end to the world within the generation: it institutionalized and individualized its eschatology and usually ignored the hallucinogenic excesses of the apocalyptic vision. Yet the fundamentalist forms by which it has returned in our time do not suggest a marginal exception, but something more like the return of the repressed. The extravagant moral dualism of the apocalyptic perspective, which can resolve the tensions of worldly life only by destroying the world, has returned with the full secular force of U.S. industrial-imperial power in this decade. Reinforcing the moral dualism is a theological dualism, in which an absolutely transcendent Deity reigns from outside his "creation," utterly independent of that world. This in turn yields a temporal dualism of beginning and end: creation is at the start, and eschatology refers to a literal conclusion.

And so there is some causal link between the ancient vision of a world at the "disposal" of a controlling Lord and that world of disposable products, itself subject to human control and human disposal of its resources, brought into being by modern technology. The sacred story ends in the apocalyptic tribulations of the end-time, preordained by the Divine dominance; the secular derivative ends—despite its belief in endless progress and its repudiation of supernaturalism—in some combination of whimpers and bangs brought on by the ecocidal and omnicidal measures of a politics of domination. Although both present supposedly hopeful visions of the future, both involve the destruction of the Earth. The latter, with its vision of endless progress by way of endless exploitation, seems to have developed the science with which to effectively and unconsciously fulfill on a worldly plane the other-worldly vision of the apocalyptic. One can surmise that the development therefore of scientific modernity, despite its apparent secularizing focus, is still inspired by biblical apocalyptic. Both in fact drive toward the end of time and the world: neither respects the spatiotemporal rhythms of earthly ecology. And, for both, woman, in her association with bodiliness, becomes the metaphor and recipient of the subjugation and externalization of nature. Woman, as whore, old wife, witch, is the embodiment of time, which is to be used up, which is running away.[6]

The link between the kind of science and the kind of theology that worked together to create the present situation is suggested by biologist/physicist and Nobel recipient Ilya Prigogine: "The 'mechanized' nature of modern science, created and ruled according to a plan that totally dominates it, but of which it is unaware, glorifies its creator, and was thus admirably suited to the needs of both theologians and physicists. . . . The debasement of nature is parallel to the glorification of all that eludes it, God and man [sic]."[7] Prigogine and coauthor Isabelle Stengers never mention the additional parallelism so obvious to feminists, that of the debasement of woman to the glory of a *he-man* God and the men who bear his image. But let us return to the original text:

> Then I saw a great white throne, and the One who sat upon it; from his presence earth and heaven vanished away, and no place was left for them. (Rev. 20:1)

No place was left for them—the natural universe, whose extension is identical with the extension of space, loses place. This at the moment when its time is up. From the vantage point of White transcendence, the apotheosis of masculine rule, the One precludes the many. The universe seems to condense itself in the vision to a single unifying centerpoint, which realizes itself by annihilating the spatiotemporal world. A pristine simplicity is achieved, in which the New Jerusalem, the bride, of "gold bright as clear glass," of twelve gates each "being made from a single pearl," can be erected for the eternal bliss of the sons of light. "All this is the victor's heritage" (Rev. 20:21). The debasement of nature is parallel to the glorification of all that eludes it, God and man.

The architect of this "victor's heritage" glories in a cosmic minimalism: "The city had no need of sun or moon to shine upon it; for the glory of God gave it light" (Rev. 21:22). "And there was no longer any sea." To elude nature is to elude its evolutionary complexity, to transcend diversity. That the sea is eliminated from the new creation is no accident: the first creation of Genesis inherits the old Babylonian identification of the sea with the primordial; with the female, chaos, the Tehom. The oceanic womb of life, construed in various Hebrew scriptures as a monster to be contained, is now eternally vanquished, replaced by the purely paternal creation. But even the relatively austere diversity of planetary bodies is eliminated, and a glory-light of immaterial transcendence shines on the desired future. This drive to transcendent unity is, of course, a profound impetus in all patriarchal spirituality, and it always achieves its ends at the expense of nature and multiplicity. I am also suggesting that it pertains to the present ecological situation.

Consider what is happening to planetary multiplicity today: "As forests disappear, as the soils erode, and as lakes and soils acidify and become polluted, the number of plant and animal species diminishes. This reduction in the diversity of life on earth may well have unforeseen long-term consequences."[8]

Indeed. And the long term is precisely what the apocalyptic deadline shortchanges for the sake of a specific sort of present intensity. (This is an ironic reversal of original intent: what operates as self-denial for the sake of future reward in fact functions to justify the systemic hedonism that wastes the future for the sake of present consumption.) What is the relation between the elimination of complexity and the elimination of the future? And what, precisely, is the ecofeminist relation?

Certainly modern complexity, ambiguity, and pluralism have created a horror of any more "progress"—not without good reason! The syndrome of future shock accounts in part for the massive recursion to simplistic, premodern, apocalyptic solutions to the moral and spiritual perplexities of the late modern age. But why has it come to this?

Let me suggest, further, that the relation between complexity and future concerns essentially the very nature of relatedness. To relate is to complicate. Whether we imagine a relation to our body, a tree, an intimate friend, an enemy, global society, or the ecosphere, to bring consciousness to the relation is to sustain complexity. And quite apart from any human consciousness, the evolutionary processes in nature all demonstrate complexity within ecological relatedness.

We are, as is everything that is, an instance of becoming-in-relation. Nothing is independent of anything else. This is the fundamental ecological vision, applicable to human culture as well as to nonhuman communities. The others always influence us, however much we screen out, deny, simplify. To embrace the influx of otherness into self, to acknowledge that even what we despise becomes a part of our experience and therefore of ourselves—this is to live in the consciousness of our interconnectedness. Yet the dominant cultures of the West have systematically stifled this sort of consciousness. In the words of Agnes Whistling Elk, a Canadian native shaman: "White people have this thing that says, 'I'm not a snake. I'm not a squirrel. I'm something important.' They separate, and that's their tragedy."[9] This is a tragedy of momentous proportions, which threatens to annihilate the squirrels and the snakes, any native peoples who survived White genocides, and, of course, life itself, to which these White separatists seem to see themselves as an exception—precisely by separation.

Many of us have felt and argued that women have been the caretakers of relation, that the dominant separate self of the culture is the male ego. Yet we must at the same time acknowledge that inasmuch as this female relatedness has survived, it has been the very means of women's entrapment, our dependency. And the dependency is no more ecologically viable than the illusion of an independent ego; indeed, ironically, it has led to our own modes of separation, of social isolation as well as the disconnection from our bodily knowledge. So Agnes Whistling Elk may perceive rightly, as a woman of color, that all White people, including White feminists, suffer from a destructive and self-deceptive separation. Perhaps we—White women—can only begin to regain the wisdom and power of relation as we move into contact with non-White, nonpatriarchal, and nonmodern modes of connection with the physical world.

This relatedness does not present itself as something single, simple, or conclusive. Note, for instance, the extraordinary complexity of the spiritual paths of Native Americans and other shamanistic and Earth-centered peoples. Every bird or stone or ancestor might embody the sacred and needs to be heard, heeded, internalized as "medicine." Relatedness is not, as classical monotheism might have it, a matter of the One Other, or the One who is Other. At any moment we meet an infinite plurality, most of which we do indeed screen out, bundle and reduce into manageable perceptual and cognitive categories. To attune ourselves to this plurality means to live with the untold, indeed unspeakable, complexity it poses for us. For as we take in the many, we ourselves are many. The cohesion we achieve is not simple oneness, but, in philosopher and mathematician Alfred North Whitehead's language, a "composite unification." No unitary subject underlies—and therefore "controls"—the spatial and temporal multiplicity that informs every moment of our experience. Our nature is not that of a separate essence; rather, the nature of things—of all things natural, which nothing eludes but by self-deception—is this fluid complication out of which the "essence" of something must compose itself. The self arises, as does the self of every cosmic creature, moment by moment in new conjunctions of influence and creativity. Its continuity composes itself out of its creativity, as it spins long-term futures on the basis of its long-term memory. The deep past and the worldly future matter *naturally* to the connective self. For it knows its own emergence from and extension into an endless network of relations.[10]

If this is so, then relation is cumulative in its complexity. And time itself is the complex pattern of relationships. Complexity can no more be evaded than nature itself. At least if one is growing with and not against the grain of reality. To honor reality is to attend care-fully to the diversity of each moment—the many cannot be purged, wasted, flung like the devil: "the cowardly, the faithless, and the vile, murderers, fornicators, sorcerers, idolaters, and liars of every kind" into "the lake that burns with sulphurous flames" (Rev. 21:8).

The dualistic solution to the problem of evil is characteristic of the great monotheisms: simplification by Oneness never quite unifies reality, never quite works—it always has the cumulative impact of its discarded waste products to dispose of. (Hence sulphurous fumes?) No wonder time must end in some final conflagration—the cosmos cannot contain all the garbage. In this worldview that at the most intimate, emotional levels as well as the ecological and economic levels refuses to recycle the past, the force of denied diversity appears as chaos and evil. Thus, already in the first creation epic, the *Enuma Elish* (the Babylonian creation myth from the late second millennium B.C.), the male warrior God Marduk establishes his universe by conquering the first mother, the Great Goddess Tiamat—who as the primordial ocean is interpreted as a monster of chaos. The biblical version is the story of Genesis, in which the word of God creates His world out of the Tehom—the Hebrew equivalent of Tiamat.[11] So the Bible opens with the creation of a world out of the primal sea, in which chaos is not yet fully defeated; and the Bible ends with the destruction of that world, in which diversity and fluidity still had their ways, and its replacement by one with no sea. While we can argue that Genesis represents a critique and transformation of the warrior myth, in Revelation he returns full force: "From his mouth there went a sharp sword with which to smite the nations; for he it is who shall rule them with an iron rod" (Rev. 19:20).

This messianic figure, also called the "Lamb," mocks the relational complexity required by Jesus' own teaching of the justice of love, even of others and enemies. This second coming—less of Jesus than of the Babylonian Marduk—poses a simpler solution, the final solution. For Jesus of Nazareth, eschatology referred, as with the earlier prophets, to a just version of *this* world, and its timing was unpredictable, even to himself. The point was to "pay heed, watch—for you know not the time" (Matt. 24:42). *Watch*—attend consciously, alert to the possibilities for relation and transformation flooding in upon us *now*. We are not to waste those opportunities, but to relish the eschatological banquet now, by opening community to include those who are radically other, poor, needy, disdained. In its better moments, the eschatological future is not a literal end but a creative edge—the moment of the fullness of time in which a new plenitude of relations is realized. Anxiety is healed not by elimination of complexity but by the cosmic trust of the lilies.

If time is the complex of relations in which diversity unfolds, then end-time is a logical consequence of the debasement of diversity and of relation. Temporality is the mark of physicality, of body and woman and all that complexity that resists control, that undermines the unitary ego, and that mocks the male hero. Relationship and sensuality have been assigned to women, and the Earth itself has been feminized and ravaged accordingly. Feminist theory has well mapped the long history of religious, philosophical, and scientific projection of "nature" onto woman's body and of woman's body onto the Earth. Ruling-class men, especially but not exclusively those raised within the domains of Western monotheism, have seen themselves as godlike exceptions to nature, diversity, and death. And so, along with women, the diversity of peoples, of races, of religions, and of species have suffered irreversible degradation during the course of patriarchal history. Yet it is not these suffering ones, but those who have inflicted the suffering who seem most to want out, who threaten to bring on the final death, the escape from time and relation and, by a perverse logic, from death itself. For apocalypticism portrays the death of everything as the way to the eternal life of the privileged few.

Science has been the needed and perhaps unwitting tool of the apocalyptic literalization. As Prigogine and Stengers analyze modern science, its classical insistence on a single, immutable, timeless, and universally dominant truth and its describing nature as a simple and homogeneous machine continued the theistic assumptions of simplicity and control—and of the transcendent mind of either scientist or God. But they offer an interesting hope by claiming that, at least in theory, contemporary science has moved to a new time-bound pluralism: "Both at the macroscopic and microscopic levels, the natural sciences have thus rid themselves of a conception of objective reality that implied that novelty and diversity had to be denied in the name of immutable universal control." They show how this shift has emerged along with a new valorization of time (which even Einstein could not accept), that is, of natural processes that are irreversible. Irreversibility is the basis of the thesis that order always emerges out of chaos (of randomness or irreversibility); that "today interest is shifting from substance to relation, to communication, to time. . . . Our universe has a pluralistic, complex character."[12]

Perhaps this new valorization of time, especially in conjunction with pluralism and relation, signals a certain conversion within the White male power elite. But in itself, such a theoretical shift is only interesting. We are now working under imperative deadlines. However, in conjunction with political movements linking ecology, social justice, and feminism, it signals an alternative to the deadly and self-contradictory mix of technological mechanism (based on time-reversible process) with apocalyptic eschatology (an archaic form of irreversibility: history moves from a beginning to an end).

What we need is a reduced and sensitive technology cooperating with the exhaustible, irreversible, spontaneous, and pluralistic character of the universe and the Earth. To achieve this we also need a new understanding of human socioecology—one that cherishes our own diversity rather than exploiting it through hierarchies of state, race, class, and gender. We therefore need to propagate a spirituality that imagines an open and sustainable future, one that looks lovingly on time as the garden of all the relations that have been and will be, that works practically to effect change where it is possible.

Such a spirituality cannot disconnect itself from the biblical heritage altogether. Some of us at least can afford to (and perhaps cannot afford not to) tap the eschatological energies of the classical prophets and of the Mary and Jesus of the synoptic gospels, for whom "prophecy" referred to the denunciation of injustices against the vulnerable and the vision of a lush future in *this* world for all who partake in justice and wisdom. None of these ancient texts come free of their own sexism and nationalism. We cannot find there a point of pure and undiluted liberation, yet there is much radical wisdom there to recycle.

When we revere the complexity of our own and each other's relations and situations, rather than seeking a feminist purity, we have the chance of extending our work effectively and multilaterally into the culture at large.

But here enters eschatology. For while apocalyptic eschatology may bear responsibility for the creation of a sense of time as coming to an end, in a larger and older sense, eschatology in the context of the prophetic cry for justice may be responsible for a sense of the irreversibility of history itself. That is, the sense of history as dramatic unfolding rather than cyclic repetition has its strongest sources in biblical consciousness.

A deliteralized, deapocalypticized eschatology can better serve the feminist project of a socially and historically responsible ecocentrism. Mary's *Magnificat*, for instance, proclaiming the eschatological "year of the Lord's favor," the "good news to the poor," suggests—like all liberation theology, biblical and contemporary—the opening of the sacred community to be realized now, though its fuller realization is still in the future. Such reformed eschatology might give us some leverage for addressing the end-time mode of eschatological consciousness with a modicum of empathy—therefore giving us the chance of affecting it. Without an ecocentric consciousness, liberation eschatology will neglect the natural environment for the sake of small gains now for the poor, undermining the soil, the water, and the air from which everyone's future must flow.

We also need an eschatological consciousness in the sense that we are *watching* now with acute consciousness of the risk to all life; that we are aware that though some processes of damage are still reversible, others are not; that we are in an edgy time, without endless time ahead—indeed, that we are in an end-time. The end of what time? Either of Earth's capacity to support human and most other societies; or of patriarchal history and its time sense (or lack thereof). That is, ending end-time means beginning again with a new, full concept of time—a time that has space for us all and a space that has time for us all—a helical time.

For such a concept of time we draw from whatever Earth-centered, native sources may still speak to us. From them we begin to learn the way of the creatures, of our creatureliness, so that our bodies, our ancestors, and our communities can again speak wisdom to and through us. Women in the past two decades have reopened access to Goddess religions in which woman was neither reducible to, nor separable from, Earth—any more than was any other earthly thing. In a culture that has led to an apocalyptic displacement of the universe in which we dwell, projecting a White warrior experience of alienation into the infinite, to be simply at home again, in our bodies, our worlds, is to become ecocentric: "eco," from *oikos,* the greek word for "home," which is also the root of "economy." This will mean being at home on the edge of time, not fighting against time but with it. It will mean finding economic/ecological niches for all the wildness of diverse creatures who still, however nervously, populate our planet. Many, too many, are gone, irreversibly, forever. Many will be lost before there is time to save them. But we can take their memory into the creation of a future out of the sacred abundance remaining to us. There is no centralized rule in the universe, no simplicity that will save us. But there is the rhythm by which, again and again, we center ourselves, embody ourselves— make a home for ourselves—amidst the multiplicity. We need no new heaven and Earth. We have this Earth, this sky, this water to renew.

NOTES

1. Grace Halsell, *Prophecy and Politics: Militant Evangelicals on the Path to Nuclear War* (Westport, CT: Lawrence Hill, 1986), provides a useful introduction to the subject.

2. For an excellent collection of essays on the varieties of contemporary apocalypticism, see Saul Friedlander (ed.), *Visions of Apocalypse: End or Rebirth* (New York: Holmes and Meier, 1985).

3. This is the famous Armageddon passage, responsible for the fundamentalist conviction. [See also Hal Lindsay, *The Late Great Planet Earth* (Grand Rapids, MI: Zondervan, 1970) (a book that seems to have sold more copies than any book since the Bible), who argues that God has foreordained a nuclear Armageddon. This necessitates unconditional support of the policies of Israel, as the Jews must be "ingathered" before it can occur.] This and subsequent biblical citations are from *The New English Bible* (New York: Oxford and Cambridge University Presses, 1970).

4. *The New York Times* (June 23, 1988), A22.

5. Lester R. Brown (ed.), *State of the World 1988: A Worldwatch Institute Report on Progress Toward a Sustainable Society* (New York: Norton, 1988).

6. See Carolyn Merchant, *The Death of Nature: Women, Ecology and the Scientific Revolution* (San Francisco: Harper & Row, 1980), for an excellent account of the link between the rise of modernity, the witch persecutions, and the industrial assault on nature.

7. Ilya Prigogine and Isabelle Stengers, *Order Out of Chaos: Man's New Dialogue with Nature* (New York: Bantam, 1984), 51.

8. Brown, *State of the World 1988,* 8.

9. As cited, whether altogether literally or not I cannot tell, by Lynn Andrews in *Medicine Woman* (San Francisco: Harper & Row, 1981), 107.

10. I have argued all this extensively in *From a Broken Web: Separation, Sexism and Self* (Boston: Beacon, 1986).

11. Ibid. For source references and a discussion of the hero myth, notably of Marduk, in its connection to the separative impulses of patriarchal selfhood, see chap. 3.

12. Prigogine and Stengers, *Order Out of Chaos,* 8f.

21

ECOFEMINISM, REVERENCE FOR LIFE, AND FEMINIST THEOLOGICAL ETHICS

Lois K. Daly

Feminist theological ethics claims to be informed by an analysis of the interlocking dualisms of patriarchal Western culture. These include the dualisms of male/female, mind/body, and human/nature. In fact, as feminists argue, none of these dualisms will be overcome or transformed until the connections between and among them are named and understood. This means that we cannot rest with examining the consequences of subjugating body to mind or female to male. We must also look at the ways in which the distinction between what is human and what is nonhuman authorizes the widespread destruction of individual animals, their habitats, and the earth itself. And, in doing theological ethics, we must also explore what this means for understanding the relationship between human beings and the divine. In other words, feminist theological ethics must ask about the implications of a transformed human/nonhuman relationship for understanding the human/divine relationship.

This essay will describe the connections between feminist concern about the status of women and the status of nonhuman nature, point to a theological ethic that reconsiders the relationship between human beings and other living beings, and explore the theological and ethical implications of those two steps. Reverence for life, as articulated by Albert Schweitzer, will serve as a primary resource in this project. Though decidedly not feminist in any self-conscious way, Schweitzer's position does provide resources for reconceptualizing the relationship between human beings and the nonhuman, or "natural," world and for examining the theological implications of such a reconceptualization. This theological task, the task of conceptualizing the relationship between human beings and God in light of a different way of thinking about human life in relation to the nonhuman world, is critical for feminist theological ethics.

ECOFEMINISM

Ecofeminists, or ecological feminists, are those feminists who analyze the interconnections between the status of women and the status of nonhuman nature. At the heart of this analysis are four central claims: (1) the oppression of women and the oppression of nature are interconnected; (2) these connections must be uncovered in order to understand both the oppression of women and the oppression of nature; (3) feminist analysis must include ecological insights; and (4) a feminist perspective must be a part of any proposed ecological solutions (Warren, 4). A closer look at each of these claims will illuminate the concerns of ecofeminism.

The Oppression of Women and the Oppression of Nature Are Interconnected

One way to talk about the connections between women and nature is to describe the parallel ways they have been treated in Western patriarchal society. First, the traditional role of both women and nature has been instrumental (Plumwood, 120). Women's role has been to serve the needs and desires of men. Traditionally, women were not considered to have a life except in relation to a man, whether father, brother, husband, or son. Likewise, nonhuman nature has provided the resources to meet human needs for food, shelter, and recreation. Nature had no purpose except to provide for human wants. In both cases the instrumental role led to instrumental value. Women were valued to the extent that they fulfilled their role. Nature was valued in relation to human interests either in the present or the future. Women and nature had little or no meaning independent of men.

A second parallel in the treatment of women and nature lies in the way the dominant thought has attempted "to impose sharp separation on a natural continuum" in order to maximize difference (Plumwood, 120). In other words, men are identified as strong and rational while women are seen as weak and emotional. In this division of traits those men who are sensitive and those women who are intellectually or athletically inclined are marginalized. They are overlooked in the typical (stereotypical) description of men as opposed to women. The same holds true for distinctions between what is human and what is not. The human being is conscious, the nonhuman plant or animal is not; the human is able to plan for the future, to understand a present predicament, the nonhuman simply reacts to a situation out of instinct. These distinctions are drawn sharply in order to protect the privilege and place of those thought to be more important.

These parallels are instructive but they do not explain why they developed. Two theologians were among the feminists who first articulated the link between women and nature in patriarchal culture. They were Rosemary

Ruether, in *New Woman/New Earth* (1975), and Elizabeth Dodson Gray, in *Green Paradise Lost* (1979). Both of them focused on the dualisms that characterize patriarchy, in particular the dualisms of mind/body and nature/culture. In her work Ruether traces the historical development of these dualisms in Western culture. She points to the way in which Greek thought, namely dualistic thought, was imported into ancient Hebraic culture. The triumph of this dualism came in the development of a transcendent or hierarchical dualism in which men

> master nature, not by basing themselves on it and exalting it as an independent divine power, but by subordinating it and linking their essential selves with a transcendent principle beyond nature which is pictured as intellectual and male. This image of transcendent, male spiritual deity is a projection of the ego or consciousness of ruling-class males, who envision a reality, beyond the physical processes that gave them birth, as the true source of their being. Men locate their true origins and natures in this transcendent sphere, which thereby also gives them power over the lower sphere of "female" nature (Ruether 1975, 13–14).

In this way, transcendent dualism incorporates and reinforces the dualisms of mind/body and nature/culture as well as male/female. In addition these distinctions are read into other social relations, including class and race. As a result, ruling-class males lump together those whom Ruether calls the "body people": women, slaves, and barbarians (Ruether 1975, 14; see also Plumwood, 121–22).

While agreeing with the reasons for the development of transcendent dualism, Dodson Gray's response to it differs from Ruether's. Ruether's tack is to reject transcendental dualism outright; Dodson Gray appears to embrace the dualism but to reevaluate the pairs. In other words, she maintains the distinction but insists that being more closely tied to nature does not detract from women's worth. Instead, for Dodson Gray, it enhances it. As others have pointed out, Dodson Gray "come[s] dangerously close to implicitly accepting the polarities which are part of the dualism, and to trying to fix up the result by a reversal of the valuation which would have men joining women in immanence and identifying the authentic self as the body" (Plumwood, 125).

A similar division of opinion can also be traced in other feminist writings. It is the difference between the nature feminists and social feminists (Griscom 1981, 5). The nature feminists are those who celebrate women's biological difference and claim some measure of superiority as a result of it. The social feminists are those who recognize the interstructuring of race, class, and sex, but who tend to avoid discussing nature exploitation precisely because it invites attention to biological difference. Both kinds of feminists have positive points to express, but another sort of feminism, one that transcends these, is needed in order to understand the connections between the oppression of women and the oppression of nature.

These Connections Must Be Uncovered
in Order to Understand Both the Oppression of Women
and the Oppression of Nature

Feminist analysis of the transcendent dualism identified by Ruether shows that there are three basic assumptions that govern the way the dualism's elements are treated (see Ruether 1975, 1983). These assumptions lie behind the parallels between the oppression of women and nature described above. First, the elements in the dualism are perceived as higher and lower relative to each other. The higher is deemed more worthy or valuable than the lower. Second, the lower element is understood to serve the higher. In fact, the value of the lower is derived in instrumental fashion. Third, the two elements are described as polar opposites. That is, "the traits taken to be virtuous and defining for one side are those which maximize distance from the other side" (Plumwood, 132). In other words, men are "not women" and women are "not men." The same holds true in traditional conceptions of human and nonhuman nature. These three assumptions lead to a logic of domination that repeatedly identifies differences and controls them in such a way as to protect the "higher" element in the dualism. In this way, from the point of view of the "higher," difference automatically implies inferiority.

In patriarchal culture these three assumptions are at work in a "nest of assumptions" that also includes (1) the identification of women with the physical and nature, (2) the identification of men with the intellectual, and (3) the dualistic assumption of the inferiority of the physical and the superiority of the mental (Plumwood, 133). Once this nest of assumptions is unpacked the differences between the social feminists and nature feminists and the deficiency of each become more clear. On the one hand, the social feminists simply reject the identification of women with nature and the physical and insist that women have the same talents and characteristics as men. These feminists focus on the interaction of sexism, racism, and classism (Griscom, 6). On the other hand, the nature feminists embrace the identification of women with nature but deny that nature or the physical is inferior. But neither of these responses represents a sufficient challenge to the dualistic assumptions themselves since both leave part unquestioned. Social feminists do not ask about the assumed inferiority of nature, and nature feminists do not ask about the assumed identification of women with nature. In this way, both "remain within the framework in which the problem has arisen, and . . . leave its central structures intact" (Plumwood, 133).

A thoroughgoing ecofeminism must challenge each of the dualisms of patriarchal culture (see King, 12–16). The issue is not whether women are closer to nature, since that question arises only in the context of the nature/culture dualism in the first place. Rather, the task is to overcome the nature/culture dualism itself. The task can be accomplished first by admitting that "gender identity is neither fully natural nor fully cultural," and that neither is inherently oppressive or liberating (King, 13). Second, ecofeminists need to learn what both the social feminists and nature feminists already know. From social feminists we learn that "while it is possible to discuss women and nature without reference to class and race, such discussion risks remaining white and elite" (Griscom, 6). And nature feminists remind us that there is no human/nonhuman dichotomy and that our bodies are worth celebrating (Griscom, 8).

Feminist Analysis Must Include Ecological Insights

One result of the way the oppression of women and the oppression of nature are linked in these dualisms is that feminist thought and practice must incorporate ecological insights. To do otherwise would not sufficiently challenge the structures of patriarchal domination. The most direct way to illustrate this is to discuss the repercussions of the feminist assertion of women's full humanity in light of the interlocking dualisms described above. The fact that male/female, human/nature, and mind/body dualism are all closely linked together means that feminism cannot rest with proclaiming women's full humanity. To do this without also raising the question of the human/nature relationship would be simply to buy into the male-defined human being. In other words, if women and men are now to be reconceptualized non-dualistically, the choices available are either to buy into the male definition of the human (as the social feminists tend to do) or to engage in a reconceptualization of humanity as well. But, as soon as we begin to redefine humanity, the question of the human/nature dualism arises (Plumwood, 134–35). This is also the case when we ask about the status of race or class. Thus, any thorough challenge to the male/female dichotomy must also take on the other dualisms that structure Western patriarchy.

At this point it becomes clear that ecofeminism is not just another branch of feminism. Rather, ecofeminists are taking the feminist critique of dualism another step. What ecofeminism aims for transcends the differences between social and nature feminists. What is needed is an integrative and transformative feminism that moves beyond the current debate among these competing feminisms. Such a feminism would: (1) unmask the interconnections between all systems of oppression; (2) acknowledge the diversity of women's experiences and the experiences of other oppressed groups; (3) reject the logic of domination and the patriarchal conceptual framework in order to prevent concerns for ecology from degenerating into white middle-class anxiety; (4) rethink what it is to be human, that is, to see ourselves as "both co-members of ecological community and yet different from other members of it"; (5) recast traditional ethics to underscore the importance of values such as care, reciprocity, and diversity; and (6) challenge the patriarchal bias in technology research and analysis and the use of science for the destruction of the earth (Warren, 18–20).

A Feminist Perspective Must Be Part of
Any Proposed Ecological Solutions

Just as feminism must challenge all of patriarchy's dualisms, including the human/nature dichotomy, ecological solutions and environmental ethics must include a feminist perspective:

> Otherwise, the ecological movement will fail to make the conceptual connections between the oppression of women and the oppression of nature (and to link these to other systems of oppression), and will risk utilizing strategies and implementing solutions which contribute to the continued subordination of women [and others] (Warren, 8).

In particular, two issues in the ecological movement and environmental ethics need to be addressed in the context of ecofeminism: the status of hierarchy and dualism, and the place of feeling.

As already indicated, ecofeminism works at overcoming dualism and hierarchy. Much of current environmental ethics, however, attempts to establish hierarchies of value for ranking different parts of nature (Kheel, 137). It does this by debating whether particular "rights" ought to be extended to certain classes of animals (Singer). This is another way of assigning rights to some and excluding them from others and of judging the value of one part as more or less than that of another. These judgments, then, operate within the same framework of dualistic assumptions. As a result, this debate merely moves the dualism, as it were; it does not abandon it. Human/nonhuman may no longer be the operative dualism; instead, sentient/nonsentient or some other replaces it.

Another way in which environmental ethics has perpetuated traditional dualist thought lies in its dependence on reason and its exclusion of feeling or emotion in dealing with nature. The dualism of reason/emotion is another dualism under attack by feminists. In this case environmental ethics has sought to determine by reason alone what beings have value and in what ranking and what rules ought to govern human interactions with nature (Kheel, 141). This procedure is flawed according to ecofeminists since "the attempt to formulate universal, rational rules of conduct ignores the constantly changing nature of reality. It also neglects the emotional-instinctive or spontaneous component in each particular situation, for in the end, emotion cannot be contained by boundaries and rules" (Kheel, 141).

Ethics must find a way to include feeling, but including feeling does not mean excluding reason. Again, the task is to overcome the exclusive dualism.

Ecofeminism, then, involves a thoroughgoing analysis of the dualisms that structure patriarchal culture. In particular ecofeminists analyze the link between the oppression of women and of nature by focusing on the hierarchies established by mind/body, nature/culture, male/female, and human/nonhuman dualisms. The goal is to reconceptualize these relationships in nonhierarchical, nonpatriarchal ways. In this way, ecofeminists envision a new way of seeing the world and strive toward a new way of living in the world as co-members of the ecological community.

What ecofeminism lacks, however, is an analysis of what Ruether and Dodson Gray agreed was hierarchical or transcendent dualism, the dualism that they think undergirds the others. Ecofeminists, largely philosophers and social scientists, have not attended to the specifically theological dimensions of patriarchy. Meanwhile, feminist theologians and ethicists have focused primarily on the interrelationship of sexism, racism, and classism without sufficiently articulating or naming the interconnections between these forms of oppression and the oppression of nature. Yet the analysis of these critically important social justice questions would be strengthened when it is understood that the same dualistic assumptions are operative in each of these forms of oppression.

Furthermore, feminist theology needs to explore the relationship between human beings and God in light of those dualistic assumptions and the impact of the new way of seeing human beings that results from linking the oppression of nature with other forms of oppression. When reconceptualizing the male/female dualism entails reconceptualizing the human/nature relation because male/female is embedded in human/nature, as ecofeminists argue, then the human/divine relationship also needs reworking, since male/female is also embedded in human/divine. In other words, if feminist theology is serious in attempting to transform patriarchal dualisms, it must go further than reworking the dualistic imagery used to refer to God; it must discover how the images themselves support a dualistic relationship between human beings and God with the same assumptions as the traditional male/female and human/nonhuman dualisms.

Two contemporary theologians, Isabel Carter Heyward (1982) and Sallie McFague (1987), have begun this task. They contrast their respective conceptions of God with the traditional idea of a God "set apart from human experience . . . by the nature of 'His' impassivity" (Heyward, 7), or the idea of a "monarchical" God (McFague, 63–69). In other words, both challenge the dualistic assumptions that typically characterize the relationship between human beings and God. They argue that human beings are not simply subordinate to God but are co-workers with God, and consequently, that human beings are not simply instrumentally related to God and that God and human beings are not polar opposites. For Heyward, God is the "power in relation" (Heyward, 2), while for McFague, God is more appropriately conceived using the models of mother, lover, and friend within the context of the image of the world as God's body (McFague, xi).

What I am suggesting is a position that goes further than these authors even while it shares certain characteristics with them. The main difference lies in the extent to which Heyward and McFague have really reworked their conception of the relationship between human beings and the nonhuman world. In Heyward's case it is clear that she wants to include the creation in the relationships effected by God as the power in relation; however, this desire appears to be qualified. For example, Heyward writes:

In relation to God, as in any relation, God is affected by humanity and creation, just as we are affected by God. With us, by us, through us, God lives, God becomes, God changes, God speaks, God acts, God suffers and God dies in the world. . . . The constancy of God is the activity of God in the world wherever, whenever, and for whatever reason, humanity acts to create, liberate, and bless humanity (Heyward, 9).

Creation, including the nonhuman elements, may be included in what affects God, but what happens to it in the talk about God's activity in the world? Is it only God's activity when the activity benefits humanity? Even more absent is any discussion of the kind of behavior toward the nonhuman world required of human beings in order to "incarnate God."

McFague goes further than Heyward when she discusses the necessity of adopting an "evolutionary, ecological perspective" due to our interconnections and interdependence with aspects of the world (McFague, 7–8) and when she includes in her descriptions of the models of mother, lover, and friend an explanation of the ethic which follows from the model. These are, respectively, the ethics of justice, healing, and companionship (pp. 116–24, 146–56, 174–80). What is missing in these ethics is a frank discussion of the hard decisions that confront us as soon as we begin to see "ourselves as gardeners, caretakers, mothers and fathers, stewards, trustees, lovers, priests, co-creators, and friends" of the world (p. 13). In other words, how far does McFague's transformation of the dualistic relationship between human beings and the nonhuman world go?

Finally, neither Heyward nor McFague does what ecofeminists claim must be done, namely, to articulate the links between forms of oppression, especially the oppression of women and of nature. Heyward's and McFague's concentration on the transformation of the human/divine relationship away from dualist assumptions is extremely helpful, but it needs to be joined with concrete descriptions of and efforts to transform the other dualisms that structure Western patriarchy. In other words, Heyward and McFague appear to reconceptualize the divine/human dualism without sufficiently exploring the consequences for other powerful dualisms, including but not limited to male/female and human/nonhuman.

REVERENCE FOR LIFE

Albert Schweitzer's notion of reverence for life provides some clues for feminist theological and ethical efforts to reexamine the relationship between human beings and the nonhuman world and between human beings and God despite the fact that he offers no analysis of oppression. Instead, what Schweitzer does is begin with a description of human beings that links us both with nonhuman nature and with God in a way that does not appear to presuppose those dualistic assumptions of subordination, instrumentality, and polarity. For this reason, his position is highly instructive.

Schweitzer begins with a description of the self as "life which wills to live, in the midst of life which wills to live." This, he says, is "the most immediate and comprehensive fact of consciousness" (Schweitzer 1949/1981, 309). As will-to-live, the self is volitional, free, driven to perfect itself, and living in relation to others who will to live. More important, however, is the fact that Schweitzer refuses to describe the self simply as "life," for "life continues to be a mystery too great to understand" (Schweitzer 1936/1962, 182–183). He knows only that life is good since the self continues to will to live.

Ethics, for Schweitzer, emerges with thinking about the experience of the will-to-live. There are two kinds of knowing for Schweitzer: intuitive and scientific. The intuitive is an inward reflection on the contents of the will-to-live. By living out these ideas, the self finds meaning and purpose in its actions (Schweitzer 1949/1981, 282). Scientific knowing, the second kind of knowing, is knowledge of the world. Science describes "the phenomena in which life in its innumerable forms appears and passes"; it may sometimes "discover life where we did not previously expect it." Hence, scientific knowledge "compels our attention to the mystery of the will-to-live which we see stirring everywhere" (Schweitzer 1949/1981, 308). Together, the two kinds of knowing allow the self to describe what science finds by using an analogy with itself as will-to-live. In this way the self knows and, for Schweitzer, feels that "the will-to-live is every-where present, even as in me" (Schweitzer 1936/1962, 185). The self, therefore, becomes aware of its inward relation to the wills-to-live present in the world.

Schweitzer gives one important qualification to both kinds of knowing: neither one can explain what life is. "We cannot understand what happens in the universe. . . . It creates while it destroys and destroys while it creates, and therefore it remains to us a riddle" (Schweitzer 1934, 1520). As a result human beings have no grounds for placing themselves at the center of a moral universe or at the apex of moral order in the universe. "We are entirely ignorant of what significance we have for the earth. How much less then may we presume to try to attribute to the infinite universe a meaning which has us for its object, or which can be explained in terms of our existence!" (Schweitzer 1949/1981, 273).

Because no purposiveness or prioritizing of phenomena is evident in the events of the world, no hierarchy of meaning and value can be constructed from the evidence of intuitive or scientific thought. As Schweitzer points out, "we like to imagine that Man is nature's goal; but facts do not support that belief" (Schweitzer 1936/1962, 181).

The inability to find meaning in the world and the recognition of the interrelationship of all wills-to-live lead to what Schweitzer calls an ethical mysticism. This mysticism is a mysticism of the will. The volition found in the will-to-live becomes an activist ethic. As Schweitzer explains:

Ethics alone can put me in true relationship with the universe by my serving it, cooperating with it; not by trying to understand it. . . . Only by serving every kind of life do I enter the service of that Creative Will whence all life emanates. I do not understand it; but I do know (and it is sufficient to live by) that by serving life, I serve the Creative Will. This is the mystical significance of ethics (Schweitzer 1936/1962, 189).

Union with the Creative Will, or infinite will-to-live, Schweitzer's philosophical name for God, is achieved through active service and devotion to all that lives. Hence as an ethical mysticism, Schweitzer's is directed toward those particular manifestations of the infinite will-to-live that come within the reach of the individual.

Schweitzer's mysticism, then, provides him a way to combine the drive for self-perfection, which is contained in the will-to-live, and devotion to others. Self-perfection in the context of this mysticism becomes a drive to attain union with that which the human will-to-live manifests, namely, the infinite will-to-live (Schweitzer 1949/1981, 301–2). In human beings, as Schweitzer points out, "the craving for perfection is given in such a way that we aim at raising to their highest material and spiritual value both ourselves and every existing thing which is open to our influence" (Schweitzer 1949/1981, 282). That is, I make a reality of my own dedication to the infinite only by devoting myself to its manifestations. "Whenever my life devotes itself in any way to life, my finite will-to-live experiences union with the infinite will in which all life is one" (Schweitzer 1949/1981, 313). Self-perfection, or self-fulfillment, is therefore, reciprocally related to devotion to others.

In addition, Schweitzer's mysticism provides another way into his refusal to place human beings at the center of the moral universe. The self as will-to-live is not the source of its own value. Instead, the will-to-live given in the self has value as a result of its relationship to the infinite. The source or origin of value is the universal will-to-live or infinite being. As Schweitzer points out, through the will-to-live

my existence joins in pursuing the aims of the mysterious universal will of which I am a manifestation. . . . With consciousness and with volition I devote myself to Being. I become of service to the ideas which it thinks out in me; I become imaginative force like that which works mysteriously in nature, and thus I give my existence a meaning from within outwards (Schweitzer 1949/1981, 305).

Meaning comes not simply from my own estimation but also from the fact that my will-to-live is a manifestation of the universal will-to-live. At the same time, all other wills-to-live are also manifestations of that same universal. Hence their value and my value have the same source. The fact that the self cannot discern the meaning of any of these lives from the world as it is experienced means that it cannot determine that any one manifestation of the will-to-live is more important or more valuable than any other manifestation. The mystical and mysterious relatedness of every will-to-live in the universal will-to-live prohibits assigning gradations of value to individual manifestations of the will-to-live, whether in humans or viruses. The will-to-live establishes value but not distinctions in it. Therefore, Schweitzer insists, all attempts to bring ethics and epistemology together must be renounced (Schweitzer 1949/1981, 289).

The ethic that follows from thinking about the will-to-live is the ethic of reverence for life. The self lives in the midst of other wills-to-live. Hence Schweitzer says, "If I am a thinking being, I must regard other life than my own with equal reverence" (Schweitzer 1936/1962, 185). Actions in accord with my will-to-live, such as upbuilding, deepening, and enhancing the optimism, value, and affirmation given in the will-to-live, are required in relation to other manifestations of the will-to-live (Kraus, 47). "Ethics consist . . . in my experiencing the compulsion to show to all will-to-live the same reverence as I do to my own" (Schweitzer 1949/1981, 309). In the language of Schweitzer's mysticism, "reverence for life means to be in the grasp of the infinite, inexplicable, forward-urging Will in which all Being is grounded" (Schweitzer 1949/1981, 283).

According to Schweitzer, the ethic of reverence for life cannot foster, condone, or excuse injuring or killing of any sort. Three reasons support this judgment. First, reverence for life is what Schweitzer calls an absolute ethic. That is, its claim is absolute because it arises from the inner necessity of the will-to-live to be true to itself. Second, reverence for life is a universal ethic. The inner compulsion to show reverence to life extends to all that can in any way be considered as life.

> The absolute ethics of the will-to-live must reverence every form of life, seeking so far as possible to refrain from destroying any life, regardless of its particular type. It says of no instance of life, "this has no value." It cannot make any such exceptions, for it is built upon reverence for life as such (Schweitzer 1960, 187–88).

Neither species nor sentience presents a barrier that qualifies this universality.

The third reason why the ethic of reverence for life does not justify killing or injury is its refusal to allow human beings to locate themselves at the center of a moral universe, its inability to base any ranking of value on information about the world that comes from external sources. There is no moral hierarchy that says that decisions to destroy infectious bacteria in human beings or other animals are the right decisions. There is no sure way to judge any being, human or not, as less worthy and therefore insignificant enough to allow it to be killed.

> The ethics of reverence for life makes no distinction between higher and lower, more precious and less precious lives. It has good reasons for this omission. For what are we doing, when we establish hard and fast gradations in value

between living organisms, but judging them in relation to ourselves, by whether they seem to stand closer to us or farther from us. This is a wholly subjective standard. How can we know what importance other living organisms have in themselves and in terms of the universe? (Schweitzer 1965, 47).

Universality, absoluteness, and the absence of any clear objective moral order "out there" prevent Schweitzer's reverence for life from condoning any form of killing or harming of life. His ethic will not compromise; it points to limitless responsibility.

These reasons clearly do not mean that choices to kill are not made. Schweitzer knows that human beings as well as other forms of life depend for life on killing and that, in many situations, decisions to save one means death to another (Schweitzer 1965, 22–23). This is all part of what he calls the "dilemma" of the will-to-live (Schweitzer 1949/1953, 181).

According to Schweitzer we must recognize that "the universe provides us with the dreary spectacle of manifestations of the will to live continually opposed to each other. One life preserves itself by fighting and destroying other lives" (Schweitzer 1965, 24–25). Conflict in the world prevents Schweitzer from being able to find a basis for ethics in the patterns and purposes seen in the world. Hence, he turns inward to the will-to-live. It is precisely Schweitzer's realistic description of the world in terms of conflict that drives him to the ethic of reverence for life. The only sure meaning and purpose for activity comes, for Schweitzer, in the certainty of the volition of the will-to-live found and experienced in the self.

Because of its absolute and universal character, then, the ethic of reverence for life cannot provide any specific guidelines for making life-and-death decisions even though it knows these decisions must be made. The fact that reason and the will-to-live can find no objective moral ordering means that there are no objective moral standards by which to judge. Reverence for life

> knows that the mystery of life is always too profound for us, and that its value is beyond our capacity to estimate. We happen to believe that man's life is more important than any other form of which we know. But we cannot prove any such comparison of value from what we know of the world's development. True, in practice we are forced to choose. At times we have to decide *arbitrarily* which forms of life, and even which particular individuals, we shall save, and which we shall destroy (Schweitzer 1936/1962, 188).

The decision, for Schweitzer, is always subjective, arbitrary:

> In ethical conflicts, man can arrive only at subjective decisions. No one can decide for him at what point, on each occasion, lies the extreme limit of possibility for his persistence in the preservation and furtherance of life. He alone has to judge this issue, by letting himself be guided by a feeling of the highest possible responsibility towards other life (Schweitzer 1949/1981, 317–318).

No one else knows the limit of one's ability to aid and protect another. The ethic of reverence of life means limitless personal responsibility. In decisions to harm or destroy one "bears the responsibility for the life which is sacrificed" (Schweitzer 1949/1953, 181).

Schweitzer's restriction of ethics to activity that does no harm reveals the extent to which reverence for life is not an unbreakable rule or law.

> In the conflict between the maintenance of my own existence and the destruction of, or injury to, that of another, I can never unite the ethical and the necessary to form a relative ethical; I must choose between ethical and necessary, and, if I choose the latter, must take it upon myself to incur guilt by an act of injury to life (Schweitzer 1949/1981, 324).

The necessity of killing or harming does not challenge the authority or validity of reverence for life. As absolute and universal, reverence for life continues its demands even in the face of overwhelming odds, namely, the fact that the will-to-live is divided against itself. It may be, for example, that it is better to kill a suffering animal than to watch it slowly die (see Schweitzer 1960, 83–84). The tension between the ethical and necessary is maintained by facing the reality of conflict. "We are living in truth, when we experience these conflicts more profoundly. The good conscience is an invention of the devil" (Schweitzer 1949/1981, 318).

A pressing issue facing individuals who must kill is the intensity of guilt incurred in actions that kill or harm and the possibilities there are to alleviate that guilt. For Schweitzer the principal way to do this is to increase service to others: "Some atonement for that guilt can be found by the man who pledges himself to neglect no opportunity to succor creatures in distress. . . . When we help an insect out of a difficulty, we are only trying to compensate for man's ever-renewed sins against other creatures" (Schweitzer 1965, 23, 49).

His answer, then, is renewed determination to reverence all forms of life. Again, the reality of destruction does not compromise the demand. Part of the reason for this is the mystical nature of reverence for life. "The more we act in accordance with the principle of reverence for life, the more we are gripped by the desire to preserve and benefit life" (Schweitzer 1965, 31). "Reverence for life means to be in the grasp of the infinite, inexplicable, forward-urging Will in which all Being is grounded" (Schweitzer 1949/1981, 283).

According to Schweitzer, the ethic of reverence for life has a profoundly religious character (1949/1953, 182). This is most clearly seen in his mysticism. Reverence for life is a way of relating to the "multiform manifestations of the will-to-live," which comprise the world. Only through action in devotion to others do I come in contact with the infinite will-to-live, God. Religion is not, for Schweitzer, a matter of accepting creeds or knowing the history of dogma. Instead, it is the ethic of reverence for life (Schweitzer 1934, 1521).

In a letter to Oskar Kraus, one of Schweitzer's early critics, Schweitzer explains his use of language with respect to philosophy and religion.

> Hitherto it has been my principle never to express in my philosophy more than I have experienced as a result of absolutely logical reflection. That is why I never speak in philosophy of "God" but only of the "universal will-to-live." But if I speak the traditional language of religion, I use the word "God" in its historical definiteness and indefiniteness, just as I speak in ethics of "Love" in place of "Reverence for Life" (Kraus 1944, 42).

Schweitzer's philosophy is at the same time his theology. The universal will-to-live manifest in the world and in my will-to-live is Schweitzer's way of speaking philosophically about God. And reverence for life is the ethic of love, the ethic of Jesus. In fact for Schweitzer, "Christianity, as the most profound religion, is to me at the same time the most profound philosophy" (Schweitzer 1939, 90).

Schweitzer defines Christianity as an "ethical theism" (Schweitzer 1939, 80–81). But Christianity's theism, Schweitzer argues, is ambiguous: "It presupposes a God who is an ethical Personality, and who is, therefore, so to speak, outside the world . . . [and] it must hold fast the belief that God is the sum total of the forces working in the world—that all that is, is in God" (Schweitzer 1939, 81).

This ambiguity is not resolved in Christian faith. As Schweitzer puts it: "In the world He is impersonal Force, within me He reveals Himself as Personality. . . . They are one; but how they are one, I do not understand" (Schweitzer 1939, 83). Theism and pantheism remain unreconciled. This ambiguity in the conception of God is not something that concerns Schweitzer. Attention to intellectual conceptions of God is, for Schweitzer, an abstraction. Concern about the particular relation of theism to pantheism leads one away from active devotion to the individual manifestations of the will-to-live in the world. Christianity, according to Schweitzer, is more a way of acting in the world than a way of knowing, and this way of acting is not dependent on a full or complete understanding of how the world works or of God's intrinsic nature. Piety, according to Schweitzer, "depends not on man being able to subscribe to a historically traditional conception of God, but on his being seized by the spirit and walking in it" (cited in Langfeldt, 52–53). Ultimately, "theism does not stand in opposition to pantheism, but rises out of it as the ethically definite of the indefinite" (cited in Langfeldt, 51).

For Schweitzer, Christians are called to surrender themselves to the ethical will of God. This surrender corresponds exactly with how Schweitzer develops the contents of the will-to-live: Service to other forms of life is also service to God. Christianity, therefore, appeals not only to the historical revelation but also to "that inward one which corresponds with, and continually confirms the historical revelation" (Schweitzer 1939, 83). Experience of the will-to-live corresponds with and confirms, then, the teachings of the historical Jesus. For Schweitzer, this means the teachings of the kingdom, especially as they are found in the Sermon on the Mount. These are Jesus' teachings concerning love. In response to them the will-to-live as devotion to others becomes the will-to-love. Devotion to others construed as will-to-love is at the heart of Christianity, according to Schweitzer, in the same way that devotion to others is a necessary part of self-perfection in a philosophical construal. For both philosophy and theology, it is service to others as individuals that brings about union with the ultimate.

Christianity, according to Schweitzer, provides no more account of the world, its meaning and purpose, than reason. The inward revelation of God as universal will-to-love and the self as one of its manifestations does not reveal anything which makes life less mysterious or tells of the final destiny of human beings.

> When Christianity becomes conscious of its innermost nature, it realizes that it is godliness rising out of inward constraint. The highest knowledge is to know that we are surrounded by mystery. Neither knowledge nor hope for the future can be the pivot of our life or determine its direction. It is intended to be solely determined by our allowing ourselves to be gripped by the ethical God, who reveals Himself in us, and by our yielding our will to His (Schweitzer 1939, 78).

> Moreover, Christianity
> assigns man a place in this world and commands him to live in it and to work in it in the spirit of the ethical God. Further, Christianity gives him the assurance that thereby God's purpose for the world and for man is being fulfilled; it cannot, however, explain how. For what significance have the ethical character and the ethical activity of the religious individual in the infinite happenings of the universe? What do they accomplish? We must admit that the only answer we have to this question is, that thereby the will of God is fulfilled (Schweitzer 1939, 73–74).

Christian teachings do not give human beings a privileged place in relation to other manifestations of the will-to-live. What Christianity does is confirm what we already experience through our own will-to-live in its relations to others.

TOWARD AN ECOFEMINIST
THEOLOGICAL ETHIC

Although I want to argue that Schweitzer's position provides clues for feminist theological ethics, it is important to point out two places where his thought is seriously lacking. First, Schweitzer has little sense of the sociality of the self. Instead, his will-to-live is the radical individual, who, despite being related to other wills-to-live in an ethical mysticism, does not really live socially or communally. The human will-to-live works, according to Schweitzer, to better the situation of other wills-to-live as individuals. Furthermore, he focuses his attention so exclusively on the individual and the individual's actions that the ways in which lives are shaped and affected by social structures are ignored. Significantly, justice is not a high priority for Schweitzer (Schweitzer 1939, 18–19). For feminists, particularly those who are schooled in the social feminist analysis of the structures of oppression, this is a serious failure. Schweitzer writes as if most suffering takes place as a result of individuals acting on other individuals. Feminist analysis insists, in contrast, that social structures and cultural expectations affect not only the conditions under which people live but also severely restrict the choices they perceive themselves to have.

The second problem is a consequence of the first: Schweitzer does no social analysis. For Schweitzer, human beings are ahistorical individuals, who learn to reverence life through self-reflection. There is no attention to social structures which limit or enhance those individuals. As a result, Schweitzer does not address institutionalized oppression in any way. For example, his position is a good example of the way in which *man,* as male, is taken as normative for both male and female without any hint that male experience is not normative for females. He makes no effort to rethink the meaning of the human (or *man,* as he would say) that experiences itself as will-to-live and that is one manifestation among others of the infinite will-to-live. In other words, although Schweitzer reworks the human/nonhuman dichotomy by using the will-to-live terminology, he fails to take seriously the destructiveness of the male/female dualism embedded in the traditional conceptions of human/nonhuman relationships. And, despite his home in Africa and his attention to individual patients, there is no analysis of two other destructive dualisms embedded in a traditional description of human beings: racism and classism.

Nevertheless, Schweitzer's position clearly involves a reevaluation of the relationship between human beings and nonhuman forms of life along the lines suggested by ecofeminists. That is, despite the absence of any analysis of oppression, Schweitzer does attack the dualistic structure of Western patriarchy. The relationship between human beings and nonhuman forms of life is not characterized by subordination, instrumentality, or polarity. Schweitzer has no basis for judging that nonhuman lives simply serve human interests or that they have no value apart from their service to human lives. He refuses to construct a moral hierarchy with human beings at the top. And, his use of "will-to-live" as the description of all that lives means that the polarity assumption has also been discarded. Human and nonhuman cannot be polar opposites since both are manifestations of the same will-to-live.

Furthermore, Schweitzer's use of will-to-live to describe not only all living beings but also the divine suggests a transformation in the divine/human relationship away from the transcendent dualism feminist theologians criticize. Human beings and God are not conceived as polar opposites or as over against each other. God is not, according to Schweitzer, an external "other," external to the world or to human beings. As Schweitzer explains, "I carry out the will of the universal will-to-live which reveals itself in me. I live my life in God, in the mysterious divine personality which I do not know as such in the world, but only experience as mysterious Will within myself" (Schweitzer 1949/1981, 79). This idea of living life in God sounds very much like Isabel Carter Heyward's notion that human beings "incarnate God" as they work to bring about justice in the world (Heyward, 159).

It may be argued, however, that Schweitzer retains at least one dualism even while he transforms others. In particular, Schweitzer is open to challenge concerning his apparently exclusive attention to all that lives. Using "will-to-live" as the primary category suggests that nonliving, nonhuman nature, such as rocks, air, and water, is excluded from the ethic of reverence for life. Feminists, in contrast, are increasingly calling for ways to include the so-called nonliving as morally significant (see Warren and Kheel). For the most part Schweitzer's will-to-live refers to plant and animal life, although, in at least one place, he does include the crystal as a form of will-to-live (Schweitzer 1949/1981, 282). In addition, he uses the language of "Being" in several places as well (Schweitzer 1949/1981, 304–6). These suggest some attention to nonliving nature. A more fruitful way to look at this issue is to recall Schweitzer's openness to science and scientific knowledge. As science through its investigations increasingly blurs the distinction between living and nonliving, will-to-live will become a less accurate way to describe what Schweitzer is trying to express.

One way for Schweitzer to include the nonliving as relevant is to emphasize the relatedness of wills-to-live, or the fact that "I am life which wills to live, *in the midst of* life which wills to live" (emphasis added). This relatedness, or interrelatedness in the context of Schweitzer's mysticism, in addition to his insistence that we do not know what life is (which means that we have no grounds for limiting it) moves Schweitzer in the direction of including the nonliving in moral discussions. Further, the possibility of seeing rocks and water as morally relevant tests Schweitzer's insistence that the reason something has value is not its analogical proximity to human life but its relationship to the divine as somehow a manifestation of the universal will-to-live.

The weight of evidence concerning the retention of hierarchical dualism in Schweitzer's thought suggests that he is more interested in transforming such dualisms. In addition to his use of "will-to-live" in the context of the human/nonhuman dualism, there are at least two other patriarchal dualisms that Schweitzer refuses to maintain. First, like feminists, Schweitzer does not divorce reason from intuition or affectivity. The two kinds of knowing for Schweitzer work in concert with each other to describe the self's relations with others in the world and to allow the self to feel those relations. Moreover, one of the most important elements in Schweitzer's ethic is compassion, and reverence itself is not a rational category. In these ways Schweitzer's ethic embraces the feelings and affectivity of the agent. In like manner feminists insist that the whole person be involved in judging and acting (Harrison, 3–21). As Marti Kheel points out, "We cannot even begin to talk about the issue of ethics unless we admit that we care (or feel something)" (Kheel, 144).

Second, Schweitzer's position works to transform the dualism of mind and body. Schweitzer's description of human beings as participants in the dilemma of the will-to-live, or its self-division, is done in such a way that he does not disparage the body. In other words, if Schweitzer was a firm supporter of a mind/body dualism, the fact that the body lives at the expense of other wills-to-live provides an occasion to deny bodily needs in favor of the "superior" mind. Schweitzer does not do this. Instead, it is the self as a whole as will-to-live that lives at the expense of others. And it is the self as a whole that must work to overcome the dilemma. Clearly feminist ethicists also attack the mind/body dualism.

In addition to overcoming these dualisms, Schweitzer's articulation of the ethic of reverence for life shares certain key features with feminist theological ethics. First, he depends on experience for his description of the interrelatedness and interdependence of all of life. For Schweitzer, the experience of the individual will-to-live in the midst of other wills-to-live presupposes a network of relation and interrelation. In Schweitzer's ethical mysticism, each being is a manifestation of the universal will-to-live and as such is related to every other being. More important, this experience of the self as will-to-live provides the only basis for understanding the self and others, including God. Feminists likewise depend on women's experience of themselves in relationship to others for their description of the world. For both, then, experience is crucial.

Second, both Schweitzer and feminists refuse to systematize ethics. Neither proposes absolute principles, which must be obeyed no matter what the situation or consequences; nor do they propose a telos or utilitarian goal. In both cases there is attention to the situation and an attempt to respond to the situation as it presents itself. For Schweitzer, ethics cannot be systematized because reverence for life, including love and compassion, must attend to the situation in which it finds itself. For example, in one situation compassion may mean saving a bird at the expense of the worms and bugs it will eat. In another circumstance, however, it may mean allowing the bird to remain where it has fallen in order to protect some other life, whether the worms and bugs, an injured cow, or the starving child I am trying to assist. In either case reverence for life cannot be removed or abstracted from the situation. Schweitzer's vision of ethics, then, sounds very much like the ethics of care that many feminists describe (see Warren and Gilligan).

Third, both feminist theological ethics and Schweitzer's ethic are activist ethics. Feminists are not simply interested in theory; rather we are interested in transforming oppressive social structures and living in nonpatriarchal ways. That entails concrete activity. Similarly, Schweitzer's reverence for life is far more than a way to reflect on the relationship between self and world. Reverence for life seeks to aid those in need and to transform the conditions of the will-to-live in the world. It does not accept present circumstances, especially the dilemma of the will-to-live as eternally or supernaturally given. The world as populated by manifold manifestations of the universal will-to-live is not static.

Fourth, Schweitzer's ethic is life-affirming. This includes not only his optimism about the possibilities for constructive action but also his attention to this world. Schweitzer's ethic does not support any form of nihilistic rejection of this world or any sort of religious otherworldliness. Individuals, for Schweitzer, come into contact with the divine not by withdrawing from others but by actively serving them in this world. This ethical mysticism lies at the heart of Schweitzer's position. It supports the sort of world-affirming and life-affirming ethic insisted upon by feminists such as Beverly Harrison, Isabel Carter Heyward, and Sallie McFague.

To conclude: Ecofeminist concerns and Schweitzer's reverence for life provide both challenges and resources for feminist theological ethics. Ecofeminists help us to see the connections between forms of oppression maintained by patriarchy at the level of dualistic assumptions. At the same time they challenge us not to lose sight of those connections when we move to the specifically theological dualism of human/divine. Schweitzer's ethic of reverence for life provides an example of an ethic that takes very seriously a non-dualistic description of the relationships between human beings and the world and between human beings and God. He challenges us to add to this the analysis of the dualistic structures that characterize human social relationships.

In short, what feminist theological ethics must recognize is that three fundamental relationships must be addressed simultaneously. These three relationships—between human beings and the nonhuman world, between human beings and God, and among human beings—are all defined dualistically by Western patriarchy. What we must see is that the way in which human beings are described in one of these relationships affects all the others. What we must remember is that no one or two of these relationships will be transformed without the transformation of all three.

WORKS CITED

Gilligan, Carol. *In a Different Voice.* Cambridge, MA: Harvard University Press, 1982.

Gray, Elizabeth Dodson. *Green Paradise Lost.* Wellesley, MA: Roundtable Press, 1979.

Griscom, Joan L. "On Healing the Nature/History Split in Feminist Thought." *Heresies: A Feminist Journal of Art and Politics* 4, no. 1 (1981): 4–9.

Harrison, Beverly. *Making the Connections.* Ed. Carol S. Robb. Boston: Beacon Press, 1985.

Heyward, Isabel Carter. *The Redemption of God: A Theology of Mutual Relation.* Washington, D.C.: University Press of America, 1982.

Kheel, Marti. "The Liberation of Nature: A Circular Affair," *Environmental Ethics* 7 (Summer 1985):135–49.

King, Ynestra. "Feminism and the Revolt of Nature." *Heresies: A Feminist Journal of Art and Politics* 4, no. 1 (1981):12–16.

Kraus, Oskar. *Albert Schweitzer: His Work and His Philosophy.* Trans. I. G. McCalman. London: Adam and Charles Black, 1944.

Langfeldt, Gabriel. *Albert Schweitzer: A Study of His Philosophy of Life.* Trans. Maurice Michael. London: George Allen and Unwin, 1960.

McFague, Sallie. *Models of God: Theology for an Ecological, Nuclear Age.* Philadelphia: Fortress Press, 1987.

Plumwood, Val. "Ecofeminism: An Overview and Discussion of Positions and Arguments," *Australasian Journal of Philosophy* 64, Suppl. (June 1986):120–138.

Ruether, Rosemary Radford. *New Woman/New Earth.* New York: Seabury Press, 1975.

———. *Sexism and God-Talk: Toward a Feminist Theology.* Boston: Beacon Press, 1983.

Schweitzer, Albert. "Religion and Modern Civilization." *The Christian Century* 51 (28 November 1934):1519–21.

———. "The Ethics of Reverence for Life," *Christendom* 1 (Winter 1936): 225–39. Reprinted in Henry Clark, *The Ethical Mysticism of Albert Schweitzer: A Study of the Sources and Significance of Schweitzer's "Philosophy of Civilization."* Boston: Beacon Press, 1962, pp. 180–94.

———. *Christianity and the Religions of the World.* Trans. Johanna Powers. New York: Henry Holt, 1939.

———. *Out of My Life and Thought: An Autobiography.* Trans. C. T. Campion. New York: Holt, Rinehart and Winston, 1949. Reprint ed. New York: New American Library, 1953.

———. *The Philosophy of Civilization.* Trans. C. T. Campion. New York: Macmillan, 1949. Reprint ed. Tallahassee, FL: University Presses of Florida, 1981.

———. *Indian Thought and Its Development.* Trans. Mrs. Charles I. B. Russell. Boston: Beacon Press, 1960.

———. *The Teaching of Reverence for Life.* Trans. Richard and Clara Winston. New York: Holt, Rinehart and Winston, 1965.

Singer, Peter. *Animal Liberation: A New Ethics for Our Treatment of Animals.* New York: Avon Books, 1975.

Warren, Karen. "Feminism and Ecology: Making Connections," *Environmental Ethics* 9 (Spring 1987):3–20.

22

MEDALS ON OUR BLOUSES?

A Feminist Theological Look at Women in Combat

Mary E. Hunt

INTRODUCTION

The question of women in combat came to public attention during the United States invasion into Panama in late 1989. As a feminist theologian I was concerned then about both the tone of the discussion—once again women were the problem, not combat—and the results—a no-win situation for women, damned to discrimination if they could not fight and damned to combat if they could. This reality presents a dilemma for religious feminists who believe in the equality of women but reject combat as a solution to global conflict. This no-win dynamic is reminiscent of the struggle for equality in the boardroom though we may reject capitalism, equality at the altar although we may reject patriarchal religions, and so forth. The military case presents an ethical dilemma that has important public policy consequences.

Little did I dream that the current Gulf crisis would emerge, adding plenty of anecdotal and analytic data to my earlier concern. At this writing, thousands of U.S. servicewomen are baking in the desert along with their male counterparts. Some may be home in body bags by the time this paper is discussed. The issues take on even greater urgency than they did following the Panama incursion, when no one really raised the question until a U.S. victory over a weak opponent was assured. This time such a victory is not as likely. Ironically, tabloid stories of grandmothers going off to war and style section accounts of husbands left behind struggling to find the Pampers are the flimsy substance of the current public debate. Will women simply fight and talk about it later?

There are more than 225,000 women in the U.S. combined armed services

---

This paper was originally presented at the 1990 American Academy of Religion meeting of the Religion, Peace and War Group.

making up 11 percent of the total; estimates of their numbers in the Middle East indicate that they are probably about 10 percent of the total there, or about 20,000 of the admitted 200,000 U.S. troops currently dispatched to the region. Officially they are in noncombat roles, but the threat of chemical warfare and the rigor of the conditions in Saudi Arabia render that distinction dubious if not moot.

That many women have seen and will see combat duty is a foregone conclusion. What begs analysis is whether this is a feminist achievement or a patriarchal ploy. Is it proof that women can and should do anything men do, or a good example of how even feminism can be co-opted to serve the ends of patriarchal power structures.

My perspective as a white feminist theologian, nurtured in the antiwar wing of progressive Catholicism and affiliated with the women-church movement, is indicative of the tension. On the one hand, I urge women's equality in and access to all avenues of society. On the other hand, I oppose combat almost without nuance. Thus I am left in a kind of feminist limbo, having to sanction, at least implicitly, something that I oppose in the name of affirming something that I support. This is a familiar position for those whose "just war" theory and "lesser of two evils" approaches have paved the ethical way. The challenge for feminist ethics is how to move from the dualistic approaches that former methodologies represent to an integrated approach, from having to choose between two options to being able to embrace several values at once.

The further challenge is how to influence public policy in a way that is fair to women who seek equality in the military realm; that is, if some want to fight, far be it from me to prevent them, and at the same time to reflect feminist values commensurate with equality; namely, peace, justice, and cooperation. I have made no pretense about solving this ethical Rubick's Cube, but I offer several contributions to the process in this paper.

First, I will lay out some of the central issues that shape the debate in an effort to handle the many objections that arise on both sides. Second, I will mention new problems that arise for women in combat within a patriarchal context. That is, all other things being unequal, there is a contradiction between the supposed equality of women in combat and the reality of the unequal burden that always accrues to women in a patriarchal culture. Finally, I will ask the question, "What's a religious feminist for peace to do?" and offer a considered, if tentative, response that affirms the values of equality, as well as peace, justice, and cooperation. While this paper is not intended to close the debate, it is intended to present a model of feminist ethical thinking that can be applied in other equally difficult matters.

It is only fair at the outset to underscore the fact that I embrace the notion of women in the military with all the enthusiasm I reserve for women in the episcopacy, and perhaps a little less. While I understand that cosmetic changes alter the aesthetic, I am not persuaded that they finally change structures at all.

Rather, I suspect that in certain instances, as in the case of women in hierarchical leadership in sacramental churches, such additions of women to the structures may serve to maintain rather than to dismantle those structures. I will use analogies to Roman Catholic Church polity and theopolitics in my analysis since it is the social organization most nearly like the military: hierarchical by design, de facto and de jure excluding women from leadership and decision-making roles, and using outmoded reasons for doing so that mask the real issue; namely, whether this model of religion, like this model of military, is good for anyone, male or female.

My basic worry about women in combat is the liberal claim that equality demands it. I wonder if there aren't really places, the combat-ready military for one, where alleged equality is really the diminution of the human spirit beginning with women's and including men's, hence reinforcing rather than shifting the power equation. The mere suggestion places me well beyond the pale of liberal feminism to a position where deep structural change is not a dream for our children but a demand on ourselves.

Many issues beg attention in this debate, but the following are the most prominent ones.

ARE WOMEN QUALIFIED FOR COMBAT?

Inevitably the point is raised about women's competence and suitability for combat. In 1990 this sounds like a pitifully pedestrian concern about women's strength and spunk when evidence is plentiful that some women, like some men, are more than qualified for combat. Since modern warfare is based more on technology than brute strength, and since some women's physical strength surpasses some men's, this issue no longer commands sustained discussion except to point out how outdated it is.

Women's performance in basic training, officer candidate schools, and the service academies is sufficient evidence of the fact that some women (or some men) can and do qualify for military service, including combat. Politely speaking, combat does not require the highest mental, physical, or spiritual capacity known to humanity. Just as some men are not physically and/or psychologically suited for combat, neither are some women. The point is that one qualified woman would be enough to justify inclusion of women in combat on the grounds of equal access, just as one Afro-American, one Hispanic and/or one Asian-American man was, in principle, sufficient to integrate the ranks.

The persistence of such trivial concerns has shaped the public debate on this issue. It serves an important negative function, namely, to obscure from public view the deeper issues at hand. In the case of racial integration of the military, for example, this false, misleading debate about qualifications kept from public view the fact that previously marginalized people were soon to be represented among the casualties in far greater numbers than their percentages in the population as a whole. Indeed they were quickly considered to be quite well qualified for fighting and death. In short, the same racism and economic injustice that kept the military closed to some qualified participants prevailed in society, paradoxically catapulting the same people into the combat branches as soon as the doors opened.

Women face a similar fate on the combat question. There is already a huge increase in the percentage of women of color in the military for reasons of racial and economic disadvantage in society as a whole and the lure of alleged but elusive equality in the military. Dr. Kristin Herzog reports this: "In 1981, for example, 42% of the women in the U.S. Army were black, while only 11% of the population were black. According to a Defense Department report of 1988, 50% of active duty enlisted women in the Army were by then minority women."[1]

Distracting discussions about qualifications serve to make combat attractive. What is stunning is how something forbidden can be made to look desirable, how the carrot of equality can be used to obscure the stick of discrimination. Now the combat ranks are full of Afro-American and Hispanic young men whose parents have "earned" for them the right to risk chemical warfare in the desert. Something is indeed wrong with this picture. Under no circumstances should equality be abrogated. But those who have been discriminated against need to be just as vigilant that they are not being set up to be discriminated against again. The question is always whether what we seek is worthy of our children or whether we must struggle to change the object of our efforts.

SHOULD WOMEN BE IN COMBAT?

The obvious question needs an equally obvious answer. Asking the question this way borders on the disingenuous, another effort at "warspeak" when plain English will do. When the question is asked in this way, it is presumed that women are not in combat and that it is an ethical question that those who would protect women's virtue are asking for women's well-being. The fact is that women are in combat already, virtue or no. It is time to reframe the question to reflect the reality.

Captain Linda Bray led her troops in Panama to a dog kennel where enemy troops were alleged to have been hiding. Gunfire was exchanged. This is combat by any definition, and Captain Bray is a woman. Hence my claim that women are engaging in combat is proved albeit by an incident that was embarrassing to the military when it handed out combat medals. The question would be usefully reframed as "What does it mean that women are in combat?"—this being the concern of those who stress strict equality; or "Should anyone be in combat?" or "How can we avoid combat?" These questions, virtually absent from public debate, are kept at bay by continually asking the wrong "should" question for which the answer, though devilish for the upper brass, is now an open secret.

Congresswoman Patricia Schroeder (D–Colorado) proposed legislation to test combat roles for women (HR-3868 January 23, 1990). The bill was referred to the House Armed Services Committee, where it was sent to a subcommittee and never saw the light of legislative day. It will be reintroduced in early 1991 as Congresswoman Schroeder and colleagues endeavor to resolve unfair employ-ment practices that are on the surface of the current controversy, a situation exacerbated by the Gulf buildup.

Legislation of this sort is a first tactical step toward equal access to combat. Feminist politicians understandably deal with the immediate situation—in this case, women who are being discriminated against on the job. Feminist lawmakers tend to leave aside the kinds of questions that I see as the essence of a feminist analysis; namely, should anyone go into combat? Reelection in a pluralistic society requires that they contend with a wide spectrum of political opinion; the questions I offer can be seen as too "fringe" for strategizing. However, I cannot urge strongly enough the need for feminist ethics to take place within an activist framework so that such questions increasingly inform public debate.

An analogous situation prevails in the Roman Catholic discussion of whether or not women should be priests. The fact is that some women are priests, minus licit ordination, of course. Some women function sacramentally and ministeri-ally as priests. They are simply not recognized, paid, or promoted as priests— good reasons to use whatever means necessary to achieve that kind of equality. That is what Congresswoman Schroeder's bill would do for women in combat; that is, recognize the reality and compensate accordingly, a reasonable approach.

But the crucial questions get lost if feminist theologians do not move beyond the liberalism of women's equality. In the case of priesthood, a deeper analysis is needed of whether the model of clerical, celibate, hierarchical priesthood of women and men is the most adequate one for the needs of the church. Analogously, is adding women to the combat pool a step forward, or does it implicitly legitimate something that women would do better to denounce? Once again, the right to serve and the qualifications of women are not under debate. They are assumed. What is central is whether such service is a step forward or, as I perceive it, a reinforcement of the status quo in both church and the military.

IS WAR MALE AND PEACE FEMALE?

Another issue that begs attention is whether war is really a male construct, something that women will imitate when given the chance but would probably not come up with on their own. I am increasingly leery of any back-to-nature brands of feminism that make earth mothers of all females, positing certain qualities of harmony and well-being to women, while saddling men with the blame for aggressive, bellicose behavior. I have met enough pacifist men and been involved in enough feminist battles to know the difference.

Still, a realistic approach is the historical route whereby one can claim that at the very least most wars have taken place on men's watches. That is, at times in history when men have held sway, which would be most of recorded history, conflicts have been solved by fighting rather than by developing consensus. Women, on the other hand, have been responsible for a range of antiwar efforts, prominent recent ones including the Jeannette Rankin Brigade during the Vietnam War, the Greenham Common and Seneca Peace Encampments against nuclear weapons, the Madres de Plaza de Mayo, and other groups of relatives of disappeared persons in Latin America, the leaders of which are usually women.

Those who oppose women in combat and those who romanticize women's goodness share this mistakenly essentialist worldview. But women should not be saddled with the additional burden of peacemaking when few have access to decisions about war. Likewise, men should not be exempt from such social responsibility in the name of some nonexistent hormone. The point is to ask the right question about war rather than to seek to assign gender where it does not correspond.

ARE THERE BENEFITS FOR
WOMEN IN THE MILITARY?

The most persuasive case for women advancing in the military, something that combat hastens, is the practical case in terms of employment and future benefits. While it is true that combat is a sure route to decorations and promotions and for this reason women should have access, such arguments miss another point, namely, the erosion of military benefits at a time when those who sign up are disproportionately poor, people of color, and lacking in basic educational skills.

The G.I. Bill, long considered a ticket to higher education after military service, now requires that military personnel contribute financially during the time served in order to be eligible afterwards. This is something many women who struggle to make ends meet on a military salary, especially if they have children, cannot afford and/or do not think they will ever use. Hence they lose out from the beginning due to inadequate counseling and the economic disadvantage with which they began their service. So much for an equal opportunity employer in an unequal society.

Likewise, many military training programs that attract women have little transfer value outside the military. For example, where is a woman trained in tank warfare going to ply her trade once she leaves the military? This is also a problem for men, of course, but like all problems in a patriarchal society, it is especially burdensome to women who face prejudice and discrimination outside the military even if they do not face it inside. Sex discrimination is such that even a remotely related job would, in all likelihood, go to a male veteran before a female.

The much-touted military discipline, "guaranteed to make a man out of you," is similarly dubious for women. Hazing and harassment that bonded men to other men in the homosocial environment that characterized the military in "the good old days" has not been redesigned to take into account women's ways of bonding. To the contrary, women are actually punished for demanding equality. While it is alleged that they are subjected to the same treatment as underlings by their superiors as men, the fact is that such treatment of women in a patriarchal military is far worse than for any man.

Sexual harassment is common. Abuse, even rapes, have been reported. The notorious case of a woman student at the U.S. Naval Academy, Gwen Marie Dreyer, being chained to a urinal by eight of her male classmates, then photographed for their pleasure just before the Army-Navy football game, touched off an investigation of that institution. The Committee on Women's Issues, including Senator Barbara Mikulski (D–Maryland), found recently that "there are structural impediments to assimilation of women" at Annapolis and that "breakdown in civility and discipline contributes to sexual harassment at the academy."[2] Further, "The negative attitudes and inappropriate actions of this minority [those who oppose women in the Academy] exert such a disproportionate influence on the Naval Academy climate that most midshipmen readily acknowledge that women are not accepted as equals in the brigade." It is reported that "low-level sexual harassment can pass as normal operating procedure" among some students and faculty.[3]

The Academy is said to lag behind the Navy as a whole in the acceptance of women, not surprising since resistance to change is strongest at the top of a hierarchy. It is logical to assume that this is the case in the other branches as well. Note the same pattern with Catholic clergy resisting women's ordination more strongly than laity. Ms. Dreyer is now finishing her college years elsewhere; her assailants had their leave privileges limited and received letters of reprimand but continue their ascent up the ladder. One can even imagine some of their future superiors reading the letters with a certain pride in the young men who did their best to show women their place in the military. Proposed solutions include increasing the number of women on the faculty as role models, keeping the committee intact, and disciplining sexual discrimination cases more severely, none of which addresses the structural issue at all.

The catch-22 for women in the military, and especially for women in combat, is that they must conform to a norm in which what is feminine is inferior. Recruits are taunted with the epithet "girls" if they do not perform properly. It is one thing for a young man to have stereotypically masculine traits ingrained into him, quite another for women. Women must choose between participating in the implicit degradation of all women by tolerating the abusive macho practices, or distinguish themselves as feminists, worse, be accused of being lesbians because they maintain their integrity as women in a system in which being a woman under any circumstance is wrong. This dynamic leaves me pessimistic about rapid changes in military life even if women enter combat, and fearful that women who do will be victimized by enemies on both sides, including their would-be comrades. Who would want her daughter in such a situation?

Even patriotism is gender-linked in a patriarchal society. While for men the ultimate expression of loyalty to one's country is to serve honorably in the military, in combat if necessary, women are given a very different message. To serve in the military, other than as a nurse or in some other support position, is at best anomalous, at worst invading men's territory, in short unpatriotic. It never occurs to people that groups like Women's International League for Peace and Freedom, Women Strike for Peace, and similar groups express a kind of patriotism that both women and men would do well to imitate. Rather, the gender-bound nature of patriotism, like every other gender-bound dimension of society, is kept under wraps until women cross the gender line as in the case of combat. Then it rears its ugly head, confusing those who do not perceive the message and punishing those who do.

This analysis, while only a hint at the complexity at hand, helps to highlight the feminist dilemma around women in combat. It is further complicated by the problems that such women face when they seek combat positions in a society in which fundamental equality in other arenas is denied.

Reports from the Gulf indicate that some women volunteered for desert duty without telling their husbands, afraid that if they discussed it, their husbands would try to talk them out of it. Instead, they simply indicated their willingness to their commanding officers and went. This variation on the old need for spousal permission, circumvented so often by enterprising women throughout history, points toward the kinds of problems that accrue when women enter combat without accompanying changes in a patriarchal society. It is important to stress that these problems are not created by women, nor are they any reason to withhold from women their legitimate right to equality, but they are part of the social equation and are ignored at women's peril.

The major impact is on children who, despite feminists' best efforts at shared responsibility, are generally cared for by women. While there are cases in the current "Operation Desert Shield" where both parents are on duty with children being left in the care of grandparents, future combat for women may mean increasing problems for children especially if, as is the case with many women in the military, the mother is a single parent.

Some U.S. military bases are coping with the problems by augmenting counseling programs in their schools. But most admit that this is an unprecedented situation, though I suspect that they do not consciously take account of the women factor, which is one reason that it is different from earlier wars. No one knows what impact the loss of female life will have on children, and no one wants to find out. But that it will be different is certain due to the cultural trappings of motherhood and womanhood in patriarchy, as well as to the loss of primary caregivers.

It does not follow that women should not be in combat, but that men ought to assume an equal role in childrearing. Such not being the case, women's entrance into combat, and the injuries and deaths that will inevitably result, will bear disproportionately on children. Our society seems reluctant to equalize such responsibilities outside the combat situation and/or to develop adequate support structures for most children. Perhaps women's increased participation in the military will have the unexpected side benefit of hastening the day when men assume their fair share of childrearing.

Women themselves will suffer from heavier burdens than simply their guns. One noncombat female soldier has already been made the subject of controversy. She was ordered by her commanding officer to keep her blouse on over her T-shirt in the searing desert heat, while male soldiers presumably went shirtless, when "outright Saudi male hostility" greeted her innocent act.[4] The clash of cultural values between Americans and Saudis, exaggerated by dubious American claims at acceptance of women in the face of fundamentalist Islamic discrimination, leaves women soldiers with the war of sexism to fight, as well as the military battle. Right now there is no combat pay for either.

The option for women to join the military and, if I am correct in my assumptions about combat, the option to enter combat present young women with choices that simply did not exist in the same way a generation ago. While some hail this as a step forward made possible by feminism, others, myself included, have deep reservations about such enthusiasm.

The least discussed theme is sounded by Retired Navy Captain Sue Young, who claims that the Pentagon simply cannot afford to deny women access to the military, eventually, I conclude, to combat, because "we just don't have the manpower—as in male—to run the military." Until women realize this and understand that their participation in combat is all but assured due to demographics, changing attitudes, and continued escalating U.S. military mentality, they will be duped into begging for equality where cultural prejudices, macho attitudes, and male resistance can easily translate into a dangerous situation for them.

This difficult scenario admits of no easy feminist solution. Involved are not only deeply held beliefs about the inferiority of women, but also economic, political, and racial structures that guarantee that the impact of such beliefs will be felt most profoundly by young, poor women of color, who will be the first female cannon fodder when combat is officially opened to women, and the ones to suffer most economically if it is not. Any proposal is tentative at best, but to leave such an analysis without at least some sketch of next steps would be irresponsible.

I suggest three preliminary moves toward resolving the question from a feminist perspective. First, it is important to insist on reframing the question, beginning with acknowledging that women are in combat and then asking whether *anyone* should be. Women have learned that how such questions are framed, indeed who frames the questions, determines the answers. Admittedly this sounds idealistic in the face of a massive military buildup that has been supported by an overwhelming majority of the U. S. population. But it cannot be forgotten that religious opposition to the Vietnam War was a major factor in the U.S. withdrawal. Such opposition is articulated strategically not simply by disagreeing with policy but by restating the issues according to another reading of the data.

Rather than denying women access to combat, we can redirect the analysis to question whether anyone, male or female, is usefully dispatched to combat at a time when nuclear, chemical, and even some conventional weapons virtually assure mass destruction. We are not talking about hand-to-hand combat, with national security at risk due to women's lack of upper body strength. The issues are too serious to be obscured by the red herring of women in combat. There is, after all, a war going on. That is the issue.

A second feminist ethical move is to take the debate to where women are, to listen to their perceptions, and to theorize out of that base. This kind of grassroots, participatory ethical model avoids the pitfalls of dogmatic liberal feminism wherein mostly white women in no danger of combat make decisions for those who are faced with the choice. More important, it avoids the pitfalls of patriarchy by educating women to listen to one another instead of to the conventional wisdom, especially in this kind of life-death situation. It is hard to imagine many women mustering enthusiasm for the proposal, especially if their daughters are in line.

Women's lives have always been considered expendable in a patriarchal society, so there is reason to think that once combat is open to women, it would serve the interests of society to fill the ranks with women. Such a sinister plot may seem more the stuff of a Margaret Atwood novel than of a civilized country, but the U.S. track record on abortion, for example, seems to indicate that women's well-being is a low priority. As in the abortion case, I trust women to make responsible decisions as women have made throughout history. Opening combat to women and then coping with the massive numbers of women who conscientiously object would be a strong statement. Support for such a move will be garnered by inviting women to discuss these matters and then to strategize creatively on the basis of their discussions. I would bet on this or another equally creative option as an alternative to gung-ho militarism from most women.

Finally, a third feminist move is to broaden the ethical umbrella to include men in the company of those who, in the name of equality, stress peace, justice, and cooperation. This is perhaps the most promising strategy because it accomplishes two goals at once. On the one hand, it models equality by insisting that whatever solutions we hope to implement will have to include women and men working together (in sharp contrast to the military decisions about women in combat that are made by all-male combat-trained soldiers). On the other hand, it offers an alternative to the "equality at any price" liberalism that would tolerate women in combat in order to achieve that goal. It takes account of the reality of unequal power dynamics for women and men that assure that equality is impossible in patriarchy and that women will always pay disproportionately for their rights.

This strategy is also practical since it gives peace groups a concrete "both-and" goal. Both gender equality and peace can be pursued through creative educational programs, counseling for women and men about alternatives to military service that will result in job skills and express their patriotism. Children of both genders can see their moms and dads resisting participation in a military machine that would happily take both of them. And even men and women in the military can consider their role in preventing future wars. Obviously this is a long-term, perhaps unachievable goal, but it acts a trajectory for educational programs, lobbying, resistance efforts, tax withholding, and other effective strategies that women and men can engage in together before it is too late.

NOTES

1. Dr. Kristin Herzog, "Peacemaker Woman? Theological Perspectives on Women, War and Peace," Occasional Paper No. 3, Published by Theology in Global Context Association, New York, 1989, 14. Dr. Herzog refers to Cynthia Enloe, "Women in NATO Militaries—A Conference Report," in Judith Stiehm, ed., *Women and Men's Wars* (New York: Pergamon Press, 1983), 330–331, and *Military Women in the Department of Defense,* vol. VI (Washington, D.C.: Dept. of Defense, July 1988).

2. Reported by Lisa Leff, "Sex Bias Study Takes Naval Academy to Task," *The Washington Post,* October 10, 1990, B3.

3. Excerpted from the review and reported by Felicity Barringer in "Four Reports Cite Naval Academy for Rife Sexism," in *The New York Times,* October 10, 1990, A12.

4. Report filed from Saudi Arabia, "Saudis Accept U. S. Servicewomen Grudgingly," *The New York Times,* August 16, 1990, A17.